DATE DUE

PACLI 1/11
1400117
PACLI 3/11
1440095

An unidentified water-colour of a stage scene from the Burney
Collection, British Museum (see p. 183)

CHANGEABLE SCENERY

*

ITS ORIGIN AND DEVELOPMENT
IN THE BRITISH THEATRE

by

RICHARD SOUTHERN

FABER AND FABER LIMITED
24 Russell Square
London

First published in mcmlii
by Faber and Faber Limited
24 Russell Square, London W.C.1

AN ACKNOWLEDGEMENT

★

THE decision when to call a book of this nature 'finished' is a hard one. Strictly it should never be until the writer is sure that all the relevant evidence is collected. Accept such a counsel of perfection, however, and there will be no book. New evidence continues to come to light—often of such a nature as not only to bring new facts but to modify the interpretation of a whole succession of old ones.

Decision on the time to publish is as hard to make as decision on the time to sail a passenger steamer when one does not know how many tickets have been sold, and when there has been no advertisement of the date of departure; but one cannot wait for ever, else the voyage never takes place. As she stands out to sea there gather behind on the quay first one and then another who should have made up her complement; but we are sailing without them. And sail, I feel, we must.

There is so much to be gathered in the little-studied subject of the way the British staged their theatre-shows since the time movable scenery was introduced, that one unaided man can scarcely hope to compass it. It is usual on occasions such as this to make acknowledgements to all who have helped. I owe a great deal to collections, the courteous keepers of collections, to writers, to stage carpenters, to owners, to students, and to friends, but I would rather here not particularize. I would much like to say 'Thank-you' and 'Skål' to Marianne Tingström who for many months worked on the dreariest and most exacting of the typing and re-typing; and then I have to make one acknowledgement which must stand above all others. This is to the work of the late Dr. W. J. Lawrence.

Of all theatre-students, W. J. Lawrence was, I believe, the first to grasp how thoroughly the physical conditions of the staging of shows affect any study of the theatre. The living theatre is contained not in drama but in the staging of a show. 'How were shows staged?' was a question W. J. Lawrence constantly asked, and in 1887, at Newcastle, Co. Down, he wrote on the fly-page of a virgin notebook this title: *Data collected for the construction of a History of the rise and progress of Stage Scenery & Mechanical Appliances showing the influence which the accessories of the theatre have always possessed, from primitive to recent times, over the drama*

[5]

itself. To which is added some a/c of the Lives of the Most celebrated Scenic Artists.

This notebook he filled with relevant quotations and his own deductions and comments. To it he added a second, in which he wrote 'Finis' in 1890. Between 1892 and 1894 he added a third and began an Index. In '96 he finished the fifth; in '98 the sixth; and in '99 he wrote 'The End'. But 1901 saw an eighth book, '03 a ninth and a tenth and the beginning of an eleventh, and then the pace slackened and a set of loose pages for a twelfth volume finally closed with 'Finished at 32, Shelbourne Road, Dublin; Sept. 14, 1912, in the 50th year of my age.'

In 1937 he told me: 'For forty years past I have been making intermittent research with the view of writing a General History of Scene Painting and Stage Mounting. About a lustrum ago I realized that the subject was much too big for full discussion within reasonable bounds and abandoned the project. Beyond a few magazine and newspaper articles I have made no use of the material, which reposes in a series of typewritten notebooks with a separate general index. At my advanced age, seventy-five, I am little likely to make further use of all this data. If, in the course of your labours, you should find yourself up against a dead wall (a predicament in which in earlier years I was often landed), the possibilities are that I could give you a serviceable leg-up.'

In 1939 he put these notebooks in my possession. The war then separated us and in October 1939 I had my last letter from him.

I cannot adequately describe the wealth of scholarship and study in these twelve volumes of forty years of work. But not their least value to me was their intimate example of a method of research. Throughout the work is visible the most vigilant self-criticism; often a recantation is made of an earlier, false conclusion (sometimes so succinctly as with a single stroke of the pen and the cry 'Bosh' in the margin—but even then is added the date of the enlightenment!) and I was afforded priceless glimpses of the labour behind such books as *The Elizabethan Playhouse and Other Studies.*

Upon this work I have depended much. It has formed the basis for a great deal of added material—especially pictorial. The conclusions I alone am responsible for, and with new evidence there has often been a need to differ or to extend, but without W. J. Lawrence this book would not have the present form nor, possibly, an existence at all.

R. S.

HAMPTON HILL, 1951

CONTENTS

***

[7]

CONTENTS

PART THREE

The Revolution in Changeable Scenery in the Public Theatre of the Nineteenth Century, and the Rise of 'The Art of the Theatre'

ILLUSTRATIONS

─────────────── ★ ───────────────

PLATES

An unidentified water-colour of a stage scene from the
Burney Collection, British Museum
(by courtesy of Far and Wide)   *Frontispiece in colour*

[9]

ILLUSTRATIONS

[10]

ILLUSTRATIONS

ILLUSTRATIONS

FIGURES IN THE TEXT

FIGURES IN THE TEXT

[13]

PART ONE

THE RISE OF
CHANGEABLE SCENERY
AT COURT

I

THE SPECTACLE OF CHANGING
SCENERY

(A PRELIMINARY SURVEY OF THE COURSE OF VISIBLE
SCENE-CHANGE FROM INIGO JONES TO IRVING)

---------------------------------★---------------------------------

Scene-change a visible thing—Purpose of front curtains not to hide scene-change—Early examples of purpose of front curtain—Early examples of visible scene-change—Persistence of visible scene-change in the eighteenth century—The passing of visible scene-change

---------------------------------★---------------------------------

THERE is one remarkable fact to be found in a study of scenes and scene-changing which outshines even the intriguing details of the machinery by which the scene-changes were worked. This fact is both surprising and important; it controls the whole structure of scenery and supplies the prime reason for stage machinery; it clears up many puzzles in the staging of plays of the past, and its recognition is an essential to any understanding of the development of scenery today. This fact is that the changing of scenes was intended to be visible; it was part of the show; it came into existence purely to be watched.

When we come to study the origin and development of scene-changing in England we shall find it to be a story of how a marvellous show grew up to become a suite of shows by presenting not one marvel but a number of successive marvels. At first no more was attempted than the drawing apart at the English court of two portions of a painted set piece to disclose another set piece behind, but as scenery grew in form and began to develop its modern anatomy of parts—the pairs of side wings, the borders, and the back scene—so ingenuity rose to each occasion of the development; and the more complicated the elements grew the more ways were found to change them all by visible transformation as part of the spectacle, instead of by covering the stage (as we do now) with a curtain and occasioning a wait for the old pieces to be taken down and those of a new scene set up. This would seem a barbarous arrangement to the minds of the early scenery-designers.

A further surprising thing is that this system of marvellous transformation which grew up in the court spectacle soon became a settled part of regular, commercial theatre procedure, and scene-changing remained visible up to a period almost within living memory.

This system of changing scenery without dropping a curtain which was widespread in all Renaissance theatre seems to offer a puzzle to some investigators; for instance, Professor Allardyce Nicoll wrote in *The Development of the Theatre* (1st edition, 1927, p. 103), concerning a 'painted front curtain' in Ariosto's plays, that 'This curtain . . . was designed, however, not to form a means of concealing change of scene but to surprise the audience by the sudden revelation of the scenic glory in the first act. Much as these Renascence theorists experimented, it is surprising to note how they, and their successors, failed to realize the opportunities which a front curtain offered to an ambitious machinist and manager.'

Moreover, Dr. W. J. Lawrence, in *Those Nut-cracking Elizabethans* (p. 122), remarks that the 'helpfulness' of the front curtain 'was long in dawning upon the players' as an agent to hide the stage when they had to change the scenery.

We must beware of thus imputing a modern attitude concerning scene-change to the Renaissance machinist. Our modern attitude to scene-change is slightly covert. We hide it because it breaks the 'illusion' of a drama by underlining its artificiality—or because it provides a sensation that competes with the action of the plot. The Renaissance machinist himself had few such reservations. To him scene-change was an aspect of his theatre, though some of his contemporaries held very different views and decried it as sensationalism and a distraction, putting its features in the most unfavourable terms, and reviling those who delighted in it as witless—but the non-use of the curtain was undoubtedly deliberate. Some of this criticism we shall review later, but at the moment we have to preface more detailed study by a brief note on when the custom of visible scene-change arose and how long it lasted, thus demarking the period of time to be covered in this book.

It was in the days of Inigo Jones that the system of changeable scenery was first elaborated in England. A glance through the text of Simpson and Bell's *Designs by Inigo Jones for Masques and Plays at Court* is sufficient to show Jones's general method. In a special ornamental border or frame, more or less like our modern proscenium arch in principle, the curtain was hung to screen the stage at the outset, but not to conceal the subsequent changes of scenery. Let us for a moment look at this curtain which appeared to be such a useful agent for concealing scene-changes, but which was in fact never employed for this purpose.

The curtain was, for *The Masque of Blacknesse*, a 'Landtschap, consisting of small woods' which fell downwards and revealed an artificial sea. Concerning this particular curtain the above-mentioned work also says (p. 7) that 'In a British Museum manuscript of the masque (Royal MS. 17 B. xxxi) this landscape is "drawne uppon a doune right cloth, strayned for the scene", which is described not as falling, but as opening "in manner of a curtine".'

What the 'manner of a curtine' is is not quite clear, but here there is certainly a suggestion of parting in the centre and a sideways movement, and we read two lines farther on that 'In *Tethys' Festival* the description begins "On the Trauers which serued as a curtaine for the first Scene, was figured a darke cloude, interser[ted] with certaine sparkling starres, which, at the sound of a loud musick, being instantly drawne, the Scene was discouered".'

This use of the word 'traverse' is so exactly suggestive of our modern usage, which employs a pair of curtains dividing centrally and drawing to the sides on runners by working lines, that one is inclined to take its meaning for granted. But the suggestion is not necessarily proof of identity; the word 'strain' in the first reference is today regularly used to denote the action in covering a framework with canvas, and in the second reference the 'trauers which serued as a curtaine' almost suggests that it was used *instead of* a curtain, and was therefore something different—though what it might be we must leave for the moment; our point now is merely to mark the use of a curtain (or some equivalent) at the opening of the show.

Thus, before *Coelum Britannicum* a curtain 'flew up on the sudden'. In *Salmacida Spolia*, for the opening, 'A Curtayne flying up, a horrid Sceane appeared of storme and tempest'. But upon leaving descriptions of these opening moments of the shows we find no more mention of curtains.

The kind of phrase used to describe the changes between scenes is 'there the whole *Scene* opened' (*Oberon*, Sc. 2), 'the Scene becomes...' (*Triumph of Peace*, Sc. 3), 'The scaene again is varied into . . .' (*Coelum Britannicum*, Sc. 5), 'The Sceane is all changed' (*Temple of Love*, Sc. 3), 'The Scoene is varied, and there appeares . . .' (*Florimène*, II. 5), 'The Scoene is turned into . . .' (ibid. III. 5), 'This Scoene becomes . . .' (ibid. IV. 9), 'The Scene wholly changing, straight was perceiv'd . . .' (*Triumph of the Prince d'Amour*, Sc. 5), 'The whole Scene was transformed into . . .' (*Britannia Triumphans*, Sc. 2), 'In the further part of the Scene, the earth open'd, and there rose up a richly adorn'd palace . . .' (ibid., Sc. 4), 'The scene of night vanished; and a new and strange Prospect of Chimeras appear'd . . .' (*Luminalia*, Sc. 2), 'The scene changed into a calme . . . ' (*Salmacida Spolia*, Sc. 2).

And there are many other instances of such scene-changes, all characterized by the suggestion of a visible transformation from one scene to another.

Exactly similar are the notes in Davenant's script for *The Siege of Rhodes* (1656), later performed at the public Duke's Theatre, Lincoln's Inn Fields, in a fuller version. At the opening only do we find the phrase 'The Curtain being drawn up, a lightsome Sky appear'd...', then the curtain is forgotten. For the next scene we read simply '*the Scene is chang'd and the City*, Rhodes *appears....*' For the third scene, 'the further part of the scene is open'd and a Royal Pavilion appears display'd', and for the next, 'the Scene is vary'd to the Prospect of Mount *Philermus*', and for the last, 'the Scene is chang'd into a Representation of a general Assault...' We may deduce that some such technique marked Davenant's presentation in the first public, closed-in theatre of the new type, when *The Siege of Rhodes* was given there later.

How the King's Men worked in their rival Theatre Royal, Bridges Street, is a little less certain, but scenery they had to have sooner or later, since the scenic shows were so 'thronged after'. There may have been certain of the 'opposition party' among them and, concerning Professor Nicoll's surprise at the lack of use of a curtain in scene-changes, we might perhaps suppose that there was latent in that party a propensity to cover the stage with a curtain in order to hide these distracting and amusing changes; but, however that may be, they soon followed the fashion of visible scene-change set by the Duke's Men, who clearly were little likely to wish to hide their great innovation and their most sensational 'draw'—the transformation of scenes.

For the development of this technique in the early eighteenth century we must turn to different evidence which will be more conveniently included later in our review, but for a summary we may quote from Montague Summers's *The Restoration Theatre*, p. 97: '... the curtain in the Restoration theatre rose after the delivery of the Prologue and (save in a few rare instances duly to be noted) did not fall until the Epilogue had been spoken. The end of each Act was indicated by a clear stage.'

This represents practically the whole of the story up to the passing away of the system at the end of the nineteenth century. But there is the one qualification to be made—one event in the otherwise clear progress of visible scene-change. This is concerned with the use of the act drop; for a drop scene came to be employed to cover the stage at the end of each act, replacing the early custom of simply leaving the stage empty for an interval. Changes between scenes within any given act, however, took place unhidden as usual for two hundred years.

We have then to ask why, if visible scene-change was an accepted convention of the eighteenth century, some factor arose in the late nineteenth which discredited the system and caused it to be abandoned so entirely as to make the very idea strange to our present ways.

We may find some suggestion of the reason in Percy Fitzgerald's *The*

World behind the Scenes (1881). Here is a series of short passages which well illustrate an alteration of attitude towards visible scene-change, and in which it will be found that the transition was quite logical, and that it would seem to have been the act drop which formed the thin end of a wedge, later driven full in, to mark the complete separation of scene from scene which we know today.

We see that Fitzgerald is familiar with the break occasioned between *acts* by the lowering of the 'drop curtain', but that he still finds—even at his late date—a curtain-fall between *scenes* a novelty. Here are his remarks relative to the subject (p. 34):

> For the last ten years the fashion has been adopted of making each act one scene, to the detriment, it must be said, of variety and dramatic interest. In the older plays there was a constant change of scene, and the *locale* was shifted from one country to another, from indoor to outside, with almost an abrupt rapidity. The effect of these changes upon us now is disturbing and unnatural. This is really owing to the elaborate and built-up style of the scenery, the changing of which involves much 'clatter' and labour, which seems disproportioned to a short scene and the slight business that may take place there. Under the old system, where a simple 'cloth' quietly glided down, this impression was not left.

One of the factors, then, in the decay of visible scene-change was the growth of built sets—the extension, that is, of the idea of scenes constructed in relief until they became actually three-dimensional, life-sized representations, covering a greater part of the stage and very difficult to move. Now follows a passage in which the supersession of visible scene-change by another method is forecast (p. 35):

> Change of scene, however, is intimately connected with stage properties. What can be more absurd or ludicrous than to see a table and two chairs moving on the scene, of themselves apparently, but drawn on by a cord? or, more singular still, to see, on the prompter's whistle being heard, the table hurrying off at one side, the sofa and chairs at the other? After all, the invariable law that each scene can only be terminated by another taking its place, seems unmeaning. If a curtain fell for a moment or two while the change was made, it would be as logical as letting the 'drop' fall at the end of each act.

Here, then, is a suggestion—and note that by its tone it is a novel suggestion!—that the thin end of the curtain wedge that had already come to separate act from act should be driven in to split scene from scene. Notice may also be taken, in passing, of the remark that among the old-fashioned ways of facing the difficult problem of changing furniture and such incidental properties at the visible transformation of the scene was the method of pulling them off with a string. Interesting too is the reference to the audible prompter's whistle that set the old transformations in action—we are reminded of Ben Jonson's allusion in *An Expostulation with Inigo Jones* (see below, p. 89) to 'Inigo, the whistle and his men'.

A few lines farther on Fitzgerald writes: 'It will be conceived that ingenious persons would cast about for some new and effective contrivances, which should be convenient and at the same time cause wonder. The mode of changing the scene, or a portion of it, has exercised a great many.'

In this particular passage the reaction against the old method of scene-change is not, be it noted, on account of its being visible (for new methods were being sought which should also 'cause wonder' by their visual effect), but on account of an increase in complication of the parts of the scene which had outgrown the mechanics of the old system. The author goes on to describe how the porches and the flights of steps (once merely painted and easily slid off) had grown into three-dimensional built pieces, for the visible changing of which innumerable shifts of trick folding and hingeing were invented to close them preparatory to the transformation.

He then describes an idea, for which an American origin is suggested, of sinking and sliding stages and, later, another 'vigorous attempt at novelty' which anticipated the modern turn-table stage. The motive behind these experiments seems not to be the hiding of the scene-change, but the invention of a method which will allow change of more complicated forms of scenery. The panorama system is mentioned, and the rise of built stuff instead of painted stuff again stressed. Another factor of the development is mentioned in the improved lighting, whose increased power and new splendours demand plastic surfaces in place of the old painted ones. An anticipation of the 'simultaneous set' of today (itself a revival of a medieval principle) is mentioned in connexion with *Jonathan Bradford; or, the Murder at the Roadside Inn*, produced at the Surrey in 1833, and said to be 'one of the earliest of those curious attempts at dividing the stage into various rooms'.

The old inconsistence of arranging highly modelled mounds and hills in a landscape whose basis is all too palpably the flat boards of a stage is noted, together with a suggestion of many hydraulic pistons under various parts of the stage floor so that it might be broken up and its parts tilted in various directions to give the accidental variety of nature.

After all these indications of the troublous tendencies of the times straining after new marvels, the author gives us a mention of that method which was to gain ascendancy, for many years at least, over the rest. He speaks of the Lyceum performance, under Irving, of a double bill, *The Cup* and *The Corsican Brothers* (Jan. 1881). The beautifully rehearsed and well-regulated scene-change in *The Cup* is described to begin with. We have an account of 'portions of the roof, sky-borders, &c., all falling into their places quietly and with a sort of mysterious growth—

> *No sound of hammer or of axes rung;*
> *Like some tall palm the magic structure sprung.*'

But it is when we come to hear of the second part of the show that we see the great innovation. When the temple scene at the end of *The Cup* had been struck, there was set in its place the first scene of the Corsican château. 'Here again we have the elaborate carved chimney-piece, solid doors with jambs a foot deep, and bolts and locks—very different from the old days of "wobbling" canvas and light frames. All this carving is also represented by papier-mâché.'

There follows an allusion to a most ingenious trap, the ghost-glide, and then we come to the important part of the whole story; Fitzgerald quotes from 'Mr. Moy Thomas, who furnishes the agreeable *Causeries de Lundi* to the *Daily News*', as follows:

The costly nature of theatrical enterprise in these days could not perhaps be better shown than by the instance of the present revival of 'The Corsican Brothers' at the Lyceum Theatre. . . . The economical but comparatively rude system of 'wings' and grooves is on this occasion entirely dispensed with, as in the best Parisian theatres; and scenes are constructed so solidly, and with so many details, that without minute division of the work, and almost military precision in the movements of the workmen, 'waits' would become intolerably long. For these reasons no fewer than ninety carpenters, thirty gas-men, and fifteen property men, in all 135 persons, are permanently engaged in the mere task of arranging and conducting the scenes. It may here be worth mentioning that the handsome 'tableau curtain' made for this occasion, containing a thousand yards of crimson silk velvet, cost £740.

We have here two primary points to notice: firstly, that there is a direct statement that 'on this occasion' the old wings and grooves (whose nature it is our purpose to define) were at long length discarded; secondly, that an elaborate and novel 'tableau curtain' is mentioned. The use of this innovation during the tremendous scene-changes we must carefully note in the following passage.

On p. 50 Fitzgerald continues apropos of this show:

But it is in the next act that the series of elaborately set scenes succeeding each other entail the most serious difficulties, only to be overcome in one way, viz., by the employment of an enormous number of persons. There is the great Opera House scene, which stretches back the whole length of the stage, followed almost immediately by the supper scene, with its two rooms also stretching back; to be succeeded again by the remarkable forest scene, equally extensive. The difficulty, of course, is, how is one to be 'cleared away' without the clumsy aid of a carpenter's scene? The rich 'tableau curtain' comes in aid here, but the dramatic interest will not bear delay, and the curtain is only dropped for a few moments, to be raised again almost at once. . . . Yet nothing can be more simple than the elements of this Opera House scene. From the audience position one would fancy it was an elaborately built and costly structure. It is nothing but two light screens pierced with openings, but most artfully arranged and coloured. At its close down comes the rich curtains, while behind them descends the cloth with the representation of the lobby scene in the Opera House. This is followed by the double rooms of the supper party, a very striking scene. Two handsomely furnished rooms, Aubusson carpets, pianoforte, nearly twenty chairs, sofas, tables, clocks, and a supper-table covered with delicacies, champagne bottles, flowers, &c. Now it has been mentioned that this is succeeded almost instantly by a scene occupying the same space—that of the forest, requiring the minutest treatment, innumerable properties, real trees, &c. Here is what takes place, showing a marvellous specimen of prompt action. So soon as the 'curtains' are dropped the auxiliaries rush on; away to the right and left fly the portions of the Parisian drawing-room; tables, chairs, piano, sofa vanish in an instant. Men appear carrying tall saplings fixed in stands; one lays down the strip of frozen pond, another the prostrate trunk of a tree—every one from practice knowing the exact place of the particular article he is appointed to carry. Others arrive with bags of sand, which are emptied and strewn on the floor; the circular tree is put in position, the lime-light is ready. The transformation was effected, in what space of time will the reader imagine? In thirty-eight *seconds*, by the stage-manager's watch. By that time the tableau had been drawn aside, and Chateau-Renaud and his friend Maurgiron were descending to the gloomy glade after their carriage had broken down.

And there, in that blaze of adulation and glory for its successor, there passes visible scene-change, with no epitaph—an ancient system that was good enough for Jones, but which sheer elaboration and verisimilitude of scenery beat into obsolescence, and supplanted with what was at first a fractional pause in the show's life—a mere momentary breath-holding of thirty-eight seconds. Thereby opening was made for a curtain-fall at every scene's end, and a dissection of the show into such separate fragments that a spectator has now to go to the cinema for entertainment unbroken by interval distractions. The wait between the acts has become so long—thanks partly to the introduction of bars into theatres (whose profits go to the land-lord's pocket, and whose existence occasions clauses in the lease specifying fixed intervals for the audience's refreshment and the landlord's profit)—that it achieves, on occasion, the amazing space of half an hour!

Thus passed gorgeous scene-change. And thus the old, quick-fire, continuous, varied shows of the Stuarts and the Georgians, where so much was packed into the time, became less than a memory.

Having thus demonstrated in respect of scene-changing in England that it was essentially a visible effect, that it remained so for some three hundred years, and that it passed away because Victorian scenery became too elaborate to change visibly, it will be useful to ask for a moment what happened in the theatre before changeable scenery was introduced. What did it come to supplant, and why did it come?

2

THE STATIC SCENE, THE HOUSE
AND THE MOVING CLOUD

★

The static scene and changeable scenery—The two varieties of the static scene—The house and the early court masque—The overcoming of a cloud

★

SCENE-CHANGING is not essential to the theatre. There have been, in history, two ways of setting theatrical shows: one employs changeable scenery such as we know it today; the other employs what we may call a static scene.

Our present system with changeable scenery dates back in regular, public-theatre use in England only to 1661, though evidence for moving scenery in special, private performances is to be found at least as early as 1574. Our system is, then, not a very old one compared with the venerable length of the history of the theatre as a whole. Three centuries is a small part of a European story that goes back over two thousand years. For the rest of this long time a *static setting* was used on every occasion, and in every part of the world, where backgrounds to performances were provided at all. Change-of-scene is now so ingrained in the acceptance of modern theatre-goers that the conception of a non-changeable scenic system is generally somewhat difficult for them. What, in fact, was a static scene?

Speaking broadly we can find two variant ways of employing the static background in theatre shows: firstly, by using a permanent, conventional screen or façade to play before—ranging in complication from a single curtain to the elaboration of the Greek *skene* front, to the Roman *frons scaenae*, and later to the façade of the Elizabethan tiring-house—and secondly, by arranging on the stage a number of separate elements side by side each representing the setting for one scene and each used in turn but all static and visible throughout the show. Such a system was used in the 'simultaneous settings' of the Middle Ages, in the earlier court masques in England, and probably also in the Elizabethan 'private' houses (and it is very well illustrated in the early work of the French designer, Laurent Mahelot, at the Hôtel de Bourgogne).

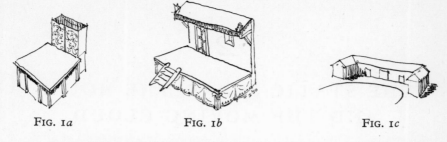

FIG. 1*a*   FIG. 1*b*   FIG. 1*c*

An element might sometimes represent a mountain or a ship or a king-dom, but in general it was a character's house, and the term 'house' became almost a technical name for it whatever it represented. Reduced therefore to its very simplest essence, the idea of static setting consisted of the use of either (*a*) a single special 'house' at the back of the stage, or (*b*) a group of 'houses' upon the stage—possibly along three sides of it.

It will not be necessary to point out to any student of theatrical presentation the great importance which the term 'house' possesses in early scenic method. In English masques of the sixteenth century (before Renaissance innovations) we read, for instance, of 'the Canvas that made all the howses for plaies', and of 'apt howses, made of Canvasse, fframed, ffashioned & paynted accordingly: as mighte best serve theier severall purposes' (see Cunningham's *Accounts of the Revels*, for 1571). The term is perhaps best known under its French form of 'mansions', which recurs almost endlessly in medieval theatre. Finally it has an Italian equivalent (exemplified, for instance, in the writing of Sabbattini) in the form of 'casa'. The 'casa', the 'mansions', and the 'howses' were all the same thing—the small constructions put up to represent the separate items of a simultaneous setting or, later, the side elements of certain, early, Renaissance, perspective scenes. An identity of purpose, of tradition, and possibly of construction, runs through all the variations.

The uses of this static house—single or multiple—upon the stages of the world have been various indeed. They range from the elemental booth, curtained at the back (probably the most ancient stage-form in history, see Fig. 1*a*) to the pierrot's stage on the sands today. An offshoot leads to the

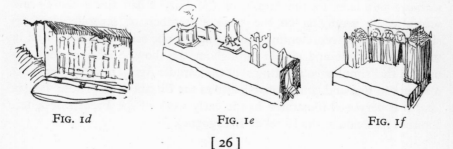

FIG. 1*d*   FIG. 1*e*   FIG. 1*f*

[26]

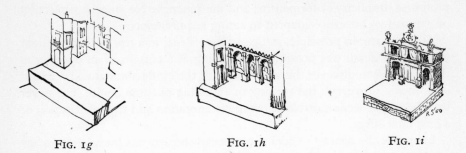

FIG. 1*g*   FIG. 1*h*   FIG. 1*i*

little Greek mime-stage, of which the house-form, backing the platform, is so evident in vase-paintings (Fig. 1*b*), then to the severe conventionalism of the classic Greek *skene* (Fig. 1*c*), and beyond to the supremely elaborate Roman façades, so like the buildings of a city that they might be the permanent expression of a pretentious town-gate of the times (Fig. 1*d*). It multiplies in the Middle Ages to become the mansions of the Mysteries, grouped informally about a town-square or lined along a trestle platform (Fig. 1*e*); it is unified again in the curtained neighbour-compartments of the Terentian stage illustrated in the Trechsel edition of 1493 (Fig. 1*f*). Under the genius of the Renaissance it spreads again into the 'street' of houses of the Serlian, perspective stage (Fig. 1*g*); then conventionalizes on the one hand into the twin, front houses flanking a formal back scene of the Venice Plautus of 1518 (Fig. 1*h*), and on the other hand into the complex, formal façade-unit backing the outdoor stages of the Rederijker societies in Holland (Fig. 1*i*)—into the formality of the arcaded front at the Teatro Olimpico—into the elaboration of the Jesuit stages. From Holland there seems a clear kinship with the tiring-house front of the Elizabethan public playhouse (Fig. 1*j*). The medieval mansions and the Serlian street combine to lead to the strange mixtures of the Hôtel de Bourgogne stage (Fig. 1*k*), and possibly our own private Elizabethan theatres. It is even left surviving today in one unique example in the staging of the Latin Westminster Play (see *Theatre Notebook*, vol. iii, No. 3). And beside and beyond all these are the classic Chinese stage, a lesson in

FIG. 1*j*   FIG. 1*k*

FIG. 1*a* to *k*. Types of non-changeable stage 'house'

profound simplicity of formalism; and the Japanese Nō stage, a perfection of national architecture adapted to acting requirements.

All these are, in principle, static settings. True, in a few of them a slight variation of detail was possible—the sliding of a curtain in an opening in the back wall to discover the space beyond; the establishment and removal of a 'scenic property'; the turning or revealing of some device, but never was the whole scene capable of complete alteration and the substitution of a new total effect.

I suppose the nearest to such a total evanishment was the wheeled stage or tableau such as was brought in and out of the banqueting hall after a prince's feast. Here at least was the element of *surprise* in early scenery—of the bursting upon the beholders' eyes of a new marvel.

The story of scene-change is the story of the introduction of this element of the marvellous upon the otherwise static stage—and of the modifications that it entailed.

Among the marvels, the most dramatic was that of movement. Either a wheeled splendour in the form of a ship or castle was borne in to the banquet hall to disgorge the players and dancers before the spectators, or the older system of simultaneous setting was maintained, and a number of marvellous items pre-set before the opening of the show and then, when all was under way, some small element would begin to move or open . . .

And with such a picture before our eyes we can bring out the first piece of direct evidence to form the foundation of a study of the development of scene-changing in England.

Such a picture, as was pointed out above, was made by the setting of shows at Queen Elizabeth's court—shows of whose details so much information is to be found in the Accounts of the Office of Revels. These details confirm our suggestion that the settings of the shows were in general upon the principle of 'static houses' such as we have glanced at above. But there is a certain added element that forms a perfect link between this chapter and the main study of the book.

The Accounts of the Office of Revels give us an incomplete but intriguing picture of show-presentation at the English court in the later sixteenth century. As a period it is significant in seeing the last phases of the medieval system of setting by means of 'houses'. But still more significant is it in giving us also a very early example of the introduction of movement for effect. That is to say of a movement of scenery not for a utilitarian reason—such as drawing aside a curtain to reveal a house interior—but for a spectacular reason, to add a marvel to the scene.

The kind of scene we have to imagine is sketched in such a reference as this (under date 26 Dec. 1579):

A History of the Duke of Millayn and the Marques of Mantua shewed at

Whitehall on St Stephens daie at nighte enacted by the Lord Chamberlaynes srv^{a}nts wholie furnyshed in this offyce some newe made and moche altered whereon was Imployed for iiij newe head attyers with traynes Scarfes, garters and other Attyers, xiij ells of Sarcenett a Cowntrie howse a Cyttye and vij paire of gloves.

Or (referring to 1 Jan. 1580):

A History of the foure sonnes of Fabyous . . . by the Earle of Warwicks s^{r}v^{a}nts . . . a Cytie, a Mounte & vi paire of gloves.

(Dr. W. J. Lawrence, in a marginal note to his copy of Cunningham, mentions a 'Play of *The Fabii* referred to by Gosson in his "Plays Confuted in Five Actions" as acted at *The Theatre*'.)

As to the making of such scenic properties as are indicated above, we know that 'patterns' were made by Hans Ewarts, William Lyzarde, and others; the Clerk of the Revels Office often puts in an item for making 'Modells'; we read of timber 'frames for the houses' being made and transported to the place of performance, being joined together with 'Long vices' and covered with canvas for the painters. We even find direct references to the execution of three of the pieces mentioned above, in the following:

Willm Lyzarde for sondry things by him browght into the offyce
Syse, cullers, pottes, nayles and pensills used and occupyed upon the payntinge of vij Cities, one villadge one Countrey howse, one battlement, iiij axes, a Braunche, lillyes and a mount for Christmas iij Holidaies;   iiij^{li}. xv^s. viij^d.

We read elsewhere of: 'Hoopes to make a Mounte; iij^s.' and presume the maker to have been John Rosse or Rose, since, as property maker, he is recorded as the builder of other 'mounts'—as witness an item for 'Tymber for the Rock (wch M^r. Rosse made for my L. of Leicesters menns playe) & for other frames for plaers howses'.

But these are all static sceneries. They help us merely to picture the common system. To the early part of the same year, however, belong certain entries with a special significance. On Shrove Sunday the Earl of Warwick's Servants performed at Whitehall *The History of the Knight of the Burnyng Rock*, and we find (presumably connected with this occasion) an interesting item concerning a piece of *borrowed* scenery—that is, not one made specially in the Office of Revels, but lent from outside and thus (it is possible to suppose) belonging to a professional company of players. However that may be, the piece was a cloud.

This cloud, we read, was 'cut to serve the rock in the plaie of the burnyng knight' and ten shillings was paid 'for the hire thereof and setting upp the same where it was borrowed'—and also to cover the cost of 'a hoope and blewe Lynnen cloth to mend the clowde that was Borrowed and cut . . .' It thus appears that (like so much borrowed scenery) it was temporarily cut to serve a special purpose, then was made good again before its return to its proper place, where, it is interesting to note, it was not only brought back but apparently 'sett upp the same' as it had been before.

The borrowed cloud was the subject of work by John Ross, the property maker, two items in whose accounts bring us to the most important feature of this cloud for our present purpose—its movement; for we find he put in for 'nayles of sondry sorts used about the Clowde and drawing it upp and downe'.

There is, of course, a possibility that this drawing up was merely a hoisting of a static piece into its position. But we find also an item 'for a coard & pullies to drawe upp the clowde', and the case for an actual moving piece of scenery is strengthened.

It is still not, however, conclusive. Special 'nayles' merely to draw it into position may be argued and the cord and pulleys might have been brought into use for no other purpose. But in an earlier reference still there appears something that may be offered as evidence conclusive that such a cloud did, on occasion, move.

This earlier cloud was not a borrowed one, for the carpenter, Rowland Robynson, included in his account an eighteen-penny 'peece of Elme boorde for the clowde'.

The occasion was a performance between 1 November 1574 and 28 February 1575. Unfortunately it is not clear for which of six rather doubt-fully mentioned plays and masques this cloud was made. But the following item concerning it, from the property maker John Ross, is of importance. We read:

To John Rosse for . . . Long boordes for the stere of a clowde; vi^s. Pulleyes for the Clowds and curteynes; iiij^s . . . Dubble gyrts to hange the soon in the Clowde; xij^d.

The fact that pulleys are here mentioned for working the curtains and that clouds are coupled in the same phrase with curtains suggests the pulleys were also for the movement of clouds, not merely to help in their erection. The first item holds the greatest significance of all. From it we learn not only that clouds moved but in what manner they were moved, namely by being drawn with cords along a long, wooden 'steering-way' or track. Beside this information, the 'sun' that hung in the same cloud by means of double 'gyrts', pales to insignificance indeed, for there we have in embryo what was to become the cardinal item of all English scene-shifting machinery for over three centuries—long boards forming a 'stere'; that is to say, as nearly as we may imagine it and basing upon a study of stage machinery in general, two strips of wood arranged to form a channel or *groove* in which a specially prepared part of the scene-piece slid (or it might be a pair of such grooves).

Whether it were for a play or a masque, we take this 'stere of a clowde' in 1574–5 as the starting-point in this study of scenery and scene-movement. Here, for effect and for effect alone, a steering way was provided as a guide for the spectacle of a moving cloud among other, but static, pieces, and it seems that it was thus that the conception of moving scenery entered the theatre. The reason, we must note, was to create wonder and delight, not to symbolize a change in the scene of action.

To such a motive also we can ascribe the significant stage-direction of some thirty-four years later in *The Triumph of Time* (from *Four Plays in One*, 1608): 'One half of a cloud drawn, singers are discovered, then the other half drawn, Jupiter is seen in glory.'

Let us remember such things came to a world which had always known a 'static stage'. The stage had had a static scene for two thousand years. No shadow of a conception could have then existed that a stage scene might become—or had any call to become—anything but a formal and static background. Against it an item of movement was a diversion and no more: it brought to the real meaning of a play no more than the closing eyes do to a French doll. It was there to satisfy the joy in man of crying 'Look! It moves!'

But those venerable, static houses of Elizabeth's diversions might well have taken two lines from the mouth of a player, and exclaimed—

> *Can such things be,*
> *And overcome us like a summer cloud . . .?*

For the device—for all that it seems a toy and no bigger than a man's hand —is to grow into one of the most pervasive and revolutionary influences the theatre has ever felt. This marvellous appearance is the herald of a transformation, in less than a hundred years, of virtually all the theatrical setting of the Western world into a system of marvellous appearances and replacements, with the brave and beautiful conventions of the static scene all lost save for two things—a particular shape to the English proscenium sides; and a very slow relinquishment of the idea of the conventional nature of scenery—for naturalistic scenes failed (rather surprisingly) to come into settled existence for nearly two centuries after the introduction of changeable scenery.

The story of this spread and growth we have here to consider. We begin by studying the development that took place in the English court from this simple beginning during the next sixty-five years, at the end of which time the triumphant masque had become a marvel so powerful that one dramatic poet was to break his court career over it, and movement had reshaped every piece of scenery on the stage and had given rise to a new form for drama.

[31]

3

MASQUES AT COURT

(THE RISE OF THE SHUTTER AND ITS FRAME)

★

The reason for the Frontispiece—The 'opening' of scenery—Traverses and shutters—Shutters in 'Florimène', 1630—In 'Passions Calmed', 1636—In 'Salmacida Spolia', 1640

★

THE staging of the court shows of the early seventeenth century came into the hands of the vivid and widely informed artist Inigo Jones— ingenious, forceful, and well able to produce work in skilful harmony with the progressive Renaissance movement. Of his work in the masques we have three forms of record: the (often elaborate) scene-descriptions (some in his own words) in the printed texts; his own original drawings and notes for the scenes; and a most important, though very small, group of plans for certain of the stages.

Jones developed the use of movement in the scenery of his masques. Not only did he extend the system of moving clouds to a remarkable degree, but he also developed another system—that of *opening* a piece of scenery to disclose a further piece behind. Again, this opening-movement was, in its origin, movement for a marvellous effect. In developing these two systems of movement the whole anatomy of the stage was altered.

The most significant anatomical alteration might be likened to one from vertebrate to crustacean structure. That is to say (if one may compare the scenery of a show to the skeleton of an animal and the action to its flesh) from hanging the flesh round a centre backbone to enclosing it in an embracing shell. In other words, where the old scenery had been a dominant central backbone (as is a maypole) for the show, the new scenery became a hollow surround, with the show taking place inside it (and, so far as the action was concerned, oddly less dependent on it; see Fig. 2a and b).

One may grasp the difference clearly if one reflects upon the consequences of parting a piece of scenery in the centre and drawing the two pieces aside to discover a scene behind. That second scene will now be 'framed' in the remnant of the first as a window is framed by drawn-back curtains. The show will seem to go back inside it. The setting for the show is now no longer centralized, with the action taking place about it: the arrangement is turned inside out and the setting develops sides and a back to form a hollow for the action—and very soon it becomes logical to add a top and complete the 'niche' in which the picture is seen.

Two things affecting the anatomy of scenery follow from this: First, that instead of being a self-contained, free-standing house, *outside* which

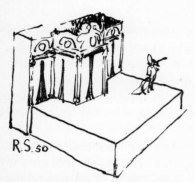
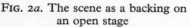

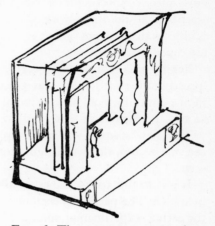

FIG. 2*a*. The scene as a backing on an open stage

FIG. 2*b*. The scene as a surround to an enclosed stage

one plays—scenery now becomes a complex of (*a*) background, (*b*) sides, and (*c*) top, *inside* which one plays.

The second thing has especially important implications. In order to make such a 'surround' tidy—to concentrate the eye within it, and to help to hide the withdrawn pieces when a scene divides to reveal another scene—some sort of fixed front frame to the picture is needed that shall (to use a technical phrase) 'mask in' all the rest, and cut it off from the remainder of the room. In short the picture has now to be isolated and a concealment must be arranged to cover its working parts.

This was a completely revolutionary idea in the shape and intention of scenery. It meant that, for the first time in the history of the theatre, the scene was isolated. Until now it had been generally an open thing, with the surrounding objects of the normal world freely jostling it elbow to elbow. The show had bravely stood competition from all the familiar sights of daily life. Round the Greek performance hung the mountains and the Attic sky. Round the medieval Mystery the streets showed unconcealed. To the early masque the banqueting hall formed a frank, unquestioned outer setting.

When scenery began to move, however, the scene became aloof; the used pieces had to be hidden away, and the prospects to come had to be kept concealed until their moment. So for the first time in history a *frontispiece* was made to frame-in the stage picture. One saw the show *through* it.

This frontispiece was, in Jones's hands, an emblematic decoration at the front of the stage, designed separately for each show, and consisting of two side pieces adjoining the walls of the hall and flanking the scene, with a cross-piece connecting their tops and reaching up to the ceiling. The whole 'arch' hid all the stage-workings and left only the acting-area visible—and visible from the front alone; no side spectators were possible as with the old, open, platform stage.

Behind this frontispiece (very similar to our present conception of a 'proscenium arch') there was placed scenery of an entirely new device, built both to form an all-embracing surround to the space within and also so as to be capable of total (and, to appearances, magic) transformation.

This new scenery was made up in essence of three sorts of elements: the side-scenes, the overhanging top pieces, and the most important back-scene.

It was to this backscene especially that the paramount capacity to move belonged. The particular method of movement had been indicated even in the earlier, experimental, masques of Inigo Jones, before he introduced the frontispiece. We read in Ben Jonson's *Hue and Cry after Cupid* (Whitehall, 1608) of a cliff scene that 'parted in the midst'. In this way scenes were to change on the English stage for close on three hundred years. Here is the birth of the idea of *opening* and *closing* the scenes, and so important was it that these backscenes should open and close in this way that by 1634 they received the special categorical name of *shutters*. They were called shutters because each backscene was in two pieces which 'parted in the midst', slid aside, and thus opened; or which moved together and so were shut.

The system of 'shutters' was the main, but not the sole, regular device of masque scenery. The shutters did not reach perfection until possibly Jones's latest masque, *Salmacida Spolia*, but before we look into the details of the full working of the whole masque system at its height it will be useful to glance in passing at the earlier stages of the shutter.

In the eight masques of the years 1603 to 1608 we have, apparently, shows with much the same type of setting as had been used in Elizabeth's day. They had decorative and elaborate constructions built in various parts of the hall and remaining permanently on view through the show—at one end a hill, at the other a grove, and so forth. In Ben Jonson's *Masque of Blacknesse* there was some advance, for a curtain concealed the scene till the time was ready to disclose it, and the whole seems to have formed a unified picture instead of a 'dispersed setting', but there is nothing yet indicative of shutters.

In 1608, with Jonson's *Hue and Cry after Cupid*, we advance to the use of a sort of framing element—like a proscenium arch possessing sides but no top, and having a cliff scene within it. This cliff 'parted in the midst' and discovered another scenic effect behind. This, as we have said, is movement for effect; but it is now something else—it can definitely be called a 'scene-change'. Here is the first flavour of the shutter idea.

It is with this 'parting in the midst' that we take a clear step forward from the opening cloud of *The Triumph of Time*. On how the parting was worked we have as yet no evidence; at present we must suppose the method was similar to that used in *Florimène* twenty-seven years later, that is to say a method involving the sliding of frames in grooves.

In Jonson's next masque, *The Masque of Queenes*, 1609, two definitely separate and successive scenes were presented, and Daniel's *Tethys' Festival*, 1610, had two changes.

Jonson's *Oberon*, in 1611, for which Jones's designs still exist, had three successive scenes, each disclosed by the opening of the back of the previous one. But in Campion's *The Lords Maske*, in 1613, we have an elaborate setting on two levels, each discovered separately. Clouds came down during the action, and while these were vanishing, 'the wood, being the underpart of the scoene, was insensibly changed and in place thereof' appeared a scene of architecture and statuary. Later 'the whole scoene' changed and became a 'prospective with Porticoes each side, which seemed to go in a great way . . .', and so forth. We should note just here the bringing over of clouds to help the scene-change and act as an agent to mask the deeper parts of the stage and provide a new 'front scene' while elements of the previous set were changed behind it.

Very similar perhaps was the setting of Beaumont's *Masque of the Inner Temple*, also in 1613, but here it is clearly stated that the 'lower descent of the mountaine was discovered' by the agency of a 'Traverse'.

It is to be admitted that, as we have already seen, the use of the word 'traverse' is sometimes puzzling, and there seems to be no reason at first sight to doubt that here it is used in its present sense of a curtain parted in the centre and drawing to the sides. A second traverse was drawn to discover the 'higher ascent of the mountaine'.

The side action of these traverses is well suited to the most becoming discovery of a scene, as witness their favourite use in the modern theatre, but such a curtain, hanging loose, as it must, is not a good surface on which to show a painted scene nor, certainly, a scene with a door in it. It is therefore with some surprise that we see in 1614, for *The Masque of Flowers*, that although there was a traverse to open the show, it was not only 'painted in *Perspective*, like the wall of a Cittie, with battlements, over which were seene the Tops of houses', but it had in the middle 'a great gate, and on either side a Temple . . . in either of which opened a little gate'. It certainly seems that, in order to open such a 'great gate', the material of the curtain must have been framed-out in some way. If so, and if the framed canvas parted in the centre and slid to either side, we have here a pair of shutters.

It would seem that the origin of the shutters lay in the traverse curtain, whose folds were flattened out—so as to present a paintable surface—by stretching the whole on a pair of frames into either of which, at need, a door could be introduced.

Much the same class of set was used for the succeeding masques (though many variations were played on the theme) until 1631. Here elaborate successions of complete scenes began to be the rule; for instance, *Albion's Triumph* by Townsend, in 1632, had a frontispiece, a curtain, and scenes of an atrium, a forum, an amphitheatre, a grove, and a landscape with White-hall in the distance.

Two years later, in Shirley's *The Triumph of Peace*, we have what I believe is the first specific mention of the word *shutter* in the inscriptions on Inigo Jones's drawings. This is not a certain point for the chronological classification of the drawings is not yet perfected, and it does not mean that shutters were not used, and called such, before this; almost certainly they are to be recognized in the descriptions of scene-changes in the printed editions of the masques; but on the sketch for the fifth scene of *The Triumph of Peace* (Design No. 188 in the catalogue by Simpson and Bell) is the note: 'not to draw ye upper shuters but ye masqu[er]s form ye under being draw[n]e'.

The full implication of the note is not clear, but the use of the word is definite. Here is the name given to those elements that were 'drawne' to discover a further scene—the *shutters*.

From now onwards in the list of masques, material for notes on shutters becomes very full. *Florimène*, 1635, calls for remark not only as being a play, or rather a pastoral, and not a masque, but as providing us with very valuable plans in which we may see exactly specified the position at which the backshutters were placed on the stage, namely in long grooves running behind the deepest set of wings. The details of these grooves will be studied in the next chapter; for the moment it suffices to say that in *Florimène* there is apparently provision for two shutters, framed by four pairs of tree wings, which remained unchanged throughout the show.

The first scene was 'the shutter o[f] ye Isle of [D]elos being for [t]he standing scaene', to quote Jones's inscription. Then followed 'The first Releiue. Tempell of Diana' (of the nature of a 'releiue' scene we shall speak in the next chapter but one). Then the Delos shutter closed again, and later opened upon the first intermedium, the design for which is inscribed '2 scene of Winter. Releiue'. Then the Delos shutters closed in and, when it was time for the second intermedium, opened again to discover a garden. This was again covered by the shutters, and upon the next opening a scene marked '4, somer. Releiue' was disclosed and, later, hidden, to be replaced on the next opening of the shutters by 'Autome. Releiue'. Then as a special finale a pair of shutters closed again and for the last time, but a different pair of shutters now, not the familiar pair showing the Isle of Delos; instead we have, '6th sceane the 2nd Temple of Diana a shutter'.

So, clearly, distinction is made between relieve scenes and shutter scenes. Shutter scenes were those painted on a pair of flat frames running together in grooves. In the case of *Florimène* 'ye sceane changes only at the Backshutters' as is noted on the plan. The wings remain standing throughout the play. This example is interesting in showing a consistent alternation of shutter and relieve scenes.

Our next reference is a particularly full and picturesque one. To find it we break the sequence of the masques at the London court and turn to Oxford. On 29 August 1636 there was presented at Christ Church a performance of Strode's *Passions Calmed, or The Settling of the Floating Island* before Charles I, the Queen and Court.

It is perhaps important to give this reference at some length, not only for its own charm and information, but also because the vital phrase in it has been the subject of a curious and somewhat misleading alternative rendering by at least one accepted authority; I italicize this phrase in the following. The source is Anthony à Wood's *The History and Antiquities of the University of Oxford* in John Gutch's edition, 1796, vol. ii, p. 408. We may conveniently begin at this point:

after the King, Queen, and two Princes had supped, they saw a Comedy acted in Christ Church Hall, but such an one it was, that it had more of the Moralist than Poet in it. And though it was well penned, yet it did not take with the Courtiers so well, as it did with the togated crew. It was intituled 'Passions Calmed', or 'The Setling of the floating Island', made by Strode the Orator, and performed by the Scholars beyond expectation. It was acted on a goodly stage, reaching from the upper end of the Hall almost to the hearth place, and had on it three or four openings on each side thereof, and partitions between them, much resembling the desks or studies in a Library, out of which the Actors issued forth. The said partitions they could draw in and out at their pleasure upon a sudden, and thrust out new in their places according to the nature of the Screen, whereon were represented Churches, Dwelling-houses, Palaces, &c. which for its variety bred very great admiration. Over all was delicate painting, resembling the Sky, Clouds, &c. At the upper end *a great fair shut of two leaves* that opened and shut without any visible help. Within which was set forth the emblem of the whole Play in a very sumptuous manner. Therein was the perfect resemblance of the billows of the Sea rolling, and an artificial Island, with Churches and Houses waving up and down and floating, as also rocks, trees and hills. Many other fine pieces of work and Landscapes did also appear at sundry openings thereof, and a Chair also seen to come gliding on the Stage without any visible help. All these representations being the first (as I have been informed) that were used on the English stage, and therefore giving great content, I have been therefore the more punctual in describing them, to the end that posterity might know that what is now seen in the Play-houses at London belonging to his Majesty, and the Duke of York, is originally due to the invention of Oxford Scholars.

The two passages of illuminating and seizing importance for us are the 'great fair shut of two leaves that opened', and the remarkably apt and vivid likening of the sliding wings to a 'Library'.

Concerning the first of these it is especially interesting to notice the rendering of two modern scholars. Professor Nicoll quotes the passage and reads 'a great fair shut[ter?] of two leaves' (see *Stuart Masques*, p. 138); but Lily B. Campbell in *Scenes and Machines on the English Stage*, p. 188, again quoting the passage, has the remarkable rendering: 'a great fair *street* of two leaves'. This seems to be an emendation that hinders rather than helps. A *street* may be at first sight more understandable than a *shut* to an ordinary reader, but there is little doubt that, with even so little special approach as we have been able to make to this point, the *great fair shut* is the cogent phrase and makes the vivid picture of what must most have struck Anthony à Wood's informant—namely the *moving scenery*.

We may perhaps pause to explain our phrase 'Anthony à Wood's informant' above. Dr. W. J. Lawrence observes in a manuscript note in my possession, included in his remarks on this passage, that

. . . the descriptions seem amazingly accurate considering that the chronicler related at second hand; but it would be interesting to know on whose authority his accounts of the scenic features of the two plays were based. At this precise juncture Wood was only 3 years & 8 months old. He relates in his Autobiography (Vol. 1, p. 6, ed. Bliss) that on the 29 August 1636 he was 'conveyed in a servant's armes . . . to the mount in' the garden of one of the canons of Christ Church, and thence 'saw the K. qu. and the rest riding downe the said street into Ch.Ch. great quadrangle'.

However this may be, the description of the 'great fair shut' is as vivid as a description from life.

In the same way the likening of the wings to a library and the statement that they were changeable are in the phrases of one who actually saw the thing. Lawrence speaks of 'Wood's apt comparison. At the Bodleian and other Oxford libraries, bookshelves are ranged at right angles at regular intervals along the two sides of the room. A "study" would be the space between two rows of shelves, as they project from the sides of the long room.'

One further word is puzzling in the passage, namely the 'Screen' according to whose nature different sets of wings were pushed out. Lawrence himself is puzzled, and his note is an interesting example of the perplexities of the student in reconstructing the nature of early scenery from incidental references:

Campion has caused me much trouble by his curious use of the word 'screen'. In what sense does Wood employ it? His 'screen' would, I think, be the back flat. For his meaning as I take it, is that the scenery at the sides altered from time to time to be in harmony with the back.

Another reading of Wood's passage would be that the word 'screen' referred to the whole setting in its entirety. It might thus stand for 'Scene'. In fact the passage gains in lucidity by reading 'scene' for 'screen'. Can the latter have been a misprint?

On second thoughts if by 'Screen' Wood meant the back flat, he would have so referred to it later, but he calls it 'a great fair shut of two leaves'. Perhaps then we would be safe in taking the word in the sense of the word 'scene' and to refer to the setting at one particular moment.

Thus in early stages we all have to fumble over a meaning. By and large, and in the light of later study, it would seem that Lawrence was right—that the 'Screen' is the scene as a whole.

Lawrence further helps us by telling us—

Mr. H. A. Evans, M.A., author of 'English Masques' writes me, in reply to enquiries:—'Both plays were undoubtedly performed in the same hall. Wood had a way of speaking of the college halls as "The Common Hall". We still talk of the "Common Room" to which the fellows retire after dinner for dessert. Christ Church Hall is a grand building about 115 ft. by 40, and 50 in height. The fire place still exists, on the south side. I do not know the exact distance from the western end, but the stage must have been deep; still the greater part of the hall would have been left for the audience.'

The depth of the stage would appear to have been about 45 ft.

'Both plays' refers to *Passions Calmed* and *The Royall Slave*—about which more in a moment. But before leaving Wood's description of *Passions Calmed* to go on to the second play we should check his remark towards the end that 'these representations' were 'the first . . . that were used on the English stage'. Even if representations at Oxford only were in question, we know of a presentation there in 1605 at which Jones had experimented with *periaktoi* (see *Stuart Masques*, p. 63), and if the London court be allowed into the question, we have already seen even in this brief introduction that many 'representations' of this nature had already been essayed.

Before leaving Wood it is not without interest to add his reference to the other play, Cartwright's *The Royall Slave*. Not only is it vivid as was the last, but it leads us to a very significant piece of knowledge concerning the *borrowing* of scenery—a subject on which we have already touched in our account of the cloud, and stressed because of its hint that professional players had some use even at this early date for items at least of scenery:

Tuesday, August 30, [1636] . . . the King and the Queen went to Christ Church, retired and supped privately, and about 8 of the clock went into the Common Hall there to see another Comedy called 'The Royall Slave', made by Mr. Will Cartwright of that House. It contained much more variety than that of 'Passions Calmed'. Within the shuts were seen a curious Temple, and the sun shining over it, delightful forests also, and other prospects. Within the great shuts mentioned before, were seen villages, and men visibly appearing in them, going up and down, here and there, about their business. The Interludes thereof were represented with as much variety of scenes and motions as the great wit of Inigo Jones (well skilled in setting out a Court Maske to the best advantage) could extend unto. It was very well pen'd and acted and the strangeness of the Persian habits gave great content. All men came forth very well contented, and full of applause of what they had seen and heard. 'It was the day of St. Felix', (as the Chancellor [Laud] observed), 'and all things went happy.' . . .

In November following, the Queen sent to the Chancellor that he would procure of Christ Church the Persian attire of the Royall Slave and other apparell wherein it was acted, to the end that she might see her own Players act it over again, and whether they could do it as well as 'twas done by the University. Whereupon the Chancellor caused the Cloaths and Perspectives of the Stage to be sent to Hampton Court in a Waggon, for which the University received from her a letter of thanks. So that all of it being fitted for use (the author thereof being then present) 'twas acted soon after, but by all mens confession, the Players came short of the University Actors. At the same time the Chancellor desired of the King and Queen that neither the Play, or Cloaths, nor Stage, might come into the hands and use of the common Players abroad, which were graciously granted.

There are thus incidental avenues which might well be explored had we time, but we must be content to accept this valuable colour to the general picture which it is the purpose of this study finally to paint, and turn to pursue our specific subject—the shutters and how they worked.

The year after *The Royall Slave*, namely in 1637–8, there was published at Ravenna what became one of the most famous works on the technique of early scenery. What influence it had upon English designers we do not know, but the traditional technique which it discusses must have been the same as that from which English practice sprang, for it was the typical European method of handling the new device of scenery. The book is the well-known *Pratica di Fabricar Scene e Machine ne' Teatri* by Nicola Sabbattini. A French translation by Mlles Canavaggia and M. Louis Jouvet was published in 1942, a German version was done in 1926 and an English translation exists in manuscript in the writer's collection. This manuscript contains the following passage relevant to Sabbattini's system of using grooves for shutter scenes. He discusses the subject in Chapters 13 and 15 of his Second Part. The backscenes only are made to work in grooves. Along the line upon the stage at which the backscene is to slide in two halves—'a groove must be made with two lengths of wood; it must be as long as from one side of the stage to the other and not more than an inch and a half deep, and should be well polished; smooth and soaped on the inside . . . it should be exactly as wide as the thickness of the battens of the backscene frame . . .', and he continues to discuss the opening of the scene in grooves, saying in Chapter 13 that the halves of the scene are held upright in the grooves by braces from the back wall of the stage and, in Chapter 15, adding an improved method by which the scenes slide on wheels in the lower grooves, each half of the backscene possessing backward-extending arms for support, which engage in a groove built into the sky-wall at the back and painted to match the sky. In Chapters 43, 44, 46, and 47 he discusses the movement of clouds in grooves, and here there may be something very close to John Ross's system of 1574—over half a century before.

These, however, are diversions from our study of the English masque and we return to the development of the shutters in London, and to our review of the mentions of the term in Jones's drawings. The next reference is brief: for Lodowick Carlell's *The Passionate Lovers* in 1638, Jones made a drawing (No. 319; see *Stuart Masques*, p. 146) on which there occurs as an inscription: 'The Wood 6 sceane. [The first scene, *struck out*] the wood a shutter in ye 2d part of Mr. Lodowicks play'.

Next comes *Salmacida Spolia* in 1640, the last and most informative of the masques with its many designs and its detailed and annotated plans. We shall shortly take this great masque as a subject for special analysis of the culminating masque technique; for the present we scan it lightly for information on shutters.

It is here we get the word 'shutter' applied to the wings as well as the back, in the term 'side shutters'. References to shutters in the annotations are as follows (see later Pl. 3);

The ground-plan is entitled 'Ground platt of a sceane where ye side peeces of ye sceane doe altogither change with ye back shutters . . .' In the drawing the following letters refer to shutters:

'D: Backshutters below.'
'I: The space for Releiues betwixt ye backshutters and backcloth when ye seates were lett downe under ye stage.'

There were three backshutter grooves, and four grooves in each of the four pairs of side-shutter sets of grooves.

Other references to shutters in inscriptions on the *Salmacida Spolia* drawings at Chatsworth are:

On that numbered 329, 'Zepherus behind ye 4 side shutter thrust forth in a grooue'. This is a cloud machine.

No. 340: '3 sceane of mountaynes the way to the seate of Honor K: & Q: masque 1640: a shutter'.

No. 349 bears the interesting memorandum: 'King and Queenes masque 1640. The great cloude wch comes fourth and opens and discouers ye Queenes seatte in a bright cloude.' 'To trye yf this great cloude may com dou[n]e betwene the groufes and then bee drawne open'; 'and whether ye shutters and this great cloude may not bee drawne a way boath togeather.' This might suggest that the shutters were moved by a machine to which the machinery of the moving cloud could be coupled, though it may refer to no more than a doubt that, in movement, one might foul the other.

The other references to shutters, making the full total of all that I have found in Jones's ascribed drawings, are:

On a sketch, No. 362, said to be for Habington's play *The Queen of Arragon*, 1640, 'Cleodora': 'first sceane a shutter of a fortified Towne & a Campe a farr off'. Then comes No. 364 from the same play: '3 sceane. A shutter with statues & figures a farr of:'

Among the less certain, or unidentified, drawings there is one connected with 'The Tragic Scene' (No. 366) which has the following cryptic notes on the back (possibly not related with the obverse):

shuters. the common sceane

[Cabinett 1. *struck out*]		cabinett	1.
a wrak & port	1.	the dreame	1.
princes hir chãber	1.	cabinett varied	1.
a desart	1.	a cattafalk	
too campes	1.		
princes chãber	1.		
the kinges chãber or prospectt	1.		

The mention on No. 375 is also interesting: 'ye 4th sceane a Chamber—a shutter sett back & so yt one might passe by'. The significance of this note will be mentioned on p. 138.

Among the unidentified scenes is No. 396: 'Wood of a new forme being a shutter [wood of Relieve 6 sceane *struck out*].'

And No. 397: 'The seuenth sceane a Prospect of Trees and houses a shutter'.

And No. 398: 'first sceane a pallas in trees pinted a shutter'.

And lastly No. 401, which is a glade in a mountain valley and simply has 'shutter of this sceane', being presumably the deeper part of a whole set, taken apart from the framing wings and designed separately.

Those are all the occasions of the use of the word 'shutter' that I have been able to find in Jones's notes on his drawings. Three of John Webb's designs for *The Siege of Rhodes* bear the word 'shutter' and will be discussed later. These are all the occasions of the use of the word that I have found before the Restoration.

4

MASQUES AT COURT

(THE GROOVES)

★

A Study of Lansdowne manuscript 1171 for information on grooves

WE have described the circumstances in which the ancient custom of static scenery was broken by the introduction of movement. We have seen that this movement was introduced purely for spectacular effect. We have described the appearances of particular pieces of scenery invented to exploit this effect, and found that the technical name of these pieces was 'shutters'.

We have now to ask how much can be found out about the way in which these shutters worked, and how their movement was made possible.

The first moving cloud worked, as we have noted, in a 'stere' or groove. In this chapter we shall find ample evidence of the development of the groove idea to become the essential element of visible scene-change in England.

The evidence we have on the early groove is virtually restricted to one source, but that is a remarkably full source. We shall find nothing so widely informative in our study for some two hundred years. This source is the major source of information on the working of all early British scenery and therefore deserves study in some detail here.

It consists of a number of papers bound together and now reposing in the British Museum under the title of Lansdowne MS. No. 1171. Some account of this manuscript was given in *Theatre Notebook*, vol. ii, No. 1, by the present writer, and the plates reproduced here are from this publication.

Lansdowne MS. No. 1171 is possibly the most important document yet discovered concerning the technical methods not only of the court masques but of that mechanical system by which the scenery of the first theatres of the Restoration was worked.

True, its bearing upon the methods used in the first public theatres of the Restoration is subject to confirmation, but when it is remembered, first that John Webb is the author of the latest pair of drawings included in the manuscript, second that the show for which those drawings were made was written by Sir William Davenant, third that Davenant and Webb are supposed to have been associated in the opening of the new playhouse in Lisle's Tennis Court, which set the pattern in 1661 for all its successors and broke the tradition of the earlier Elizabethan type of house, and, last, that the very show for which the above-mentioned plans of Webb's were made was, only five years later, the same show which (in an extended version) opened the career of the tennis-court playhouse—then the combination of all these facts makes it highly likely that the system illustrated in the manuscript was closely related to that introduced into the first regular public playhouse to use scenery at the opening of the new era in 1661.

If then the manuscript is evidence to us not only of masque technique but is also presumptive evidence of the scenic system upon which the whole career of post-Restoration scenery (including, ultimately, our own) is based, then it assumes very considerable importance and must be allowed to be something no serious student of the development of the theatre can ignore.

No complete reproduction of this manuscript had apparently ever been made before save on the occasion mentioned above, therefore no apology is needed for reproducing the plates here, though individual pages have been reproduced in line copies by Reyher, and in photographs by Allardyce Nicoll, W. G. Keith, and others.

The manuscript consists of ten drawings of various sizes bound together at a later date and with no apparent order. Some considerable study has been made of certain of these, notably by William Grant Keith in *The Burlington Magazine* (vol. xxv, pp. 29 et seq.), to whom we owe a highly valuable identification. Some of the drawings are uninscribed and unidentified, some bear copious notes and are clearly named as belonging to a given play and date. The notes have, in nearly all cases (but with at least two very important exceptions), been carefully transcribed and published in *Designs by Inigo Jones for Masques and Plays at Court*.

The subjects of the drawings are briefly as follows:

ff. 1b and 2. Double-spread containing on f. 2 a section through the stage and scene for *Salmacida Spolia* (1640), and on f. 1b a list of explanatory notes (see accompanying Pl. 2).

ff. 3b and 4. Double-spread containing a ground-plan of the above (see Pl. 3). Both these items are ascribed by Keith to John Webb's hand.

ff. 5b and 6. A long drawing, folded in four, containing a ground-plan of the stage and of the auditorium for *Florimène* (1635). attributed by Keith to Jones's hand (see Pl. 4).

ff. 6b and 7. A somewhat smaller double-spread bound in upside down, showing the section of a so-far-unidentified stage (see Pl. 5).

ff. 8*b* and 9. Double-spread showing plan of stage and auditorium for a so-far-unidentified show (see Pl. 7).

ff. 10*b* and 11. Two drawings on separate sheets, the former being a plan (see Pl. 10) and the latter a section (see Pl. 11) by John Webb. These have been identified by Keith as for *The Siege of Rhodes* on its Rutland House performance in 1656. Note: the folios in the manuscript have been confusingly numbered in the top right-hand corners by some later hand, and though some figures have been altered the whole needs renumbering before consistent reference can be made—hence the discrepancy between the folio numbers in the present review and those used by Keith.

ff. 12*b* and 13. Two separate drawings inscribed as for *Florimène*. Both are studies in technical perspective. The former shows a curious attempt at setting up a skeleton perspective from a plan (see Pl. 8) and the latter gives a brief sketch-section of a stage with certain sight-lines towards the bases of the wings (see Pl. 9).

ff. 14*b* and 15. Double-spread showing an alternative ground-plan of the stage only, in *Florimène* (see Pl. 16).

All the last three are ascribed by Keith to Webb's hand.

An examination of these drawings for information on grooves shows that the first evidence from the chronological point of view, though still leaving the subject in some mystery, does give us a real starting-point. It is in the two plans for the staging of *Florimène*, a French pastoral, at court in 1635 (see Pls. 4 and 16).

The first shows the plan of the stage and full hall. On the stage are curious bipartite wings like our modern hinged, or 'booked', wings, but set with the 'knuckle' (or angle) pointing towards the audience, not away from it. There are four pairs. Immediately behind these is a line across the whole stage, with, behind, an arrangement, to either side, of two pairs of shorter lines that would appear to have been hidden behind the wings directly in front. Behind these again, in the centre of the stage, are three, separate, medium-length lines, and then a long, double one.

When we turn, however, to the second plan for the same show, *Florimène*, where the stage only is shown, we see a difference in respect of some of these lines. The pairs directly behind the wings now extend to meet in the middle of the stage. Moreover, this plan bears an inscription:

First Ground platt of that kind of sceane with triangular frames on ye sydes where there is but one standing sceane and ye sceane changes only at the Back-shutters comparted by ye scene for ye Pastorall of Florimene in the hall at Whitehall 1635.

The only place in these two drawings where particular difference occurs is in this group of lines behind the wings. In the first the lines are confined to the side leaving a centre opening: in the second they are brought in to the centre and form the back of the scene. It is, now, highly likely that if they are closed in, or *shut*, and so form the *back* of the scene, then they must be those *Backshutters* referred to in the legend. We interpret this legend as meaning that the plan shows a particular arrangement of scenery wherein the sides are composed of 'triangular' wings (that is, each forming two sides of a triangle), and that these wings are 'standing', that is to say they remain unchanged throughout the show. The only change of scene which does occur is achieved by dividing the backscene and sliding it apart in two halves, or by shutting together over it two fresh pieces to meet and form a new complete back piece. Two such pairs of shutters would enable two scenes to be alternated. Our question at the moment is, *How did the shutters shut and open?*

Let us turn to Pl. 5. Here is a longitudinal section of a stage, as yet unidentified. At a point on the stage floor roughly corresponding with the long line across on Pl. 4, is shown a step down; immediately behind are two uprights reaching up from the stage to a square beam, a little less than half-way to the roof. These two uprights are our 'shutters' shown in side view. How are they supported? There are three small squares at the feet of the shutters, and similarly at the heads. If we take these to be the end-sections of strips of wood fixed to the stage floor and, correspondingly, on the cross-beam above, in order to form 'ways' or tramlines for the shutters to run in, we then begin to see our answer: here are grooves.

We may notice in passing that the upper half of this backscene is composed of a similar, but hanging, piece, constructed so as to have its head running also in a grooved way, suspended from the roof.

Let us examine further pages in the manuscript before we seek to crystallize our argument. Pl. 7 shows a plan of another stage. Here again it is unidentified, but here again is seen an arrangement similar to the open shutters of our first plan of *Florimène*.

We turn now to Pls. 2 and 3. And here we find our principal information. These show a section and plan respectively, of the stage and scenery for Sir William Davenant's *Salmacida Spolia*, presented in 1640. *Salmacida Spolia* was possibly one of the most notable shows in English theatrical history, so far as concerns its contribution to the technical story and its influence on the whole successive form of stage presentation. In *Salmacida Spolia* there was not merely a change of one or two elements of the back scenery, but four complete changes of every piece visible—wings and borders as well as 'backshutters' or backscenes. This is the first English show of which we have graphic record of such an achievement. And in this achievement, grooves played a part *sine qua non*.

The drawings are full and contain great detail; much of the detail we shall analyse later, but it suffices for our present purpose concerning grooves to note the following:

On the drawing of the section there occurs a lengthy inscription entitled:

Profyle of ye sceane when ye sceane doth wholy change aswell on ye sydes as at ye back shutters, and when ye syde peeces are made to change by running in groues.

Here is our first certainty. We are now launched on our story, for here we have grooves shown as such and specifically named as such. The 'hero' of our biography takes on a recognizable individuality.

Coming to details, we find these grooves situated at the bottom and at the head of each group of wings. There are four of these groups, with four wings in each group. The back, or fifth, set of grooves carries, as the ground-plan shows, not wings but backshutters, this time to the number of three. These groups of grooves are all of similar appearance, consisting of a flat backboard with strips fastened along it (or grooves channelled out of it) so forming the 'groues', in which the pieces 'are made to change', as described in the legend, by sliding to and fro.

There follows a series of elucidatory remarks applying to the lettered parts of the two drawings. Among them, the following refer to grooves:

B. The side shutters which runne in groues & change ye sceane 4: seuerall tymes.

G. A crosse peece of tymber which went in ye groues to which ye seate was fastened . . .

L. Peeces of tymber which bore upp ye groues of ye backshutters & ye back-cloth.

R. The peeces of Clouds which came downe from ye roofe before ye upper part of ye syde shutters whereby ye grooues aboue were hidden & also ye howse behind them:
    These Clouds also went in grooues marked S: & changed with ye sceanes below:

V. The upper back shutters which were also hung in grooues and changed as ye others did.

There is one other example of the grooves in this manuscript, again as used in an historically important show—one which was to have a great influence on the groove's future life, and one by which it was to gain its introduction to its proper career and full use in the public theatre—the show is Davenant's *The Siege of Rhodes*, as it was first privately performed in 1656, with scenes by John Webb, at Davenant's house.

This performance at Rutland House has frequently been discussed—by William Grant Keith in *The Burlington Magazine* (vol. xxv, pp. 29 et seq.), by Montague Summers in *The Playhouse of Pepys* (chap. 1), and elsewhere

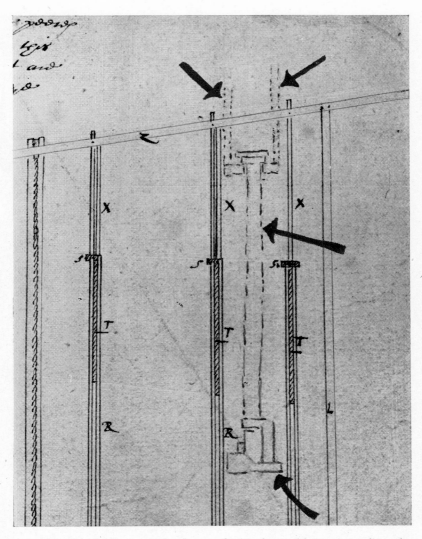

1. Detail of Pl. 2, with signs of cloud machine strengthened.
(Pls. 1–11 and Pl. 16 are from Lansdowne MS. 1171, British
Museum)

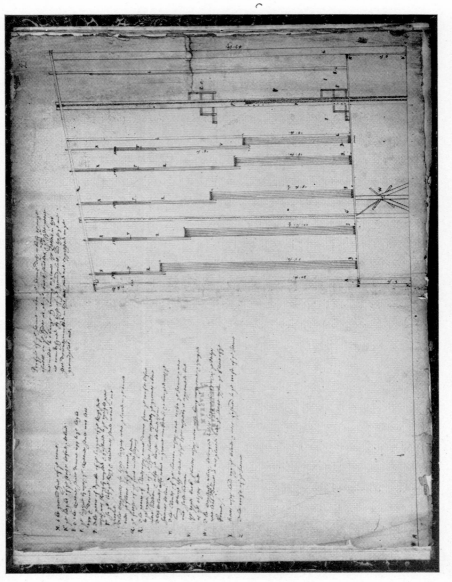

2. Section for *Salmacida Spolia*, 1640

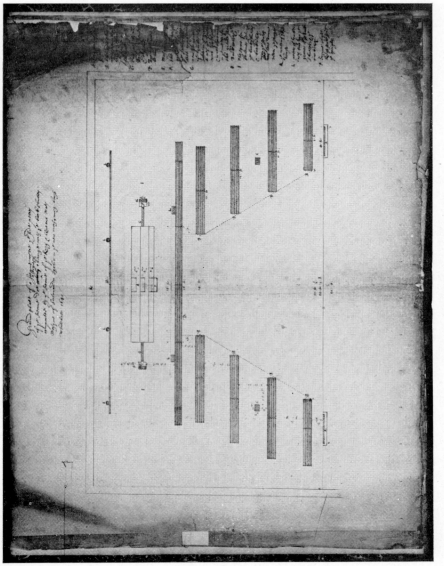

3. Plan for *Salmacida Spolia*, 1640

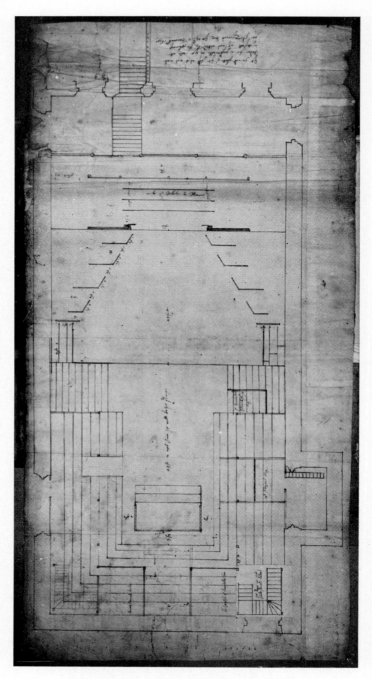

4. Plan of stage and hall for *Florimène*, 1635

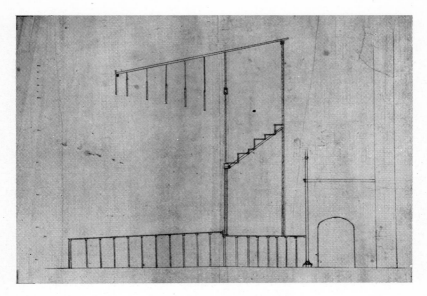

5. Section of unidentified stage

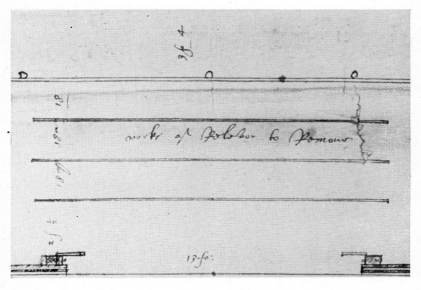

6. Detail of Pl. 4

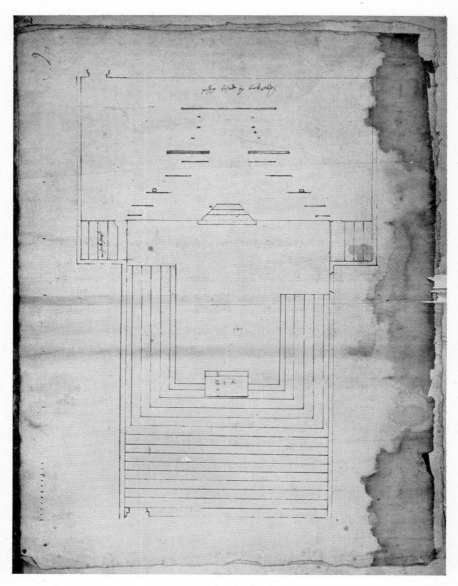

7. Plan of unidentified stage

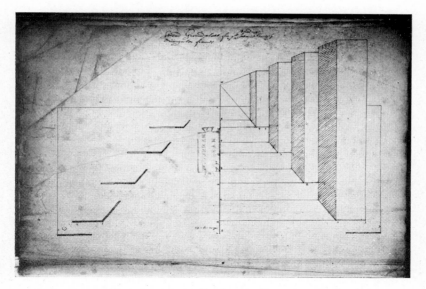

8. Perspective study for *Florimène*, 1635

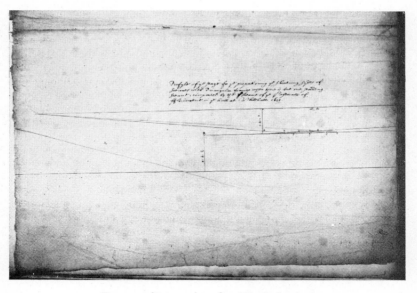

9. Perspective section for *Florimène*, 1635

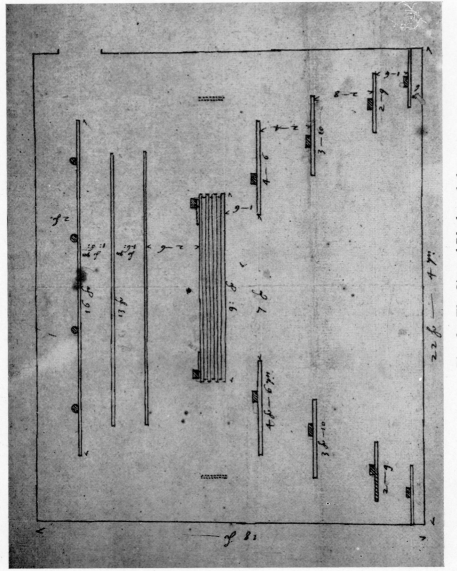

10. Plan for *The Siege of Rhodes*, 1656

—and its importance as an occasion in English theatre history is recognized. The stage was small, measuring 22 ft. 4 in. wide and 18 ft. deep; and the backscenes were only 9 ft. wide by 7 ft. 6 in. high. This is in marked contrast with the dimensions of the stage for *Salmacida Spolia* which is shown as 55 ft. 9 in. wide and 48 ft. deep with a proscenium-opening 30 ft. high—unusual figures even for a stage today.

The general features of arrangement in *The Siege of Rhodes* are discussed by Keith (op. cit.) and will be given here only briefly; two special details have, however, suffered confusion and these will be considered at length.

This stage of 1656, which was possibly to serve as the basic pattern for the scenic arrangements of the public stages of the Restoration and early-Georgian periods, is shown in the plan and section (Pls. 10 and 11) to be as follows.

The stage was divided into two equal sections, of which the front was built at a slope of 1 in 27, and the back was level, dropping down by a step of 4 in. from the summit of the slope. A simple *frontispiece* was built 6 in. back from the front of the stage, with plain upright sides and a top-piece sloping slightly forward. Three pairs of posts were arranged behind in converging pairs to support the wings. This system of supporting wings against posts only obtained when the wings were intended to stay permanently in position throughout the whole show. In other shows (such, for instance, as *Salmacida Spolia*) when the wings had to be changed they were held in grooves. Over each pair of wings a border ran across the stage from side to side to frame-in the top of the scene. These borders are shown in Webb's section as—rather interestingly—not touching the tops of the wings, and thus apparently leaving a gap between wing and border above, through which the audience would see the side walls of the stage (a fault which Jones specifically guarded against). It is, however, highly probable that these borders were in fact slightly arched, and though at the centre they rose to the elevation shown in the drawings, yet at the ends they dropped to the wing-tops. The question however, arises: Did they drop in front of, or behind, the wings?

In most normal stage-procedure in England a border edge was arranged to drop in front of the corresponding wing-top. It thus hid the upper edge of the wing, and this, as will be shown, was a highly necessary piece of concealment. This section of Webb's is, however, interesting in showing the borders directly *above* the wings—neither in front nor behind. Further, in the well-known drawing at Chatsworth (reproduced in Keith's article) showing a view of the frontispiece of *The Siege of Rhodes*, and of the wings behind, it appears that the wing-tops are profiled, or cut to the shape of the summits of the rocks painted upon them (see Pl. 25a). Such an edge would appear to have been lost if the borders came in front of it. Webb then may either have used an unorthodox arrangement on the ground that his wings had not to be shifted, or on the other hand it may well be that he in point of fact did *not* profile their tops after all but finished them off with a strip of sky and a straight-cut edge, just below which the irregular outline of the rock-summits was merely painted. In this case his border could conveniently have hung just in front of this edge and joined with it in painting-effect.

When now, however, we resume our process up the stage we find elements represented on the farther, flat half of it which have set investigators much more puzzling problems.

Immediately behind the step comes the complex unit which we now identify with the working of the *shutters*. Behind this again are three lines, the first two of which are named by Keith as the 'releive' scenes and the last as the backcloth. All these will bear detailed examination.

To begin with the grooves. The chief inconsistence which has puzzled students in the matter of the *Rhodes* grooves is that there is indication in the play, and in Webb's scene-designs, of only *three* shutters needed for the performance. Each of these may be examined in the drawings and carefully checked against the text of the play. And yet in the diagrams of plan and section in the manuscript there has been held by authorities to be clear indication of grooves for *four* shutters. Even Mr. Keith finds difficulty on this score and solves it only very tentatively by supposing one of those shutters was in some way connected with the make-up of a 'releive' scene.

In point of fact I believe a different solution, consistent with the figures, may be found which considerably assists our knowledge of later stage machinery. Let us examine these lines which at first sight appear to indicate the presence of four shutter-scenes.

We may begin with the section (Pl. 11). At the foot of the grooves the configuration of the lines in the drawing is such that we appear to see three small blocks on the stage floor separating four uprights, each composed of a pair of lines. This interpretation most investigators have accepted. But in studying the upper grooves it becomes clear that the right-hand pair of lines of the four is not securely nested in a groove; its forward edge is unconfined and touches directly the back of the border. Can this pair of lines then represent something other than the end-section of a shutter? Once this possibility be accepted the whole conception changes. Let us now for a moment suppose that *no shutters at all* are shown in this section. Those upright lines then have some other meaning. What may it be?

Referring to the plan we see that these pairs of lines, whatever they are, represent something slightly longer than the intervening strips which we noticed as blocks in the end-section. This again might tend to the view that they represented shutters slightly longer than the grooves. But here we see that neither the front pair nor the back pair are supplied with final confining strips. Those in front might conceivably be held back by the riser of the step in the stage which comes just in front (though that involves an unworkmanlike friction against the painted surface), but the pair at the back of the group come without any interruption dead against two mysterious short strips which project inwards from either shaded upright post.

The meaning of these short strips we hope to suggest later, but at the moment we may go so far as to say that they certainly appear more likely to represent a piece of scenery than an empty interval. Thus we may argue that what comes immediately in front of the two short strips is more likely to represent an interval than a piece of scenery, since two pieces of scenery running close together would involve scratching.

The new conception now arises that perhaps what have been hitherto considered the 'intervals' between each pair of lines represent in fact the shutters themselves (or spaces for them) and that what we had supposed to be the shutters are really something to do with a means for separating them and perhaps for assisting them to slide.

In support of such a reading is the unavoidable fact that there are *three* shutter scenes in the play, and *three* of these 'gaps' between the pairs of lines.

Turning now to the section again, the objector immediately inquires how we may explain the fact that these 'intervals', or separating-pieces between what we now claim to be the positions of shutters, are shown as being slotted into the headboard above, just as it might be supposed the shutter-frames might be slotted into grooves?

Once such a question is boldly faced it becomes apparent that there is one answer and that this may exactly explain the situation; namely that the upright pairs of lines are not shutters but four narrow *vertical posts* at either end of the grooves separating the upper grooves from the lower and built in to form one solid framework with these. A method which, when one comes to think of it, is far more workmanlike than to support the upper grooves only by the two uprights at their hinder edge and the short stay from the ceiling. These latter are there merely to keep the single solid framework in place, not to support the weight of the upper grooves, for which latter purpose they would be, considering the lateral thrusts suffered by the shutters in changes, insufficiently strong.

If now we have to picture an upper and a lower set of grooves separated at either end by four narrow uprights, we are offered three intervals for the running of three shutters between them, but how then do we explain the three small 'blocks' below on the stage and coming between these uprights in positions where we would suppose the shutters should run?

[51]

The answer may be suggested by considering the upper grooves. Here we have what appears to be firstly a grooved element to hold the scenes and secondly a sort of backboard above to which this is fixed. But what is the structural use of such a backboard? Its function is already discharged, it would seem, by the ungrooved portion of the member below—the function of a supporting bed for the ridges between the grooves.

At this point the need for questioning John Webb's ethics as a careful draughtsman arises. Once we face that question we find, alas, that those ethics were not too sound. In many of his drawings Webb was guilty of errors of measurement and confusions of statement—the height of the stage in the section, for instance, to take these drawings alone, is given as 2 ft. 6 in., but the height of the stage shown on the elevation of the proscenium arch is 3 ft. Indeed, a study of Webb's work will bring the suggestion that he was often very hard put to control his medium of plans, sections, and elevational representations, and frequently had recourse to corrections.

Since there is no logical interpretation, then, of his groove-sketch as it stands, the only possible alternative left must claim the right to consideration, and that is that the conformation of the actual carpentry is not here quite exactly represented.

The only arrangement that will fit both the practicalities of carpentry and be consistent (with certain likely reservations) with the detail of the drawing would seem to be as is described below, and this we offer as our theory of how the pre-Restoration groove was constructed. Since, however, a merely verbal description of a complicated three-dimensional machine is never likely to be fully communicative, it seemed better to study this theory in actual practice as far as possible. To this end a scale model was made of the whole arrangement and made in a somewhat unusual way—John Webb's original designs for the scenery of *The Siege of Rhodes* (see Pl. 25) were specially photographed with the valuable assistance of the photographers of Messrs. Common Ground Ltd. (and the information included in a film-strip); with their help, enlargements were made under the present writer's direction of each of the details of scenery in the designs so that all were reproduced to the same scale of half an inch to one foot. These were mounted and cut out separately, and assembled according to the theory outlined here and later in this book. For their assembly a model of Webb's stage was made to the same scale and a careful reconstruction of the groove element. This reconstruction is shown in place on the stage in Pl. 12.

The photograph may perhaps be considered as a tentative representation of what the actual stage looked like as it was being arranged for the show. The step down about the middle is shown, together with the holes in the stage floor for the insertion of posts to support the wings; and the backcloth is represented in position. A line round the side walls of the model stands for the join between the actual walls and the ceiling-level at Rutland House. On the far side the mounted photograph of one of the backscenes is visible, cut in two halves and leaning against the wall as a pair of shutters might before being put into position. In the centre of the stage, just behind the step, is what interests us most at this point—the model of the groove element itself. This may be referred to as an aid in understanding the following description. Pl. 13 shows the same stage but with the three pairs of shutters now in position (the deepest pair half-closed) and the wings set up on the far side of the stage. Further photographs of the model showing progress in the erection of the scenes will be referred to in a later chapter.

Beginning now at the top of the grooves, suppose a flat plank of wood to act as the inverted basis to which the rest is built. Below this we suggest four strips of timber of such dimensions as 3 in. × 1 in. placed on edge longitudinally along the whole surface. Between these, acting as distance-pieces and again placed on edge, are three strips of narrower timber, possibly 2 in. × 1 in., and each a couple of inches shorter than the first strips; these it is which are shown as projecting down between the uprights. Now into each end of the wider strips is jointed a vertical piece of 3 in. × 1 in. forming, with the corresponding piece in the lower grooves, a complete open rectangular frame. Four of these frames, with their upper and lower separating strips, formed the whole and supplied the three intervals or 'ways' in which the shutters ran.

All that would be needed to make Webb's drawing true to this arrangement would be to carry up the pairs of vertical lines in the section to meet the first horizontal line above them. Then we should claim that the three squares at the bottom on the stage floor represented, not divisions between shutters, but the beds of grooves upon which the shutters ran—grooves whose walls are concealed behind the intervening uprights which rise upwards between each bed. Similarly above, the down-projecting elements of the 'battlemented' line do not represent the separating groove-walls between four shutters, but the beds between four concealed strips which thus afford openings for *three* shutters.

Such a claim to explain a drawing on the basis of the inaccuracy of the draughtsman needs special support. It would be good to be able to show that in the work of his master, Inigo Jones, instance could be found of a similar detail there correctly portrayed but, in its treatment, open to misunderstanding, at a superficial glance, of just the sort suggested above.

There is, I think, something more than a mere coincidence in the fact that exactly such an instance can be shown. It is in the section for *Salmacida Spolia* reproduced on Pl. 2. This diagram, though probably from the hand of Webb, is taken to be a copy from Inigo Jones who undoubtedly was the designer of this masque. There, just under the bottom of the collection of lower backshutter grooves, a tiny diagram (showing as no more than a short line in Pl. 2) has been inset showing the 'battlemented' profile of the groove-ends. This is correctly drawn in the section itself so it would appear not to be an emendation but, more likely, an emphasis of some point too easily confused.

Here the matter is irrefutable. The drawing of the section clearly shows eight lines, indicating four uprights and three intervening open spaces for shutters. (And we know that three backshutters were in fact required in the scene-plot of *Salmacida Spolia*.) But here the uprights are correctly shown rising not from the groove *beds* but *from the intervening walls between them*. The evidence is reinforced, in this diagram, by the wing, or side-shutter, grooves. Of these the masque demanded four (and a note on the ground-plan says specifically that these side shutters 'runne in groues & change yᵉ sceane 4: seuerall tymes').

Here, then, is incontrovertible proof that a groove-group designed to hold four scenes was represented on section by means of *five* uprights and four beds, and similarly, one to hold three scenes showed *four* uprights and three intervals. This is exactly what we have shown the section for *The Siege of Rhodes* to do, and we may now summarize our theory of the construction of these grooves by describing them as composed of four rectangular wooden frames measuring about 7 ft. 8 in. high by 11 ft. 2 in. wide by 1 in. thick, and built of timber some 3 in. wide. These were assembled flat against each other but separated by $1\frac{1}{2}$ in.-thick distance-strips, each a couple of inches deep, running along top and bottom. The whole was stood on edge on the stage, battened together across the top edges, and stayed in position by two tall posts behind and a timber from the ceiling. This will be considered when we deal in full with the staging of the whole show in its place. The scene-drawings are reproduced and discussed by Keith in *The Burlington Magazine*.

So much for the contribution of the volume of plans in the Lansdowne MS. It is clear that there are clues therein to many subjects beyond grooves, but we cannot essay too much at once. We may summarize our information as follows.

Grooves were employed by Inigo Jones as early at least as 1635, for guiding the movement of pieces of scenery during a scene-change.

At first they were only used to guide the two halves of a backscene as it closed, or slid open, but by 1640 the system was extended.

Firstly, in each wing position there were two sets of grooves, one at the feet of the wings, resting on the stage, the other suspended from above, grooves-down, and supporting the tops of the wings. All the wings for the various scenes of the show were set in their grooves at the beginning, and the particular pieces for the first scene were pushed on into position, the rest, belonging to other scenes, were drawn back in the grooves and were hidden. The wings were called the *Side Shutters*.

Secondly, the backscenes (or those, at least, composed of a flat painted surface, for the relieve scene, as we shall study later, had nothing to do with grooves) were bisected down the middle, and slid together or apart, at need, in similar grooves, this time, of course, much longer, and now extending right across the acting-area of the stage. The backscene itself was called a *Backshutter*.

Thirdly, there might be, above the backshutter, an *Upper Backshutter*, constituting the upper half of the backscene, and itself sundering and slid-ing apart to reveal a group of deities in heaven or some such elevated vision. These upper backshutters hung, and were engaged in, a groove only at the upper edge.

Finally, there was a curious further piece of scenery, a sort of cross between a side border and an upper wing. Jones calls them: 'R. The peeces of Clouds which came downe from ye roofe before ye upper part of ye syde shutters, whereby ye grooues aboue' (that is, the grooves that held the wing-tops) 'were hidden and also ye howse behind them: These Clouds also went in grooues marked S: and changed with ye sceanes below'.

But it seems that the borders proper did not change; they were 'T: the clouds of ye heaven which went crosse ye sceane and were hung betwixt the Clouds of ye sydes whereby it appeared but one sole heaven'.

The long 'ends' of the border did, then, hang in grooves, and joined border proper to wing-top, and themselves changed at need (as from stormy sky to fair), but the central, true border remained.

We have, then, grooves for four different types of scenery, the back-shutters, the wings, the upper backshutters, and the side clouds.

In passing, we may note Jones's desire to hide these grooves so that they should not mar his effect. Yet at two points they must have presented special difficulties: how, when the backshutters were opened, was the empty groove across the back of the floor of the stage hidden? (We have seen that on some stages it was concealed by a step, but not on all.) And how, when both lower shutters and upper shutters were open together, were the grooves above the lower shutters concealed from sight?—in other words, how were they prevented from spanning with an ugly horizontal band any scene combining the vault of heaven above with a stretch of distant landscape beneath? (With the technical constitution of this occasionally-disclosed deep scene of far landscape, or other view, disclosed when all backshutters were open, we shall deal later.)

The answers to the above two questions are not yet immediately clear.

[55]

They will emerge after a closer study of the elements of scenes later, but first we shall have occasion to see how the problem remained a problem throughout the history of grooves, and eventually occasioned a special set of machinery to avoid it.

In addition we may note another, slightly different, use of the groove, where guidance was given for the movement of some flying god or chariot or piece of scenery that had to rise or descend before the audience.

The groove, then, forms the principle by which movement was controlled on the stage. Whenever the scenes had to be shifted, or when an 'effect' was presented involving a flying actor or a moving cloud, the groove was laid under contribution for the control of the movement.

The groove at this time was also to be found on the Continent. That inexhaustible observer of the novelties of the new Renaissance age, the German, Furttenbach, noted it in his accounts of methods of staging collected in his travels, and some record of it may be read in his *Mannhafter Kunstspiegel*, published in 1663. His information adds little, however, to the examples given by Inigo Jones. Nicola Sabbattini in *Pratica di fabricar scene e machine ne' teatri* (1637-8) and Andrea Pozzo in his treatise on *Perspective* both refer to grooves.

So much then for our immediate question concerning the method by which shutters were worked in grooves. We now have to answer another, quite different, question, reference to which has been made above more than once, and which we have put off till this moment; the question is, What was the nature of that sort of scene which served as an alternative to the shutter scenes, and which did not work in grooves?

5

MASQUES AT COURT

(THE 'SCENES OF RELIEVE')

--- ★ ---

The position of relieves in plans—The meaning of the word 'relieve'—The representation of relieves in designs—'The Queen of Arragon', 1640—The planes of relief—The framing of relieves—'Salmacida Spolia', 1640

--- ★ ---

THE kind of scene which formed the alternative to the more usual shutter scenes was called the 'scene of relieve'. Few scholars have ventured upon a theory of the make-up of relieve scenes. Montague Summers alluded to them, without clarifying his term, as 'moulded scenes' (which a recent book has reduced to absurdity because, misunderstanding his phrase, it has described a relieve scene as a scene with mouldings on), and William Grant Keith frankly regards their nature as not precisely to be determined.

We must try to define more clearly than has been done hitherto just what a scene of relieve appears to have been. We have hinted above at the position of this type of scene on the stage as being 'behind the shutters'. We have to begin our study of it by substantiating this hint at its position, and to do so we turn again to the plans in the Lansdowne MS.

In the first two plans (see Pls. 2 and 3) we see that there is mentioned in the notes something which is called 'The space for Releiues betwixt ye backshutters and backcloth when ye seates were lett downe under ye stage' (those 'seates' were certain disappearing pieces connected with the cloud machinery).

The first piece of evidence then is that the space at the back of the stage 'betwixt ye backshutters and backcloth', besides affording opportunity for the manipulation of certain effects of rising or descending figures, was available also, upon the clearing away of the machinery, for relieves. We thus establish their position, which we shall find is the same in all the drawings.

It is very important for true understanding that we should avoid a fixed idea that backshutters came right at the back of the stage; they were never situated deeper than about two-thirds of the distance between front and back of stage, and the significance of the term *back* which qualifies them is not that they formed the back limit of scenery, but only that they formed the back of that part of the scenery which worked on the shutter principle. In *Salmacida Spolia* the wings, too, slid in grooves, and were then called *side* shutters. Backshutters are so called not because they are at the back of the stage, but so as to distinguish them from the side shutters; backshutters are intermediate in position, and when they are all fully open a further depth of stage is still revealed behind them. In this the scenes of relieve were set.

Further than this these two drawings give us no information. Neither on plan nor section is any diagrammatic indication made of these relieves nor any further mention in the inscriptions.

On turning to Pl. 4 we are offered a little more. Here is the plan of the complete theatre—stage and auditorium—'as it was made redye for a pasterall in the hall at whitthall wch was akted by the ffrench on St. Thomas day the 23th of december 1635'.

This earlier plan may perhaps be expected in the circumstances to show a less elaborately developed technique. It is taken by all authorities to be for the performance of *Florimène*, and the system of scene-change is here clearly simpler than that in *Salmacida Spolia*, although the actual plan inscribed *Florimène*, on Pl. 16, is slightly different in measurements. In *Salmacida Spolia* both wings and backshutters changed with the scenes, while here the wings are of an older type and stand through the show and only the backshutters change.

But behind these backshutters we have a definite piece of evidence: in the place appointed for relieves, that is between the backshutter and the backcloth (both clearly marked), are three simple parallel lines, the first is $2\frac{1}{2}$ ft. back from the shutters, with 18 in. separating it from the second, and again the second from the third, and the third from the backcloth. Between backcloth and back wall of stage is 3 ft. 4 in. (see Pl. 4).

Most interesting of all is the inscription on these three lines, which is not noted in the *Designs by Inigo Jones for Masques and Plays at Court*, and which to my knowledge has not been remarked by any other authority. It reads (see Pl. 6): 'works of Relevo to Remouv'. These relieves then can be definitely stated to have been movable, that is capable of being set and struck.

Pl. 5 offers us no information on our subject save that the section there drawn shows that the deeper part of the stage—that extending from just in front of the first backshutter to the back wall—was here flat in contradistinction to the raked front part of the stage, and that it dropped, by a step, a few inches below the top of that raked part, being in fact no higher than the very front of the stage near the audience.

Pl. 7 offers something more. Here is an unnamed plan of a stage showing what is presumably a proscenium with four pairs of simple wings behind, a set of backshutters shown open, and, near the back wall of the stage, a backcloth. Between shutters and backcloth there are no lines as in the *Florimène* plan, but there are instead six tiny squares arranged in pairs, flanking the opening behind the shutters.

These are very similar in appearance to other squares on the plans for *The Siege of Rhodes* where they represent vertical posts. We find them also in the plan for *Salmacida Spolia* in three positions, two behind the backshutters, four behind the backcloth (all lettered L), and one either side intermediate between the second and third sets of wings, where they are lettered C. The inscription clearly describes L as 'peeces of tymber which bore upp ye groues of ye backshutters, and ye backcloth', and C (less clearly) as 'Engynes by which Deityes ascend and discend'. Fortunately these are all clearly shown on the accompanying section and leave no doubt that they were all square posts of wood reaching up to the roof over the stage.

In the plan we are discussing there are two similar squares also directly behind the second pair of wings.

When we turn over to Pl. 10, the plan for *The Siege of Rhodes*, we find these supports not only behind the backcloth and shutters as usual but behind each wing, though we do not now find any in the space between shutters and cloth. Instead we find here a reversion to the *Florimène* method of representation, and 2 ft. 6 in. behind the shutters we have a 13-ft. long line; 1 ft. 6 in. back from that, a second; and then 1 ft. 6 in. away again, the backcloth, with 2 ft. between it and the back wall. Here, then, only two lines are shown in the space for relieves instead of three as in *Florimène*. In the accompanying section (Pl. 11) we see the side view of all the upright supports, and may notice that here only two pairs of these reach to the roof above the stage, those behind the proscenium and those behind the shutters. We have further an item of great interest: the only representation to my knowledge of scenes of relieve in section. There are two double lines rising, the first pair to just above the shutters, and the second a trifle higher.

On Pls. 8 and 9 we have little to help us save a very slight indication that the upper part of the stage behind the wings was flat, not raked like the rest.

On Pl. 16 we have a plan inscribed as being for *Florimène*, showing the backshutters closed, and three lines between them and the backcloth. This plan is especially interesting in bearing the inscription against these lines: 'Works of Releivo'. Here then is the specific name applied to these lines. It should be noted here that though no indication of removal is present, this inscription, like that on Pl. 6, does use the word 'works' and use it in the plural. This either implies that many relieves could be set here one after another, or that a relieve scene had several parts.

Summarizing the information on the plans we have, behind the back-shutters of these stages, usually a step down and then a flat area of stage instead of a continuation of the rake. At the back of this is a wide backcloth in every case, and in some cases three lines or two lines, all a little longer than the width of the opening between the shutters, and which, in one case, are inscribed 'works of Relevo to Remouv'. In one case also these lines are replaced by three pairs of squares that possibly represent supporting timbers.

A final point concerning the plans: in Pls. 4, 10, and 16 a small feature is noticeable directly behind the position of the shutters which is in the nature of a very short line on either side, drawn inwards from the wooden supports upholding the backshutter grooves, and projecting from these towards the centre of the stage.

Turning now from the plans to the word itself to see what information can be gained there and to inquire into its probable significance; it is found in Jones's notes in a variety of spellings—

Releue (see *Designs*, p. 11 and p. 132)
Releiue (pp. 76, 99, 100, 101, 119, 130, 131, 132)
releaue (p. 109)
relievo (p. 136)
Relieve (p. 140)
Relevo (Lansdowne MS., f. 6)
Releive (*Rhodes*, Sc. 3)
of Releaue (see below)
hole Releaue (see below).

But, confusing though the word may have been to their orthography, the question is, What did it convey to Jones's and Webb's minds?

The theories hitherto advanced by authorities as to the nature of the relieve scene turn upon the interpretation of the word 'relieve'. It may mean one of two things: either that what is said to be 'of relieve' was modelled, or that it was composed of separate flat planes. The same ambiguity attaches to our modern phrase 'in relief'; it may either signify that the object is partly modelled or 'bossed out', or it may signify that part of the object is detached from the background and, though itself flat, stands out in relief against that ground; thus a cut-out cardboard figure placed in front of a flat ground in a tobacconist's window may be said to be in relief, or thrown into relief, against that ground. The distinction is between essentially flat, cut-out things against a ground and things actually modelled in three dimensions and not necessarily set before a separate ground.

The question then arises: Was a scene of relieve a modelled scene in three dimensions, or was it composed of one, or more, flat, two-dimensional planes, cut out and placed before a background? And over this question there is disagreement. Montague Summers talks of '"the relieves", or scenes in relief, moulded scenes', while William Grant Keith, though also using the phrase 'in relief', tends, guardedly, to suggest the arrangement was one of different planes.

A certain amount of support may seem to be given to the former view by certain usages of the word in the descriptions of the scenes printed in the published scripts of the masques. Thus in the text of *Hymenaei* we read concerning the scene that: 'On the sides . . . were placed two great *Statues*, fayn'd of Gold . . . bearing up the Cloudes, which were of *Releue*, embossed, and tralucent, as Naturalls', or this from *The Lords' Masque*, where the scene 'was divided into two parts from the roofe to the floore, the lower part being first discovered there appeared a Wood in *prospective*, the inner-most part being of releaue or whole round, the rest painted'. Such evidence would seem to settle the matter without any question that to be 'of relieve' meant to be modelled in the 'whole round'.

There are such arguments against this interpretation, however, that we may begin to suppose it likely that 'of whole round' is a mistake or mis-interpretation arising from the deceptive artifice of the cut scenery—or at least this is so in some cases—since it is inconsistent to suppose (referring to the last quotation) that the foreground was painted and the background built. The reverse is the usual arrangement when such a mixture of painted and built stuff is employed. But apart from this there are some five objec-tions to the theory of modelled scenery.

The first objection is that, without exception, the plans and sections that we possess, showing relieves, state them as flat things with no indication of any forward projection.

Secondly, it will be shown that there is much reason to suppose the short lines projecting inwards from the uprights supporting the shutter-grooves were part of the relieves, and these could not have been modelled, for in all occasions they are within a few inches of the back of the shutter-grooves, and in one occasion (*Siege of Rhodes*, Pl. 10) actually touching them.

Thirdly, we may raise the objection that modelled scenery seems, artistically, highly unlikely to be used in conjunction with flat, painted wings and interspersed among flat, painted shutter-scenes. An inconsistence of technique arises since, with any system of lighting that we may suppose to have been used on the masque stages, unpleasant cast shadows would have been almost impossible to avoid were part of the scenery modelled and the rest flat-painted.

Fourthly, we may turn to Jones's own words. On the back of No. 286 is an account of certain work in connexion with staging:

> for ye masques the Mr Carpenter
> for ye stage shutters and cloudes—12
> and putting bourdes togeather for
> sceanes of releaue

It is difficult to see why the 'putting of bourdes togeather' in connexion with 'sceanes of releaue' should have been an item of any importance were the resulting sheets of wood merely to be used as bases or backboards for modelling upon—any rough battening-out at the back would have sufficed, and such, one imagines, would have been so subsidiary a job as not to need separate itemizing.

There is, however, a special department of stage carpentry where such putting together of boards would have been, and—on rare occasions, for its use is almost obsolete—still is today, a matter of some technical importance and a vital preparation for scenery. This matter is perhaps worth considering in detail before we go on to our fifth and last objection. Frederick Lloyds, in a treatise on *Scene Painting* (1875), describes it in words which so closely suggest an operation identical with that conjured up by Jones's phrase that we may quote him at length. He says on p. 69:

Procure a few boards of good deal, with as few knots in them as possible, each a quarter of an inch thick, 11 inches wide, and 12 feet long, rough planed on each side, and carefully at the edges where they have to be joined. Three of them should be laid flat on a sufficiently large bench, and the edges joined together with some good glue. This being dry, some cork canvas, or scrim canvas, as it is sometimes called, which can be had wherever the canvas was bought, must be glued on to the boards. . . . When dry, prime them on both sides with good stout priming, and you will then have what is called a *sheet of profile* ready for use. For small work, single boards can be used and prepared in exactly the same way.

The similarity of the process to that suggested in Jones's line is as striking as anything could well be, even when the latter is couched in such brief, enigmatic words. But when we realize that the purpose of these *sheets of profile* is to be attached to the edge of a canvased framework, projecting over, so that the whole piece can be painted and *cut out to any required shape*—that, in short, cutting-out is the essential end of this joining of boards together—we see at once that we are before a technique which would allow one at least of the applications of the phrase 'in relief' to be achieved—namely the situating of a cut-out shape before a background. And in Jones's note this putting of 'bourdes togeather' is specifically stated to be 'for sceanes of releaue'.

We now turn to our last objection to the theory that relieves were modelled, and this time again to Jones's own words.

On the fly-leaf of Jones's copy of Palladio's book on Architecture appears a long note in Jones's hand describing Palladio's Teatro Olimpico at Vicenza. (The full text is given in William Grant Keith's article 'A Theatre Project by Inigo Jones' in *The Burlington Magazine* for August 1917.) It is headed 'Vicensa. Sundaie ye 23 of September 1613', and the relevant passages are as follows (discussing the perspective built scenes on the stage of this theatre):

All the houses on ye sides ar of Releave the windoues look out and maad with bourdes inwardes to maak a thicknes the collombs wear flatt but round tourd the edges ye stattues of marbel and bronze finto [feigned] I mean thos in shortning ar flatt but of hole Releave wh sheaw strangly a neear but a farr of well. . . .

The figures of realeave in shortning ar of Carta Pasta they are maad flatt as I saide to anenswear the narrownes of the shortning neeces [niches] in wh the stande.

Here we have three occasions of the use of the word 'releave' and in two of these Jones takes specific care to emphasize that he is talking of something *flat* (not modelled), something in fact cut out of cardboard. In the other occasion—the first—of the use of the word he again employs it to describe something cut out—that is, houses with practicable windows and with columns—though now undoubtedly these partake of the third dimension, for he describes thickness-pieces to the windows.

We may conclude, then, that though the word relieve may, on occasion, be applicable to something with three-dimensional elements, yet it is not used specifically to denote that quality, but its true employment is to describe something which is cut out, and which may be quite flat. A 'relieve' is a cut-out. 'I mean thos' statues in perspective, or 'in shortning ar flatt but of hole Releave', that is to say are flat, but wholly cut out round the edge.

Surely it is impossible to deny what is more than an implication and amounts to a direct statement that the phrase 'of hole Releave' could apply to something flat.

Upon a proscenium stage a cut-out cannot generally be left, like a sculpture, in free space, it must have a background. A 'scene of relieve' is then a combination of cut-out and background.

We may now turn to the designs for scenes for instances of relieve scenes. Those scenes inscribed 'Shutter' we have already discussed. A large number of the remaining scenes are not inscribed as belonging to either type, and these we may pass, lacking any direct indication of their make-up. This leaves us with only a mere handful out of the great collection, but all have one important point in common: they are inscribed with the word 'relieve' —or with some other spelling of the same word.

Taking the sequence and numbering of the drawings from the *Designs of*

[63]

Inigo Jones, above mentioned, we find the first record chronologically of any such inscription is on the drawing No. 166. This design is ascribed to Walter Montagu's *The Shepheard's Paradise*, performed 8 January 1633, and the inscription reads, 'The 8th sceane a Temple of Releiue'.

On the next drawing, No. 167, similarly ascribed, we have 'Loves Cabinett of Relieue'.

The next use of the word is on No. 245, a scene from *Florimène*, which is inscribed 'The first Releiue. Tempell of Diana for ye pastorall of Florimene 1635', and 'only an Architraue and ye Celing in squares'.

No. 246 has '2 scene of Winter Releiue'.

No. 249 has '[3 *struck out*] 4. somer. Releiue'.

No. 250 has 'Autome Releiue'.

All the above are for *Florimène*.

No. 355 is for *Salmacida Spolia*, and is inscribed (among other things irrelevant to our subject) 'D Bridge of releiue annswer[ing] to ye sceane of Architecture. E ground before which hidd ye underpart of ye releiue'.

No. 359, for the same play, has: 'Releiue [sceane *struck out*] of Deityes belonging to ye sceane of Architecture in ye King & Queenes Masque 1640'.

No. 361 (ascribed to *The Queen of Arragon*) has marked on it 'Citti of releue'.

No. 363 (for the same) has 'Cleodora', '2 sceane of Releiue'.

No. 396 (unidentified) has 'Wood of a new forme being a shutter [wood of Relieve 6 sceane *struck out*]'.

To these drawings of Inigo Jones we may add two from John Webb's designs for *The Siege of Rhodes*, the plan and section for which we have seen in the Lansdowne MS. These are inscribed: '3rd Scene. Releive. To draw ye upper part of ye valance of ye Canopy at   fo: high', and the other simply '4: Scene Relei'.

Our evidence then is scarce. Only thirteen drawings bear the inscription 'Relieve', namely two from *The Shepheard's Paradise*, four from *Florimène*, two from *Salmacida Spolia*, two from (it is said) *The Queen of Arragon*, one unidentified, and two by Webb from *The Siege of Rhodes*. But we shall see in a moment that the evidence is sufficient to have considerable weight.

If we now turn our attention from the relieve pieces themselves towards the background in front of which they stood, we may make further progress in understanding the form.

Firstly, the Lansdowne plans show in every case a *backcloth* (in Pls. 2 and 3 even specifically so named) at the back of the stage. It is always separated by a sufficient distance from the back wall to allow an actor's passage behind, and it is of considerable width—far wider than any other

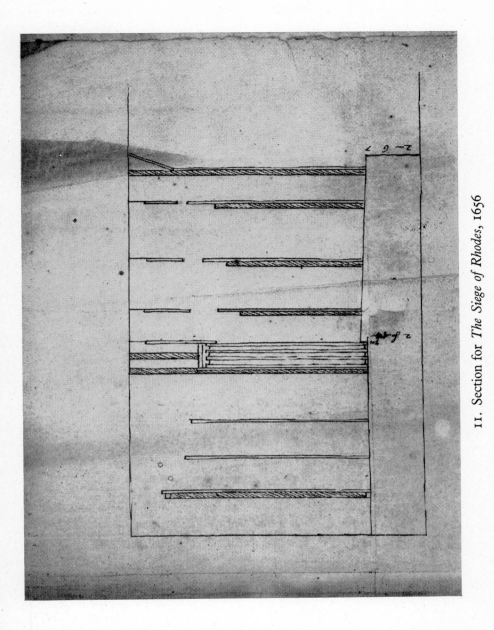

II. Section for *The Siege of Rhodes*, 1656

12. Model reconstruction by the author of grooves for *The Siege of Rhodes*

13. The model showing shutters and wings

14. The model showing a scene of relieve

15. Model of full stage showing first shutter scene

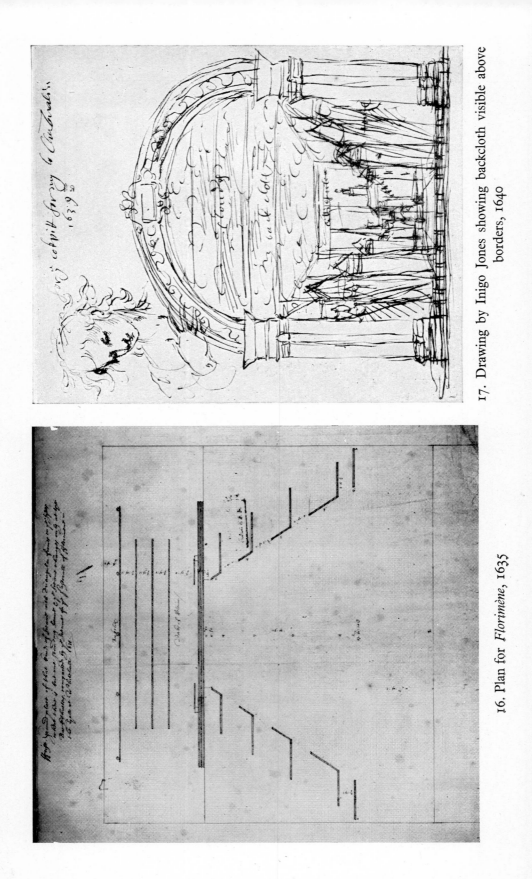

17. Drawing by Inigo Jones showing backcloth visible above borders, 1640

16. Plan for *Florimène*, 1635

piece of scenery on the stage, stretching as it does to within a few feet of the side-walls. On no single drawing is there any indication that this backcloth was movable.

A very important second piece of information is to be found in one of the drawings, No. 361, and this needs discussing in detail. Here (see Pl. 17) there is a view of houses designated a 'citti of releue' seen between two rows of tent wings; and above this is seen (and marked) the 'backcloth', and above again, 'cloudes'. We have then direct evidence that when a 'relieve' was showing, the backcloth might be visible too, above the piece in relief.

Concerning this particular drawing, however, there is a curious point of great interest. The sketch is one of the lightest, suggestive notes and perhaps not perfect in detail, though on the other hand it may well possess a hurried, diagrammatic telescoping of all the elements of masque scenery—some of its lines may mark the position of closed shutters, while at the same time a relieve scene is shown as if seen through them.

There is a notable difference in the proportions of this scene from any-thing we can see on our stages today, in that the proscenium opening is appreciably higher than it is wide. This at once raises problems in the masking and disposition of the pieces of scenery which are unusual to our modern technique. The top of the proscenium opening is arched, but the highest wings only reach up to a little above half the height of the opening. At once the query arises: How was the comparatively vast area above these wings masked-in? Modern technique takes it for granted that any border must hang across the stage low enough to touch the top of its related pair of wings, but the remarkable thing is that if we take the summary horizontal lines, crossing the sky in this drawing, to represent the edges of borders, then that particular one of them suggesting a border low enough to touch the wings runs across the very portion of the heavens *upon which the word 'backcloth' is written*. Furthermore, *beneath* that word 'backcloth' is indica-tion of still further 'cloudes' identical with those above, which, we suppose, were represented on borders. Was it then possible to see a portion of the backcloth up in the air *over* one of the borders?

And again, if these horizontal lines in the sky are to be taken as indicating the edges of borders—and it is almost impossible to see what else they could represent—how did the first border (situated right up at the top in the crown of the arch) mask the first pair of tent wings that do not reach up even as high as the spring of that same great arch?

We would welcome a chance to inspect a detailed set of plans for the working of scenery for this show, whatever it may be (for there is some reason to question its ascription in the *Designs of Inigo Jones* to Habington's *Queen of Arragon*, produced April 1640; on this matter see Allardyce

Nicoll, *Stuart Masques*, p. 144), but no such plans have been found. We may see, however, a possibility of solution in the section for *Salmacida Spolia*, also of the year 1640 (Pl. 2). Here, though the first pair of wings are of a nearly orthodox height in relation to the top of the proscenium opening, yet the deeper wings are very much shorter, while the borders above them (labelled 'T') sink in level far less steeply, so that at first sight we see almost as vast a gap between the tops of the fourth wings and their border above as we presume existed over the first wings in our present Pl. 17. But we have very clear indication how this gap in the *Salmacida Spolia* set was masked, for while 'T' in the section is defined as 'The Clouds of ye heaven which went crosse ye sceane & were hung betwixt the Clouds of ye sydes whereby it appeared but one sole heaven', yet these first clouds do not touch the wing-tops but the connexion is made by another agent—namely the 'clouds of ye sydes'—those pieces marked 'R'. Unlike the 'clouds of ye heaven' (the borders proper), which were permanently fixed in place, these pieces marked 'R' were long and drooping and were movable, and hung only at the *sides* of the stage, connecting the borders proper to the wing-tops. They are in a sense 'upper wings'.

In effect this meant that what we may call the whole border-element of the scene was tripartite, consisting of a shallow, high, fixed centre portion and two, much deeper, changeable, end-portions (in modern jargon 'short legs') reaching down to the wing-tops themselves. And, to dispel any doubt, we have in the notes to the section a very understanding and to-the-point description of them, clearly from an experienced stage designer. The pieces 'R' are defined as:

The peeces of Clouds which came downe from ye roofe before ye upper part of ye syde shutters whereby ye grooues aboue were hidden & also ye howse behind them:

These Clouds also went in grooues marked S: & changed with ye sceanes below:

That is to say, these descending side-pieces had for their function to mask the upper grooves of the wings, and also—the very point we were inquiring about—to prevent any view through at the sides, above the wings and between the high borders, of the walls of the stage beyond. (There is a most misleading and unfortunate misprint in the transcription of the above note in *Designs of Inigo Jones* (which book generally has a claim to meticulous care), for the latter half of the note is made to read 'Then (*instead of* These) Clouds also went in grooues marked S . . .' which, of course, confuses any attempt at interpretation and leads one to suppose the presence of yet further sky pieces sliding in front of those shown on the section.)

There is, however, in the section a further arrangement appearing exactly similar to that marked 'R', but this time only one pair, and situated to hang just in front of the top of the backshutters, as those marked 'R' hung in front of the side shutters, and this further feature is labelled 'V'. It is described as: 'the upper back shutters which were also hung in grooues and changed as ye others did'. (We have already distinguished between *upper* and *lower* backshutters.)

These pieces marked 'V' were shutters. What was revealed when they were opened? Immediately we begin to answer this we see a striking analogy in situation with that shown in Pl. 17. For clearly *the backcloth would be seen above the backshutter top*—or if, as in fact we presume, the lower backshutters were at such a moment also open, then the complete height of the backcloth would be revealed from stage to roof, and in front of it any cut-out flat pieces (such as a 'citti of releue') might show up bravely enough in relief against the tall backcloth.

There is apparent, however, in our hypothetical picture one awkward and inartistic blemish that clearly could not be permitted to exist unhid. This is, of course, the great irrelevant, horizontal, grooved baulk of wood in which the tops of the backshutters ran and which now spans emptily the glorious rift of sky with the nakedness of the cross-bar of an H.

It is for the disguising of this blemish that Pl. 17 has a slight suggestion, for the very point we noticed about it was that the backcloth seems to be represented as visible between what appear to be two borders. But the lower 'border' covers the horizontal line which suggests the top grooves of the backshutters. Is it in fact not a border but a cut-out piece whose purpose is to mask those upper grooves, by suggesting a floating rack or wisp of clouds across the sky? One pauses, struck by the very splendid possibilities now open in such a scene-design for such a high proscenium; and the whole scheme takes on a capacity for eloquent and magnificent dignity with its tall, distant sky against which is fretted a tracery of clouds *in relief*, and in front of the bottom of which stand the houses of a cut-out city, perhaps in several planes as are the rows of tents and the ranks of clouds. Here at length we are in a position to see how, with perfect aptness, part of these clouds (on the upper backshutter) might open in the upper height and disclose a shining glimpse of the empyrean above the houses and the lower clouds, wherein the very gods themselves would be not unworthily enthroned. We may come to the conclusion that we have perhaps forfeited a little of the glory of scenery when we no longer use the possibilities of clouds in relief.

The third point of evidence we can offer concerning the nature of the background against which we suppose the scene of relieve was shown in relief is of a somewhat different nature. So far it might be supposed that the ground of a relieve was always the sky itself. But against this we have one drawing of an interior scene which is marked as being 'of releive'.

This is the Design No. 166 (see Pl. 18), which is inscribed 'The 8th sceane a Temple of Releiue' and 'The toombes to of whight marble wth ornamentes of Brass guilte. A scelleton on each side in a shroud houlding torches. [*paper torn*] . . the farr of parte to bee open from [*torn*] wth a raill and ballester shorting [*torn*] farder arches on the sides sum'. The design is ascribed to Walter Montagu's *The Shepheard's Paradise*, performed 1633.

Here we are aided by no plans or sections and there is little we may say with certainty as to the technicalities, but this at least is clear: here is a relieve scene in which the cut portion (that is, the portion 'to bee open' in 'the farr of parte') is thrown up in relief *not* against a sky but against another painted piece of scenery representing a more distant wall of the temple. So we have a scene of relief in two definite planes, an arch and a backing.

It is to this question of planes that we must now turn our attention.

In the last-mentioned drawing it is clear that we can isolate no part of the design and suppose it to be a flat unity with a cut top-edge in relief against a sky backcloth. Here, if we are going to admit the design to be in relief at all and to accept the implication in the inscription, we must see an arrangement in at least two planes and with the second appearing as a distance behind a central cut opening in the first.

Our research then so far leads us to suppose that a scene of relieve was made of flat cut-out, or cut-into, elements sometimes against a sky back-cloth, sometimes against another painted element. We have now to inquire into the number of planes in a scene of relieve.

Clearly if there may be two painted planes represented in an interior there may also have been more than one plane represented in front of the backcloth in the exteriors. What evidence is there for or against this?

Immediately there rises to mind the pair of lines in the relieve space on the small Rutland House stage on both plan and section, and the three lines in the plan of the larger *Florimène* stage at Whitehall.

These have been taken by some authorities to represent each line a separate scene in relief, possibly on the somewhat slender evidence that there are two scenes marked 'releive' in the set of *Siege of Rhodes* drawings and two lines on the place for relieves in the plan and section, *ergo*: one line marks the relieve of one scene and the other of the other.

But in *Florimène* we have not only four interludes of the four seasons but one additional scene, the Temple of Diana (first appearance), which is also inscribed on the sketch as a relief, so we have five relief scenes and only three lines on the plan.

[68]

The supposition then arises that these separate lines marked, not each the position of a separate scene, but, all, the positions of different parts of one scene. And all the parts would be removed (cf. 'works of relevo to remouv') and be replaced by another set of pieces for the next relieve scene.

The question we need to answer is: Is there any evidence that any exterior scene was so cut into two planes for the little Rutland House stage, or into three planes for the larger Whitehall stage?

An answer is given to this in the drawings for the design of the last scene of *Salmacida Spolia*. In this scene, behind a set of street wings, there was placed a bridge in the distance and a view beyond of houses, as is shown in Design No. 355. This drawing is fortunately inscribed and we read in the margin, after a description of the cloud machines in the air above: 'D Bridge of releiue annswer[ing] to ye sceane of Architecture.' (See Pl. 24.)

The reference letters on the drawing itself have disappeared, but there is little doubt to what bridge this refers, and we are to suppose then that this bridge at the back of the scene was cut out since it was said to be 'of releiue'. If so, were the views of distant houses seen through the three arches of the bridge painted on the bridge-piece? Or were the arches cut out on one plane and the houses situated and cut out on a second plane of relief standing behind the bridge?

In regard to this question it may be objected that before we can accept the theory that scenes of relieve were cut out in separate planes we should be able to produce a set of drawings for a relieve scene in which the separate pieces are shown separately. And this we are now able to do. There are fortunately still preserved other drawings of the bridge in this scene. In one (No. 356) the bridge itself is carefully studied but the spaces in the arches *are blank*; in another (No. 357) the bridge is shown as merely a roughly hatched silhouette and the buildings in the view under it are completed in great detail.

The conclusion is inescapable that bridge and houses were considered as separate pieces.

Pressing the point still farther, it occurs to us to ask: Since the space for relieves was nearly 7 ft. deep in the *Salmacida Spolia* stage, while that on the Rutland House stage (where only two planes of relief are indicated) was only 5 ft. 6 in., was it not likely that for *Salmacida Spolia* we should have *three* planes of relief, as in *Florimène* where the space was also 7 ft. deep? Even upon this point Design No. 355 throws some light, for the last line of the notes runs: 'E ground before which hidd ye underpart of ye releiue.'

To put a comma after the word 'before' is a more legitimate emendation than to alter 'before' to 'behind', but either course would give sense to a sentence which is clearly not to be taken to mean that the bottom edge of the bridge-piece hid *in front* of anything, whatever its nature.

But if the almost obvious reading is correct we clearly have three planes—a foreground, the cut-out bridge, and the distant view—all capable of being removed and set in place in front of a sky cloth when the space for them was vacated by the lowering under the stage of a certain heavy piece of cloud machinery that also worked between the shutters and the backcloth.

Though it must be admitted that we can distinguish no letter E in the drawing, we have no doubt in applying it to the little, low line of hummocky ground forming the bank of the river, which the bridge—by a most magnificent piece of arrogant licence—does not span but bisects like a spine in the middle.

The very real value of a low profile piece like this becomes obvious at once. Without it, it could be seen that the bridge stood on the stage, but with it, the stage floor is hidden (alternatively the hole into which the cloud machine sank was hidden), and if an artist has enough confidence in his power over his audience to get away with a bridge *along*, instead of *over*, a river he will not have any difficulty in asserting to their logical sense that what is hidden behind the bank is water and not deal boards (or empty space).

In short, we have here a ground-row in all conscience—as certainly, in every respect, a ground-row as any piece could well be, and such that it might almost be taken as a type example of the term to illustrate a pictorial dictionary—yet it has been said that ground-rows were not known on the English stage until about 1770, de Loutherbourg being credited as one of their inventors. The evidence would suggest that not only is this untrue but that all the elements of scenes of relieve were ground-rows or set-pieces in some form.

Once this idea of separate planes be granted in the make-up of scenes of relieve, we may turn to attempt to define the last occupant of the relieve space which as yet we have only mentioned. This is that pair of very short lines attached to the square uprights supporting the shutter grooves and projecting thence inwards towards the centre of the stage. They are present in the full Whitehall plan; in Webb's plan of the stage itself alone, set for *Florimène*; in his Rutland House plan for *The Siege of Rhodes*, and in his plan in the Duke of Devonshire's Collection for the theatre at Whitehall.

It may well be that this pair of side pieces are in the nature of narrow profiled wings framing the scene of relieve at either side of the opening made by the drawn-back shutters. Is there any element in the design of the scenes themselves which could have been fitted to such pieces?

A glance at the designs for *Florimène* immediately confirms this. That for *Winter*, No. 246, shows unequivocal framing wing-pieces, giving added relief to the scene in relieve behind, in which they were, of course, further helped by the step down in the stage at this point, and this drawing seems to indicate even this step.

For the second intermedium, *Spring*, though No. 247 seems to offer immediate further confirmation, there are several points on which one hesitates. To begin with, the opening here is of very different proportions from that of the other three intermedium drawings; it alone among them is not inscribed, its squaring-up is different, the meeting of the tree wings (themselves far wider than any other relief-frame pair that we can find) above, in an arch over the drawing, is so very hard to reconcile with the full perspective of the *Florimène* 'Standing scene' in No. 243, wherefrom one cannot avoid the conclusion that the last sky border would fall over the tops of these trees and throw the whole woefully out of scale, and when finally we compare the note of this scene in *The Argument of the Pastorall of Florimene with the Discription of the Scoenes and Intermedij*, 1635, p. 7, which reads, for *Spring*, 'the scoene is varied, and there appeares a spacious Garden, with walkes, perterraes, close Arbours, and cypresse trees, and in the farthest part stands a delicious Villa, all of which figureth the spring', we begin to feel we are not justified in following the authors of *Designs of Inigo Jones* in including this among the drawings for *Florimène*. Any of the above points might conceivably have been reconciled, but all together seem to point to another provenance for the drawing.

The sketch (No. 249) for the third intermedium, however, which is in strict uniformity with the others, shows again the narrow side pieces in the form of summer trees, and the fourth for *Autumn* (No. 250), despite its being of an open unwooded country, brings in almost perversely two ill-defined verdant uprights at the sides.

We have no plans for *The Shepheards Paradise*, but it is interesting to note that No. 166 has a formal border at sides and bottom of a similar nature.

The fact that neither the *Salmacida Spolia* plans nor that reproduced in Pl. 7 from the Lansdowne MS. show these small framing wings would suggest that they were not invariably used in shows having scenes of relieve.

In *The Siege of Rhodes* drawings (see Pl. 25) the two relieve scenes are, however, furnished with these framing pieces; the first relieve—that of Solyman's throne—has columns at either side, while the second (and this is worth noting), which shows the prospect of Mount Philermus, has a high, shaded, city wall *on one side only*, so, presumably, this framing element could on occasion be dispensed with altogether, or it could be used only on one side.

On both the above drawings a depth of 4 in. is cut off from the bottom of the scene and hatched separately, corresponding with the depth of the step down at the shutters.

We may begin to see how a relieve scene was portrayed upon its cut-out planes once we recognize how certain of the drawings we possess for such scenes are so composed that some feature of the subject is arranged to act as what we have called a 'framing element'. Frequently this framing element is hatched with lines which suggest it is in shadow, or lit differently from the main subject. Both Webb's designs for the relieves of *The Siege of Rhodes* are informative here, especially the second for Mount Philermus. Keith says that it 'may very well have been made up of three separate parts, of which the city wall and the immediate foreground would form the first; the hilly background, the second; the sky, the third. In this connexion it will be observed how the city wall and foreground are very heavily shaded; so much so, indeed, as practically to cut the drawing into two parts'.

We would but amend this excellent description to read, in the opening sentence, 'made up of *four* separate parts', and in the final phrase, 'into two (or more) *planes*', and we may hazard the following suggestion for its technical realization on the stage.

Referring back to the 'two mysterious short strips which project inwards from either shaded upright post' which we mentioned above in connexion with Pl. 10, it will be clear that no more suitable position could be found for such a 'framing element' than this. We notice that these two short strips appear, both in the plan and in the section, to be slid in between the last shutter-groove and the posts behind—from which posts there is, indeed, a section cut away to take them (see also the photograph of the model in Pl. 12).

We may then divide the landscape in this design into planes, as shown on the model in Pl. 14. Let us, however, refer to the other relieve scene before finalizing our views. Turning to the other relieve scene in *The Siege of Rhodes*, that of Solyman's throne, we find it again amenable to our theory. Here the paired columns on either side, with their intervening drapery and the small portion of tessellated pavement between, would be represented on the two framing pieces. The throne, the canopy, and the rest of the pavement on the first plane, and the distant tents and the ground they stand on, on the second. The sky would be on the backcloth. The throne-piece would then reach to the top of the stage and disappear out of sight as is suggested by the section. The note at the side of the drawing: 'to draw ye upper part of ye valance of ye canopy at fo: high', may well be an unfinished reminder that the upper sight-lines from the audience would rise diagonally and disclose, under the last border, more of the roof of the canopy than is shown in the elevational drawing; hence it would be better to deepen the

valance by raising its upper edge to prevent the roof becoming disproportionately deep.

At this point we must deal with a curious problem that may already have
presented itself to some readers; the two drawings now under discussion
are squared-up for enlarging in exactly the same way as are those for the
shutter scenes in the same play. In the shutter scenes this can be understood, for all the picture is in one plane and can be accurately enlarged by
drawing its elements in proportionately enlarged squares (just as a scene-
painter does today), but if the relieve scene is supposed to represent a
composition in several planes—that is *in perspective*—what is the use of
squaring it up? For each plane would have to be enlarged to a different
degree to present the perspective effect of the drawing.

In answer to this it is interesting to note that we encounter many strong
indications that drawings of stage scenes in several planes were formerly
often *not* made in perspective but in elevation. Andrea Pozzo is at pains,
in his two-part treatise on Perspective, to show the difference between the
perspective view of a scene and its setting-up in elevation, and the value
of the elevation to a scene-painter. Angelo Carboni has an elaborate design
to be executed in many parts which is a true elevation, not a perspective
of the scene, as I have shown at length in 'The Staging of Eighteenth-
century Designs for Scenery' in the *Journal of the Royal Institute of British
Architects* for 10 August 1935. Of course the strict elevation is the only
proper working drawing to make of the front aspect of scenery, provided it is
put into the hands of workmen whose need is for clear dimension in all
the parts, and not into the hands of outside persons who may erroneously
suppose an elevation represents a true view of the scene. This latter supposition would be erroneous because it is, of course, the perspective view
which illustrates the proper diminution of the distant parts comparable
with the real effect on placing the elements in their separate planes, whereas
the elevation would not—but the perspective is of no use as a working
drawing at all to a craftsman since it offers him no means of measuring the
parts to guide his carpentry. Reflection will show that it would be useless
to square-up a scene-sketch for enlargement unless all its elements are to
the same scale, whereas in a perspective drawing of a subject in many
planes the scale naturally decreases progressively as the elements appear at
deeper distances. In an elevational drawing, however, the design is drawn
with all its parts, near as well as distant, to the same scale, and so can be
safely squared-up for enlargement.

Webb's note about the valance written in the margin of his drawing for
Solyman's throne (even though he has left out the specific figure) certainly
would be far less workmanlike if the drawing were in perspective, not in
elevation. But in elevation we presume it to be.

Concerning the second relieve of Mount Philermus, the cutting-up of the landscape into planes is open to a number of possible choices, any one of which may have been Webb's own choice. But there arises a serious difficulty, however it is cut out, when one turns to his section of the stage. Here *both* relieve lines are shown to reach to the top of the line of sight. What then is the use of the backcloth behind them, which presumably they would completely hide? One may allow that the presumed front plane of Solyman's throne might reach up out of sight, but we supposed the second plane, showing the distant tents, was lower and allowed the backcloth to be seen over it. But in the Philermus relieve scene there is no element of the open country that can be stretched to reach up out of sight. What then is the meaning of the section?

The only possible solution—if our theory on the nature of these scenes is correct—is that what we are shown on the section are two vertical posts, each being one of a pair standing either side the stage and serving to uphold the ends of any piece of scenery placed between them, whether low or high, just as three similar pairs of posts were indicated in Pl. 7. These posts are roughly suggested in the model in Pl. 14, where a tentative essay at the arrangement of the relieves and their frame is shown. Pl. 15 gives a view of the same model from the front, now completed with the frontispiece and displaying one of the shutter scenes.

A reflection arising (though it is one incapable, I believe, at our present stage of research, of any substantiation) is that since these little framing wings are so often found hatched over in the designs and so suggest a darker element, it may have been that there was stationed behind them a special set of lights whose function was to illuminate the cut-outs beyond. If the above supposition is true, and if the nature of relieve scenes was as we suppose, their general theatrical impression must have been such as could hardly have been surpassed for delight and intriguing effect even in our own day.

An interesting guess can be made at the contemporary name for these framing elements of relieve scenes. Among the 'Accounts for Work on the Cockpit in Court and the Hall Theatre', published by Eleanore Boswell in *The Restoration Court Stage* (Harvard, 1932), there is on p. 255 an item due to Robert Streeter 'ffor paynting ye sceane of boscage being a paire of shutters & a paire of side Releises'. Miss Boswell herself suggests the emendation 'side Releives', and if this be so, perhaps we have here not only the term by which such pieces were known, but a curious suggestion that they were (at any rate by 1674, by which time many innovations had come about) also usable in front of a shutter—possibly in the first shutter-grooves while the shutter itself was in the last.

The above conclusions may be summarized as follows. Scenes of relieve were not modelled but composed of flat parts. The parts were cut out and stood 'in relief' against either a backcloth (presumably a blue sky) or a special backing. The cut-out pieces could be arranged in two or more planes. They were removable and possibly supported against vertical uprights. They were sometimes framed by tall, narrow profile-strips in the nature of wings. The relieves were analogous to our ground-rows and set-pieces both in that, as ground-rows some were set to conceal the stage floor behind, and as set-pieces in that they were placed in position beforehand to be discovered at the opening of shutters. On the other hand, a shutter scene was in one plane (for the moment I am disregarding the associated wings and borders) and was not necessarily previously set and then dis-covered, but could be 'closed in', taking its position in sight of the audience. But no relieve scene could be changed in sight of the audience. And finally, a piece in relieve (as opposed to a whole scene in relieve) meant a cut-out piece standing or hanging (as a cloud) in front of a background, that is to say in relief from it.

To conclude these three chapters on the staging of the later masques, it would perhaps be informative to turn away from our arbitrary references to separate points in many masques according to which best illustrated a current problem, and to seek to give some idea of the effect of the staging of one selected masque from the opening scene to the end. For this purpose we will take the latest and technically the most mature masque which Inigo Jones set—Sir William Davenant's *Salmacida Spolia*.

To the plan and section (in Pls. 2 and 3) we have already referred many times and we should be familiar with the general set-up. Here to follow is a full quotation from the stage directions of the printed script of 1640 (1639 old style) with notes on the effects in each scene. (A version of the whole masque is available in the valuable book *English Masques* by H. A. Evans, M.A.)

A Curtayne flying up, a horrid Sceane appeared of storme and tempest: no glimpse of the Sun was seene, as if darkness, confusion, and deformity, had possest the world, and driven light to Heaven, the trees bending, as forced by a gust of winde, their branches rent from their trunkes, and some torne up by the roots: a farre off was a darke wrought sea, with rowling billowes, breaking against the rockes, with rayne, lightning and thunder: in the midst was a globe of the Earth, which at an instant falling on fire, was turned into a Fury, her hayre upright, mixt with snakes, her body leane wrinkled and of a swarthy colour, her breasts hung bagging downe to her waste, to which with a knot of serpents was girt red bases, and under it tawny skirts downe to her feet: in her hand she brandisht a sable Torch, and looking a Scanse with hollow envious eyes came downe in to the Roome.

For this scene we possess a vivid drawing (No. 323) by Jones. If the sea with its wrecked ship actually moved it is perhaps possible that this was a relieve scene; on the other hand it was undramatic to open with one's full powers displayed, and since only three shutters are shown on the plans perhaps the stormy sea was merely painted, or had a transparent sky with a lightning effect. Above the wings hung stormy side-borders, and in the centre of the sky the borders proper were probably plain blue (Pl. 19).

For the Furies we have three costume—or make-up—drawings (Nos. 324–6).

The first Fury delivers a speech of envy against the peace of England and then is joined by the other three who dance an antimasque.

This Antimasque being past, the Sceane changed into a calme, the skie serene, a farre off *Zephyrus* appeared breathing a gentle gale: in the Landskip were Corne fields and pleasant Trees, sustayning Vines fraught with grapes, and in some of the furthest parts Villages; with all such things as might expresse a Country in peace, rich, and fruitfull. There came breaking out of the Heavens a silver Chariot, in which sate two persons, the one a woman in a watchet garment, her dressing of silver mixt with bulrushes, representing Concord: somewhat below her sate the good Genius of Great *Britaine*, a yong man in a carnation garment, embroidered all with flowers, an Anticke sword hung in a skarfe, a garland on his head, and in his hand a branch of Platan mixt with eares of corn: these in their dissent sung together.

For this scene also we have a drawing (No. 328). Here it is most likely that the storm wings were drawn off revealing calm tree wings, and the stormy side-borders slid aside to reveal sunny clouds flanking the same central blue sky. The backscene probably closed in on shutters (Pl. 20).

Zephyrus most likely appeared in the cloud machine which we shall discuss in a few moments. We possess a sketch (No. 329) of his head blowing a breeze out of the cloud. Concord and Great Britain descended in their chariot on the machine situated between the second and third wings on the stage left (for which see Pls. 2 and 3).

The chariot descended to the stage, the figures dismounted, and a short dialogue followed:

Being arrived at the Earth, and descended from the Chariot, they sang this short Dialogue, and then departed severall wayes to incite the beloved people to honest pleasures and recreations which have ever beene peculiar to this Nation.

The 'beloved people' are the British.

After this, a vast succession of *ballets-divertissements* followed, of the most fantastical nature and extending to twenty separate numbers. All were antimasques, or semi-grotesque contrasts to the main dance that was yet to come. We possess nine costume drawings for these 'entries' (Nos. 330–8).

The Antimasques being past, all the Sceane was changed into craggy rockes and inaccessible mountaynes, in the upper parts where any earth could fasten, were some tres, but of strange formes, such as only grow in remote parts of the Alpes, and in desolate places; the furthest of these was hollow in the middest, and seemed to be cut through by art, as the *Pausilipo* neer *Naples*, & so high as the top pierced the clouds, all which represented the difficult way which Heroes are to passe ere they come to the Throne of Honour.

The Chorus of the beloved people came forth (led by Concord & the good Genius of Great *Britaine*,) their habits being various and rich, they goe up to the State and sing.

The wings and shutters drew off, then, to reveal this great Throne of Honour scene, set in the midst of 'inaccessible mountaynes', and the main design is preserved in Drawing No. 339 (see Pl. 21). From a duplicate drawing by John Webb (No. 340) we learn that this is a shutter scene, and this is of vital importance in our reconstruction. The scene is remarkable for the racks of cloud streaming across it; a scale inscribed at the side of the drawing suggests that the cloud above the top of the distant mountain is 14 ft. above the stage. Reference to Pl. 2 shows that this is the height of the grooves holding the tops of the lower backshutters; this cloud then presumably has a function—it is a separate piece fixed before the grooves and intended to hide them when later both upper and lower scenes are open together. Thus we may deduce that the scene before us is a 'two-storied' scene and that all the portion above the cloud-wraith is painted on the upper backshutter. The whole back effect is some 26 ft. high by 14 ft. wide, see Fig. 3a. The Chorus of the 'beloved people' comes forth from the wings, advances to the front of the stage, descends by steps from the stage into the hall, crosses the empty dancing-place in the nearer part of the auditorium, approaches the State, or royal canopy, and sings. The song, however, is not to the King but to the Queen Mother, Mary de Medicis. This is for the very good reason that both King Charles I and Queen Henrietta Maria are at this moment (all unknowing what was to befall within a decade) behind the scenes preparing for a spectacular entrance.

The song ended they return up to the Stage, and divide themselves on each side; then the further part of the Sceane disappeard, and the Kings Majesty and the rest of the Masquers were discovered, sitting on the Throne of Honour, his Majesty highest in a seat of Gold, and the rest of the Lords about him: this Throne was adorned with Palme trees, betweene which stood statues of the ancient Heroes: in the under parts on each side lay captives bound in severall postures, lying on trophees of armours, shields, and Antique weapons, all his Throne being fayned of Goldsmiths worke. The habit of his Majesty and the Masquers was of watchet, richly embroydered with silver, long stockins set up of white: Their caps silver with scrowles of gold, and plumes of white feathers.

Miss Linthicum in *Costume in Elizabethan Drama* defines watchet as 'light or pale blue inclining towards green'.

Some consideration must now be given to the scenic effect described above. We see that 'the further part of the Sceane disappeard' and the King was discovered among his masquers seated upon the throne of honour. For this we suppose that the lower backshutters withdrew and that beyond, in the space of the relieves, there had been set ready a duplicate hill (see Fig. 3*b*), this time built with stepped seats and forming an arch 'cutt throw' as we read in the margin of Jones's relevant sketch (No. 351)—'and a landscip seene beyound all'. What is now to follow is an effect of great magnificence. The King descends from the hill with the masquers and, after the chorus has sung a six-stanza song to him—

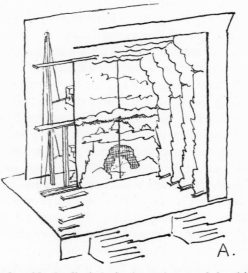

FIG. 3*a. Salmacida Spolia* (1640), the make-up of the third scene

. . . there came softly from the upper part of the Heavens, a huge cloud of various colours, but pleasant to the sight, which discending to the midst of the Sceane open'd, and within it was a transparent brightnes of thin exhalations, such as the Gods are feigned to descend in: in the most eminent place of which, her Majesty sate, representing the chiefe Heroin, environed with her martiall Ladies; and from over her head were darted lightsome Rayes that illuminated her seat, and all the Ladies about her participated more or lesse of that light, as they sate neere or further off: this brightnesse with many streakes of thin vapours about it, such as are seene in a fayre evening skie softly discended: and as it came neere to the Earth, the seat of Honour by little and little vanished, as if it gave way to these Heavenly Graces. The Queenes Majesty and her Ladies were in Amazonian habits of carnation, embroidered with silver, with plumed Helmes, Bandrickes with Antique swords hanging by their sides, all as rich as might be, but the strangenes of the Habits was most admired.

We may identify the lower 'Kings Seate' and the upper 'Queenes seate' without difficulty in the section (Pl. 2) and we are informed in the notes to the drawing that they both 'went in one groove' but we notice that they were worked by different lines (see Fig. 3a).

What is not, however, so easy to see is that the section also contains information as to how the fascinating 'Huge cloud' itself worked. For up above, in the space between the fourth border and the upper backshutters, certain very faint pencil or chalk lines are visible. These have been enlarged and emphasized for distinction in Pl. 1. It may readily be seen that the conformation indicated by these lines is very like the principle shown in Furttenbach's *Architectura Recreationis* in his 'Profilo' of a Comic Scene

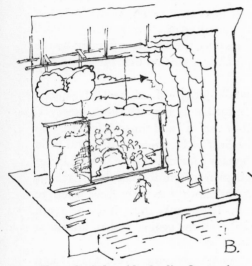

FIG. 3b. *Salmacida Spolia*, Sc. 3, the lower shutters open and the cloud moving across

FIG. 3c. *Salmacida Spolia*, Sc. 3, the cloud sinking and opening with the upper shutters, to reveal the Queen

(numbered 23) situated at just the same part of the stage and designed for just the same purpose—the drawing over of a cloud. Two struts project down, in Jones's drawing, from the timbers of the 'roof' over the stage and appear to carry the two members of an overhead 'railway'. Slung between the latter is a vertical piece ending at the bottom with what appears to be some sort of foothold or seating, or possibly a second railway on which the moving halves of an opening cloud might run.

Design No. 349 (Pl. 23) shows such a cloud from Jones's hand, and it is inscribed with the note, 'The great cloude wch comes fourth and opens and discouers ye Queenes seatte in a bright cloude.' 'To trye yf this great cloude may com dou[n]e betwene the groufes and then bee drawne open'; 'and whether ye shutters and this great cloude may not bee drawne a way boath togeather.'

The problems in understanding this inscription are largely solved if what we have deciphered as a cloud machine is actually such. What happened was that this great cloud, built in two parts, was drawn across from the side to the centre of the scene and in front of the upper backshutters (Fig. 3b), then lowered till its base rested level with the top of the lower backshutters; there the two parts were drawn open 'and makes a great ouall' (see inscription on No. 351)—or rather the bottom and ends of a great oval, the top being supplied by a strip of 'cloudes fixt on ye topp' and 'ouer that seate' behind, in which the Queen with her ladies sat already prepared (Fig. 3c). Before, however, she could be thus revealed in her glory, the upper backshutters had of course to be opened also, and hence Jones's query 'whether ye shutters and this great cloude may not bee drawne a way boath togeather'. The spectacle of the Queen and her ladies once revealed is suggested by the sketch in No. 350 (see Pl. 22), upon which it is written that there be 'raies of tinsell ou[e]r ye Queene'.

The marvels now continue. The whole glory—cloud, seat, masquers, backing, and all—begins to descend. Immediately beneath them, however, is the King's seat; this must be got out of the way and thus we find that, as the glory 'came neare to the Earth, the Seat of Honour by little and little vanished, as if it gave way to these Heavenly Graces'. Where it went is not far to seek, for the notes on the ground-plan inform us that the 'space for Releiues betwixt ye backshutters and backcloth' was only free 'when ye seates were lett downe under ye stage'. They sank, then, into the room below. But the cloud disengages itself, 'shuttes againe and is drawne a waye ouer ye sceane'.

We possess eight drawings for the King's costume (Nos. 341–8) and three (Nos. 352–4) for the Queen's.

As Queen Henrietta Maria and her Ladies descended a four-stanza song was sung to them, then—

When this heavenly seat touched the Earth, the Kings Majesty tooke out the Queene, and the Lords the Ladies, and came downe into the Roome, and danc't their entry, betwixt which and the second dance was this song.

And a three-stanza song follows. The main masquing dance (from which the masques took their name) is the social climax of the show. After it the King and the Queen left the scene and took their seats under the State (having blessed the eyes of the beholders with this gracious performance) to watch the rest of the show, and this was the signal for the last great scene-change and the theatrical climax.

The second Dance ended, and their Majesties being seated under the State, the Sceane was changed into magnificent buildings composed of severall selected peeces of Architecture: in the furthest part was a Bridge over a River, where many people, coaches, horses, and such like were seene to passe to and fro: beyond this

18. Inigo Jones's design for an interior relieve scene in *The Shepheard's Paradise*, 1633

19. Inigo Jones's design for the storm scene in *Salmacida Spolia*, 1640

20. The peaceful scene in *Salmacida Spolia*

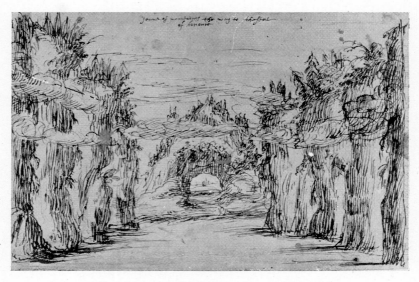

21. The throne of honour scene in *Salmacida Spolia*

22. The Queen's cloud-throne in *Salmacida Spolia*

23. The great cloud in *Salmacida Spolia*

24. The scene of architecture in *Salmacida Spolia*

on the shore were buildings in Prospective, which shooting far from the eye shewed as the suburbs of a great city.

From the highest part of the Heavens came forth a cloud far in the Sceane, in which were eight persons richly attired representing the spheares; this joyning with two other clouds which appeard at that instant full of Musicke covered all the upper part of the Sceane, and at that instant beyond all these, a Heaven opened full of Deities, which celestiall Prospect with the Chorus below filled all the whole Sceane with apparitions and harmony.

Drawing No. 355 illustrates this scene (Pl. 24); Nos. 356–8 are details of the bridge (which we have discussed) and Nos. 359 and 360 are studies of the chorus of deities in the heavens for which all three cloud machines were used at once (to say nothing of two more ranks of wholly painted deities).

This was clearly a relieve scene. Notice the clever device by which one relieve scene was made to follow another directly; the Queen's cloud, after coming half-way down to the stage, opened. It then slowly sank farther to the stage to allow the Queen to dismount. At this point, however, it wholly covered the opening of the lower shutters. The mount of honour could then be struck and, the King's seat having been lowered out of the way, the bridge could then be set in the space, ready for discovery. Upon cue the empty cloud could rise, the rock wings be drawn off to reveal the street wings, and the whole transformation effected ready for the descent of the choruses of deities.

A short song was sung by the whole assembled chorus, then—

After this song the Spheares past through the Ayre, and all the Deities ascended, and so concluded this Masque: which was generally approoved of, especially by all Strangers that were present, to be the noblest and most ingenuous that had been done heere in that kind.

The Invention, Ornament, Sceans and Apparitions, with their Descriptions, were made by INIGO IONES, Surveyor Generall of his Majesties Workes.

What was spoken or sung, by WILLIAM DAVENANT, her Majesties Servant.

The Subject was set downe by them both.

The Musicke was composed by LEWIS RICHARD, Master of her Majesties Musicke.

FINIS

6

FIRST INTERLUDE

(THE GREAT SCENIC CONTROVERSY AND THE ANATOMY OF SCENERY)

———————————— ★ ————————————

A CLOSE technical examination is always arduous to follow, and just as a profound scene of emotional drama brings a desire for relief, so now an Interlude may relax the tension and, moreover, allow a glance about one, as it were, to consider other aspects and implications.

There are certain implications arising from this study of the factual development of changeable scenery that require considering in order to make our picture complete. This is the excuse for introducing the word 'interlude' into the title of this chapter and of certain later chapters. Not only is it a relief from technical study, and with perhaps a lighter note, but it is to remind ourselves that there are other aspects of movable scenery beside the practical ones, and that to grasp the whole significance upon the living theatre we must take our nose a little back from the details.

In this interlude chapter, and in the interludes that come later, it may be convenient to break the chronological sequence of our study and to range history where best we can find our matter. In the following account of how scenery aroused a lasting quarrel, we shall then ride somewhat ahead in selection of references and return to steady development by date later on.

It should be fully realized that from the beginning there was another school of thought about changeable scenery—one that opposed its arrival and attacked its continuance. Business interests became involved and the attacks grew virulent and the attitude stayed. We may trace it from the origin of changeable scenery up to the present day.

To understand the controversy we have to go back to that extraordinary, fecund, generative period where so many of the characteristics of our present theatre sprang, that of the masque at the Stuart court.

There, under James I, the first wedding of spectacle to stage took place. Spectacle there had been before in Elizabeth's day and in Henry VIII's; and—completely separately—the dramatic stage had been before, not merely 'been', but, in that being, had reached an apogee of its long existence.

But James's court was to see the richest parts of each fused, under the lambence of the Renaissance mind, in one feast of brilliance that could boast the simultaneous radiance of such first luminaries as Ben Jonson and Inigo Jones, master-poet with master-architect.

The married name of the united arts was The Masque. Then hard upon this too-brilliant wedding followed the divorce, upon grounds of incompatibility of temperament.

Jonson turned on Jones and all his ways, and the purlieus of the court were dinned with as fierce a stream of invective as ever passed a master-word-stringer's lips. The union was dissolved, and behind it there was left among the offspring a flourishing babe with vitality so rude and lusty, and nature so unbiddable, that it is vociferous in our own day almost as it was in theirs. This child of Jonson's union with Jones was The Great Scenic Controversy.

Since an understanding of the meaning of scenery in the theatre is impossible without a knowledge of those stresses causing, and those resulting from, this controversy, it would be well to look at its origin in some detail.

Ben Jonson was a *playwright*; Inigo Jones was (for the purposes of this instance) a scene-designer for *masques*. It is true that Jonson was also a poet for masques, and Jones was occasionally a setter of plays. Indeed, had not this dual exercise been present in each there might have been no clash, but because Jonson brought the dramatic playwright's sense of the pre-eminence of the poet in the play against Jones's architect's sense that a masque must stand or fall by its visual qualities, he came to resent the rivalry of this other department beside the poet's, supposing he should have as undisputed credit for the whole creation as a playwright can claim for his drama, which is frequently above setting as a masque is not.

A masque is a different thing from a play or drama. Had the development of the English theatre proceeded uninterrupted in the same terms as the development of English playwriting, the theatre of today would have been a very different place to enter and to see, and the Elizabethan public play-house with its platform stage might have been still with us, more or less modified as the progress of playwriting had prescribed, but still alive. And the Restoration would then have seen no revolution in the form of the public theatre and its stage, a revolution that brought a completely new technique of stage-presentation and another art into the theatre, which the old school has never ceased to deplore and to decry—a revolution which brought changeable scenery to our stage.

But this uninterrupted development was not to be. The Renaissance mind imported the new factor, it blended the glories of other arts into a fusion with the old play-poet's tradition and transmuted the whole into something rich and—to him—strange. It created theatrical spectacle, and the playwright arose in his wrath and called it prostitution.

He failed before the weight of public opinion which favoured the new theatrical form, but he never gave in with good grace, and still he produces a school which fights to suppress scenery, to prescribe limits for it, to dictate the nature of its expression, to ensure it should be little-welcomed, lopped and not trained—what the writer wants, not what the artist wants. He could not ban it from the theatre. It came and it came to stay; the audience approved it, indeed hailed it with delight—a delight that brought from him gibe upon gibe, jealous invective and bitter insult. But the public continued to enjoy spectacle, and the playwright found he could not get the people to come to his play unless he dressed it with some pretence at scenery. But he saw to it that it was only a gelded and infertile travesty of the suggestive fascinations which graced the spectacle stage that he permitted to come beside his own play. He poured his heart of scorn on all machines and effects, he decried with his trained pen all who cared to go and see them. Yet scenery had for all that come to stay. Indeed popular usage has now sanctioned the suggestion of *scenery*, primarily, to the mind when the phrase *the art of the theatre* is in question. In some contexts the two are synonymous, 'the art of the theatre' *means* scenery.

The 'Art Theatre' must have, and must care deeply about, scenery, else it cannot pretend to the name, but the ordinary playhouse of the typical three-act drama has never learned what to do with scenery, and has many times produced playwrights who hate its very existence and tread it under their feet in rage at any controversial opportunity.

How does this inimical attitude arise? Why should the art of literature act so cuckoo-like in the theatre to the child of its host, the art of the theatre itself?

According to our policy we seek to supply what material we can for an answer by looking at how it all came about, rather than take sides when the din is at its height. Let history have its say.

What does it tell us of the difference between play and masque?

It must be very clearly understood that not all royal performances of this time consisted of masques. Many plays were presented at court. The court play-stage sometimes differed in form from the court masque-stage, and the first public theatres which came into being in and after the Restoration of 1660 were formed on a plan deriving points from both types of stage.

Some of the court plays certainly had scenery, some may have been presented very similarly to the masques. But the Elizabethan play form was not designed for the masque stage, and its conventions fitted ill with it. Hence there was at length a different way arrived at for the presentation of plays at court, which was to contribute to the birth of the modern proscenium arch.

But what was it that made the presentation of a play differ from that of a masque at all?

To begin with, a play was something in itself, it already existed as a literary work of art on its own. It was a definite, unified, and complete creation with its own rules, forms, and standards of criticism. A masque, on the other hand (and hereupon we raise the flames of the Ben Jonson–Inigo Jones controversy), was a subject with only a partial existence in its written state. Indeed when only written, it was not a masque, but the script for a masque. A masque truly existed only as a theatrical performance—a combination of allegory, dance, speech, effects, *and scenery*. A masque was an occasion for scenery *sine qua non*. It was by its intrinsic nature a scenic, theatre occasion, not a poem on paper nor even a poem recited. A masque stood not as the presentation of a playwright's plots and characterization, but purely and alone as an entertainment and a spectacle. It may, admittedly, have included the poems of a very distinguished poet among its parts, but the masque was the sum of, and the actual performance of the sum of, those parts. It was for princely entertainment; and that which entertained, among other things, was the feast to the eye. Its very reason was splendour.

A play on the Elizabethan stage was a different thing. A play's quality rested in the contribution of its playwright; its situations, its characters, and the interplay of these on each other as the playwright had created them were the material of the performance. The shape of the performance and the lack of scenery arose from two factors: the material of the play, and the physical considerations arising from the entrance, interplay, and exit of the actors presenting that material. The actors alone were the vehicle of the play, and, instead of its being scenery that arose as a concomitant of the Elizabethan drama, there arose instead a particular code of conventions relating to the shape of the stage and to the provision upon it of certain adjuncts—the whole system being entirely different from a scenic system. The first physical consideration was of helping the players, of supplying a raised playing-space so that they might be seen of the people, of providing a background to that space against which the people might see them and against which their action might be mounted. The background and its *et ceteras* were aids to action, never were they much in the nature of pictorial representationalism on the stage inspired by the locality or atmosphere of the scene played upon it. Provision had to be made for means of ingress and egress upon that stage, which took the natural form of doors in the background. Beyond these primaries, however, there arose certain secondary developments, designed to make the presenting of the playwright's material more effective, and these it was, and the ingenious use of them by players and playwright alike, that gave visual interest to the show—these and not a painted changeable scene. Noticeable among them were the windows and balconies of the background which arose from the fact that the scene of action of so many early plays is outside a house, whereby advantage can be taken of the amusing variations in levels (always effective with an audience) made possible by playing from the windows or balconies of such a house. Hence actual windows and balconies became accessories to the acting-area and took a place in the tradition of the physical stage, bringing to Mahomet the windows or balconies once pressed into service by the players visiting inn-yards, or great halls possessing minstrel galleries above their screens. Also, among these secondary physical appurtenances of any area for presenting plays comes the further feature of a smaller, curtained, additional area at the back, which might be disclosed or hidden at will and could be employed for the playing of more sharply particularized scenes which might be rendered more theatrically effective by being played in a recess, as certain other scenes had proved more theatrically amusing when played from a window.

One can compile a list of some hundreds of instances in Elizabethan plays where the playwright invoked the assistance of such an inner stage, with its sense of surprise, its sense of change, of cosy concealment, of intriguing possibilities, of sudden and incisive punctuation of the general action. These factors of the platform-stage—a permanent raised area, a background behind it, entrance doors on to it, galleries and windows above it, and a further and concealable little stage beyond it—had become the conditions of the form of playwriting or had developed alongside this, each reacting upon the other, so that they had become exigencies of the very medium, integral parts of theatrical tradition.

Since so it was, it will be understood that a company of traditional actors presenting a play, and not a masque, would not be well served if, on their coming to court to perform, they were introduced upon the masque stage with its entirely different form. Their show would take an alien flavour, if indeed they attempted to go on with it at all. It would, in its presentation, cease to be like a play as plays were known, because its script would in most cases be unsuited for the occasion and for the stage. A new kind of play would have to be written in a new form or the stage would have to be modified to give the players some approximation of the conditions that were traditional to them, that their whole presentation had been designed to follow, and that the play itself had been written to be consistent with. Presentation of a play on a masque stage would have entailed either fundamental reconstruction or have deteriorated into an artistic solecism—abuse of the medium.

[86]

(Gerald Eades Bentley has, in his article in *Shakespeare Survey*, I, called 'Shakespeare and the Blackfriars Theatre', given very cogent reasons for supposing that when at length the public-playhouse companies came to perform extensively indoors in the 'private houses' a notable revision of the form of playwriting had to come about.)

Therefore the court made two kinds of stages, for masques and for plays, and as we have seen, it was upon the former that scenery rose to its great elaboration. Ben Jonson's first encounter with Inigo Jones upon this stage was in 1605 and the masque was *The Masque of Blacknesse*. At the end of the introduction, which describes the appearance of the scene at the opening, are the words: 'So much for the bodily part, which was of Master Ynigo Jones his design and act.'

Even here the implication in ascribing to Jones the bodily part seems to be that reservation was made of all the spiritual part by Jonson himself— not, if so, a quite just division. But we have now to see what happened in the years that followed.

This is difficult. That there arose strife between Jonson and Jones is clear. It may have been brought to a head by disagreement as to whose name should come on the programme first. Jones may have been overbearing, Jonson jealous; the personalities are hard to assess at this distance of time. What is apposite to our story is that there was a conflict, and that the principles of this conflict have ever since affected the position and the very nature of changeable scenery in the theatre. As far as this is so, the conflict is our concern.

Whatever happened in the years that followed, we come to a signal event in 1635—a flame that burst from the explosion, the sign of the breach. It took the form of the following verses drawn up and handed about in private, then, at the instance perhaps of Howel, recalled and, as far as possible, every copy destroyed. But the recall was ineffectual, for we still have these lines, which some refuse to ascribe in full to Jonson, but which few have discounted entirely as being no evidence of a real and personal attack:

AN EXPOSTULATION, WITH INIGO JONES

Master Surveyour, you that first beganne
From Thirty pounds, in pipkins, to the man
You are: from them, leap'd forth an Architect,
Able to talke of Euclide! and correct
Both him, and Archimede! Damne Archytas
The Noblest Inginere, that ever was!
Controll Ctesibius! over-beareing us
With mistooke names, out of Vitruvius!

[87]

FIRST INTERLUDE

Drawne Aristotle on us! and thence showne
How much ARCHITECTONICE *is your owne!*
Whether the building of the Stage, or Scene!
Or making of the properties, it meane!
Vizors, or Anticks! or it comprehend
Some-thing, you Sur-ship doth not yet intend!
By all your titles, and whole stile at ones,
Of Tire-man, Mounte-banke, and Justice Jones,
I do salute you! Are you fitted, yet?
Will any of these express your Place? or Witt?
Or are you so ambitious, 'bove your Peeres,
You would be 'an Asinigo, by your ears?
Why, much good doo 't you! Bee what beast you will,
You' will be as LANGLEY *said, an Inigo still.*
What makes your wretchedness to bray so loud,
In Towne, and Court? Are you growne riche? and proud?
Your trappings will not change you. Change your mind.
No velvet sheath you weare, will alter kind.
A wodden dagger, is a dagger of Wood,
Though gold, or Ivory hafts, would make it good.
What is the cause you pomp it soe? I aske;
And all men eccho, you have made a masque!
I chime that too: And I have mett with those,
That doe cry up the Machine! and the showes!
The Majesty of Juno, in the cloudes!
And peering forth of Iris, in the shrowdes!
The' ascent of Ladie Fame! which none could spie,
Not they that sided her, Dame Poetry,
Dame History, Dame Architecture too,
And Good'y' Sculpture, brought, with much adoo,
To hold her up. O showes! Showes! mighty showes!
The eloquence of Masques! what need of prose,
Or verse or sense, t' express immortall you?
You are the Spectacles of state! Tis true
Court Hiero-gly-phicks! and all Arts afford,
In the mere perspective of an inch bord!
You aske no more then certaine politique eyes!
Eyes, that can peirce into the mysteries
Of many colours! read them! and reveale
Mythologie, there, painted on slit-deale!
O to make bords to speake! there is a taske!
Painting, and Carpentry, are the soule of Masque!
Pack with your pedling Poetry, to the Stage,
This is the Money-gett, Mechanick age!
To plant the Musique, where no eare cann reach!
Attire the persons, as no thought can teach
Sense, what they are! Which by a specious, fine
Terme of you Architects, is call'd DESIGNE!
But, in the practiz'd truth, DESTRUCTION *is*
Of any art, by side, what he calls his!

FIRST INTERLUDE

Whether! O whether will this Tire-man growe?
His name is Εκενοποιός, wee all knowe,
The maker of the properties! in summe,
The Scene! the Ingine! but he is now come
To be the Musique-master! Fabler, too!
Hee is, or would-bee, the mayne Dominus doo-
All, i' the worke! And so shall still, for Ben:
Bee Inigo, the whistle, and his men!
Hee's warne on his feete, now; hee sayes! and can
Swimme without Corke! Why, thanke the good Queene Anne,
I am too fatt, to' envy him. Hee too leane
To be worth envy. Hence-forth, I doe meane
To pitty him: as smileing at his feate
Of Lanterne-Lerrey; with fuliginous heate,
Whirling his whimsey's, by a subtilty
Suck'd from the veines of shop-phylosophy!
What would he doo, now gi'ing his mind that way,
In præsentation of some puppet-play?
Should but the King his justice-hood imploy
In setting forth of such a solemne toy,
How would he firke, like Adam over-doo
Up, and about! Dive into cellars too,
Disguis'd! and thence drag forth enormitie!
Discover Vice! commit absurdity!
Under the moral! shew he had a pate
Moulded, or stroakt up, to survay a state!
O wise Surveyor! Wiser Architect!
But wisest Inigo! who can reflect
On the new priming of thy old signe-Posts;
Reviving, with fresh colours, the pale ghosts
Of thy dead standards: or (with miracle) see
Thy twice conceiv'd, thrice paid-for Imag'rie,
And not fall downe before it? and confesse
Allmighty Architecture? who no lesse
A Goddess is, then painted cloth, Dele-boards,
Vermilion, Lake, or Cinnopar, affords
Expression for! with that unbounded line,
Aym'd at, in thy Omnipotent DESIGNE!
What Poesy, ere was painted on a Wall,
That may compare with thee? what Story shall
Of all the worthies, hope t' out-last thy one,
So the materials bee, of Purbeck Stone!
Live long the feasting Roome. And e're thou burne
Againe, thy Architect to ashes turne!
Whom, not ten fires, nor a Parliament can,
With all remonstrance, make an honest Man!

(From Bernard H. Newdigate's edition of *The Poems of Ben Jonson*, Shake-speare Head Press, St. Aldate's, Oxford, 1936; as is also the following.)

FIRST INTERLUDE

TO INIGO MARQUESSE WOULD-BEE
A Corollarie

But 'cause thou hear'st the Mighty King of Spaine
Hath made his Inigo Marquesse, would'st thou faine
Our Charles should make thee such? t'will not become
All Kings, to doe the self-same deeds with some!
Beside, his man may merit it, and bee
A noble honest soule! what's this to thee?
Hee may have skill, and judgement, to designe
Citties, and Temples! Thou a Cave for wine,
Or ale! Hee build a Pallace! Thou a shop,
With slyding windowes, and false lights a 'top!
Hee draw a Forum, with quadrivial streets!
Thou paint a Lane, where Thumbe, the Pygmie meets.
Hee some Colossus, to bestride the Seas,
From the fam'd Pillars of old Hercules!
Thy Canvas-Gyant att some channell a'mes,
Or Dowgate torrent, falling into Thames!
And stradling, shewes the boyes browne-paper fleet,
Yearely set out, there, to sayle downe the street!
Your workes thus differing; troth, let so your stile:
Content thee to bee Pancridg-Earle the while;
An Earle of show: for all thy worth is show!
But when thou turn'st a real Inigo,
Or can'st of truth, the least intrenchment pitch,
Wee'le have thee stil'd, the Marquesse of New-ditch.

We may avoid discussing the values of the personalities here contained, but some lines we must examine.

What is the cause you pomp it soe? I aske;
And all men eccho, you have made a masque!

Here is implication that Jones's contribution to the court shows was recognized by 'all men' as effective, even creative. And then follows the first of those hard gibes from playwrights, lashing the spectator for being pleased with stage effects—

I have mett with those,
That doe cry up the Machine! and the showes!

As an interesting side-point, it is to be noted that in none of this was Jones accused of bungling in his effects; rather the machinery of 'the ascent of Ladie Fame' was so well contrived that 'none could spie, not they that sided her'.

Jealousy seems to find its full expression in the satiric:

O showes! Showes! mighty showes!
The eloquence of Masques! what need of prose,
Or verse or sense, t' express immortall you?

The references to inch-board and slit deal are interesting as being suggestive of carpentry and cut-out shapes. But 'to make bords to speake' were no small feat, and surely legitimate art?

There is patent suggestion that Jonson felt his poetics overcome by Jones's 'painting and carpentry', in the too-hot allegation that the result of Jones's work was not 'Design'—'specious fine terme of Architects'!—but 'Destruction, of any art beside' his own.

A few lines later there is a very interesting suggestion that Jones, beside setting the masques, took a hand in their musical parts, and maybe 'fabler' even indicates that he had to do with the scenario writing—in other words, that he was on a fair way to becoming a *producer* in the modern stage sense. And it is not out of the way to note than when a scene-designer makes a serious effort to take upon him the tasks of a producer, there generally results a type of show that, in the end, contributes to the progress of the art of theatre.

The idea at the close seems to be that Jones had, when all is said and done, only a perishable medium, which could never expect to live as long as the words of Jonson might. But history has strangely preserved the ephemeralities of the architect, and these toys made history for the stage, and a mark in the theatre that, at any rate to our own day, has not been erased.

The core of the disagreement seems to be that the script of the acted play is all that matters in theatre; the rest will pass away, the rest is a vehicle, a mere means of imparting the precious script to the people. Should those people become enamoured of the vehicle and not the script, they are base empty-heads, and desecrators of the theatre, the mistake is theirs. And it follows that all theatre based on an empty script is poor theatre, and, even more sweeping, that all theatre based on a good script is good theatre.

It is further held that the setting can do disservice to its play by being too good of its own quality. It must never possess any quality of itself, or in any respect exist for its own sake alone. Therefore all machines and effects are anathema, all pantomimes scorned. The play in a single scene is upheld as a model of the 'unities', and an example for all to follow.

And one may go on. The terms of the conflict are innumerable. But the gist of it comes to be that changeable scenery, the subject of our present study, does not sort well with plays, the material of the dramatic stage. The pure playwright's play does not want scenery. Or it wants scenery bound in every character by the hand of the playwright—a faithful execution of his idea of the scene of his action. Complete, but adding nothing; perhaps real to the point of life, but entirely unsensational in effect; attracting attention to itself in no detail.

If this is true—and the claim is often made—what is the use of studying at this length a subject so confined, or making a history of a craft so cribbed?

[91]

One reason is that our theatrical past shows how another attitude towards scenery, and another valuation of it, exist in the theatre. There emerges, from the dim shadows of bygone wings and vanished managerial offices, a host of other theatre-men beside the pure playwrights—men of the theatre foremost and of the desk after—who hold another view. They hold the painter and his products as tools in their medium to exploit to the full. (And note too that many of these men hold the dramatist and his products as mere tools also.) These men are not by any means all designers—there is also a vast proportion of the showmen; of the Astleys, the Cochrans, the Riches, the Irvings, the Davenants—yes, the Davenants, and with this name we come to a class who add fuel to the fire of the controversy; for here, in the very ranks of the dissenters, are to be found men from the poets themselves, playwrights who have squared the circle, solved the enigma, embraced the whole art of the theatre, envisaged a new voice for the art—conceivers of dramatic spectacle.

Davenant was the first of these, and with him we turn to the question of how the influence of the Jonson–Jones controversy passed on into the regular theatres to rage there as fiercely as at court.

To all intents, Jonson's swan-song among his masques was *Chloridia* (1631), though *Love's Welcome* was performed at Bolsover in 1634. And in 1635 there was performed at the Banqueting House, Whitehall, *The Temple of Love*, by a poet whose name does not appear before on the list of masques, though it was to appear again—Sir William Davenant. Jones's latest and richest settings were for Davenant's scripts—*Britannia Triumphans*, *Luminalia*, and, greatest of all the masques, *Salmacida Spolia*.

There rested in Sir William Davenant special qualities that make his place assured in any history of setting. Firstly he was one of the two links between the post-Elizabethan stage and the Restoration theatre yet unborn. He and Killigrew opened respectively the first two theatres, the Duke's Theatre, Lincoln's Inn Fields (1661), for the Duke's Men, was Davenant's, and the Theatre Royal, Vere Street (1660), for the King's Men, the rival company, was Killigrew's. These two theatres held monopolies from the Crown and they began the whole story of the modern stage. Killigrew came from what we may term the Jonson party, having worked in the public theatre that still belonged to the Elizabethan days, a successor after Shakespeare and Jonson. Davenant came from the court, and the full heady infection of the masque's brilliance (though he had had plays produced in the old playhouses too). He came to the new public theatre, not to carry on a tradition, but as an innovator, to found a new one.

Secondly, he seems to have been one of the very few playwrights of merit who conceived their shows in terms of scenery as well as words. Besides

Montague Summers's statement in *The Playhouse of Pepys* (p. 4) that 'all Davenant's activities were designedly leading up to the establishment of the first English picture-stage, the new Duke's Theatre in Lincoln's Inn Fields, which opened on Friday, 28th June, 1661', we have such notes as that in the title of Davenant's play *The Cruelty of the Spaniards in Peru*, which reads: '*Exprest by Instrumentall and Vocall Musick, and by the Art of Perspective in Scenes*'. Similarly, in his next work, *The History of Sir Francis Drake*, the same phrase was used: 'exprest . . . by the Art of Perspective in Scenes'.

Thirdly, Davenant created *The Siege of Rhodes*, produced in the inter-regnum and set by John Webb in the masque tradition.

Davenant and the Duke's Men formed the rival company to Killigrew and the King's Men, and among the weapons of this rivalry was Davenant's interest in scenes. The theatre above mentioned in Lincoln's Inn Fields was supplemented in 1671 by the Duke's Theatre in Dorset Garden—in Professor Nicoll's words, 'a very large theatre, and later abandoned except for the production of spectacular pieces'. Dorset Garden carried these marvels upon its boards and formed the gateway of their career and nursed the infant scenery upon its bosom. Sir William Davenant himself did not live to see it. He died in 1668, but in the smaller, earlier theatre of Lincoln's Inn Fields he had, as we quoted from Summers, laid the foundation of his achievement and there inaugurated the type of show that his son, Charles Davenant, and others at length brought to the great stage at Dorset Garden.

It is in the development there of this type of show linked, as we have seen above, directly to Jones and the masques, that we find the Great Scenic Controversy raising its head again. We find the story set out in the columns of an English *Cyclopaedia*, and as there are contained in its pages some of the most informative passages about the nature of scenery on the British stage that I have yet found in all my study, it is necessary to break off for a moment to introduce it.

I have found it very convenient in developing the theme of this book to refer on occasion to this work which I name briefly for convenience as Rees's *Cyclopaedia*. Since, however, it was not published until 1803–19, the proper place for a detailed study of its information is somewhat far on in my book (namely at the opening of Part 3, in Chapter 13, where material from the early nineteenth century is considered). To delay all mention of the information in the *Cyclopaedia* until that chapter, appeared to hamper unduly the interpretation of some of the earlier evidence. I have, therefore, when it seemed to me both justifiable and enlightening to do so, made reference to material in Rees in an anticipatory sense (as here) even when studying evidence dating from perhaps a century and a half before Rees was written. The full title of the work is *Cyclopaedia, or universal*

Dictionary of Arts, Sciences and Literature, illustrated with numerous Engravings, published in London from 1803 to 1819 in various volumes under the care of Dr. Abraham Rees. The main article in the *Cyclopaedia* of interest to us will be examined in detail later; at present we have to refer to another article under the heading of—surprisingly enough—'Dramatic Music.' Here we read:

Sir William D'Avenant dying in 1668, while his new theatre in Dorset Garden was building, the patent, and management, devolved on his widow, lady D'Avenant, and his son Mr. Charles, afterwards Dr. D'Avenant, well known as a political writer and civilian, who pursued sir William's plans. The new house was opened in 1671; but the public still more inclining to favour the king's company at Drury-lane than this, obliged Mr. D'Avenant to have recourse to a new species of entertainments, which were afterwards called dramatic operas, and of which kind were the Tempest, Macbeth, Psyche, Circe, and some others, all 'set off,' says Cibber, 'with the most expensive decorations of scenes and habits, and with the best voices and dancers.'

(We interrupt for a moment. The writer has just quoted Cibber. He goes on quoting Cibber, and in a further quotation and in his own mild comments upon it there comes to light just the same controversy as burned in Jonson's *Expostulation*—and this at almost the birth of public-stage scenery.)

'This sensual supply of sight and sound,' continues he [Cibber], 'coming in to the assistance of the weaker party, it was no wonder they should grow too hard for sense and simple nature, when it is considered how many more people there are, who can see and hear, than can think and judge.'

There he records the familiar attack of the literary writer on the scenic show; and it seems—perhaps because writers manifestly write more books than other folks—that this attitude to scenery is the majority view, or so far at least as the literary evidence of the past can tell us, and therefore it is with especial interest that we find the writer of this note in Rees's *Cyclopaedia* joining issue with Cibber and taking up cudgels for the minority (who allow the scene's claim to be a legitimate department of theatre art on its own merit), and he answers Cibber's somewhat crabbed and Puritan attack in good style. He goes on by saying of it:

Thus men without taste or ears for music ever comfort themselves with imagining that their contempt for what they neither feel nor understand is a mark of superior wisdom, and that every lover of music is a fool. This is the language of almost all writers on the subject. The ingenious author of the 'Biographica Dramatica' tells us, that 'the preference given to D'Avenant's theatre, on account of its scenery and decorations, alarmed those belonging to the rival house. To stop the progress of the public taste, and divert it towards themselves, they endeavoured to ridicule the performances which were so much followed. The person employed for this purpose was Thomas Duffet, (a writer of miserable farces,) who parodied the Tempest, Macbeth, and Psyche; these efforts were, however, ineffectual.' This is fair and historical; but after saying that 'the duke's theatre continued to be frequented;' when he adds, 'the victory of sound and shew over *sense* and *reason* was as complete in the theatre at this period, as it has often been since,' it seems as if sense and reason had for a moment quitted this agreeable, and, in general, accurate and candid writer. . . . But it does not clearly appear, because music and decorations were added to Shakespeare's Tempest and Macbeth, that one theatre was in greater want of sense at this time than another. . . . In the censure of these musical dramas, which has been retailed from one writer to another, ever since the middle of Charles the second's reign to the present time, the subject seems never to have been candidly and fairly examined; and, indeed, it appears as if there had been no great cause of complaint against the public taste for frequenting such representations, particularly those written by Shakespeare, in which the principal characters were performed by Mr. and Mrs. Betterton, as was the case in Macbeth, though music, machinery, and dancing were profusely added to the treat.

And so our writer closes his article on '*Dramatic Music* attempted in England, previous to the Italian opera'.

What a storm in a teacup it would all seem—save that it is not by any means made little by an intervening stretch of past time: the struggle dissociates itself from the old days and comes rushing up to us now, like an image in a concave mirror, in our daily work in the theatre. In spite of all reason, all experience, and all brave attempts, the difference has never yet been resolved. Still we quarrel over the place and rights of scenery, and Craig is as vituperative now as ever Jonson was, but with him the diatribe is sped from the theatre-man, not from the poet-playwright. It transfixes those that do not make the most of scenery, not those who make too much of it. A champion on this other side is welcome, but the quarrel does not seem to be made less bitter nor the issue any clearer.

The interim, between Davenant's day and our own, is as full of the controversy; when the eighteenth century had half run its course we are given another typical example of just the same attitude to scenery, not now by a famous name, but in a brochure entitled *The Actor; or, A Treatise on the Art of Playing*, Anon., London, 1755. We read there, on p. 254, this passage in which almost every line refers to some aspect or another of the Great Controversy:

There is one thing more, on which the truth of representation in a great measure depends; it is foreign to the player, but the manager must add it, or else all that has been inculcated will be ineffectual. This is the scenery and decorations.

Something is necessary in this, but too much is faulty; we should not have the scenes of a play like those of an *English pantomime*, or an *Italian Opera*; because we would not have them engross that attention which is more due to the player. If, for this reason, we do not expect, or desire, to see real sheep upon the wooden plain or temples change into rocks, or deserts rise to groves and gardens; yet we would not see a lady pulling off her capuchin in the street, or hear the conversation of a couple of rakes in a lady's bed-chamber. The changes must not be violent or many, but there must be some. Even where the conduct of the play does not require it the imagination of the audience does; the eye is tired with the sameness even tho' it be proper. We have had a late instance of this. In the play of *Phaedra and Hippolitus* [Revived Drury Lane, 28 Nov. 1751] the author has observed the unity of the place so well that all the scenes are transacted in one spot, in an outer court of the palace. Mr. Garrick saw this, he had a good scene prepared and it stood the whole time of the play. The manager was right; critics will say the author also was right; but the audience was disgusted . . .

Most interesting is our warning to distinguish the *drama* from *pantomime* and *opera*; the two last are the descendants of Davenant and his Duke's Houses, the former is the playwright's tradition with a literary ancestry as long as one's arm.

'We should not have the scenes of a play like those of an *English pantomime* or an *Italian Opera*.' What distinction is intended here? When we recognize it we shall encounter a fundamental idea of very cardinal significance in the meaning of scenery.

The scenery of a pantomime or an opera was a special thing, a confection having a merit of its own, an adornment along with all the other richnesses —the singing, or the folly, or the music, or the romance—all contributing to the pleasure of the theatre. (If well done, these things became indeed the Art of pleasure; if not well done, then simply the trappings or, at worst, the palls of pleasure.) But the scenery of a play was a plain background—a painted alcove and draped curtain, a dado and panel—now no feature of itself, but the unnotable handmaiden of a plot, a screen for the poet's play to act against.

But there was one thing that both sceneries had in common. *Neither, in any degree of conception whatever, had as its aim the presentment of an illusion of reality*. No vision of Heaven in an opera sought really to portray the actual clouds nor the true god—how should it! It showed decorative clouds and embodied fantasies. No foreign country was portrayed, in those days, by the representation of a given clime. Verily that would defeat the fancy. Neither did any room in a play ever have the faintest intention of *looking* like a room; how was that possible on wings and flats? Nor no garden intended the spectator to forget what he saw was presented on a stage. Those were not the prime intentions of scenery. Stage illusion had not as its original subject the illusion of reality. What a fantastic idea!

And yet that is probably the hardest point for the general person of today to grasp. The skill of painters in the eighteenth and nineteenth centuries became so great that they could delude the eye. (That is as old a trick, in truth, almost as the art of painting itself, not confined to any century, as witness the famous grapes of Zeuxis.) But we may too easily fail to see that this delusion of the eye was not the sole aim of the painters—it was merely a gesture of their skill—a source almost of amusement to a competent workman; but nothing more. It was of no significance in itself.

As the painters of the Victorian era expanded this excellence of handling at the dictates of their age, we have come to be misled into supposing this was the only aim of their art. Study of scene history as a whole teaches us otherwise.

To give a pictorial statement of, or comment upon, a thing is a very different matter from giving a visual imitation of a thing's appearance— but we shall have occasion later to add more material to this subject.

To return to the *Actor* treatise; there is an odd suggestion of *naïveté* throughout this passage which is generally fair and moderate in tone, but the writer definitely words himself like an adherent of Jonson rather than a light dallier after the ephemeralities of Jones. (Incidentally, I have never known the players in a pantomime allow even the most gorgeous scenery to engross attention due to them, though I have known the scenery of an opera be spoilt unendurably by the insipidity of the acting!) After all, however, note this one thing: the author talks of scenery, whatever its possibilities of abuse, as an essential thing—'the manager *must* add it or else all that has been inculcated will be ineffectual'—and, most remarkable of all, 'The changes must not be violent or many, but there must be some. *Even where the conduct of the play does not require it . . .*'! The Great Scenic Controversy was rarely about whether scenery and scene-changes should exist in the theatre or not but about the extent to which they should be subordinated to the drama or allowed to exploit their presence for their own sake.

Cibber attacked the scenes of the late seventeenth century, *The Actor* spoke of those of the first half of the eighteenth, and next Boaden speaks against those of the end of the eighteenth. In Chapter 19 of his *Memoirs of Mrs. Siddons* this adherent of the 'Jonson Party' says:

But neither tragedy nor comedy ever seemed with me to derive a benefit proportioned to the pains that have been taken in the scenic department of our stages. When the scenes are first drawn on, or the roller descends, the work exhibited is considered a few moments as a work of art—the persons who move before it then engross the attention,—at their exit it is raised or drawn off, and is speedily forgotten, or seen with indifference the second time. If the perspective, as to the actor standing in front of the scene, was so accurate that the whole effect should be delusive, and the impression be of actual sky, and land, and building (though an objection will always remain to the abrupt junction of the borders with the tops of the scenes—the wings, and the scoring line where the flats meet each other— the grooves in which they move, the boarded stage and other difficulties hitherto insurmountable), I could understand the object of those who expend so much money on their elaboration—but I confess I am of opinion, that they should never do more than suggest to the imagination; and that it would not be desirable that the spectator should lose his senses to the point of forgetting that he is in a regular theatre, and enjoying a work of art invented for his amusement and his instruction by a poet, and acted by another artist of corresponding talent called a player. All beyond this is the dream of ignorance and inexperience.

I have already hinted at my impression that the powers of the truly great comedian, using the term to express an actor of either species of the drama, are superior to all this aid; his commerce is with the judgement and the passions—it is vitality operating upon kindred life, man awaking the sympathies of man. When we have such a being as Mrs. Siddons before us in Lady Macbeth, what signifies the order or disorder of the picture of a castle behind her, or whether the shadows lie upwards or downwards on the mouldings of a midnight apartment? It is to the terror of her eye, it is to the vehement and commanding sweep of her action—it is to the perfection of her voice that I am captive, and I must pity the man who, not being the painter of the canvas, is at leisure to inquire how it is executed.

Balanced, and just, as much of this is, there is the same sting in the tail to prick the folk who let an eye wander from the actor to the stage, and whose imagination (in the conceit of Leigh Hunt) desired to take a walk in the scenery.

The body of the passage calls our glance to that other bone of contention in the scenic theatre—the meaning of 'stage illusion'. It might be supposed that an adherent of the 'Jonson Party' in the Great Scenic Controversy would uphold the opinion that stage illusion means the delusion of reality, and Boaden actually speaks of a view that 'the whole effect should be delusive, and the impression be of actual sky and land and building', but he speaks of the view as a mistaken one; his opinion is that the scenes 'should never do more than suggest to the imagination'—yet after ascribing such a sacred appeal to their purpose he can go on to say that all that matters in a regular theatre is that a man should feel that he is before a work of art 'invented for his instruction and amusement by a poet' and 'acted by another artist of corresponding talent called a player', the rest—the scenery—is 'the dream of ignorance and inexperience'! But maybe Boaden had a very wide conception of the sphere of a poet—he might have included Inigo Jones—or he might not!

Boaden quotes a letter of Burke's:

The dresses, the scenes, the decorations of every kind, I am told, are in a new style of splendour and magnificence; whether to the advantage of our dramatic taste on the whole I very much doubt. It is a show and a spectacle, not a play, that is exhibited.

Moderate and impersonal words, these; but still the same old story.

It is with almost a relief that we turn to Rees again and find his author taking up the cudgels, albeit with the properest moderation, for the other side:

In the earlier ages, although dramatic entertainments were very popular, especially among the Grecians and Romans, more attention seems to have been paid to the genius and labour of the poet, than to that of the mechanist or decorator. The names of Æschylus, Aristophanes, Terence, Plautus, and many others, have reached us, while those of the mechanics employed (if there were such) have sunk into oblivion. Whether the mechanical and decorative taste of the ancients was equal to the genius of their poets, it is wholly foreign from the design of this article to inquire. In the present state of dramatic representation we find, by experience, that Cinderella, and Mother Goose, generally fascinate the spectators more than even the most eminent works of Shakspeare. If this be a proof of decay or perversion of literary taste, it is also at least a very strong one of the progress of the mechanical arts, and of the effect which they produce upon the public mind even in matters of amusement.

At the end of the century it was William Telbin, speaking again from this other party, who made his defence against the same old attack, that scenery (this time, we may guess, it was Irving's scenery) had too much attention and money spent upon it, and who gave us a most interesting technical passage in this defence that we shall have occasion to analyse on p. 384.

In our own day just the same wrangle continues. Now perhaps there is a fresh field for its flourishing—and a fertile one indeed—for the amateur player has come into the light again and many are the books by amateur writers and amateur authorities on the theatre that profess to teach him his business. We find: 'The scenery is the setting for the actor. It has no justification in itself' (C. B. Purdom, *Producing Plays*, 1930). And a professional stage-manager such as Frank Napier has even gone so far as to state (with italics and all): '*The fundamental purpose of scenery is to help the actor and nothing else*' (*Curtains for Stage Settings*, 1937). Even in the Art Theatre the austere attitude towards the danger of scenery is to be found; Professor Una Ellis-Fermor, in *The Irish Dramatic Movement* (1939), sums up W. B. Yeats's views on scenery with the following quotations from his writing:

If Yeats was 'the advocate of the poetry as against the actor', he was equally 'the advocate of the actor as against the scenery'. . . . 'The background should be of as little importance as the background of a portrait group, and it should, when possible, be of one colour or of one tint. . . .' 'The poet cannot evoke a picture to the mind's eye if a second-rate painter has set his imagination of it before the bodily eye; but decoration and suggestion will . . . never become obtrusive or wearisome. The actor and the words put into his mouth are always the one thing that matters, and the scene should never mean anything to the imagination until the actor is in front of it.' (*Samhain*, 1904).

But we are heading fast for a digression. We have proved the existence of A Great Scenic Controversy. We purposed no more. Its echoes will haunt us through all our examination of scenery. We shall never escape it. Every student intending to design for the theatre should know of the battle which—be it covert or open—he will have to plunge into. For us there remains but a closing word and we return to our history.

We may now well understand the descendants of the 'Jonson Party'—though forced to pander to public taste by the inclusion of scenery for their shows—holding the setting in a lesser regard, and playing in any adequate stock scenery with no more pricks of conscience than a bluestocking permits on her frocks, while Jones's successors, as they prepare entrancing special designs and ingenuities, see the subject in the light of a coquette: the one is sufficient unto herself without trimmings, and the other knows the world is more graced by her presence. The one has solid worth, the other real delightfulness; the former is content with anything out of the wardrobe, the latter is special and extravagant. The first is unvarnished, the second effective.

We may well understand, then, that the theatrical setting has been considered by one party as a trumpery matter, of no importance, save as a subject for economy, and by the other as an essential part of its craft.

But above all their views rises the one convention neither could escape, that just as the two sorts of women nowadays have got to wear clothes, so both parties in the theatre must have scenery; for though the incidence of the 'evil' may have sprung from the demonstrative whim of one side only, yet a fashion was set thereby which the other might contemn but not ignore—and nudism, whether of clothes or scenery, had to await conception as an idea until the twentieth century.

How fatally easy it is to take sides in a controversy! A latent 'Irish' pugnaciousness seems invoked by discussion on movable scenery. One involves oneself against one's will. Yet when one returns to an impartial viewpoint the reflection occurs that it is not scenery that inspires this controversy—it is movable scenery, scenery that sets out to present the appearance of the places where the action is supposed to occur. Through all the controversy there rides unshaken and unassailable as a tower—*turris fortissima*—the vision of the stage with a static scene. No one has ever impugned that or called its technique in question. Or have they?

A restless stirring makes itself felt in our mind and, listening uneasily to the new schools of thought that argue about the theatre today, we begin to ask if perhaps they may not have something right in them—if we may not be on the threshold of a new era of theatrical presentation. Perhaps it is another phantom. But one thing is certain: it can hurt no one if we equip ourselves to meet whatever is coming by a very searching inquiry into what has been.

To return to our technical approach, and in preparation for the details of the next chapter, it is useful to close this interlude by asking: What did English scenery represent at its beginning? What is the nature of the traditional English scene? And is there in that nature anything which would itself give birth to a controversy?

When we refer to 'the traditional English scene' we refer to something which a French theatre-man today might well call by a different and possibly unexpected name (though one quite familiar to him), that is, *la scène à l'italienne*. His phrase is interesting not only because of its reference to the theory of the Italian origin of the style of scenery we are discussing, but for the reflection which arises from the use of the word *scène*. To us a scene is the scenery, to the French *la scène* is the stage—it could never be equivalent (as our English word 'scene' is) to the German *Bühnenbild*. Yet the power of the English words 'scene' and 'scenery' is very great. Their descent from the Greek *skene*—the building that backed the playing area—need not occupy us here, but what is also interesting is that the implication in our two words of 'something to look at' is so great that they spread out of the theatre and came to be used to name that thing so dear to most circumspective Englishmen—the vision of a landscape, a view.

The Oxford English Dictionary defines 'scene' in this sense as: '(9) A view . . . of a place (1653)', and 'scenery' as: '(3) The general appearance of a place and its natural features, regarded from the picturesque point of view: the aggregate of picturesque features in a landscape (1784).' The theatrical use of 'scene' as 'painted hangings'—from which these later meanings derived, and which has the root meaning of the word—is dated 1540. (The same word signifying 'stage' in the French sense is quoted later as 1638.) The other word 'scenery' was used of stage scenes in 1774 but transferred to landscapes only by 1784.

Whether these dates are finally correct or not, the interesting fact is that our landscape-word, 'scenery', was derived from the theatre. I have not found any other language which made this applied use of the word 'scene'. 'The scene', then, to the English had enough significance to become transferred to non-theatrical uses.

Let us inquire a little further into the original elements of an English scene to learn, if we can, just what significance they had to an Englishman.

A scene was made fundamentally of two different sorts of scene-pieces—the backscene and the wings, whether the former be flat or in planes. True, there were also the borders hanging above which often enter quite considerably into the picture, but these are in the nature rather of necessary adjuncts; they are the least important of the three main constituents. Taking the backscene first, what is there to be noticed about its appearance and the nature of the designs it bore, and the relation these had to the show? To begin with, it is essential to any full setting. Once the system of full scenery, as opposed to detail setting, is accepted, the backscene must be there to close the back of the set and hide the crass and concrete walls of the theatre.

But having made that point and established that its relation to the stage is concrete and easily definable, we find on the other hand that its relation to the show is far more difficult to put down in set terms. What, to come to fundamentals, is to be painted on a backscene?

We must consider this question in the broad light of the past and of established tradition, not merely judge the matter from the narrow standpoint of today—whence, perhaps, to give an answer seems far too easy. What was painted at the outset on the early backscenes; what did they portray? We find it was not necessarily a picture of the place where the action was imagined to occur. That place may, indeed, in early scripts be only very vaguely indicated or completely passed over.

Many of the earliest backscenes in Italy seem to have borne a painting of houses—sometimes a topographical view of some city—or later to have presented a painting of a purely imaginative vista—of gardens, of the sea, of heaven, or of hell. This topographical local view is especially to be noticed. In England, for instance, we have a record of a stock, Court backscene, just after the Restoration, giving a portrait of Denmark House.

In all these manifestations there is a common quality; the subject of the backscene seems to have been presented in its own right—not as a subordinate factor in the plot of the show. It was a view of Venice or Denmark House for the joy of having a view of Venice or Denmark House at the back of an action which admittedly might have taken place in either of the spots, but which was backed by that scene rather because they liked to have that scene in the theatre than because the plot was laid in a locality where such a background would logically be visible.

Or it was a view of hell, not seen from the standpoint of a collaborator with the playwright and arranged only to suit his script, but conceived apart from the play as a subject sufficient in itself to merit the enjoyment of a creator—an opportunity not a condition.

It is somewhat more easy to understand how this attitude to the backscene came to inform its origin when one considers the particular nature of the script of the early spectacle show (as opposed to dramatic plays), and of the show itself.

They were shows composed for show, not to exploit a constructed plot or to justify any demands of logic nor conform to any strict canons of treatment of character or faithful representation of life. Consequently it did not matter so much exactly *what* the backscene's relation to the plot was. The link was in slightly different terms. A backscene was required: it might be very definitely laid down what it was to represent, but the reason its subject was definitely decided was not so much inherent in the script of the play as in the needs or possibilities of the show, and of making a sensational or charming setting to the spectacle.

In short, the backscene bore to the show a relation more closely resembling that of the backcloth in a music hall to its turn than that of the modern stage-setting to its specific scene of the drama. This is indeed to be expected, for there was more resembling the nature of the music-hall show in these early scenic spectacles than there was resembling the spirit of a modern play production. The early backscene was a background to the stage in its own right, not a subsidiary adjunct to the play.

It is for this reason that early writers on scenery make remarks about the design of scenes that have what seems at first an oddly absolute flavour to modern ears; for instance, Serlio in a famous passage says that in a Comic Scene (note: *any* Comic Scene, not the comic scene in a particular play) 'the Houses must be made as if they were for common or ordinarie people . . . but specially there must not want a brawthell or bawdy house, and a great Inn, and a Church; such things of necessity to be therein'. Remark the insistence of the last phrase. Again of Tragic Scenes he says, 'you must make none but stately houses'; and in 'Satiricall Scenes' you 'must place all those things that be rude and rusticall'. This is far away indeed from that parrot-cry at the opening of modern primers on scene-design which say the first thing before all else is to read the play through carefully!

Thus, then, in approaching the subjects of the next chapters we should remember that a scene might be a 'shutter' scene or a 'scene of relieve', but we should not be too certain that what is represented upon it will have quite the relation to the show that we expect today.

Turning now to the framing element of the backscene—the side-scenes or wings—we find a curious technical matter about their placing which is worth mentioning at once before we go on to consider the subject painted upon them.

In the first place a wing is necessarily limited in width. It must be high to suit the height of the proscenium opening, but it must not be so wide as to become inconvenient to handle or to pack or to travel; this limits its width to a nominal 6 ft. at the most—often it was much narrower. But one 6-ft. wing will not mask the side of a normal-sized set on its own, and so it follows there must be several wings set one behind the other, according to the size of the wings and of the stage. Now if these wings are to mask the stage-side most adequately, a simple plan upon a sheet of paper will show that the effective angle at which to set them is definitely diagonal, so that each is directly facing not the bulk of the audience but the outermost seat on the opposite side of the house. A stage which is set with wings according to this rule will be set most economically; were the same wings turned parallel to the proscenium opening, they would not mask—spaces would be seen between them from the side seats and to remedy this fault they would have to be placed nearer together and hence they would need an increase of number to mask a given length of side.

The principle is much the same as that of a Venetian blind, which when 'closed' (that is with the slats turned at an angle) effectually masks a window, but with its slats horizontal (analogous to wings parallel with the audience) allows a view through.

It follows then that the best position for wings is at an angle with regard to the bulk of the audience, and so we place them today. But in earlier days they were not always set diagonally; they were in most periods set 'straight'. We shall see how the requirements of changeable scenery influenced this angle.

As will now be readily seen, the effect of a row of wings exercises a somewhat restricting influence on the design of a set. Very few interior scenes nowadays can have their side-walls adequately represented on a row of wings, and the vast majority of the scenes on our stage today are interiors. Further, only certain classes of exterior scene (such as woods) can be, with any degree of freedom, represented by sets with wings. No wide, open country scene, for instance, may be suggested without the closing influence of a double row of trees, no mountain-top that is not imagined between avenues of rock pillars, and no sea-scene that is not stretched to the very limits either of ingenuity or ingenuousness by arrangements of ships and sails, or wholly conventional clouds. The wings like much else in scenery have been the subject for great controversy.

The classic wing, then, is a free-standing, tall, narrow piece of scenery. Rows of wings frame the backscene at either side. What relation in the beginning did the wing bear to the scene as a complete composition—was it an intimate part of the pictorial conception of the whole, bearing equal value with the backscene, or was it a mere adjunct with a different importance? Was it part of the scene or part of the frame of the scene?

In explanation of the last question I would point out that we are now turning our attention to elements of scenery which may be conceived in slightly different terms from the backscene that we discussed above. When we dealt with the backscene we emphasized that it was the kernel of the scene—in short, scenery in the essential meaning of the word. But the other elements of the setting, the wings and the borders, may not be scenically essential in just the same way; they may be functional rather than representational.

A word on this distinction may not be out of place here. In my book *Stage Setting* I suggested that a study of contemporary setting as a whole leads to the division of the elements of any set into two classes; firstly we have that piece or those pieces which specifically stamp the nature of the particular scene of the show—which apply to no other scene, and which must be changed before another scene can proceed; and secondly we may have those pieces which are not so intimately bound up with the nature of one scene in particular, and are more in the nature of a general surround to the scenery proper, fitting the latter to the stage, and themselves capable of remaining unchanged—or with little change—throughout a number of scenes in a show. This divergence of function may be marked by reserving for the first kind the name of *scenery* proper, and by thinking of the rest rather as the *stage setting*. All that the eye sees in the stage picture is not necessarily scenery.

The distinction is one which arises early in any study of the general development of theatrical presentation. A couple of illustrations should serve to clarify the point. In the classic theatre, authorities inform us that the spectacle took place before the *proskenion* (the *frons scaenae* of the Romans) which was the façade of the *skene*-building, and in front also of such extensions (the *paraskenia*, for example) as were added to that building. This formed the *stage setting* to the day's theatrical presentation as a whole, but it could not be called scenery.

We understand, however, that specific scenes were particularized, though to what extent is not decided, by placing in, or before, this façade details of painted scenery which were changed at the transition from one scene to another.

We have then to conceive (*a*) a general architectural setting for shows, not particularized in any special way, and (*b*) the placing in this setting of relatively smaller painted pieces of scenery of a nature we are not prepared to describe here in detail, but about which two things are clear; they, unlike the architectural setting, were changed for the different scenes and, further, they form not the whole of the stage picture but only a detail of it, the setting filling out the rest.

Offering, as it were, a transition between the classic theatre and the modern we have the form of the Elizabethan playhouse. Here again we find the same idea: the stage itself formed the background of the show—the stage with its essential adjunct, the façade of the tiring-house. These with the whole interior of the playhouse were the *setting* for the show—*scenery* was only an added detail now and then—a throne, a table, a tent, a little set-up disclosed within the tiring-house by the drawing of a curtain, or frankly built out on the stage itself. Whatever its detail this little piece of scenery was but part of the total picture perceived by the spectator. Scenery was originally a small thing on the stage and did not occupy its whole area.

At the present day, in a simple set on any little-theatre stage we may find the need for economy enforcing something of the same principle. Here the setting of the stage is not so likely to be an architectural background as it was in Greece, owing to the particular nature of modern stage-planning, but it will very often take the form of an arrangement of curtains or other

[105]

such neutral things. This is in no way to be called scenery, it is only the stage-setting for scenery and, upon the presentation of a show, painted or built or other details of scenery are placed in or before those curtains to stamp the nature of the scene; and these have to be changed before another scene can be presented. Scenery here is the core or essence of the visual side of the show, while the stage-setting is as it were a frame or mount to set off the scenery. To take the analogy from jewellery, the one is the stone, the other—and the same word is used—is its setting.

In studying the English stage wing we have, then, to remember that the elements of a stage picture may be divided into the central, changeable, particular feature and the subordinate (though possibly larger) and more general feature which may be said to be a mount or setting for it. This duality is what we have to bear in mind when we consider the question: Was the wing, in its original essence, part of the scene proper or part of the frame of the scene?

We must review the evidence in the present book before giving a final answer, but on the point of beginning the review we may hint that we shall frequently find wings not thought of as having to be of a piece with the backscene, and also we shall find backscenes that have but the lightest regard for the logic of the drama. In these two attitudes towards the main elements of scenery we find something of the meaning of theatre, as well as fertile seeds of controversy.

To make a unity of things which are disparate is good. To make a unity of things carefully selected so as to belong is good. The one results in a Contrast, the other in a Harmony. It is the attempt to make a unity with things which are disparate by chopping their very nature so as to fit them, which is bad in all ages and all walks of life. This results in mutilation and embarrassment.

We must remember the opposite liberties to blend or to contrast now that the parts of the scene-picture suffer this emphasis on a need for unity.

PART TWO

THE DEVELOPMENT OF
CHANGEABLE SCENERY IN THE
PUBLIC THEATRE OF THE
SEVENTEENTH AND EIGHTEENTH
CENTURIES

7

DAVENANT AND
THE SIEGE OF RHODES, 1661

★

*'The Siege of Rhodes', Part One—'The Siege of Rhodes', Part Two—The
Engine and the Machine*

★

WITH this chapter we leave the nursery of changeable scenery,
which was the royal court, and go on to survey its introduction
into the regular English public theatre, and note its fortunes and
developments there as it begins its three-century journey to our own day.

Our method will be to place in chronological order such contemporary
references as we have found that seem to be informative upon the nature
and use of changeable scenery and to comment upon them, both in the light
of experience gained in the study of earlier periods and (when it is indis-
pensable for illumination) in the light of what can be learned from later
evidence but which may be as yet hidden from the reader.

The first reference to the introduction of changeable scenery as a regular
thing in the professional theatre in England is naturally a highly important
one and must be studied in some detail. Unfortunately it is not well documented from the point of view of practical facts, and we shall be put to some
ranging at large for details to give the picture shape at all.

Sir William Davenant had made experiments during the Commonwealth
at his own home with new forms of theatrical shows. Something about this
work may be read in the first chapter of Montague Summers's *The Playhouse of Pepys*.

When the Restoration sanctioned theatres once more, Davenant opened,
in 1661, his public playhouse in Lisle's Tennis Court, which we now know
as the Duke's Theatre, Lincoln's Inn Fields, and his first presentation was
a revival of *The Siege of Rhodes* (the staging of which at Rutland House in
1656 we have already discussed). This was immediately followed by a newly
written *The Siege of Rhodes, Part Two*. So much is established fact. But
whether the details of staging of *The Siege of Rhodes, Part One*, at the Duke's
Theatre were the same as the details of staging at Rutland House five years

[109]

earlier we have still to decide. And for the staging of the Second Part we have no plans or designs as we have for the First Part. However, with the memory of Webb's drawings for the First Part tentatively in mind we turn now to study the printed texts of the two plays for enlightenment on their staging at the Duke's Theatre. We shall find little direct evidence of the details of scenery, but we shall find so remarkable a reflection of the function of scenery as conceived in Davenant's mind that our whole ensuing study will be coloured by it. We have therefore now to examine the stage-directions of the printed editions in detail.

The edition dated 1656 was printed to mark the occasion of the experimental private performance at Rutland House. Its title-page reads:

THE SIEGE OF RHODES Made a Representation by the Art of Prospective in Scenes, And the Story sung in *Recitative* Musick. At the back part of *Rutland*-House in the upper end of *Aldersgate*-Street LONDON [Decoration] *LONDON* Printed by J. M. for *Henry Herringman*, and are to be sold at his Shop, at the Sign of the *Anchor*, on the Lower-Walk in the *New-Exchange*, 1656.

The title-page of the edition dated 1659 is the same except for the date and for the substitution of 'At the Cock-Pit in *DRURY* Lane' for the reference to Rutland House.

This edition marked a further presentation of the show, this time in a public theatre, but not as yet, be it noted, a public theatre that we know to have been regularly equipped for scenic shows. It is presumable that the Cockpit in Drury Lane had at this period a platform stage related to the little-known stages of the typical Elizabethan private houses and that the theatre would have been specially fitted up for *The Siege of Rhodes*, as a masquing hall was specially fitted up for the occasion. It is unlikely that scenery was dispensed with at this presentation since Davenant so clearly conceived of it as being part of his show, but as yet he had not set a precedent for all shows.

The title-page of the edition dated 1663 is different:

THE SIEGE OF RHODES The First and Second Part; As they were lately Represented at His Highness the Duke of *YORK'S* Theatre in *Lincolns-Inn-Fields*. The First Part being lately Enlarg'd. Written by Sir William D'avenant [Decoration] *LONDON* Printed for *Henry Herringman*, and are to be sold at his shop, at the Sign of the *Anchor*, on the Lower-walk in the *New-Exchange*. 1663.

Editions 1656 and 1659 begin with an Address to the Reader concerning the narrowness of Rutland House stage.

Edition 1663 begins with a dedication to the Earl of Clarendon and then goes on to describe the scene.

(And it is implied that these descriptions refer equally to the Duke's Theatre performance as they did in earlier editions to the smaller performances at Rutland House and the Cockpit. This point is important. Had dissimilar scenery been used on this occasion from that at Rutland House, it is more likely that the scene-descriptions in the script would have been rewritten or at least altered, for certain portions of the play itself are altered. But the scene-descriptions are *not* altered or added to; they stand exactly as they stood in the first edition, when they referred, in accurate detail, to the designs made by John Webb of which we have full record. The above argument is given unusual weight because Davenant as a playwright paid an unprecedented attention to scenery, even regarding it (as his title-page suggests) as part of the essential vehicle and medium of his drama— 'made a Representation by the Art of Prospective in Scenes . . .' Such an attitude had probably existed in no English playwright before. Thus it is very likely that when a new edition of his play, marking the occasion of a fresh presentation, bears the same scene-descriptions, then this argues the retention of the same design of scenery. Admittedly the scenes may have been repainted and probably remade, for Rutland House had only a minute stage. But the presumption, at present, seems fair that the same designs were used—see Pl. 25.)

These are the descriptions then of the scenes of the two parts 'as' (so the title-page states) 'they were lately Represented at His Highness the Duke of *YORK'S* Theatre in *Lincolns-Inn-Fields*'.

The Ornament which encompass'd the Scene, consisted of several Columns, of gross Rustick work; which bore up a large Freese. In the middle of the Freese was a Compartiment, wherein was written RHODES. The Compartiment was supported by divers Habiliments of War; intermix'd with the Military Ensigns of those several Nations who were famous for defence of that Island; which were the *French*, *Germans*, and *Spaniards*, the *Italians*, *Avergnois*, and *English*: The Renown of the English valor, made the Grand Master *Villerius*, to select their Station to be most frequently commanded by himself. The principal enrichment of the Freese was a Crimson Drapery, whereon several Trophies of Arms were fixt, Those on the Right hand, representing such as are chiefly in use amongst the Western Nations; together with the proper Cognizance of the Order of the *Rhodian* Knights; and on the left, such as are most esteem'd in the Eastern Countries; and on an Antique Shield the Crescent of the *Ottomans*.

The Scene before the First Entry.

The Curtain being drawn up, a lightsome Sky appear'd, discov'ring a Maritime Coast, full of craggy Rocks, and high Cliffs, with several Verdures naturally growing upon such Scituations; and afar off, the true Prospect of the City of RHODES, when it was in prosperous estate; with so much view of the Gardens and Hills about it, as the narrowness of the Room could allow the Scene. In that part of the Horizon, terminated by the Sea, was represented the *Turkish* Fleet, making towards a Promontory, some few miles distant from the Town.

The ENTRY *is prepared by Instrumental Musick.*

The First Entry.

This 'first entry' is the opening act of the play. Upon the stage an Admiral

[111]

and Villerius, Grand Master of Rhodes, speak, and to them comes Alphonso, the hero, who is also Ianthe's new-wed husband. He is urged to leave Rhodes and return to her in Sicily to escape the coming attack by Solyman and the Turks. He refuses and stays. They all go out.

There now immediately enter Ianthe and her two women who are in Sicily, and Ianthe proposes to go to Rhodes to share her husband's danger. *But no scene has been changed!* This 'prospect' of Rhodes in the distance serves to set both a scene inside Rhodes and a scene in Sicily. (We have an illustration of its presumed appearance in Pl. 15, and, there, it is a shutter scene. See also Pls. 25*a* and 25*b*.)

A chorus sung 'By Souldiers of several Nations' brings us to the 'End of the first Entry'.

The Scene is chang'd, and the City, Rhodes, *appears beleaguer'd at Sea and Land*.

The Entry is again prepar'd by Instrumental Musick.

The Second Entry.

In this new scene Villerius and the Admiral speak again, still in the same situation as before, though the backscene is now changed. Thus we may change scenery while the characters remain in one spot, or change characters and place while leaving the backscene unaltered. This particular attitude to scenery as a decorative adjunct to a theatrical presentation or as an accompaniment to the progress of mood of the play, and not as a representation of the background of the characters, is of importance in assessing the original estimate in which it was held (Pl. 25*c*).

Alphonso again joins the others and, after speech, they leave the stage empty. Next, *with no change of scenery*, on come Solyman and Pirrhus—of the opposing forces! To them Mustapha leads in the captured Ianthe. She is offered safe passage into Rhodes by Solyman and, further, safe passage out again with her husband. They '*exeunt* several ways'. There follows a chorus of women, presumably sung inside Rhodes, for they are setting about its defence.

So comes '*The End of the Second Entry*'. Next—

The further part of the Scene is open'd, and a Royal Pavilion appears display'd; Representing *Solyman*'s Imperial Throne; and about it are discern'd the Quarters of his *Bassa*'s, and Inferiour Officers.

The ENTRY *is again prepar'd by Instrumental Musick.*

The Third Entry.

Enter *Solyman, Pirrhus, Mustapha.*

Solyman orders a day's pause to allow Ianthe and Alphonso to escape from Rhodes (see Pl. 25*d*); they all go out and—

The Scene is chang'd to that of the Town Besieg'd.

Enter *Villerius, Admiral, Alphonso, Ianthe.*

They discuss the strange chivalric situation and Alphonso points out that honour stops his leaving Rhodes. They go, and then (into the same scenery) enter Roxolana, Pirrhus, and Rustan. Roxolana is Solyman's queen (and is a new character imported into the First Part only at this edition, having found her birth in the Second Part when that was written for the opening of the Duke's Theatre). She comes to his camp outside Rhodes in jealousy, hearing of his clemency to Ianthe. A chorus sung by Men and Women ends the third entry on a light note. Then—

The Scene is vary'd to the Prospect of Mount *Philermus*: Artificers appearing at work about that Castle which was there, with wonderful expedition, erected by *Solyman*. His great Army is discovered in the Plain below, drawn up in *Battalia*, as if it were prepar'd for a general Assault.

The Entry *is again prepar'd by Instrumental Musick.*

The Fourth Entry.

Enter *Solyman, Pirrhus, Mustapha.*

(For this see Pls. 14 and 25*e*.) Solyman hears of his refused passport and issues orders that Ianthe and Alphonso are to be spared in the imminent attack. This is a short scene of forty lines. The characters *exeunt*, and then, with no signal of a new entry, we find—

The Scene returns to that of the Town Besieg'd.

Enter *Alphonso, Ianthe.*

They quarrel, Alphonso suspecting unjustly Solyman's reasons for offering safeguard to Ianthe. They part in anger. Villerius and the Admiral enter and warn of an attack, bewailing Alphonso's distraction. Into the same scenery now come Roxolana with two of her women and Pirrhus and Rustan. (Note how this convention of scene-sequence is much like the 'opposing camps' convention in the Elizabethan playhouse.) Roxolana shows growing jealousy. Haly (a new character who is a Eunuch Bassa) enters and announces the attack. All 'exeunt *severall wayes*' and a chorus of wives finishes the entry. Then—

The Scene is chang'd into a Representation of a general Assault given to the Town; the greatest fury of the Army being discern'd at the English Station.

The Entry is again prepar'd by Instrumental Musick.

The Fifth Entry.

Pirrhus and Mustapha with Solyman call urgent encouragement. Then, though there is no indication of their exit, Alphonso appears, having failed to stem a retreat. The Admiral calls him back, crying that Ianthe in disguise lies wounded at the English bulwark. They leave, and Pirrhus (from the Turkish side) enters to tell of a change in the fortune of the fight (for this see Pl. 25*f*). Next—

The Scene returns to that of the Castle on Mount Philermus.

Solyman has a speech of sixteen lines, then—

The Scene is chang'd to that of the Town Besieg'd.

Enter *Villerius, Admiral, Ianthe.*

She in a Night-Gown and a Chair is brought in.

She despises her wound and bewails Alphonso's alteration. 'Enter *Alphonso* wounded, led in by two Mutes', and the pair are reconciled. A scene follows where Solyman briefly chides Roxolana for her jealousy, then a final chorus brings us to the end of the Fifth Entry and 'The Curtain is let fall'.

Before going on to analyse the Second Part, some observations will be useful in the way of general recapitulation of significant matter in the First Part.

To me the most remarkable thing about this 'first' play to use changeable scenery is that the changes of scenery were not made to coincide with the changes of dramatic scene. This is remarkable because the author was for the first time in English history faced with an unprecedented possibility— the possibility of backing a scene of action in his play with a relevant setting of full scenery on the stage; and then, when his scene of action in the play changed, of removing the setting of scenery and replacing it with a fresh one relevant to the new action. This possibility existed and Davenant must have seen it. Yet the possibility was completely and studiedly ignored. *He did not employ his scenery in this way.* He took a quite different course and exploited a quite other possibility of the new medium offered to his hand. Davenant did not introduce scenery as an illusionistic setting but, instead, thought out a quite profound conception of it as an accompaniment to the exposition of the plot used in a sort of counterpoint.

Thus, for the First Entry in *The Siege of Rhodes, Part One*—in what we today should call the 'first act'—we have three distinct developments of the action—what we should call 'scene 1', 'scene 2', and 'scene 3'—and in the first of these three characters speak as it were inside the city of Rhodes; in the second 'scene' the action shifts to Sicily and three women speak who are preparing to go to Rhodes—a journey across the Ionian Sea and the Sea of Candia—and in the third 'scene' we have a chorus of 'Souldiers of several Nations' presumably in Rhodes once again.

Yet the setting conceived for all this 'act' (or *entry*) is (see Pl. 15) a green-covered stage with rock wings either side and a painting at the back of a bird's-eye view of a sea-port at the foot of rolling hills and facing a sea on whose horizon appear the threatening Turkish ships. This is indeed an admirable accompaniment to the opening mood of the play; it helps to give the atmosphere for the story by illustrating for us a peaceful city under an imminent threat, but it is not, in any but the most remote sense, a presentation of the actual surroundings of imagined human encounters. It is high convention of the theatre, but is not within hailing distance of being naturalism. It is scenery in the stage sense of the decking of a stage, but not scenery in the landscape sense of a background seen behind people.

In the Second Act (or Entry) we are presented with a new shutter as backscene, upon which we now see Rhodes depicted from the landward side, and look over its towers to our left to glimpse the sea and the attacking fleet once more; but now, upon the hilly country to our right, the Turkish camp is pitched with warlike engines and cannon that already discharge their shot upon the town. Despite this change of scene, and despite the fact that it still shows us Rhodes from without the walls, the act opens exactly as before with a scene between the beleaguered generals in the city. Presumably they enter and exit on the spectator's left where the walls of Rhodes are glimpsed. After them comes the second 'scene' where, for the first time, we see the enemy, with Solyman in his majesty appearing in the field. We suppose him entering from our right and looking across to the town he attacks. Ianthe, captured in her sea trip, is brought to him and chivalrously passed on towards Rhodes. They '*exeunt* several ways'—presumably Ianthe crosses to our left to go out into Rhodes and Solyman and his generals withdraw to our right towards their camp. Now follows a third 'scene' where the women of Rhodes sing in chorus of its defence. The structure of the second 'act' is then similar to the first.

Now what happens is a drawing of the scenery-shutters to reveal the first relieve scene, showing Solyman's Camp and Throne, and, as always, a space of time is left to view the scene while 'the Entry is again prepar'd by Instrumental Musick'.

The third 'act' *does* include a change of scenery. After continuing Solyman's scene in the relieve camp, we find the second pair of shutters is closed again and a scene with the Rhodians follows. This is in consonance with our modern conception of scenery, for surely a Rhodian scene could not be acted in the setting of a Turkish camp! Yet, immediately after, the third scene of the act takes place where Roxolana and others are introduced as speaking from Solyman's camp. Yet there is no indication of a scene-change, and she speaks before the shutter showing the Turkish artillery outside Rhodes. This scene is, in point of fact, an interpolation made for the revival in order to introduce Roxolana who did not exist in previous editions of the First Part, but who was to play so important a role in the Second Part.

[115]

Now the sequence of the 'act' is picked up again and a chorus concludes it, reviewing in an almost abstracted way the relation of Ianthe and Alphonso —scarcely it would seem in any particular geographical situation at all; a mere general comment.

The introduction of the Fourth Act (or Entry) is on usual lines; the shutters are opened for the Prospect of Mount Philermus and a pause is made for surveying it to the accompaniment of instrumental music. This is the second relieve scene—to which we have referred in some detail in a previous chapter—and we have in it again a view of a camp on rolling hills to our right with a glimpse of the walls of Rhodes to our left.

Before this rolling country Solyman acts the first short scene and no other action of the plot occurs; the shutters now close for the second scene of the act and bring us to Rhodes beleaguered again. Before these shutters Alphonso and Ianthe (supposed in Rhodes) play their quarrel scene. After this is over Roxolana of the opposing forces takes the stage again before the same shutter and, last, the usual chorus draws the entry to an end and the Fifth and last Act opens.

This 'Fifth Entry' begins before a new pair of shutters (the third in the play) depicting a distant Rhodes almost smothered in a horde of attackers. A Turkish scene is quickly succeeded by a Rhodian scene before the same shutter, and then comes a return to the relieve of Mount Philermus to present a very short speech from Solyman. The Rhodes-beseiged shutters from the earlier acts then close once more, and before them a Rhodian scene is played in which Ianthe and Alphonso are reconciled, and lastly Solyman rebukes the jealousy of Roxolana to conclude the play.

This interpolation of the battle-shutter at the opening of the last act well provides dramatically for a passage of intense action in the development of the plot, and yet it is with special interest that we note a return at the end to the less-sensational second pair of shutters (which it might seem would set the action back in mood to the opening of the siege) as a setting for the reconciliation and conclusion.

In the Second Part we open with a notable change of styling; there are no 'entries' now, instead we begin—

Act the First, Scene the First.

The *SCENE* is a Prospect of *Rhodes* beleaguer'd at Sea and Land by the Fleet and Army of *SOLYMAN*.

Enter Alphonso, Admiral, Marshal of Rhodes.

They bewail lack of reinforcements and plan a desperate sortie, though Villerius counsels—

Where shall the softer Sex their safety find?
When you with num'rous Foes lye dead,
(I mean asleep in Honour's Bed)
They then may subject be
To all the wild and fouler force
Of rudest Victory;

Into a discussion of treaty then comes '*A shout within, and a Noise of forcing of Doors*', and the people pray Ianthe be sent to intercede with Solyman. Alphonso goes out, then 'Enter *Ianthe* and her two Women at the other Door.' The Marshal insists on her embassage to conclude the act. Then—

The same Scene continues.

The Second Act.

A great Noise is heard of the People within.

Enter *Villerius, Admiral, Marshal.*

After their speeches Alphonso and Ianthe enter to them, and much shouting of the people without, spurs them to send Ianthe, and she agrees to go. Then—

The Scene is Chang'd to the Camp of *Solyman*, the Tents and Guards seem near, and part of *Rhodes* at a distance.

Enter *Solyman, Pirrhus, Rustan.*

Solyman exults at signs of treaty and prepares to receive Ianthe and they leave. Roxolana and her court then take the stage. After this—

The Scene continues.

The Third Act.

'Enter *Solyman, Mustapha, Pirrhus, Rustan*' and later Mustapha and Ianthe. Ianthe is presented to Solyman; he delays her return, but sends her to lodge with Roxolana. Then—

The Scene returns to that of the Town Besieg'd.

Enter *Admiral.*

Later Villerius and the Marshal come in and then Alphonso. This is a purely Rhodian scene. In it suspicion of Ianthe and Solyman grows among the Rhodians as her absence is lengthened. Then—

The Scene returns to that of the Camp.

Enter *Roxolana, Haly.*

Roxolana expresses anger at having to keep Ianthe. To them comes Mustapha. This is purely a Turkish scene, and it concludes the Third Act. There is a change of scene in the interval for—

The Scene returns to that of the Town Beleaguer'd.

The Fourth Act.

Enter *Solyman, Mustapha, Rustan.*

These discuss Roxolana's reaction before this scene outside the walls of Rhodes. Pirrhus comes to them and then they go out and the action switches to the Rhodian party in the same scenery, and Villerius, Alphonso, the Admiral, and the Marshal come on and describe the reception of a letter from Roxolana suggesting Ianthe's seduction of Solyman. After this—

The Scene is Chang'd.

Being wholly fill'd with *Roxolana*'s Rich Pavilion, Wherein is discern'd at distance, *Ianthe* sleeping on a Couch; *Roxolana* at one End of it, and *Haly* at the other; Guards of Eunuchs are Discover'd at the wings of the Pavilion; *Roxolana* having a *Turkish* Embroidered Handkerchief in her left hand, And a naked Ponyard in her right.

This is a long scene in which the two women recognize each other's purposes and are reconciled. This ends the Fourth Act and then—

The Scene is chang'd to a Prospect of *Rhodes* by night, and the Grand Masters Palace on Fire.

The Fifth Act.

Enter *Solyman, Pirrhus, Rustan.*

The battle begins. They leave and the Rhodians take the stage to make an attack. Then 'A Symphony expressing a Battail is play'd awhile'. Solyman enters and organizes a counter-attack, and '*A Symphony sounds a Battail again*'. After this—

The Scene Returns to the Town Besieg'd.

Here the action is first between the Turks and then between the Rhodians. The battle is now over. Then to conclude—

The Scene returns to *Roxolana*'s Pavilion.

Enter *Ianthe* in her Night Dress.

Roxolana is present, and others; Alphonso is brought in prisoner; he has a scene as prisoner with Ianthe, and then follows a general reconciliation of all parties to conclude the play.

Reviewing now this Second Part as we did the First we notice straight away the new use of the word 'Act' instead of 'Entry'. This is retained through the part. But the use of the term 'Scene', as in 'Scene the First' is not retained and no 'Scene the Second' is found nor any subsequent reference to scenes by numbers, though the sentence 'the Scene is changed' is used.

For this Second Part we have, as has been said, no drawings. We are therefore uncertain which were shutter scenes and which relieve scenes. It is likely the first scene was on shutters, but whether the same pair was used as for Part One, Second Entry, we have no means of telling. Since the latter was described as the City of Rhodes 'beleaguer'd at Sea and Land' and the opening scene of the Second Part was also a 'prospect of *Rhodes* beleaguer'd at Sea and Land by the Fleet and Army of *SOLYMAN*', it is very possible they were the same.

Yet the action suggests we are in an interior, for as the scene (which concerns the Rhodian characters) proceeds, a new and highly significant stage-direction occurs—namely, the 'Noise of forcing of Doors' and, shortly after, the exit of Alphonso and the entrance of Ianthe *at the other Door*. This is clear and certain evidence that the stage of the Duke's Theatre, Lincoln's Inn Fields, was different from the stage at Rutland House and different from the stage of the masques. It possessed a feature in common with the public playhouses of the pre-Commonwealth period; it had doors of entrance for the players.

From this we may conclude that the form of the new playhouse already anticipated, in respect of its forestage and proscenium, the form which was to become characteristic of the whole Restoration and Georgian public theatre in England that was to follow—that is to say, a form with a deep forestage, flanked by entrance doors in the proscenium sides, and standing in front of an 'inner' stage which was primarily intended as a scenic area and possibly less as an acting area—the acting area being mainly confined to the forestage. Maybe this notable convention was still only in its infancy here, but however that may be, Ianthe entered at a door (and there was a second door elsewhere—presumably opposite—since she enters 'at the other Door').

The interesting question now arises—where did the characters of the First Part chiefly enter in this revised version? Was it by these new doors which were now present since they were used in the Second Part, or was it in their old manner through the wings as they must have done at Rutland House, where there were no doors? This we have not sufficient evidence to answer.

What we do know is that they entered by doors in the Second Part; and the fact that the backscene may have represented an exterior scene at the same time is no bar to this, as the merest glance at Restoration stage-directions will show.

This first scene now continues to the end of the First Act, and we have no variation as in Part One, but go straight through into the Second Act without a change, where the business of the First Act is developed. Then during this Second Act comes the first change of scene, bringing us the Camp of Solyman.

So far the logical modern relation of a background to the action played in front of it is observed—the opening act contained only Rhodian

[119]

characters, and now for Solyman's entry in the Second Act we have this change to a camp. At its make-up we cannot guess. There is a slight suggestion in the phrase '*Rhodes* at a distance' that it might be a relieve, but this is by no means certain.

This same scene contains no Rhodian intervention, and remains through the next interval into the Third Act, where the Turks continue the plot.

After a time, what we presume are shutters close and bring us back to the first setting. Here the action is only Rhodian. Then, still within the same Third Act, the shutters open and the camp is revealed, again for purely Turkish action.

We now open the Fourth Act with a return to the (presumed) shutter of the Town Beleaguer'd and see a Rhodian action before it. Then a complete change takes place and we open up to what would appear to be an interior—the only definite one in the two parts—showing Roxolana's Rich Pavilion. Here a number of figures is discovered and we must argue a scene of some elaboration and depth. Here also we have the first scene with which rock wings would probably be seriously inconsistent, and we wonder if the somewhat vague reference to the Guards of Eunuchs discovered 'at the Wings of the Pavilion' may not allude to a change of side-shutters as in *Salmacida Spolia*. (The early use of the word 'wings' would then have a special interest.) The action of the scene is consistently Turkish.

Next something of a variety occurs in tempo. There closes-in, to open the last act, what is possibly a shutter, showing Rhodes by night and the Grand Master's Palace on fire. The opening action is Turkish, but this is succeeded by a Rhodian action immediately preceding an attack (of which the fire already shown on the backscene is presumably the result) and then a musical interlude—'A Symphony expressing a Battail is play'd awhile'. Thereafter a Turkish action shows Solyman urging a counter-attack in the same setting, then 'A Symphony sounds a Battail again' and the 'scene Returns to the Town Beseiged'. We are back to our first setting, and before it we see first a Rhodian and then a Turkish action, prior to the great last scene for which we return to Roxolana's Pavilion and see the reconciliation of all the parties.

It seems that this may well be all we shall know of the staging of *The Siege of Rhodes*—unless further material is brought to light. It tells us very little of the factual technique of scene-changing (for this we shall have to argue on from what we studied before and back from what comes later), but we learn much of the regard in which scenery was held. We presume the continuance of side-scenes (or wings), of shutter scenes and relieve scenes and, from these, deduce the use of grooves.

But before we leave this play there is one remaining point in the script which contains a faint clue about the nature of the scenery. The clue lies in Davenant's Prologue to the Second Part. One line only holds this special significance, but we quote the context pretty fully since it all touches our subject:

> But many Trav'lers here as Judges come;
> From Paris, Florence, Venice, and from Rome:
> Who will describe, when any Scene we draw,
> By each of ours, all that they ever Saw.
> Those praising, for extensive breadth and height,
> And inward distance to deceive the sight.
> When greater Objects, moving in broad Space,
> You rank with lesser, in this narrow Place,
> Then we like Chess-men, on a Chess-board are,
> And seem to play like Pawns the Rhodian Warr.
> Oh Money! Money! if the WITTS would dress,
> With Ornaments, the present face of Peace;
> And to our Poet half that Treasure spare,
> Which Faction gets from Fools to nourish Warr;
> Then his contracted Scenes should wider be,
> And move by greater Engines, till you see
> (Whilst you Securely sit) fierce Armies meet,
> And raging Seas disperse a fighting Fleet.

The significant line is that, in richer circumstances, the poet's scenes should be bigger and *move by greater Engines*. These scenes, then, had 'engines'.

It is perhaps worth while to make a distinction and some observations at this point. Why does Davenant use the word 'engine'? The question arises because the obvious word to us would be 'machine'. Did the word 'engine' signify in this context something different from a machine?

'Machine' in English theatrical parlance came to be used so widely that it covered in the end all devices effecting movement upon the stage (and it is in this sense that we shall use it in this book), but its earlier uses seem rather to intend reference to devices for flying figures or to objects actually themselves in movement on the stage—such, for instance, as a turning globe. The word is used by Ben Jonson as early as 1606 when in *The Masque of Queens* he employs it (with a slightly unfamiliar flavour) to accredit Inigo Jones with 'the invention, and the architecture of the whole scene, and machine', thus anticipating by half a century the date for the word in its theatrical use given by *The Oxford English Dictionary*, which is 1658. Inigo Jones uses the word 'engine' in the marginal notes on his drawings. If this be so, it becomes interesting to ask why, when one word was already in use, another was imported beside it. Can there have been originally a distinction?

We find that the word 'machine' is derived from the Greek root signifying 'contrivance'. Pierre Sonrel in his *Traité de Scénographie* adds a special footnote on the word:

> Etymologically the machine is 'un instrument propre à exécuter', from the Greek *Mechane* which, through *mechos*, is attached to the root 'medomai'—I reflect, I machine something, I govern, I command. Whence, in opposition to the *tool*, which is only *the instrument of someone*, the *machine* is *the instrument which commands a whole series of movements*.

'Engine' is perhaps a subtler and an older word. It is cognate with the word 'ingenious' and all the *gen-* roots connected with begetting. Its first meaning in *The Oxford English Dictionary* is 'mother wit; genius'. Chiefly it may be said to signify an 'appliance' or a 'means'. It does not essentially imply movement—a trap or a snare is an 'engine'; it is not a mechanism which itself moves or works so much as the means by which action or work may be achieved in something else. A machine is complete in itself, an engine is designed to make something else possible. It is a means, not an effect. It is more closely related to the humble tool than the independent self-sufficing, autocratic machine.

This distinction established, we may make two significant observations about *The Siege of Rhodes* passage. First, there are in this play no flying effects or mechanically moving devices at all. Second, it may not perhaps be thought too curious, if we point out that Davenant's phrase is: that his scenes would be wider and *move* by greater engines: not be wider and *be moved* by great engines. If there be anything in this fine point at all, it is that the engines are not referred to as the *agents* of the movement so much as the *means* of the movement. 'Move' is here an intransitive verb, not a transitive one. The scenes themselves move, not the engines move the scenes. '*By* greater engines' thus implies a means or an aid to their movement rather than a cause of it. In fact a *guide*.

Whether the details of this reasoning be right or wrong it seems fairly certain that what Davenant had in mind when he spoke of engines was the grooves. We find grooves reaching amazing dimensions in the nineteenth century (as our consideration of Contant on p. 332 will show), and we found them remarkably small in Webb's plans for the first *Siege of Rhodes*. About these, Davenant had much the same plea in vivid phrases, referring to Rutland House:

> It has been often wisht that our scenes . . . had not been confin'd to eleven foot in height, and about fifteen in depth. . . . This is so narrow an allowance for the fleet of *Solyman* the Magnificent, his army, the Island of *Rhodes*, and the varieties attending the siege of the city, that I fear you will think we invite you to such a contracted trifle as that of the *Caesars* carved upon a nut.

Davenant had clearly had experience of bigger and more elaborate grooves than this, and of the greater scenery that went with them, since he

had co-operated with Jones on *Salmacida Spolia*, and thus we may understand his appeal for means to introduce, in this new theatre of his, larger
grooves and a system more capable of large-scale effects since he had known
them before and would seek to touch their standard again in his work in
the public theatre.

Whether he succeeded or not in his own lifetime we do not know. But
we shall see the groove grow in the next two centuries to a final peak of
elaboration and serve, in all this period, as faithfully as its nature would
allow, the interests of its one *raison d'être*—visible scene-change.

8

SCENES AND CHANGES
IN THE SEVENTEENTH CENTURY

★

*Dryden's 'The Wild Gallant', 1663—'The Adventures of Five Hours', 1662–3
—'The Change of Crownes', 1667—Dryden's 'An Evening's Love', 1668—
Development in the position of the shutter—The 'manet' convention—
Orrery's 'Guzman' and the flat scene, 1669—Profiled or open flat scenes
—The motions of the flat scenes, Aphra Behn's 'Sir Patient Fancy', 1678
—Wings in 'Theodosius', 1680—Changes in 'Albion and Albanius', 1685—
Frontispiece to Eccles's 'Theater Musick', 1699—Grooves on the Restoration
Court stage, 1674–90*

★

OUR intention in this study as a whole is to collect and examine direct, contemporary statements, either verbal, pictorial, or diagrammatic, about the details and arrangement of scenery and about the machinery by which it worked. But in the period directly ahead of us such direct statements are so few as to be non-existent. We have then to fall back on implications—at any rate for the first few decades of the Restoration. Restoration plays teem with suggestive stage-directions. These stage-directions are rarely directly explanatory; some require special knowledge of the shape of the theatre and its proscenium, and some of the general system of scenic machinery in use. Our knowledge of both these subjects is in its infancy at present, but, with such an approach as we have made so far in this book on the particular subject of machinery, it is, I think, permissible to build some interpretation of certain at least of the stage-directions in order to sketch a preliminary picture of the technique of the times; and such an interpretation will have to serve us for a while in the lack of more secure evidence in the form of direct statement. With this qualification we begin a study of changeable scenery in the Restoration public theatre by a study of certain significant stage-directions.

As far as our present knowledge goes there was at this period no system of scene-changing known in England save that elaborated in the masques and which we presume was imported by John Webb to the public theatre for *The Siege of Rhodes*. We have yet to consolidate this belief, but we are able to say that an examination of stage-directions with the picture of this particular scenic system at the back of our minds does not seem to bring us against any inconsistence grave enough to lead us to abandon it—and, on the contrary, it enlightens much. Realizing our temerity, then, we set out into the uncharted.

We have noted that the shutter scene of the court stage was characterized by drawing apart, or closing in, the two halves of a painted canvas scene mounted on a pair of wooden frames and running in grooves behind the last set of wings; was this system continued? When we step across the interregnum into the mass of stage-directions in the printed plays of the period we have to exercise a certain caution. We must beware of using the material in a printed play as evidence of scenic procedure in that play's first performance. The printed copy may be a later edition marking the occasion of a revival; thus we may read a stage-direction indicating the presence of scenery in a play first produced in the pre-Commonwealth period, but we must not fail to remember that these directions probably apply to a later revival, and are therefore no evidence for the method of staging used at first. But apart from this matter, there are, in the directions of plays belonging to the period 1660–9, sufficient records of the scene *closing in*, or of the scene *opening*, to make it appear that the employment of a system analogous to the shutters is inevitable. If the principle of the shutter, or divided back-scene, was not carried on into the public theatre, then it was replaced by something so similar as to be at least a development of it. But the word 'shutter' was not used. Instead we have the term 'scene'. We read so often that 'the scene draws' or 'opens', or that 'the scene closes in', that one is embarrassed to know which occasions to pick as examples.

Perhaps Dryden's *The Wild Gallant* will instance more than one of the above points. The quarto was published in 1669, but the first performance was at the Theatre Royal, Vere Street, in 1663. It was, however, revived in 1667—two years before its publication—at the Theatre Royal, Bridges Street, lineal successor of the former theatre but, unlike it, equipped for scenes, and the script bears signs of both occasions. As an instance of the first occasion, reference is made in the dialogue (see Summers, *The Restoration Theatre*, p. 151, note 33) to the arras background, an item of the old Jacobean platform stage, whose lines the little transitional Vere Street theatre closely followed. But by the time the King's Men transferred to their second house in Bridges Street, in 1663, they had had to accept the scenic style of presentation imposed by their rivals, the Duke's Men, and the revival of *The Wild Gallant* at its second theatre was undoubtedly scenic. Thus we read (and this instances the revival) in Act V, Sc. i–ii, '*The Scene opens, and discovers* Constance'. Here then is a mixture of two techniques; the 'arras' and the 'shutters'. But we are chiefly interested at the moment in this *opening* of the scenery.

'The scene opens' is indeed a very fitting sentence to find at the beginning of a review of scene-changing. It immediately calls our attention to the fact that we must now realize that this stage-direction is a literal statement concerning the scenery; it does not mean simply *the scene of the play begins*, but that the *scenery* actually *opened*. Similarly 'the scene closes' is not a mere announcement of the end of the action but an equally literal statement that the two halves of the backscene were drawn together—that 'shutters' were closed.

The misleading similarity between this direction for the movement of scenery and an author's flourish, equivalent to 'Finis', at the end of his work, has led to a curious and charming usage as late as the 1890's. F. Anstey published in 1892, in book form, a collection of his pieces from *Punch* under the title of *Voces Populi*. Each consisted of an amusing scene of life written in dialogue and with imitation stage-directions. The piece entitled 'Bricks without Straw' describes the difficulties of a curate who seeks to comment upon a set of lantern slides which he has not seen before. It ends with: '[*Collapse of Curate as Scene Closes in.*' Now here there can be no reference to the drawing over of a new piece of scenery since the little sketch is not theatrical in the first place. What is significant is that the phrase 'closes in' had become so accepted a part of the language that it was permissible to a writer to employ it—in a context alluding to theatrical usage—as a final line to a literary trifle which was itself not theatrical. It has all the requisite flavour of finality to end an article, yet in its origin it signified, with a quite literal meaning, not a termination but a trans-formation of scenery.

To clinch this argument we may note that 'The scene opens' is not usually found at the beginning of a play but only between scenes, nor is 'the scene closes' found at the end but only when a transition to a further scene is involved. It is the *curtain* which ends the show, not the closing of the scene —the closing of the scene, on the contrary, initiates a new part of the show. This with all respect to *The Oxford English Dictionary*'s definition under *Scene*, 3*b*, with its exceptional example from *The Empress of Morocco*.

But in early procedure it was not always necessary even to effect this alteration of scenery in order to suggest movement from one room to another. In Sir Samuel Tuke's *The Adventures of Five Hours*, produced at the Duke's Theatre, Lincoln's Inn Fields, in January 1662–3, it seems clear that a change of 'scene' could in fact be implied by a special use of the proscenium doors, but presumably without any alteration to fresh scenery in the background at all.

This play, so very successful and so well thought of in its time, is worth considering in some detail—and a convenient modern edition by B. Van Thal, very well done, is available and introduced by Montague Summers, based on the third impression of 1671.

The Adventures of Five Hours is like a Restoration mystery novel; that is to say, it compares with the modern detective story in being in a highly artificial convention, widely fashionable, and whose effect lay in the high ingenuity with which the theme was handled within the rules of the form. Like it also, it offers possibility for sketches of characterization and humour. The atmosphere is 'cloak and dagger' to the last degree: the theme, chivalry and honour; and the form is that of confused intentions and identities, and the whole is heightened by being set throughout in candle-light, starlight, or pretended pitch-darkness—pretended, because on the Restoration stage darkness was suggested by the groping action of the players, not by the lowering of the lights. The plot is so highly complicated and ingenious that no attempt will be made here to spoil what is in truth a very pretty piece of work by any synopsis—the whole may be read in its modern edition. The first two acts are reasonably straightforward, but with the third we enter among intriguing points, and some detail will be needed in the description. If this makes our less-studied passages suggest a bald-ness in the rest of the play, it must be disregarded as a gross misrepre-sentation.

The First ACT. The SCENE Don *HENRIQUE'S* House.

This is the sole direction and the place of action is unchanged throughout the act; there is no indication at first whether an interior or an exterior of the house is to be supposed, but the text suggests that we are in a room. The characters enter by the proscenium doors, of which there seem to be more than two. No reference whatever is made to the wings or side-scenes in the script and it is not easy to suppose just what happened in this matter. We learn that Porcia (sister to Henrique) has a chamber near by and that this gives on to the 'remotest part of all the Garden' by a 'Back-door'. Chairs are brought in at the end for a song.

The Second *ACT*. The SCENE The City of *SEVIL*.

This is a street scene since it is defined in the text as 'The Market Place behind the Jacobins'. Off this street or square there open—1, a post-house; 2, Octavio's house; 3, a street. The action is straightforward and no change is involved.

The Third *ACT*. The SCENE Don *HENRIQUE'S HOUSE*.

Camilla, Porcia, Flora *appear in a Balcone*.

This is an exterior scene, despite the title being the same as that of Act I. We find a character looking up and saying '*Not one Star appears in the Firmament*'.

What happens in the next six pages is extremely puzzling. We begin by supposing an exterior is represented but we do not know yet what is on the backscene. Camilla, Porcia, and Flora open with their lines in the balcony, in which Porcia awaits the visit of Octavio and asks her maid Flora and her friend Camilla to *'watch above with care'* in case her brother Don Henrique surprises the meeting. To aid in understanding the following analysis of the use of doors we append in Pl. 26 the nearest we can find to contemporary evidence of the appearance of a forestage—a model of Wren's drawing for a Playhouse.

Next, *'Enter* Antonio, Octavio, *and* Diego, *with their Cloaks o'r their Faces, and their Swords undrawn in their hands.'* (It seems likely they come in by the Lower Right-hand Door and that the women are waiting above the Upper Right-hand Door—these are the two doors shown in the Plate.) Octavio says:

> *Stay you here,* Antonio, *I'll step before,*
> *And give the Sign, when you hear the door open,*
> *Then come on, and follow me in.*

It is to be supposed he leaves Antonio at the Lower Door and creeps with his servant Diego to the Upper Door on the same side. He prepares to knock as a sign to Porcia. At this moment a distraction occurs on the stage (which it must not be forgotten is supposed to be wrapped in darkness), and there *'Enter at the other side of the Stage* Henrique *and* Carlos.' One may choose the Lower Left-hand Door for this (which, with its neighbour, is omitted in the model). The two are supposed to be returning home from a visit, and Don Henrique says:

> *Indeed, we have staid longer than we thought,*
> *And therefore let's go home the shorter way;*
> *The Back-door of my Garden's here at hand.*

Carlos answers,

> *It will be better than to go about.*

Now the problem is: what action do they take? Presumably they do not cross the stage—if that is what is implied by 'going about'. They are proceeding to a nearby garden door—the same door to which Porcia is, in a moment, to descend to let in Octavio. As they begin to move to this door, attention reverts to Porcia, who speaks *'above in the Balcone'* and says:

> *Would he were come, I fear the Rising Moon*
> *Will give us little time.*

The curious stage-direction now follows: 'Octavio *knocks upon the Hilt of his Sword.'* This may not be knocking at a door, but a characteristic sound (perhaps the tapping of a ring against the sword-hilt) which she recognizes. She says to him, *'I'll open the door . . .'* and presumably goes in leaving the other two women in the balcony on guard.

[128]

The next line comes from Don Henrique, who tells Carlos,

Come; we are now hard by the Garden Gate.

Octavio comes next with the remarkable line, spoken to his servant—

Let's to the door; sure she's there by this time;
Be not afraid Diego.

The remarkable point is that although Octavio was standing immediately under the balcony to hold the whispered conversation with Porcia above, yet now she has gone to open the door his line implies that he must move some way to get to the same door to meet her. This would appear to make it almost certain that the door in question is *not* the Upper Right-hand Door under the balcony, as we might have supposed, for this would make his line meaningless.

What door then was it? It cannot be the Lower Right-hand Door, for that has been stamped as an entrance from a street. It cannot be the Lower Left-hand Door because Don Henrique and Carlos entered by this after their walk. It cannot, it seems, be the Upper Left-hand Door, for Don Henrique has already said it is the short cut to his house, and his house is (on the evidence of the balcony) on the Stage Right. The only logical solution demands a *fifth* door.

Upon this fifth door two separate parties are now converging in the supposed darkness—Don Henrique and Carlos from one side of the stage, and Octavio and Diego from the other (while Antonio still waits in the shadows). The picture suggests that this fifth door is a *centre* door.

At this point expert readers may remind us that recent research points to the existence of no less than *three* doors on each side of the proscenium in certain Restoration theatres. We might accept one of these but for what follows (and for what follows, a door in the backscene seems almost unavoidable):

Diego checks Octavio's approach to the door and calls his attention to the other couple approaching it in the darkness. Octavio draws back and whispers:

let's to avoid suspicion,
Walk on at large, till they are out of distance.

They draw back, and at that very moment '*The noise of a Lock*' sounds from the door, and it begins to open.

Don Henrique sees it and starts back surprised and immediately suspicious:

Ha! at this time o' th' night?
Why what a devil can this mean?

Immediately poor Antonio, hearing the agreed signal of the opening door, advances from his corner to support his friend who, like all the rest, is acting as if he were invisible in darkness.

Porcia whispers fearfully through the door she has half-opened, '*What stay you for?*' and sees no one. Don Henrique whips to a fury. Octavio holds off. Antonio innocently walks in. Porcia sees his figure and opens the door wide:

> An. *Madam, I am not* Octavio.
> Porc. *Not* Octavio? *who are you then? and who's*
> *That shadow there?*
> Henr. *I can hold no longer; I'm thy Destiny,*
>
> > [*Draws his Sword.*

—and immediately Antonio is fighting for his life against two assailants who force him through the gate, for '*they all enter the Garden fighting*'. Don Henrique cries, '*Make fast the door*', and it slams to as Octavio and Diego run to it, only to hear Antonio's brave defiant reply spoken (significantly) '*In the Garden*'. They find the door shut and the desperate clash of swords rings over the garden wall.

It seems impossible by any manner of thinking that one of the proscenium doors could have been used for this effect. And indeed no solution appears acceptable save the one hazarded above of a centre door in the scene. But we have a further surprise to follow. Octavio cries,

> *Excluded! Cursed Fate! this Tree may help me*
> *To climb o'r;* [*He climbs up.*

This is unequivocal; he mounts the wall by (presumably) a practicable tree that has been all this time on the stage. It might be argued that (as was done in other plays) he merely climbs up to the balcony, but the suggestion lacks conviction. Five lines follow from his servant and then we reach possibly the climax of these remarkable stage-directions, for—

> *The* SCENE *changes to a Garden, out of which they issue fighting.*

There appears no conclusion but one: we are here watching an anticipation of cinema technique—a man climbs a garden wall—cut—we see him inside the garden. If shutters were used to stage this play the following is quite possible: a pair of short shutters representing a garden wall and containing a gate stood across the stage at the opening of this action. The fighters disappear through the gate and are hidden; a voice cries over the wall. Octavio climbs the wall; the fray continues and the wall opens to reveal it. Octavio's next line is,

> *Courage, brave Friend; you have* Octavio *by you.*

and the fight waxes. Don Henrique calls to his house for assistance and a servant appears announcing others to follow, but he is immediately felled and Don Henrique, tripping over him, is disarmed. '*The Rising Moon appears in the scene.*'

The end of the action is now in sight. In the moonlight Porcia runs to

[130]

Octavio. They slip away followed by Diego and with Antonio covering their retreat. Don Henrique's servants run in and remove the wounded man, and—

The SCENE *changes to the City of* SEVIL.

It is likely that the street scene of Act II closes in again at this point covering the garden and the tree. If this be so, it is for a mere matter of seconds, for only five lines are spoken as Porcia, Octavio, and his party slip across the street to temporary safety in Octavio's house. As they go in here a curious final instruction closes the scene, namely, '[Camilla *and* Flora *appear in the Balcone*.]' and immediately there follows the direction—

The SCENE *changes to Don* Henrique's *House.*

and the two women speak from their position, exactly picking up the thread of the fight scene by Camilla's exclaiming:

> *Was there ever such a Disaster, Flora?*
> *Sure, th'are all dead, so great's the silence;*
> Porcia, Porcia, *no body answers.*
>   Flor. *Madam, let us go down into the Garden.*
>   Cam. *Excuse me; that were to involve my self*
> *In this unlucky scandal; 'tis possible*
> *Affrighted with the scuffle, she's return'd*
> *Into her Quarter by the other door;*
> *Let's away thither.*   [*They go down upon the Stage.*

This they do, but immediately seeing Don Henrique coming with his men '*they go behind the door*'.

What scenery are we to suppose here? By all logic the discovery of the women in the balcony stamps a return to the garden scene; but in point of fact the following dialogue almost certainly presumes an interior. It would appear that for the first few lines in the balcony the atmosphere of the action in the garden was preserved but now in front of an interior backscene, and into this the women descend for what follows.

To approach this long passage of stage-management with the preconception of our modern usage would involve difficulties of setting that would be insoluble without cutting or rearranging the script. The implication seems unavoidable that this stage and this scenery were used somewhat differently from our modern way.

The plot now steadily develops for a while; Carlos quietens Henrique and persuades him to hand his case to justice instead of taking the law with his own fists. A fine elaboration of mistaken identity is now built up by the playwright, so intricately that it is impossible to trace it shortly here. But no stage-directions of any significance to our present study occur in the remainder of the act.

The Fourth *ACT*. The SCENE Don *OCTAVIO'S HOUSE*.

Now Octavio's problem is, having carried off Porcia, to lodge her some-where safe before pursuit catches up with them. He goes out to seek and hire a Sedan-Chair to take her under its cover. After much interplay he returns—'*Enter* Octavio, *and the* Chair-men *appear at the Door*.' He speaks to them, telling them to wait. He then discovers Porcia has been taken to another place of safety in the meantime and that, to save himself from the pursuit, he must take the Chair himself. But there is no direction as to whether he gets into the Chair; instead the curious sequence follows; Octavio says:

> *Come Chair-men away. Pray Friend, do you guide us.*
>
> > [*To* Sancho.
>
> Die. *Up with your Burden Beasts, and fall forth-with*
> *To your Half-Trot.*
>
> > [*Exeunt.*

This, especially the *exeunt*, would seem final. But immediately follows the direction (and without a sign of any change of scenery):

> [*The Chair is carried over the Stage,*
> Diego, Sancho, *and* Flora *follow*.
>
> *A noise within, Follow, follow, follow.*
>
> *Enter* Carlos, *the* Corrigidor, *and* Serjeants, *pursuing*
> Sancho, Flora, *and* Diego.

Where this is supposed to take place is not clear. It would seem the street, but no change is directed and (unless there is an omission) we presume it still is the interior of Octavio's house. But why, after the direction *exeunt* above, is the Chair carried back over the stage?

At any rate the party is apprehended. The pursuers are skilfully put off from looking into the Chair supposing it to contain Porcia, and the servants are sent to search the house for Octavio, returning, of course (since he is in the Chair), unsuccessful. Carlos directs for the Chair to be taken up and all go out.

The SCENE *changes to Don* Antonio's *Apartment in Don* Henrique's *House*. —an apartment, be it understood, with which Don Henrique has supplied Antonio without realizing his alliance with Octavio. Here the act ends with a prodigal display of very skilful ingenuity in misunderstandings.

The fifth *ACT*. The SCENE Don *CARLOS's HOUSE*.

The last act brings the most notable example of all, of the conventional use of the doors to replace a change of scenery. It opens with the following very curious passage:

> *Enter* Diego, Flora, *and* Pedro *accompanying the Chair,*
> *groaping as i'the dark.*

Pedr. *Dame* Flora, *and Signior* Diego *go in there.*
And you, my Friends, set down the Chair, and let
The Lady out; Go, there's money for you.
I'll go fetch a Candle.

> [Diego *and* Flora *go in, and the Chair being set in the*
> *door,* Octavio *goes out into the Room;* Pedro *claps*
> *to the door, and goes away.*

Enter Octavio, Diego, Flora, *at another door.*

Oct. *What! Put in all alone here i'the dark!*

> [*Groaping as i'th' dark.*

And the door shut upon me! Diego, Flora.
Die. *Here am I sir, and Mistriss* Flora *too.*

There seems only one way possible to make sense of this extraordinary
double entrance, and this is as follows. We suppose the scene to show the
interior of Don Carlos's house. It is therefore a completely new scene.
It presumably shows a hall or antechamber. Here the Chair enters with
its train, say by the Right-hand Lower Door, and crosses the stage. Pedro
opens a door on the Left side (let us suppose the Lower Door), bids Diego
and Flora go through, has the Chair set at the door, allows himself to be
masked by the Chair while Octavio slips from it through the door (or he
relies upon the supposed darkness to justify his not noticing that Octavio
is not a woman), and claps the door to after him. Then he returns across the
stage to the Right with the Chair-men, sees them out at the door they
entered by, closes it after them, and goes out himself to seek the candles—
possibly by the Upper Door on the same side. The stage is empty.

Now, presumably from the Upper Door on the Stage Left, a door not
used before in this scene, Octavio and his companions enter the stage a
second time—note the direction: '*at another door*'. The significance of
this would appear to be that they had crossed the room into which Pedro
had put them from the Chair, found a door at the far side of it, and gone on
again into a third chamber—this chamber is now the one we see on the
stage.

Truly, here the scene may well be called only '*Don Carlos's* House'!
It represents at least two rooms in the same house successively.

After some lines Flora says to Octavio:

> *Suspend a while your Apprehensions, Sir;*
> *You may escape before the Candles come;*
> *The door was wont to open on this side;*
>
> > [Octavio *goes to the door.*
>
> *If not, I have another way in store.*

Which door she alludes to here can only be guessed at; it is possibly on
the opposite side of the stage and presumably it cannot be the one they
have just entered at, for Octavio's next line is:

[133]

Flora, *I cannot make the Lock go back.*
    [Pedro *unlocks it on the other side, and coming in with a Candle,*
       meets with Octavio, and starting back and stumbling, lets the Candle
       fall, then running out again, double-locks the door.
  Die. *Nay, then, i'faith, w' are fast; I heard him give*
The Key a double turn . . .

But Flora's resource is not exhausted; soon she says:

    W'have yet some room for hope; there's a Back-stairs
    Beyond that Inner Chamber, which goes down
    Into the Garden, if the door be open,
    As certainly it is, the way is easie.

And out they all go. Then:

    The SCENE *changes to Don* Henrique's *House.*

As may well be imagined, the train of confusion becomes more entangled still as these strange events are narrated by messengers, and at length we turn again to the house where we left the fugitives:

    The SCENE *changes to Don* Carlos's *House.*

The room is the same as before, but we begin by seeing the mournful train returning by the entrance they went out at, having only reached the garden-exit to find it was locked against them. After much council the surprising event of the entrance (with key) of Porcia and Camilla occurs, most ingeniously arranged. This but contributes to the problems. Then comes another remarkable stage-direction:

    [*A Blaze of Light appears at the Window, and a noise*
      without.

Most commentators have puzzled over this, and the tendency has been to use it as evidence that the Restoration proscenium-side contained windows as well as doors and balconies. Note that the present window cannot be one of the balconies under another name since Camilla later runs to it and looks out to see Henrique and Carlos approaching, but with no break in the dialogue such as would be needed had she to mount stairs to the balcony. No, this must be a ground-floor window. Can it be in the proscenium side? It seems impossible, for these have their full quota of doors already. It follows then that, since we have found a garden gate built presumably in the scenery for one scene, we may have a window built in the scenery for this scene. So we take this as being a scenic window cut in the backshutters.

However this may be, Octavio sends Porcia and Camilla to '*that inner Room*' (possibly the vestibule between the hall and this chamber, which they entered on leaving the Chair), puts Flora and Diego after them, shuts the door, draws his sword, sets his back against the door, and awaits the entrance of Henrique and his train led by a fierce Antonio who, completely baffled by the intricacies of the plot, now suspects Octavio, his friend. A peak of ingenious artificiality follows with Antonio fighting now on one side, now on the other, as he tries to cope with the developing plot. Then comes the most amazing use of the doors in the play. Reinforcements come to Henrique against the hard-pressed Octavio. Antonio takes his side against them and cries to Octavio:

> *Trust me you must, they will surround us else;*
> *Through that narrow Passage they'l assail us*
> *With less advantage.*
>
> > [*They retire fighting off the Stage;* Henrique *and his*
> > *Men pursuing them, and* Carlos *endeavoring to stop*
> > *Don* Henrique.
>
> Henr. *What d'ye give back, ye men of mighty Fame?*
> Ant.   *Don* Henrique, *you shall quickly find, 'tis Honour,*
> *Not Fear, makes me retire.*   [*Exeunt.*

Thus the noise of the fighting dies down and the stage is left empty as the two heroes retreat down narrow passages which guard their flanks. Now what happens?

We follow the fight. The noise grows again. *Another Door* bursts open and Antonio and Octavio run in as to a respite from the fighting. The lines continue without a break:

> *Enter presently* Antonio *and* Octavio *at another*
> *Door, which* Antonio *bolts.*
>
> Ant.   *Now we shall have a breathing while at least,*
> Octavio, *and time to look about us;*
> *Pray see yon other Door be fast.*
>
> > [Octavio *steps to the Door where they went out, and*
> > Henrique *bounces at the Door they came in at.*
>
> Henr. Geraldo, *fetch an Iron Bar to force The Door.*
>
> > [*Within. Aloud.*
> > [Antonio *goes to both the Doors, to see if they be fast.*
>
> Ant.   *So, 'tis now as I could wish it;*

Doubtful as our earlier interpretations may have seemed, here we have clear statement. They retire fighting off the stage; the two pursued men enter immediately at another door and—presto!—they are in another room. One man goes to the door by which they had just left the previous room, to make it fast, and the other holds the door they have just come in by. This is almost equivalent to a panning shot through three rooms in modern cinema technique: the camera swings through an arc, leaving one room to follow through the wall the fighters' exit by a door into the next room, then across it and into a third where the fugitives pause and bar the door against pursuit.

In all this the script of the play makes no suggestion whatever of any change of scenery; the scene that stood for Henrique's house to begin, and backed the room where the fight started, still remains to back the third room into which the fight extends. It is therefore highly likely that it was not scenery of any detailed design but a general stock set, expressive of no special room in particular. It had, in short, the same very loose connexion with any naturalistic-background intention that marked the shutter scenes of *The Siege of Rhodes*.

In this final scene the denouement takes place after a breaking in of the door and a climax of confusion between all parties and an ingenious reconciliation to end.

We learn little of the factual scenery in this strange play, or of its means of changing, but we acquire a very significant insight into the particular regard in which scenes were held in the first years of their use in the regular professional theatre.

Our next reference is a short one and belongs to 1667. In this year there was performed a play whose manuscript has come down to us with its prompter's notes. Almost any such perpetuation of prompters' notes is likely to be interesting, and it is of great help to research that there are many examples of such preservation. The notes in *The Change of Crownes* are no more full nor significant than those in several other plays, but they do serve here to offer some evidence on the method of the signal-whistle that was used to bring about a scene-change in the Restoration theatre—thus linking us with the past in recalling our memory of Inigo Jones and pointing to the future in so far as references to the prompter's whistle are found as late as the nineteenth century. This play, *The Change of Crownes*, is by the Hon. Edward Howard; it was first printed in 1949 under the editorship of Dr. F. S. Boas, and its scene-plot was reviewed by the present writer in vol. iv, No. 3 of *Theatre Notebook*.

In the script we find that some twenty or thirty lines before the first scene-change in any act a mark is made: '*1st whistle ready*', and this whistle blows at the end of the scene as a signal to the stage-hands for the change. Similarly for the next change the mark is '*2nd whistle ready*', and so forth. The sequence goes back to '1st whistle' again with each act. To find a transition from one scene to the next unmarked by a whistle is suggestion that both scenes were played in the same scenery. No warning is found when the change is between the last scene of one act and the first scene of the next, since presumably the fact of the act-interval was sufficient warning to the stage-hands to stand by.

Lawrence, in his *Old Theatre Days and Ways*, p. 37, quotes a long and pleasant passage from 1734 saying that, beside using a bell to signal for music, the contemporary prompter had 'a Whistle, which hangs about his neck . . . at the least blast of it, I have seen Houses move, as it were, upon Wings, Cities turned into Forests . . .', &c.

We seek now to fill in the picture with certain added details from other sources and, keeping in mind the conventions so far revealed to us, we turn to another play of Dryden's. In his *An Evening's Love: or, The Mock-Astrologer*, produced at the Theatre Royal, Bridges Street, in 1668, we have no descriptions of scenes, but we read at the close of Act IV, Sc. i, during Wildblood's soliloquy, that—

The Scene *opens and discovers* Aurelia *and* Camilla: *behind them a Table and Lights set upon it.*
The Scene *is a Garden, with an Arbour in it. The Garden Door opens.*

And Wildblood says: 'How now! *Aurelia* and *Camilla* in expectation of Don *Melchor*, at the Garden door; I'll away, lest I prevent the design . . .'— and he goes out. Later Don Melchor enters and is taken for a ghost by the two women, one of whom overturns the table with the lights, and both run out. '*The* Scene *shuts.*' Don Melchor is left in front and he soliloquizes.

It deserves note that though it was thought worth while to indicate the opening of the scenery, yet it was not thought worth while to say what the scenery represented on any occasion in the play save in the one reference above to a garden.

At the end of Act V, Sc. i, Bellamy says, '*Maskal*, open the door.' The stage-direction follows: '*Maskal* goes to one side of the Scene, which draws and discovers *Theo. Jac. Aur. Beat. Cam. Lop. Wild.* standing all without motion in a Rank.' Later Bellamy bids Maskal shut the door and '*Maskal* goes to the Scene, and it closes'. And a host of other such references may be found for the looking, as any reader of Summers's *The Restoration Theatre* will quickly see.

An examination of these will perhaps show the reason for my apparent over-caution in affirming the carry-over of shutters into the Restoration theatre. For there is a suggestion of a certain divergence from the shutter principle. Of course it is not to be wondered at, since we are now dealing with plays newly fitted with scenery while before we dealt with masques long familiar with it and composed for it. Adaptations of technique are to be expected. The present difference is that, in the masques, when a shutter opened it either uncovered the shutter directly behind or opened up the stage in full and discovered the relieve at the back; the Restoration 'scene', on the other hand, could open either merely to change the aspect, or in order *to discover a situation or group of actors*—a discovery marked not by any great decorative surprise as was the relieve, but by a sense of the dramatic rather than the magnificent. We have not noticed in the masques —at any rate in the later ones where the backshutters had settled into their regular position on the stage—any great number of discoveries of persons by the opening of the shutters. True, instances are to be found where divinities descend by clouds in the back space reserved for relieves, and then step forward between the open shutters, but the more intimate and human sliding of shutters aside to discover a woman reading, or a couple in conversation, is new. The motive behind the opening of masque shutters was exclusively spectacular and for splendid effect; the motive for opening the Restoration scene had in addition a technical-dramatic element—to change the setting and enable the play to proceed; so that there is now a parting of the background for dramatic reasons, as well as a transformation of the scene for a visual effect.

Notice too the following point: in a masque, even if the backshutters were to open and discover an actor or a group, then it followed inevitably that that actor or group was discovered in a scene of relieve. They could not be discovered against another shutter scene, for the successive shutters were generally too close together to enable any person to be stationed between them for discovery.

But it becomes clear from later study that, on the other hand, on the Restoration public stage the successive shutters *were* spaced far enough apart for one scene to disclose, on opening, a group in front of another shutter scene and not necessarily in front of a full relieve.

There is one odd exception to this closeness of shutters in masques which we have come upon on p. 42. On Jones's drawing No. 375 we noticed the inscription 'ye 4th sceane a Chamber—a shutter sett back & so yt one might passe by'.

We were not concerned at the time to notice the unusual significance of the shutter's being *set back* so that someone *might pass by* between it and the preceding shutter, but this is the sole exception we know to the placing of backshutter grooves all close together at one point in masques. The clearness of the instruction to set the shutter back is indication that this was a variant from usual procedure.

The opening or 'drawing' of the Restoration scene came to be very widely used, until it can be said to have animated the production of plays as assuredly as, in its old decorative usage, it had multiplied the glorious visions of the masques, and as assuredly as did the old balconies and windows of the platform era animate the scripts of the Elizabethans; and it was maintained as a system in the dramatic theatre for probably much the same reason as those Elizabethan doors and windows were carried on and incorporated in the new proscenium—because of this animation of the plot, and the means it afforded of quick transition from scene to scene of the story—not for the purpose for which it was first invented—to unveil a greater and more dazzling spectacle behind. There is a close connexion, in the system of using opening backscenes, with the Elizabethan dramatic use of the inner stage and its concealing and revealing arras.

Hence it comes to be a little more easily understood that it might now become christened with a new name, which should forget the earlier function and throw up more clearly its connexion with the progress of the play. So we first have the dramatic phrase, 'the scene draws', but the technical name 'shutters' falls into disuse.

I should like to insert a word here on a certain aspect of this convention of visible scene-change which is well exemplified by our quotation from *An Evening's Love*, and which seems to have puzzled several writers. We find many instances of a scene-change of the nature above described—that is a scene-change like that where Maskal *stayed on the stage* during the transformation. This was widespread practice, but for some reason it is objected to by certain modern authorities as a manifestation of faulty technique—a shift to which old playwrights sank because they could not take the trouble to finish off their scenes properly.

It is strange to realize how fixed a law it has become in our modern dramatic technique for an author to arrange that each of his characters has an 'exit' provided for him! So fixed, that we presume to say of an author who does not provide for such an exit before the scene's end that he is a shoddy playwright who is doing his job inadequately. We exclaim 'Bad work!' without ever considering that it may, instead, be the intended employment of a significant theatre-convention rising with the rise of changeable scenery, and part of the first-flush of its new vigour.

It is, I think, of the highest importance to realize the existence of this critical attitude, for a fact of the first significance in the understanding of scenery in the theatre arises from it. I shall, therefore, quote several passages in which the attitude occurs.

R. W. Lowe in his *Life of Betterton* rates it a 'curious fact' that we find 'cases in which the characters remain on the stage while the scene is changing'. W. J. Lawrence in his earlier notes showed much the same surprise: 'a strange stage convention peculiar to the period'; 'What scenic illusion could exist amidst such crude stage subterfuges!' Discussing Southerne's *The Wives' Excuse; or, Cuckolds make Themselves*, Drury Lane, 1691, he says (and I italicize the relevant passages):

In the fourth act we have an illustration of a *strange stage convention* peculiar to the period. In the opening scene we have the company assembled after dinner at Mr. Friendall's house. Cards are proposed; and while the stage is full of people the 'Scene draws, Shews tables and Cards'. The conversation goes on while the scene is a-drawing and as soon as a few of the characters have seated themselves for play the previous scene closes in upon them leaving the remainder of the company in front. The stage direction runs 'They go to play. The scene shuts upon 'em. Wellvile and Sightly stay.' *One can hardly hazard a guess why this arrangement should have been adopted* instead of clearing the stage before the change. Whatever may be said in favour of it, *it certainly does not conduce to the illusion of the scene.* After some conversation between Sightly and Wellvile we have the direction (the two still remaining in front) 'The scene opens, the Company rises from play, and comes forward'. Finally 'They go in', and the 'Scene changes to the Garden'. Again take the fifth act; Mr. Southerne's method of making his characters discover Friendall and Witwoud in a love passage is not to bring them suddenly on the scene of action. He plants them in one scene ('Mr. Friendall's House') and to effect the discovery 'Scene draws, shews Friendall and Witwoud upon a Couch'. In all *these primitive arrangements* a good deal is left to the imagination of the spectator. The actors were supposed to have performed the journey which the removal of the scene indicated. How absurd a modern play would appear if performed according to these conventions!

Again, concerning Rowe's *Lady Jane Gray*, Drury Lane, 1715: during the last act,

In the middle of a reprimand delivered by Lady Jane Gray we have the stage direction 'The scene draws and discovers a scaffold hung with black. Executioners and Guards.' Immediately she concludes her speech with 'And see my journey's end.' None of the characters have left the stage during the change, which prefigures, of course, the journey to the scaffold. Later on the scene closes leaving Gardiner in front of the audience. To him Pembroke immediately enters and after a brief colloquy the tragedy concludes. This curious stage convention of drawing a scene in the presence of the dramatis personae. . . .

Also, with reference to Otway's *Don Carlos*, Duke's Theatre, Dorset Garden, 1676:

The 4th act opens in an Ante chamber to the Queen's apartment. In the course of the action at this juncture, the scene draws while the King and Ruy Gomez are still on the stage, and reveals to them Don John and Eboli embracing: an arrangement based upon a curiously stupid convention of the period. We have another illustration of the same device in the fifth act. While the King is speaking, 'The scene draws, and discovers the Queen alone in Mourning on her Couch, with a Lamp by her'. With this exposure, the King addresses himself to Don John, who is his companion, with 'Look where she sits, etc.' In those days, the dramatist evidently deemed it a more creditable feat to bring the mountain to Mahomet than Mahomet to the mountain!

Again, discussing Lee's *Constantine the Great*, Theatre Royal, 1684:

Act III consists of two scenes only, though the stage is altered twice. To explain this it is necessary to point out that in the second scene, the flats are drawn at the back when Arius says: 'See there the Bed's prepar'd—' One would be inclined to think it would have sufficed if Arius had merely pointed off at this speech and left the bed to the imagination of the audience. But, as I have pointed out before, scenic arrangements at this period were still in their crudity. All was conventionalism of an order easily understood of the spectators.

Finally:

During the Restoration period I have noted frequent instances of that curious convention whereby the characters were made to pass from one room to another without leaving the stage. The invariable method was to draw the back scene and disclose a second batch of dramatis personae to the one that already occupied the stage.

At the beginning of the succeeding century I note one instance of a strange reversal of this process. It occurs in Act V. scene 2 of 'The Confederacy' as produced at the Haymarket in 1705. Clip informs Gripe he wants to speak with him in the next room. Gripe: 'Ay, with all my heart. Shut the door after us. (They come forward and the scene shuts behind them.)' Then Gripe continues, 'Well, any news?'

In printing these quotations from unpublished notes I have made public material which the writer might have wished to revise, but I have quoted for two reasons: firstly because the examples of the convention are useful in themselves, and secondly because the attitude marking the accompanying notes is characteristic of so many students of the period.

That the convention of discovering characters existed there is overwhelming evidence in play after play—indeed, its existence was so real and wide that the idea could be used as a metaphor, as was neatly done by Shadwell in *The Scowrers*, Theatre Royal, 1691, when Tope says, 'Knaves do not trust themselves with drink, it draws the Scene, and discovers them'. But it is with this surprise, shown by modern writers at the convention of changing a scene with the characters on the stage, that I wish chiefly to deal. They speak of shoddy work in the dramatists, and regard the convention as merely a sign of crude failure to find anything better. Why should it be so considered? Why should not the actor *remain*, if it so suited the show?

There was once a word almost as common as the famous *exit* to describe this variant behaviour of a character at a scene's end—it was *manet*. Instead of 'he goes out', we have 'he remains'.

To give an example of this is to add yet another specimen of the above convention, and a striking one. In Mrs. Trotter's *The Fatal Friendship*, Lincoln's Inn Fields, 1698, Gramont visits Castalio in prison. At the end of the scene 'Cas *goes within the Scene*, Gra *Advances, a Scene shuts representing the outside of the Castle. Manet* Gramont.'

And why should this not be dramatic?

Let us examine this 'manet' convention realistically, and try to see it as it really took place on the stage with all its accompanying effects of atmosphere and action, and ask if it really was so untheatrical.

Let us suppose three characters talking on a shallow front scene. They build up the atmosphere, we look forward to the development. Eagerness is imparted to the audience. The plot is afoot.

Now two of the men part from the other and swing across the stage to their exit, leaving him holding the scene for an instant while they depart; maybe he takes a step or two in sympathy, or in counterbalance, to the movement of the others, and in preparation, as it were—a sort of gathering for a launching. The thing is all swift and pregnant with possibilities to come.

Suddenly the remaining actor turns on his heel. The moment has arrived, the mind is made up, the action sprung. He strides—perhaps towards the scene—perhaps far to the side to clear it, and, as if moved by a mightier urgency even than that of Life, which limits itself to the actions of men, the scene itself is animated and now plays a part and opens to the player. He swings through the gates of a new phase of action—into a new field of plot—nigh and nigh draws the climax

> With unperturbèd pace,
> Deliberate speed, majestic instancy;
> And past those noisèd scenes
> The voice comes yet more fleet . . .

I may not be justified in my adaptation of this quotation, but I think the Restoration stage manager was fully justified in his employment of this technique, it seems to me the very usage of the theatre! And as to this movement of opening in itself—even crudeness of words and vulgar misconstruction of phrase cannot rob point and truth from a remark that was to be made in the dying days of closing scenes, in a periodical for Victorian amateurs, and entirely relevant here: 'It is very effective when sliding flats suddenly and rapidly open and discover another scene behind, especially if the latter be a bright and sparkling picture' (see also p. 175).

It *is* very effective. Whatever else we may say about those words, they are words of one who had seen the thing itself in a theatre, not tried (and failed) to reconstruct it from a misunderstood script in a library.

Let us, rather than criticize the Restoration dramatists for their technique, seek to revise our own idea of scenery in their theatre. We have now to think of it no longer as a static thing. Scenery originally was a *playing* thing —it took part in the show. The whole went together. This was potentially dynamic scenery. Not a background, but an operative factor.

Without this realization, no visualizing of the early stage may ever be effectual.

We return now to the history of the shutter scenes.

We turn to Lord Orrery's play, *Guzman,* for the discovery of a great landmark in our story of backscenes. The play was produced at Lincoln's Inn Fields on Friday, 16 April 1669, though it was not published till 1693. We have, however, to select the edition of the script with some care. Here we come upon an example of one of those great disservices which well-meaning but unthinking editors may do to the cause of theatre research by indiscriminately 'tidying up' a script for a printed edition. When Lord Orrery's works were reprinted in their 1739 edition certain cuts were made in the stage-directions that had been published in the first, or 1693, edition. It would, moreover, appear that the very material cut had been notes from the prompter or stage manager referring to particularities of staging at some performance between 1669 and 1693. These notes, which cannot be later than the latter date and may be as early as the former, contain the essential matter of the present reference—namely, the new name given to the shutter scenes in the Restoration.

There is no reason, in order to explain this point, to go into detail over the script; what is important lies in the stage-directions of this first edition, and they are printed below in simple form and as a list.

Act I. The First Scene is a Piazza, with Walks of Trees, and Houses round about it.

Act II, Sc. i. The Scene with the Chimny in it.

Act II, Sc. ii. A Table and Two Swords. Enter Oviedo to Pirracco in his Chamber. [A flat Scene of a Chamber.

Act II, Sc. iii. Enter Leonora, Pastrana, and Antonia. [The Q. of Hungary's Chamber.

Act. II, Sc. iv. The new Black Scene. The Scene opens, and Francisco appears in a magical Habit (with his Closet painted about with Mathematical Instruments and Grotesque figures), with a Laurel on his Head, and a white Wand in his Hand, knocks with his foot, and four boys appear within the Scene. Flashes of Fire ready.

Act III, Sc. i. The Scene is Alcanzar's Astrological Cabinet. (later) Maria and Lucia peeping through the Scene.

Act. III, Sc. ii. A Flat Scene of a Chamber.

Act III, Sc. iii. The Scene the Piazzo. [The new flat Scene.

Act III, Sc. iv. The Scene a Field with Trees. [The Forest. (later) Fran(cisco) looks through the Scene.

Act IV, Sc. i. The New Flat Scene.

Act IV, Sc. ii. Q. of Hungary's Chamber.

Act IV, Sc. iii. The Scene is Francisco's House. [The Chamber with the Chimney in't.

Act IV, Sc. iv. The New Flat Scene.

Act IV, Sc. v. The Scene a Grove of Trees. [The Forest.

Act IV, Sc. vi. The Scene a Garden. [The Garden in *Tryphon* as a Back Scene.

Act IV, Sc. vii. The Scene the Piazzo. [The New Flat Scene.

Act IV, Sc. viii. The Scene the Astrological Cabinet. [The new black Scene. Rapping ready.

Act V, Sc. i. The New Flat Scene.

Act V, Sc. ii. Queen of Hungary's Chamber.

Let us examine the above: concerning the first scene we can say little that is certain—it might be a shutter scene, or a relieve scene, or a complete novelty. The words suggest some degree of elaboration, but not certainly enough for us to build upon.

In the Second Act, however, we have much to see. Firstly, it is divided into four scenes and the first of these is somewhat specially particularized by the wording. It is '*The* Scene with *the* Chimny in it'. Here, we may presume without exceeding the bounds of available evidence, was a practicable fireplace-opening in the backscene—possibly in the centre, possibly towards the side but most probably a real opening. Other plays (for instance Aphra Behn's *The Feign'd Curtezans; or, A Night's Intrigue*, Dorset Garden, 1679, where Sir Signal Buffoon is found 'Peeping out of the Chimny his face blackt') have indications not only of chimneys but of characters being hid in them, thus implying practicable openings; and the specific 'the' used in the direction seems to indicate a prompter's note to use a definite scene already in stock. That certain of the scenes in this show were from stock is implied by the special mention that others, in contra-distinction, were 'new' (as for instance Sc. iv of Act II) and were pre-sumably first used for this particular play.

In the second scene of this act we make the discovery which is perhaps most important to our present study. Here we have the earliest use I have yet found of the term which we infer replaced that of 'shutters'. The directions for the scene run: 'A Table and Two Swords. Enter Oviedo to Pirracco in his Chamber.' Thus the scene is presumably a discovery, but in the margin is added, '[A flat Scene of a Chamber'. There are seven mentions of this term *flat scene*: 'a flat scene of a chamber' is mentioned twice, 'the scene the Piazzo, the new flat scene' is mentioned twice, and 'the new flat scene' is mentioned three times. Perhaps the last two refer to the same item of scenery, in which case we have two different 'flat scenes' spread over the seven occasions of their use. Some attempt must be made to clear up what is implied here. The very significant history of the word we shall review in Chapter 13. In the meantime it is useful to look in detail at the remaining scenes in *Guzman* to see if we can find something common to them all but which is lacking in the 'flat scene' and thus forms a dis-tinction and makes the reason for bestowing a special name.

The remaining scenes appear to be five in number: the 'Chimny' scene; the chamber specified as 'the Q. of Hungary's'; 'the new Black Scene' which we may identify with the Astrologer's Cabinet; the 'Forest'; and the 'Garden'.

The 'Chimny' we have mentioned. The Queen of Hungary is not one of the characters in this play, but we have not far to seek for her since she appears in another play of Orrery's, *The Tragedy of Mustapha*, which was performed at court and which had a scene named the 'Queen of Hungaria's Tent'. The design for this by John Webb still remains to us.

The New Black scene was no doubt a fascinating novelty. It was clearly no stock piece but was specially prepared and tricked with mystic symbols for the event of *Guzman*, to set forth therein the 'Astrologer's Cabinet'. The last time we came upon a scene for a cabinet (or closet) it was 'Love's Cabinett, Releive' in Jones's Design No. 167. This is clearly no justification for supposing any other cabinet must also be a relieve scene, yet it appears to me we have, on the other hand, no authority for certainly describing this scene as painted all on the one flat surface of a pair of shutters. It is nowhere specified as a 'flat scene'.

We are left with a 'Forest' and a 'Garden'.

Now during the passage in the forest we learn from the text that 'Fran-(cisco) looks through the scene'. We are to suppose then that it was cut away in places—for he does not look *round* the scene but *through* it.

And in the direction concerning the Garden we have the rather obscure note '[The Garden in *Tryphon* as a Back Scene'. Does this mean that a scene borrowed from *Tryphon* (another play of Orrery's, produced at Lincoln's Inn Fields in 1668) was used for this garden, or that it stood behind another garden scene as a backing to it?—in the latter case this front garden scene must have been a cut or open scene.

The evidence is very slight. But it is just possible that if we shall ever be able to prove that *all* the above five scenes had openings in them—as we know the Chimney probably had; as we know the Forest had; as we suppose the Garden had; and as finally we find by an examination of the play (where we read (Act III, Sc. i) of Maria and Lucia peeping *through* the scene) the Astrologer's Cabinet must have had—we may then be inclined dimly to body forth a question: was not the *Flat Scene* so called because it had no openings in it, in contradistinction to those cut scenes which were to a greater or lesser extent in two planes?

I would not venture to give, without further evidence, a definite 'yes' or 'no' to the question at the end of the last paragraph. Certain later evidence seems to be against it, but on the other hand it seems probable that something at least of the truth is hinted at in it.

The evidence tending against it is a statement from Rees's *Cyclopaedia*, which we shall consider in detail in its chronological place (1803), that 'profiled or open flats' were a variety of the flat scene proper.

But this is not, after all, conclusive evidence against our theory. We have seen, and shall see, how many another term shifts its scope of application in successive centuries. It may well have been that, originally, a cut scene was not reckoned a flat scene, and that in the beginning a flat scene meant a plain scene.

But future research may reverse all this. The important point is here: At this time, whatever the terms used for them might have been, there were two kinds of scene, a plain scene and a cut or open scene, and in Rees we find the same distinction a century and a half later in the 'Flats' and the 'Profiled or open flats'.

A word now in passing upon these open scenes.

A cut backscene is no recent thing. Rousseau's character St. Preux, in his *Nouvelle Héloïse*, 1731, describing satirically the settings of contemporary opera, said that the backscene was nearly always pierced and torn that it may represent at a little distance gulfs in the earth or holes in the sky, and the evidence already given from *Guzman* that characters peeped *through* the scene is certain indication that as early as 1669 the backscene might be pierced or perforated with cutout spaces leaving a vision through of a further backscene beyond.

One is perhaps too inclined to suppose the early scene was quite flat. It was, in fact, frequently in at least two planes. The equivalents of what we today call 'cut wood scenes' seem pretty clearly indicated, in which characters might flit and flicker behind the separate trunks, and hide behind a bush to eavesdrop. And similarly in interiors there seems to be pretty strong suggestion of the same sort, since in spite of the almost exclusive use of the proscenium doors for entrance and exit, there are occasionally to be found directions that speak of a character specifically entering 'from the back' or 'through the scene'. And hence it appears that practical doors, or at least practicable openings, were in use from the very beginning, though employed only now and then, and perhaps with a sense of special effect for, for many years, the proscenium door was to remain the principal way of access to the scene.

Of the construction of a cut scene in the seventeenth century we have little evidence, but it seems highly likely that very little change or development had been made before 1850, and then (as we shall describe on p. 337) we have a perfect example. On exactly similar lines to these we may suppose (pending more specific information) the Restoration cut or open scenes would have been made.

I refer now to a play first presented at Dorset Garden in January 1678, written by Aphra Behn and entitled *Sir Patient Fancy*. In the Third Act of this play we have a fairly elaborate sequence of scenes, and we find after study that the changes involved in these could only be done if certain arrangements which are so far new to us were observed. I quote from the 1702 edition of *Plays, written by the late ingenious Mrs. BEHN* (vol. ii) the scene directions for the whole show and propose then to study in detail those of the Third Act.

'ACT the first, SCENE the first, *A Room. A Chair and a Table*' is all that refers to the scene in the First Act of the play. It is interesting to note in passing that the specific mention of a chair and table implies that such things were not the normal and inevitable accompaniments to a room scene on the Restoration stage, but, if they were specially needed, had to be specifically called for. It is clear that the system of visible scene-change would find indiscriminate use of such furniture a great embarrassment. What such furniture involved in a scene-change we shall find later.

'ACT II, SCENE I, *A Garden*' is followed by 'SCENE *changes to a Chamber*'. This chamber, a room in Sir Patient's house, gives us the start for the next act. Note how half-heartedly the numbering of the scenes is followed up; at first the numerals are faithfully added, but soon all that seems to matter is the record 'The Scene changes' or something of that sort. The interest was in the action of the change, not in the numeration of the scenes, as it is today—for I'm sure no budding playwright would ever forget the duty of writing 'Scene 3' or 'Scene 4'.

ACT III, SCENE I. *Scene draws off and discovers Lady* Knowell, Isabella, Lucretia, Lodwick, Leander, Wittmore, *Sir* Credulous, *Other Men and Women, as going to a Dance.*

SCENE II. *Lady* Knowell's *Chamber.*

SCENE. *A Garden. Enter* Maundy *by dark: Opens the Garden door.* [A short 10-line scene in which Maundy lets in Lodwick and bids him follow softly.]

SCENE *draws off, and discovers L.* Fancy, *in her Night-gown, in a Chamber as by the dark.*

SCENE *Changes again to a Garden. Enter* Isabella *and* Fanny *in their Nightgowns.*

A confus'd noise of the Serenade, the Scene draws off to Lady Fancy's *Antichamber.* [A scene of merely five lines.]

Scene changes to Lady Fancy's *Bed-chamber, discovers her as before;* Lodwick *as just risen in disorder from the Bed:*

The Scene draws over Sir Patient *and Lady: draws again and discovers the Garden,* Wittmore, Fanny *and* Isabella.

SCENE *Changes to the long street, a Pageant of an* Elephant *coming from the farther end with Sir* Credulous *on it, and several others playing on strange confused Instruments.*

Thus ends the Third Act. The rest is comparatively simple; Act IV has four scenes and Act V has one, as follows:

ACT IV. SCENE I. *Lady* Knowell's *House.*

SCENE II. *A Table and chairs.*

SCENE III. *A Hall.*

SCENE *the Lady* Fancy's *Bed-chamber.*

ACT V. SCENE I. *A Table, and Six Chairs.*

A careful examination of this very valuable example of the sequence of scenes, and of the terms used to express the changes of those scenes will lead us to postulate a somewhat important development in the use of this successor to the old shutter.

Let us try especially to reconstruct the procession of the nine scenes of the Third Act, as they must have unfolded, one by one, before the eyes of the new audience only nine years after the opening of the theatre which was Davenant's posthumous crown—the house for spectacles.

We seek to know how the various scenes were disposed over the stage. Which came in front of which? And what relation had they to take with regard to that commanding factor, the layout of the grooves?

To do this it is best to act just as a modern stage manager might do, that is, to work out a plan of the stage, putting the flat scenes in such order that they will allow the proper progressive unfolding of the play and permit the preparation of 'discovery' groups behind when these are needed.

We list briefly the scenes of the play, adding certain significant notes and giving each new piece of scenery a distinguishing symbol to keep them distinct—these symbols are shown in brackets immediately after the number of each scene:

I. I (x) Room. Chair and table (therefore ? discovery).
II. I (G1) Garden (must ? draw over).
II. 2 (y) Chamber (draws off to discover III. I).
III. I (x) Discovery of group (location not stated).
III. 2 (K) Lady Knowell's Chamber.
III. 3 (G1) Garden (with garden door; very short; draws off).
III. 4 (F1) Lady Fancy's Chamber.
III. 5 (G1) Garden (draws off).
III. 6 (F1) Lady Fancy's Antechamber (very short; drawn off).
III. 7 (F2) Lady Fancy's Bedchamber (probably practical bed).
III. 8 (F1) ? Lady Fancy's Antechamber (closes and opens to III. 9).
III. 9 (G2) Garden (figures discovered).
III. 10 (S) Long Street.
IV. I (K) Lady Knowell's House.
IV. 2 $(?x)$ Table, chairs.
IV. 3 (H) Hall.
IV. 4 (F2) Lady Fancy's Bedchamber.
V. I $(?x)$ Table, six chairs.

The scenes marked x and y are not directly specified. It is clear that II. 2 and III. I are in different scenes since II. 2 draws off to discover characters waiting in III. I; thus we give them separate symbols on a basis that will be made clear below.

The significant thing, now, about the arrangement of this whole sequence of scenes comes in the Third Act; we see that the Garden (III. 5) 'draws off' to disclose Lady Fancy's Antechamber (III. 6), and the Antechamber must in its turn draw off to disclose the Bedchamber (III. 7), therefore it is practically certain that the bedroom scene was placed behind the Antechamber and the Antechamber behind the Garden.

Furthermore, it is clear that III. 1 must be behind II. 2 since II. 2 'draws off' to discover a group of characters in III. 1.

Here, then, is some introduction to the order in which the flat scenes were stationed on the stage. Let us develop this, taking for the moment Act III only.

At the beginning of the act the scene y is left on the stage from the end of Act II. This 'draws off and discovers Lady Knowell, Isabella, Lucretia, Lodwick, Leander, Wittmore, Sir Credulous, Other Men and Women; as going to a Dance'. Where they are discovered is not stated, but there is one fact of considerable significance whatever the scene may be—namely that there must have been enough space between these two backscenes, x and y, for Lady Knowell and company to get set in front of x before the opening of the scene in front, y. This means that the two scenes must have been at least 3 ft. apart (unlike Jones's shutters). But the fact brings a further point in its train; being at so great a distance, the second scene, x, would probably not be masked at its outer edges by the same wings that masked the front scene, y, and so another pair of wings is needed between the two scenes. Therefore this second flat scene ran in grooves placed behind a second set of wings—that is to say, in a different set of flat-scene grooves altogether.

So it is inescapable that we have here a second set of grooves, and that scene y was in the front set and scene x in the set behind, see Fig. 4a.

Scene 2 is Lady Knowell's Chamber. It is likely that this was arranged not by opening the previous room scene, but by closing the new Lady Knowell's room in front of it. The new scene (K) might be in front of x, or in front of both x and y. We have no evidence at the moment, but later on we shall see that the latter arrangement fits better.

Now comes the Garden (G1). We know it must be near the front, because it has to draw off to show the next scene in Lady Fancy's Chamber (F1). It is also a very short scene and thus is likely to be shallow. We want it near the front; hence it might run in the same front set as Lady Knowell's House. However this may be, the way in which the garden was changed is clear—The scene 'draws off and discovers Lady Fancy in her Night-gown, in a chamber as by the dark'.

Now, if this again is a discovery, as it clearly must be, it presupposes as before that between the garden scene and the scene of Lady Fancy's Chamber there must have been another space. This again means that the chamber was in another set of grooves—possibly in the second, if the garden scene was as seems likely in the first, see Fig. 4b.

Scene 5 'changes again to a garden'. The 'again' seems to suggest that the same scene as that for Sc. 3 was used once more (G1), in which case it simply closed in its first grooves covering the Chamber in the second.

It then 'draws off to Lady Fancy's Anti-chamber' again, that is, pre-

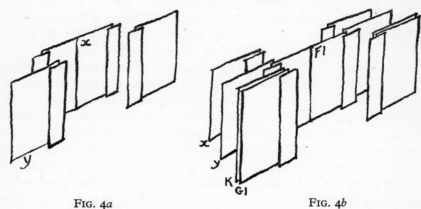

FIG. 4a   FIG. 4b

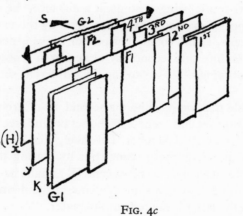

FIG. 4c

Fig. 4a to c. Possible arrangement of scenes in *Sir Patient Fancy* (1678)

sumably, to that Chamber where she was discovered in her night-gown in Sc. 4, which was still ready in the second grooves (F1).

Next comes another discovery: it is a Bed-chamber and one with presumably an actual bed in it. But this scene is disclosed by the withdrawal of a scene in the second grooves (F1), therefore it must be either in the third grooves or in a still farther set behind—which in the end turns out more convenient—that is to say, in a fourth set up till now unmentioned (F2; see Fig. 4c).

The next development is interesting. We are to lead to a Garden again, but this time a garden with people discovered. Therefore the scene already

[150]

used for Sc. 3 and Sc. 5 (G1) will not do; so a new scene must be used, and used behind the bedchamber scene. But the bedchamber scene is in the fourth grooves and in our examination of grooves we find no occasion of more than four sets used at this early period. An additional point is that there is a bed to be got rid of; we cannot just open the bedroom scene and disclose the garden (even if we suppose yet a farther set of grooves again) with the bed left standing in the middle of the lawn! And we cannot close the garden over in front of the bed because the garden scene is to have figures discovered in it at its opening. What is to be done?

The move made is interesting, not only in showing the solution, but in proving by the very presence of this solution that a special difficulty had indeed arisen, and that what we have propounded was not merely a figment of the imagination. The solution was this: the bedroom scene was closed over much as one might shut the door on it, by drawing a scene in front of it (and indeed this use of drawing-in a scene to shut the door of a room is often to be met as an acknowledged convention). There is a very suitable scene for this occasion in the second grooves—namely that for Lady Fancy's antechamber (F1), which might well be outside her bedroom (see Fig. 4c). Presumably, then, this scene is meant in the direction which follows: 'The scene draws over Sir Patient and Lady', but, the direction goes on, it 'draws again' immediately (leaving enough time for the bed to be struck and the bedroom scene to be opened, disclosing the garden (G2) beyond in the farther grooves of the same set, and for the actors who are to be discovered in that garden to take their places where the bed was) 'and discovers the Garden'. No action presumably took place before this antechamber scene; it merely hid the stage for a few seconds while the bedroom in the fourth grooves was cleared ready for the penultimate scene of the act. A procedure very similar to our use of the traverse curtain today.

Now we turn to the last scene of the act, a scene of some fancy (S). The direction says that the garden 'changes to the long street, a Pageant of an Elephant coming from the farther end with Sir Credulous on it'. What is here?

We must remember that we are already in the fourth grooves with the garden set. It is probable that this fourth set was the last set. We have as yet seen no more than two scenes in any one set of grooves, therefore it may very well be that there were only two flat-scene grooves in each set. But now we have to present a street (and one with a discovery—an elephant) behind the last grooves.

The clue lies in the word *the*: it is not *a* long street but some long street with a particular, specific quality, something famous in the scene store maybe, known as *The Long Street*. Why 'Long'? Perhaps the explanation is to be found in Fillipo Juvarra.

It is good to welcome here by mention this Italian, Juvarra, even though we are concentrating on the English theatre and do not propose, as some writers have done, to let this concentration take the form of adulation of everything across the Channel and the relegation of the English theatrical genius to the class of a mere copyist and deriver. But Juvarra's book of scene-designs and plans in the Victoria and Albert Museum deserves a reference in the scenic history of almost any country that takes any technical approach at all to its subject.

Juvarra clearly distinguishes between two types of scene which he calls respectively, *lungo* and *corto*, that is to say 'long' and 'short', and upon referring to the illuminating sketch-plans of scenes below his drawings we can see that his stage, beside possessing the usual scenic area of any stage, has also a sort of alcove at the back—a small annexe very similar to the 'inner stage' of the Elizabethans. It is an arrangement of which there are many examples in later English theatres.

Upon these plans of Juvarra's a normal set is represented as occupying only the larger of the two stages, and is then labelled *corto*, but upon occasion a scene can open up, occupying the space of both stages, its deeper parts penetrating into the recess at the back, and in this case the scene is called a *lungo* or 'long' scene.

This system is not in itself, of course, new to our study: Jones also had his shutter scenes, whose flat back was situated about two-thirds up the depth of the stage, and he, upon occasion, opened up his stage, by withdrawing all his shutters, to include the farther third and display thereon his scenes of relieve. Upon the conclusion of one of these scenes, a pair of shutters would close again in their usual position, and the stage would be 'shortened' once more, with the new scene now displayed painted on the flat shutters.

We know that just such a disposition of stage plan obtained in all the early English theatres of which we have records—namely, this annexing to the main stage of a smaller central recess opening off at the back. And so it may very well be that, on similar stages, the coincidence of the term 'long' marks a similar technique, and that Aphra Behn's 'long street' was a scene that reached back into the depths of the recess, which means that it was not a normal 'shutter' scene, but a sort of spectacular set, closely related in form and in theatrical effect to the relieve scenes of the masques.

Now the particular result of the analysis of *Sir Patient Fancy* that I promised would be interesting is this: Provided we allow room for all the discoveries mentioned in the directions, we cannot, by any sort of juggling, make do with any arrangement giving less than three separate intervals between groups of flat scenes, thus implying four sets of grooves, that is to say, a separate set of flat-scene grooves at each wing position—not a clump together only at the back, but a dispersed arrangement, each unit containing two grooves, at four different depths on the stage.

We have supposed two flat-scene grooves in each set. We have now filled all these eight grooves but one. We suppose all the scenes in the play would be set in their grooves ready for closing in, before the rise of the curtain. Therefore we have to ask whether the remaining four acts could be set with the scenes we have already put in place with only one addition—namely in the third grooves.

Act I is in one scene; possibly x, which is likely to have been an interior. Act II could be set with G1 and y, the latter being another interior in the same house. Act III we have discussed. Act IV could be set with K (Sc. 1), x (Sc. 2), F2 (Sc. 4)—leaving Sc. 3, a Hall, unaccounted for. For this we can use a fresh flat-scene (H) situated with x in the third set of grooves, thus filling the blank. Act V might be set throughout in x.

Variant arrangements are possible, with one or two of the flat scenes in other positions, but in the main the principle stands as inevitable.

Here, then, is a notable development on Inigo Jones's arrangement—the introduction of flat scenes at any part of the stage. This arrangement we now have reason to deduce obtained from the very beginning of the public theatre and was an innovation coincident with its inception.

This is definite and useful knowledge; we are not only beginning to learn something of the form of our modern backscene at its origin, but are to some extent able to picture its action—and a very positive one it was—on the show it set.

My gratitude is due to Dr. Montague Summers for putting within reach much material concerning scenery of this period, but, while I acknowledge this, I cannot leave his treatment of the subject without commenting on a statement of his that we shall find reason later to disbelieve. Discussing 'flats', as he calls them, he says on p. 97 of *The Restoration Theatre*: 'These flats were of three kinds: the usual shutters which met in the centre, or which ran across the stage; the "relieves", or scenes in relief, moulded scenes; and the cut scenes where some part was cut out to show a distant prospect or perspective extending behind. The "relieves" were an heritage from the old masque.' Four points stand in need of comment. Firstly, I have not found the use of the word 'flat' as a noun so early as this. Secondly, the relieve as I have shown was definitely *not* a variety of flat scene at all, but rather an antithesis—an entirely alternative form of scene. Thirdly (also as I have shown), the word 'relieve' does not signify a 'moulded' scene. Fourthly, to say particularly that the relieves were 'an heritage from the old masque' would seem to suggest that the other two types of scene, the plain shutters and the cut shutters, were not. This would be untrue; all three forms have direct antecedents in the masque. But apart from this, Dr. Summers's chapter is immensely valuable, those passages in it directly succeeding the above reference being especially to our present purpose, see his pp. 99 to 104. There mention is made of the use of opening flat scenes 'in order to exhibit a "situation" or a spectacular inner scene'. On p. 101 there is a phrase that is suggestive to the imagination in passing: In *The Sham Lawyer*, Drury Lane, 1697, 'Homily knocks; the Scene opens, and presents an Alcove Room. . . .' One toys with the idea that the term 'alcove' might imply that the halves of the scene were only partly drawn and disclosed a little chamber beyond . . . but that is guess-work; yet the idea seems a variation with possibilities. At least it may have been a cut scene like the Astrological Cabinet you could peep through in *Guzman*.

It is interesting to look, before we leave this subject, at the terms of Davenant's participation in the Duke's Theatre. He was allowed two shares 'towards the house rent, buildings, scaffolding and making of frames for scenes', and one 'for provision of habits, properties and scenes for a supplement of the said theatre' (in all about £1,800 per annum). Those 'frames for scenes' pretty certainly included the basic structures for the halves of flat scenes.

The next reference concerns another element of the scenery to which we have had little opportunity to refer as yet in this chapter—namely, the side-scenes or wings. We indicated at the end of Chapter 6 that it seemed likely we might find the side-scenes in early scenic convention to have been sometimes treated as separate elements and not designed as part of a unified subject with the backscene. Thus it is interesting to read this curious note in the stage-directions to Lee's *Theodosius* (1680):

Act I. *Scene* I, a stately Temple, which represents the Christian Religion, as in its first Magnificence; Being but lately establisht at Rome and Constantinople. The side Scenes shew the horrid Tortures, with which the Roman tyrants persecuted the Church: and the flat Scene, which is the limit of the prospect, discovers an Altar richly adorn'd; before it, *Constantine*, suppos'd kneels, with Commanders about him. . . .

Here, though we have a clear instance of wings designed in conjunction with the backscene, we yet have an odd variation of the expected relation. The flat scene showed a stately temple but the side-scenes did not show, as we might expect, the precincts or surroundings of that temple, nor yet an avenue leading to it, but bore each its own symbolic picture of the torments of a martyr. Here is an unexpected use of the wings, imaginative and decorative, instead of representative and subsidiary to the view, as we might have supposed all early wings would be.

(A most remarkable example of a similar convention of representing gigantic heroic figures on the wings of a scene is to be found in Pl. 16 of J. Fransen's *Les Comédiens français en Hollande au XVIIe et au XVIIIe siècles*, published by Honoré Champion, Paris, 1925.)

A further reference to the side-scenes occurs in an interesting note in Dryden's *Albion and Albanius*, Dorset Garden, 1685, where we read: 'The Scene is a Poetical Hell. The change is Total. The Upper Part of the House, as well as the Side Scenes....' We have noted already the existence of Upper Backshutters; it may be these that are referred to in the mention of the 'Upper Part of the House'. We have to remark in addition how the special inclusion of the side-scenes among those parts which suffered this vaunted 'total' change offers us some ground for supposing that, in a scene-change of this period, it was not by any means inevitable that the wings would change with the backscene. The normal change we are almost led to infer was that of the backshutters or flat scene alone, while those occasions in which the wings were involved in alteration too were sufficiently rare to justify remark on the part of the author, whose play had achieved that special effort of the stage-staff which resulted in a 'total change'.

In the First Act of the same opera is another direction which now seems to fit in far more convincingly, given upper and lower flats at the back. The scene here is 'A Street of Palaces, which lead to the Front of the *Royal-Exchange*; the great Arch is open, and the view is continued through the open part of the *Exchange*, to the Arch on the other side, and thence to as much of the Street beyond, as could, properly be taken'. (In these words is pictured one of those cut scenes of 'profiled or open flats' as vividly as one could wish—and very effective it could have been made to look on the stage—but what follows later in the scene is especially interesting to our present subject; there we read:) 'The clouds divide and Juno appears in a Machine drawn by Peacocks; while a Symphony is playing, it moves gently forward, and as it descends, it opens . . .'

It is this moving 'gently forward' that cannot be explained in any way save by some such arrangement as is here suggested. To begin with, it is unlikely that the 'clouds' spoken of refer to cloud borders, for a border, as has already been suggested, is a relatively unimportant part of the scene and exists only for the benefit of the spectators in the lower and nearer parts of the house. For any others the borders are scarcely seen, and to have an important effect make its entrance by moving *forward* through a border—even if the border be divided—is to have it make a poor and partly obscured entrance.

It is very unlikely—indeed impossible—from the words of the direction that it was the border which divided to reveal this machine. Note the

suggestion of the words 'the clouds divide and Juno *appears* in a Machine . . .'
If it was a border alone that divided to show this revelation, then it would
have been Juno's feet and not Juno that appeared up there, and the splendid,
breath-taking effect of this visitation of peacocks (that forms one of the
most elaborate machines of trick scenery) would lose all the beauty of
marvellous discovery. Moreover, we see that the peacock-chariot, after the
burst of chords which greeted its celestial disclosure, moved gently *forward*,
and only then, as the music continued, are we told that it *descends*, and
begins to open. . . .

There is no avoiding the clear implication in the words that the machine
was revealed directly in all its completeness by the opening of some sort of
shutter, and only after its clear discovery did it move and begin to work.
But it is definitely stated that the *clouds* opened and not the front of the
Royal Exchange. So there is only one conclusion left—that the Royal
Exchange was on a pair of independent lower flats and the clouds were on
a pair of upper flats and occupied the top half of the backscene.

If with this new knowledge we turn to such a collection of pictures of
contemporary settings as is contained in Nicoll's *Stuart Masques*, we find
the following. Of the forty-nine mixed English and foreign designs
illustrated there (and—from our present point of view—selected at
random) which may be said to portray full sets, the amazing figure of
thirty-two show one of two notable characteristics: either the architecture
or hill or other detail on the backscene *does not come more than half-way up*,
and leaves the upper part of the backscene plain sky (there are seventeen of
these), or the design reaches about half-way and then exhibits some feature
which might give rise to a horizontal break and, above this, continues with,
as it were, another story of the design (there are fifteen of these).

Especially is it notable that a certain type of architectural design is very
prevalent upon these scenes, which consists in essence of a sort of peristyle,
or one-storied façade below, crowned by a balustrade extending the whole
length, and thereupon is set a sort of central tower or narrow central upper
story, of the turret or lantern nature, surrounded by sky. This sort of
design is most apt for a central parting of the upper half independently to
allow a vision into the heavens above. And of such a vision there is a magnificent example in the frontispiece to the work quoted.

It is interesting to remember that Sabbattini, in his *Pratica*, recommends
that the backshutters or 'perspectives' should not be higher than the height
of the back, or shortest, pair of wings. Yet in all his three designs of full-
sets, items of architecture which are all clearly painted on the centre
'perspective' project well above the back wing-tops.

There certainly seems to be definite proof that, in masques, a system obtained of occasionally painting the upper part of a back scene upon a different piece of scenery from the lower half.

When now we turn to the Restoration public theatre, what evidence is there of such a system persisting? We have the above evidence from Dryden, and we have, in the Burney Collection at the British Museum, a hitherto unreproduced water-colour of an English stage of the highest interest which exhibits just the sort of two-storied architectural features as were noticed above in connexion with the masque drawings; this painting will be discussed in Chapter 10 (see Frontispiece).

At this point we will leave *Albion and Albanius* and the considerations arising, though some readers who know the amazing script in which, as Dryden wrote, 'The Description of the Scene and other Decorations of the Stage, I had from Mr. *Betterton*, who has spar'd neither for Industry, nor Cost, to make this Entertainment perfect, nor for Invention of the Ornaments to beautifie it', may have hoped that we should examine the details of such an elaborate show at great length. Interesting as this might have been, it would have involved us with particular embellishments of the stage and scene such as were outside the normal run of the everyday theatre. It is often misleading to base one's opinion of the state of technique of a period on some selected special example of it, for one runs the risk of mistaking the standard of everyday work. *Albion and Albanius* is an astonishing field for study to the special investigator, but it gives little that we have not learned already about the common run of ordinary scenery.

Our final reference in this chapter is a pictorial one—and such a thing is unfortunately only too rare in English seventeenth-century scenic history. It is the frontispiece published in all three volumes of John Eccles's *Theater Musick* (two in 1699 and the third in 1700). It illustrates much of the matter of this present chapter—see Fig. 5. It is not easy to deduce from the text of *Theater Musick* whether the picture is ascribable to a specific play; possibly further research may solve this point.

I have not myself been able to define certainly the significance of the presence of the motto *Vivitur Ingenio* inscribed under the arch. It is clear it was the motto written above the proscenium of Rich's Covent Garden, opened in 1732, and it appears again in identical form over the proscenium of a print entitled 'MUSTER of BAYS's Troops', showing a crowd of contemporary players on a stage with a tiny figure peeping from the proscenium balcony who is identified in a note as 'Mr. Lunn, *as a Spy from the other House*'. Since Lunn *is* Rich one supposes then that *this* house must be Drury Lane, not Covent Garden. But the details of the proscenium sides, as well as the motto, are the same as those in an indisputable print of Covent Garden used as the frontispiece of *Harlequin Horace*, 3rd edition,

1735 (reproduced in Lawrence's *The Elizabethan Playhouse*, first series, opp. p. 177).

The theatre in Eccles's print cannot, however, be Rich's Covent Garden since this was not built till 1732. Did, then, its predecessor in 1699 (which was the New Theatre, Lincoln's Inn Fields, once Davenant's Duke's Theatre and Lisle's Tennis Court) also bear this motto over the proscenium? If so, was this theatre also called the Theatre Royal at this time, as well as the one in Drury Lane? For Eccles's print also bears the legend 'The Theatre Royall'.

FIG. 5. Frontispiece to Eccles, *Theater Musick* (1699)

We know the term 'Theatre Royal' at some dates refers to either theatre. But can this present print with its great arched opening really portray a stage built in a Tennis Court? Yet, in 1699, it could only have been this theatre, or Wren's Drury Lane (which we do not suppose had an arched top to the proscenium opening), or the Duke's Theatre, Dorset Garden— for these were the only theatres that year in London. And Dorset Garden was already past its heyday.

I have to admit I do not know the answer, and must turn to the facts of the print.

It gives an illuminating illustration of the use of the classical, masque type of costume on the public stage. The principal male figure wears a semi-Roman tunic with a feathered head-dress (fallen to the stage), but the female figures are in general in contemporary fashions. The scene is flanked by four pairs (as far as can be distinguished) of classical garden wings, and the backscene appears to show a good example of a cut, flat scene, with the great arch in the front plane and the distant arcade with waterfall as a

[158]

backing. It is, broadly speaking, a conventional scene, probably not intended to portray the character of any particular place but rather to supply a general, classical, palace-garden setting. Such as it is, this print is almost the only example (putting aside the well-known *Empress of Morocco* 'sculptures') of a full set on the English public stage before 1700.

In this chapter we have endeavoured to confine ourselves to the development of scene-changing in the public theatre, but before we close it there is an important footnote to add about the private theatre at court in the Restoration period.

So great a part of our attention is taken up with the radical changes in theatre technique that took place in the new public theatres of the Restoration that we are sometimes inclined to forget that, parallel with this development, the shows at court were continued and still developed. Almost the only extensive study of this subject is contained in Eleanore Boswell's *The Restoration Court Theatre* (Harvard, 1932). Here we find much information about the post-Commonwealth work of John Webb at court, and there are certain references of considerable importance to his technical methods at this time.

Especially interesting to us is the evidence of Webb's continued use of grooves for scene-changing. We can find no direct information about the physical details of scene-handling in the Restoration public theatre, and we have had to deduce the use of grooves from such suggestions as have been discussed above—and there is much still to be learned. But in the court theatre up to the end of the seventeenth century the use of grooves is certain. Since the likelihood is strong that similar methods were used in the public theatres to those at court, we may take the following as important presumptive evidence for the use of grooves on the ordinary stage.

Of the court stage at the Hall Theatre, Whitehall, to which the following quotations refer, we have plans by John Webb, now in the Duke of Devonshire's Collection. A study of them is given in Miss Boswell's book. They add nothing new to the information given in the *Salmacida Spolia* plans, but the following vivid sidelights upon the maintenance of grooves on a stage are to be found in the accounts for work. There is to be felt in them the first intimations of one of the potential disadvantages of the groove system—its rigidity; scenery had to be placed not at discretion but where the grooves existed to take it, or else the grooves had to be altered and that might be a troublesome and recurrent undertaking. It is with such an alteration as this that our first extract is concerned, for in January of the year 1674–5 we read of a decision to 'widen the whole stage by drawing Back the side sceenes & altering the frames & Groves accordingly' (op. cit., p. 236).

Presumably this entailed prizing the grooves off the stage and shifting them outwards. Whether 'altering the frames' means merely moving the wing-pieces, or signifies some alteration to the groove supports, or alteration of the size of the framework of the scene-pieces, is not clear. It will be seen that, on a stage limited for room, the widening of the acting-area by pushing the wings outwards would result in the constriction of what might already be a very narrow wing-space off-stage, and therefore might enforce a narrowing of the wings themselves, whereupon considerable rearrangement might be entailed. Something of this is suggested in the extract from the November-to-February period directly following (p. 253): 'takeing downe ye said [*W. J. Lawrence suggests* side *for* said *since no scenes have been recently mentioned*] scenes & Cutting them less & Makeing ye groues shorter, & rayseing ye backs shutters', and in the next account: 'putting vp one paire of shutters for clouds & makeing new groues for them to slide in'.

It might be argued that since the grooves are made *shorter*, the 'lessening' of the side-scenes was in respect of their width not their height, and resulted from their being now too wide to draw back easily in their new positions nearer the side-walls of the stage, where they conceivably obstructed the passage of actors down the side-spaces to their entrances. On the other hand (as we shall see later), the groove unit was of such a shape that it is possibly more likely for the above passage to mean 'cutting the wings down in height and making the relevant groove-groups *lower*' ('shorter' signifying 'of less height').

A later reference, in November 1681 (p. 262), is interesting in two ways: firstly, in its sidelight on the work necessitated in keeping the machinery in going order: 'oyling the Scenes and cleansing the groves to make them slide and putting new ropes to them'; and secondly, in giving us one of our special problems, what does 'putting new ropes to them' mean? This is a very difficult question. It may be that no more is to be inferred than the renewal of ropes tying the upper grooves in position; if so it is of comparatively small importance. But it may equally mean something else—it may signify that the scenes themselves were moved in the grooves by a system of ropes and not merely pushed separately to and fro by hand. If this is so we may have a system of pretty elaborate mechanism concealed in the phrase. But, sadly, there is not sufficient data for us to decide, we can only defer the question of how the scenery was moved in the grooves till we have had an opportunity to discuss the use, or non-use, in England of that particular mechanical system of working the movement of scenes that came to be universally used on the Continent (see Chapter 11).

The next references are simple and (but for the intriguing penultimate word of the second reference) add little to our information, but they bring

a. Frontispiece and wings

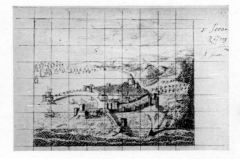

b. 1st shutter, the prospect of Rhodes

c. 2nd shutter, Rhodes beleaguered

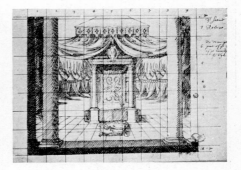

d. 1st relieve, Solyman's throne

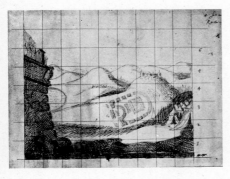

e. 2nd relieve, Mount Philermus

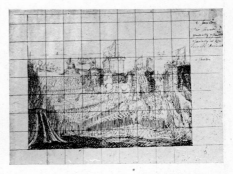

f. 3rd shutter, the general assault

25 *a-f.* John Webb's designs for *The Siege of Rhodes*, 1656

27. Debased copy of the subject in Pl. 26
with borders obliterated

26. Powel's puppet stage showing borders,
from *A Second Tale of a Tub*, 1709

us up to April and November 1690, respectively: 'sweeping & cleering the Stage & cleering the Grooves . . .' and 'Searching the Scenes in ye Theatre, & nailing & mending the Braces and brushing the groves for them to slide & soping them . . .' (p. 269).

In the frequent mentions of 'cleering' and 'cleansing' the grooves one is reminded irresistibly of the daily task of bus-cleaners brushing the filth and old tickets from between the slats on the gangway-floor between the seats of the older type of buses. It is a delightful detail to learn that these grooved ways were *soaped* (as they were in Sabbattini's day in Italy) for the easier working of the scenes in them. We shall find references later to the scenery jamming in the grooves, but only rarely do we find any suggestion of the means employed to help prevent this.

In the text of her book (see p. 151) Miss Boswell states of the scenery of the court theatre, 'The wings, shutters, and relieves slid in grooves.' We are forced to take exception to this statement so far as concerns the relieves. The relieves are a special department of scenery in which the system of changing was, as we have shown, different from that of the shutters. For the present we would content ourselves with saying that wings and flat backscenes slid in grooves but that relieves had probably little to do with them, and no evidence has yet been found to suggest there was any connexion between relieves and grooves.

Just after the turn of the century a small item concerning grooves comes to us in a translation into English (published 1707) of an Italian book on perspective written in 1693 by one of the great pioneers of scenic perspective, Andrea Pozzo. It shows that grooves were used for a time at least in Italy. The passage runs in the translation to his 'Seventy-second Figure':

Scenes for the Stage have very much Affinity with those lately describ'd, but the Point of Sight is not so easily found in these; and from the Obliquity of the Grooves in which the Scenes run, it comes to pass, that the right Lines which ought to appear parallel to the Line of the Plan, must not be drawn parallel thereto, but oblique; which is a Work of some Difficulty. This indeed may be avoided, by fixing the Grooves parallel to the Poscene; as is usual in some Places, especially in *Germany*. Nevertheless, the *Italian* Manner has this Advantage; That those who are employ'd to prompt the Actors, and shift the Scenes, *&c.* are less expos'd to Sight, in the Performance of their Business.

We need not concern ourselves now with the technical points in the above save to point out that here is one of the rare indications that wing-grooves were occasionally placed diagonally instead of parallel with the front of the stage—a matter we discussed at the end of Chapter 6. It is interesting to expand this note a little. Pozzo gives us to understand that the Italians at that date still used the wing-grooves in the oblique position and that in this respect they were superior to the German technicians. Of course it is true that oblique wings are more useful to a stage-manager than what we may call 'straight' wings. The reason is a matter of sight-lines; oblique wings mask-in the sides of the stage better, yet we shall find very few examples of oblique wings until the dawn of our own day. Italy gave them up and, in spite of what Pozzo says, never accepted them in her regular stage tradition, as witness the works of Juvarra or the Bibiena family. Why wings became set in the less advantageous position is a question which will be better answered when we have gained more infor-mation on the system of machinery which existed to move them.

The unfamiliar word 'poscene' in the above passage from Pozzo signifies the back of the stage where, as his diagrams show, the backscenes ran, also in grooves.

9

SECOND INTERLUDE

(THE DISTINCTION BETWEEN CURTAIN, DROP, AND ACT DROP)

———————————— ★ ————————————

THERE is one development of the English backscene which began before 1700 and which we must deal with separately. It was a development which, to be explained, seems to demand a somewhat freer ranging over the limitations of dates than we have permitted ourselves in this review as a whole. It therefore is a suitable matter to treat in an interlude-chapter where, as we have observed, we shall consider ourselves a little less confined to the restrictions of chronological development. This interlude moreover, about a particular variation in the make-up of the backscene, gives us the chance to offer a warning: that we should observe a distinction between three certain scenic units that are far too frequently misnamed and muddled to the detriment of any clear thinking about them.

In the last chapter we were examining a period of experiment in the theatre when a new technique was finding its forms. Before the seventeenth century is out, and before we go on to consider the stabilization of scenery in the eighteenth century, there is this last innovation of the backscene to be noted. This innovation is the introduction of a variant of the flat scene which later, in Rees, was to be placed first in his list, namely the *Drop*. Concerning the drop scene, or cloth, we have oddly enough comparatively little information, though of Rees's three varieties of flat scene it is the drop alone which has survived today.

Today, under its name of *cloth* or *backcloth*, the drop is so completely accepted as a standard element of scenic equipment that one is perhaps a little surprised to find that it is one of the latest of those elements to come into use.

Even concerning the drop there is a considerable confusion of terms owing to the quality of development in the uses of technical words—a development that marches unequally with the development of the uses of the things themselves. (And, hence, that sometimes very instructively reflects their story to him who can read.)

In this case, the term 'backcloth' (now synonymous with 'drop'), which is by far the most general name in present use for this particular piece of scenery, originally applied to something that was not a drop at all, and in this early sense we have already found it as a term as far back as Inigo Jones's plan for *Florimène* in 1635. But the essential of a cloth today is that it should be capable of being 'struck' (or taken away) easily in the change to another scene. Of this the backcloth of Jones would not allow. His was a permanency behind his scenes of relieve.

Thus there was introduced another name to designate the cloth used as a movable scene when it first came into use and that name was—logically enough in contradistinction to the 'flat' scenes which drew sideways—a *drop* scene because it rose and fell vertically instead of parting to the sides; it *dropped* from above.

Just as the earliest form of flat scene seems to have been a curtain, but of the traverse variety, so the earliest drop seems to have been a curtain, but of the roller variety.

Montague Summers states his opinion that the period of origin of the drop was about 1690, tracing it in the opera *The Prophetess* at Dorset Garden (see *The Restoration Theatre*, p. 101). He says:

There occur in Betterton's elaborate opera *The Prophetess; or, The History of Dioclesian*, Dorset Garden, April–May, 1690, a number of extremely significant and interesting stage directions, of which one or two at least require some brief, but especial notice. At the commencement of Act III, 2, we find: *A Curtain falls representing the entrance into the inner parts of a Magnificent Pallace. A noble Arch; behind it two Embroider'd Curtains, part of the first ty'd up on either side, the farther Curtain hanging down. Figures of Diana on each side of the Arch standing on large Pedestalls.* (The *two Embroider'd Curtains* are paintings on the scene.) Act IV, Scene 1, is 'Scene *the Great Curtain*'. At the end of the scene Drusilla *'waves her Wand thrice. Soft Musick is heard. Then the Curtain rises, and shews a stately Tomb . . .'*

The conclusion that these curtains, first seen on the London stage in 1690, were 'drops' is unavoidable. 'Drops' were used in the French theatre at least as early as 1664, and probably rather before that date. But it must be emphasized that 'drops' were never employed by Inigo Jones in the Caroline Masques, nor throughout the whole reign of Charles II, and to talk of 'drops' before 1690 is wholly erroneous. When these 'drops' known as 'curtains' were first introduced they were only utilized as something quite extraordinary, a device wholly belonging to opera rather than to the regular stage.

There is hereabouts the possibility of a troublesome confusion. It is important that we do what we may to warn the reader against it. We have in this connexion three essentially different pieces of stage scenery to distinguish and, unless one is watchful, the changing application of the terms marking these three items is an obstacle to their distinction.

In the first place we have the word *curtain*. Even today this is a loosely defined word in theatrical practice: *The Curtain* is generally understood to

mean the large wall of fabric folds which closes the opening of the proscenium. *The Curtain falls* is almost a household word to express the end,
the hiding away of the spectacle:

> *The curtain falls, the play is played,*
> *The beggar packs beside the beau . . .*

said W. E. Henley.

This particular curtain is the front, or proscenium, curtain, and it has
nothing whatever to do with any particular scene or any particular show.
It is part of the furnishing of the theatre. It may work in one of several
different ways: it may draw from the sides, fall inwards from the top corners
where it was bunched in festoons, or drop vertically from above. In which
latter case it may very easily be called a drop curtain.

But here the first confusion rises, for we have also to distinguish the
existence of a drop *scene*. And a hanging scene is very commonly called—
by those not strict with their terms—a *curtain* (as was the drop in the
Prophetess stage-direction). So a hanging scene may also come to be called
a *drop curtain* on occasion, though what is intended is something very
different from the proscenium curtain proper and is, instead, a standard
piece of painted scenery, not falling in the proscenium opening to shut off
the stage, but coming in any of the possible positions of a backscene,
leaving a more or less wide acting-area in front, between it and the proscenium.

It is now that confusion becomes worse confounded, since in addition to
both these very distinct things, the 'scene drop' and the 'front curtain',
there is to come in a few decades a third thing which is in its nature a drop
scene, but which falls in the position of the proscenium curtain. This is
designated the *Act Drop*, and it again is as separate in function from either
of the two preceding as they are from each other.

Perhaps the following attempt at an historical sequence will bring some
order into the confusion; but it must be said at the outset that our evidence
on this matter is still very fragmentary and we are at present able to do no
more than give a sort of interim report on the succession of events based on
the scraps we have. My putting the following on paper may occasion other
investigators to correct me with details they themselves have discovered
and so lead to the establishment of the authentic historical sequence.

The confused story of these curtains seems at present, then, best told as
follows.

At the beginning of the theatre in 1660 the front curtain rose after the
prologue had been spoken on the apron stage, and remained up until the
epilogue had been delivered, when it fell to mark the end of the show (see
Summers, *The Restoration Theatre*, p. 97).

[165]

This curtain was not a piece of painted scenery, but was of material (traditionally green in colour) and worked in the proscenium opening. Beyond it the acts and their scenes developed, the transition from act to act being marked by a pause (with perhaps a musical entr'acte) when the stage was left vacant by the players; and the transition from scene to scene, within an act, was marked by a visible transformation of the scenery. Should the opening scene of an act be different from the concluding scene of the previous act, the pause was left while the old scene was still on the stage and at the beginning of the new act the old scene drew and was replaced by that for the first scene of the subsequent act.

There now comes a qualification. On certain special occasions the front curtain *was* dropped during a show—even as early as 1664 (see Montague Summers's note to p. 57 of his 1914 edition of Buckingham's *The Rehearsal*). On such occasions it appears to have been used (much as was the 'curtain' of *The Prophetess*) to prepare for a special effect. Something at least of the nature and reason of this effect may be gained from *The Rehearsal* (performed Drury Lane 1671). It forms an especially interesting example since this play was of its nature a commentary on current stage conventions. There at the end of Act IV Bayes, the playwright-character, cried, 'Let down the curtain'. The forestage is left with the characters on it, and then the characters go out.

At the opening of Act V Bayes enters again upon the forestage with the two spectators to his play and begins:

Now, Gentlemen, I will be bold to say; I'l shew you the greatest Scene that ever *England* saw: I mean not for words, for those I do not value; but for state, shew, and magnificence. In fine I'll justifie it to be as grand to the eye every whit, I gad, as that great Scene in *Harry* the Eight, and grander too, I gad; for instead of two Bishops, I bring in here four Cardinals.

> *The Curtain is drawn up, the two usurping Kings appear in state, with the four Cardinals,* Prince Pretty-man *Prince* Volscius, Amarillis, Cloris, Parthenope, *&c. before them, Heralds and Serjeants at Arms with Maces.*

In short, a stupendous crowd effect and dazzling tableau is intended. Now if, on the Restoration stage, such a crowd-tableau were to be discovered in the normal way, by opening flats, it could not but be kept upstage at least as far as the first pair of flats. Thus not only the depth of the forestage would intervene between the tableau and audience but an additional space of possibly 9 ft. or more between the proscenium line and the position of the first grooves. And so although an effect of a vastly crowded throng would be intended, the audience would see it only across a desert of possibly 30 ft. of empty stage—a poor beginning for a multitude. (The 9 ft. is the distance still existing as late as 1876 between proscenium line and first grooves at Ipswich Theatre Royal—a space filled in by large, booked, proscenium wings—and the remaining 21 ft. is the measurement given in Wren's (presumed) Drury Lane forestage in 1674.)

Thus it is indisputable that a more dazzling effect was to drop the curtain, crowd the stage behind, draw up the curtain, and discover the throng massed down to the very proscenium opening itself.

Hence, it seems, the use of the Restoration front curtain, on occasion, during a show.

The next step in the story is that, about 1690, the customary flat scene, or form of scene which parted in the midst and drew, was supplemented by another variety of 'flat scene' which consisted of an unbroken area of painted canvas, and which *dropped* from above by means of rollers (or so we infer from what is to follow) instead of 'drawing'. This was called, in 1813 at any rate (see Rees), a *drop*. But at its origin in 1690 it was (perhaps unfortunately) called a curtain, maybe because in the particular case quoted above of *The Prophetess* it was painted to represent a curtain, or maybe because on many of the first occasions of its use it actually *was* a curtain. At any rate the name stuck, and the phrase 'back curtain' is to be found even today in inexpert usage to name a painted drop scene.

In this connexion it is very interesting to keep an eye open for any evidence which might show that a usage similar to that in a certain German print ever obtained on the English stage. The print is, so far as I know, the only evidence we have that in the seventeenth century a *traverse curtain* in the modern sense was used, behind the wings and in conjunction with scenery. The print is ascribed to the year 1655 and is reproduced in Nicoll's *The Development of the Theatre*, Fig. 196. It shows a performance on a stage, with a fringed front curtain (no proscenium arch is shown), four pairs of wings, sky borders, and a backscene representing a street in perspective. But its especial interest is that there is to be seen, with a clarity remarkable and allowing of no mistake, a curtain rod across the stage behind the last pair of wings and in front of the backscene, with a pair of fringed *traverse curtains* running upon it on rings. At the use of this traverse we can only guess, but one cannot avoid seeing in it—without any provable grounds— an epitome of the old traverse of the Elizabethan stage and the shutter principle of the masques, though exemplifying neither of these in exact detail.

The next step in the story is that, somewhere about the year 1750, the custom of marking the act intervals by no more than a stage left empty of actors was very gradually superseded by an extension of what had already become a usage upon special rare occasions—namely the dropping of the front curtain, not now in preparation for a special tableau, as had been formerly the reason (see Summers, *The Restoration Theatre*, p. 164), but

[167]

for the whole space of the interval between two acts. '. . . The curtain now fell in the act intervals as a regular thing. . . . The several houses varied in their practice, but perhaps it is not too hazardous to say that the modern employ of the curtain was admitted and began to prevail about the middle of the eighteenth century.'

The full helpfulness of the front curtain to hide and so simplify scene changes 'was long in dawning upon the players, as evidenced by the fact that it did not begin to drop regularly between the acts until the middle of the eighteenth century' (W. J. Lawrence, *Those Nut-cracking Elizabethans*, p. 122).

Now there comes another development; it is the provision of more than one 'front Curtain'—of, in fact, an additional drop directly behind the front curtain proper, but not, like it, of plain material; instead it was a painted canvas just like any drop scene, though its subject was more decorative than representational. This was used instead of the front curtain, to drop at the act-intervals, so that the front curtain devolved to its original use—only at the beginning and end of the show, while the acts were marked by the special *Act Drop*.

The reason for this innovation may perhaps have lain in the very fact that we have noticed above in Henley's lines—that a falling curtain has a sense of finality. It cuts off the stage too finally. Dropped between acts, it presented to the gaze of the waiting spectators too complete a change from the atmosphere of the artificial, theatrical world, and of the show itself, which had already been built up by the preceding scenes, and it deprives one of something of the continuity of the theatrical experience. So the alternative was invented of veiling the stage in an interval with another 'curtain', one relevant to the show, one especially painted.

The first occasion I have yet found where we see this idea in practice was, fittingly enough, in a period of considerable scenic experiment and development; it was during the régime under Garrick of the Alsatian scene-designer Phillip James De Loutherbourg at Drury Lane. Here, according to a note of W. J. Lawrence's on Henry Angelo's *Reminiscences* (2 vols., London, 1828), 'De Loutherbourg painted or designed a landscape scene which was first used as a drop curtain for the pantomime *The Wonders of Derbyshire; or, Harlequin in the Peak* in 1779. This was used at the theatre for some years afterwards.'

Percy Fitzgerald in his *World Behind the Scenes* gives the following in quotation marks (p. 13) but without specifying whence it is quoted, concerning De Loutherbourg and *The Wonders of Derbyshire*:

Here he had full scope for his pencil, and I may venture to say, never were such romantic and picturesque paintings exhibited in that theatre before. Previous to the curtain being drawn up on the first night of its performance, the drop (as it is called), alluding to the country (Derbyshire), gave you an idea of the mountains and waterfalls, most beautifully executed, exhibiting a terrific appearance.

One is at first glance puzzled by the apparent suggestion that the 'drop' showed itself *previous to* the curtain being drawn up. But Angelo (if he be the author quoted) is, I think, loose in his phrasing and merely means, 'Previous to the *drop* being raised (and the show beginning) this drop gave you an idea . . . etc.'

But it is interesting that this special cloth which, it seems, was not the backcloth to any particular scene, remained in use at the theatre for some years afterwards. One would like to know whether it remained in its original function or became a typical stock backscene. If it remained an 'act drop', it may be said to have been adopted by the theatre much as a signature tune is adopted by a dance band of today—retained from one of its signal successes to become a symbol or badge on ensuing occasions.

And this, in fact, the act drop became. Only on special occasions is a fresh act drop painted for a specific show (as that by Claud Lovat Fraser for the revival of *The Beggar's Opera* at the Lyric Theatre, Hammersmith, in 1920), but in general it became a stock piece of the theatre's furniture, like the famous drop by Byam Shaw depicting the Pantheon of Great Players which for so many years worked beside the front curtain of the Coliseum, London.

It is to be remarked that in the above quotation relating to *The Wonders of Derbyshire* no direct evidence is given that this drop of De Loutherbourg's was used in the act-intervals as well as before the opening of the play. That must remain undecided.

But however it may be, William Telbin wrote in a special article on 'Act Drops' in *The Magazine of Art*, July 1895, p. 335, that the front curtain

at any rate where it has been used during my recollection, has only been exhibited at the beginning of a piece and lowered at the end; in the interval between the acts a painted canvas, either representing drapery or other form of decoration, or a landscape (classical mostly), has been used.

He adds that,

For an act-drop to be successful a design should, in my opinion, be only suggestive, and not bear too directly upon any one special aspect of the drama, as our theatres in the vicissitudes of their existence fall into strange hands, being sublet at certain periods to tenants whose productions are as the antitheses of art to one another. . . .

Perhaps the arrangement most acceptable to architects and generally favoured by managers is the painted drapery 'blind'.

And this frequency of the use of a design of painted draperies to decorate an act drop, it may well be understood, still further tended to increase its confusion with the curtain proper.

These then are the terms we have to keep clear; the Curtain, the Act Drop, and the Drop Scene. The Curtain came with the birth of the theatre in 1660. It was used only at the beginning and end of a show (save on very rare occasions when it was dropped to precede a specially elaborate tableau).

About 1690 the Drop Scene came in to augment the variety of flat scenes.

About 1750 the curtain began to fall in act-intervals as well as at the close of the show.

In 1779 something very closely analogous to the painted Act Drop was used, and in the following century, till near the close, certain theatres used the act drop at act-intervals, relegating the front curtain to its old use at the beginning and end of a show.

With Irving a curtain was used even to hide the scene changes within acts, though his technique was full and varied and he did not stick exclusively to one method.

Today the act drop is, on the whole, rare. The front curtain is used not only for act-intervals, but to hide all scene changes within an act.

The Oxford English Dictionary has, under the word 'drop', the following: '16. In a theatre The painted curtain let down between the acts of a play to shut off the stage from the view of the audience; also called *act drop*, and (less technically) *drop-curtain*.'

It is suggested here that the drop is synonymous with act drop and with drop curtain, whereas we have seen that they are three different things, and we find no reference here whatever to that more frequent use of the word 'drop' to designate a *drop scene*, and that is an important omission. The date quoted by the *Dictionary* for the earliest use of 'drop' is 1779, and agrees with the reference to an act drop which we gave above from Angelo.

Of the method by which the drop worked we know little from direct evidence until we come to the nineteenth century. Nevertheless, enough can be said to make a pretty certain deduction.

There are three ways open to us today to work a drop: it can be flown, or it can be rolled, or it can suffer one of several shifts of part-flying, part-folding, part-lapping-up that are all mere compromises, and generally damaging in the long run to the paint or the material of the cloth. Of these three methods the first, flying, may be ruled out of seventeenth-century procedure, because the structure of early theatres would not permit it. They were not provided with sufficient head-room or flying-space to allow of a cloth being raised up out of sight.

So there remains the method of the roller. And this method was at one time so prevalent that the roller was regarded as the natural concomitant of a drop. We find writers speaking of the union of the two as if it were inevitable. Thus Harry Lancaster, writing in a series of articles cut out presumably from *The Furniture Gazette*, and preserved (but without dates) in a scrapbook compiled by H. R. Eyre, about 1875, and now in my possession, says of drops, with no hesitation or suggestion of an alternative: 'Scenes that roll down from the top of the stage, are out of the theatre called *drop-scenes*, in the theatre they are termed *cloths*.' The roller mechanism is taken for granted as the principle of all drops.

Similarly, in a manuscript note of Eyre's accompanying these cuttings, and based upon conversations with William John Burgess, scenic artist and manager of the Theatre Royal, Ipswich, in 1875, we read: 'Scenes which hang from the top of the stage and descend to it by being unrolled from off a long roller which is fastened to its [*sic*] bottom edge, are called "drops" or sometimes cloths.'

Furthermore, in Henry N. Benwell's series of articles on 'Practical Scene-painting for Amateurs' in *Amateur Work*, vol. iv, 1884–5, we read: 'Cloths—These are the scenes which work up and down on rollers from the bottom.'

In all this evidence it is strongly implied that the prime method of drop-handling was the roller, and also that that roller was at the bottom of the cloth.

Probably this method obtained right back to the beginning of drop scenes, but Rees seems to suggest that a variation did take place, during the drop's history, in the position of the roller. He informs us that:

the canvas is furled or unfurled upon a roller, placed either at the top or bottom of the scene. A difference of opinion exists as to the placing of the roller, which, as it is a mere matter of taste, may probably never be determined—both ways are used in the London theatres. The rollers, in either case, are made to revolve by means of cords tightened or slackened as may be necessary; and when the scenes are large it is usual to wind them up by means of a cylinder and a winch, as in the trap machinery.

Though Rees's writer supposed no decision would ever be made between the top-roller method and the bottom-roller method, events since have shown a decided preference for the bottom roller, and we may even say that this remark in the *Cyclopaedia* is one of the very few pieces of evidence we have that a top-roller method was ever in general use. We can find no pictorial illustration of it, and to discover another mention is difficult.

But we know a good deal about the bottom-roller method. We can illustrate it by (Fig. 6) a cut from Frederick Lloyds's book on *Scene Painting* (no date, but about 1875) which though so late (like much else of this evidence on drops) may be admitted since the method is one which either exists or does not—time is not likely to vary it in detail at any period or impose any development upon it.

The roller of the drop was a curious beast. As time went on it came to be famous for its tricks. One of these tricks was a failure to roll evenly if one did not take great care to see that the ropes were prevented from overriding and trapping the edges of the cloth as it wound up. If they were allowed to do so, it never came down again. And the care needed to ensure this even rolling caused Eyre to take down this quaint and interesting note from Burgess's lips: 'The seams of the canvas should run horizontally, because the seams of the canvas if running perpendicular each turn it takes round the roller gathers one on the other and at last becomes so large as to cause the colour to crack off.' Though the English is free, the meaning is plain and pertinent.

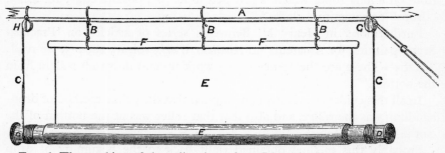

FIG. 6. The working of the roller drop, from Lloyds's *Scene Painting* (1875)

These rollers were often of considerable size—even reasonably short ones, no more than 15 or 16 ft. long, amounting to 5 in. and more in diameter.

When a drop was being raised the whole weight of the roller depended from the lines at either end; its centre was unsupported, and it was of great importance that the roller should not sag, since then it would not roll evenly. It was therefore the practice, for lightness and strength, to use a hollow roller, which the carpenter made up himself by glueing long strips of deal around the edges of a row of polygonal former-pieces, planing the whole to a true cylinder, and finally canvasing it. Disks of wood were fixed to the end of the complete roller to prevent the lines riding off.

Another shocking trick of the roller-beast depended upon its voracious grasping quality; this, perhaps unexpected, vice is revealed to us in the following: the roller was the method adopted to work the Act Drop as well as the Drop Scene, and, as late as 1890 and 1893, we find the two following references which admirably supplement each other and render further comment unnecessary.

The first consists in a letter in *The Era*, 28 October 1893, from G. Edmonds of the Princess's Theatre:

Sir: Now that the opening of new theatres—with their up-to-date improvements

FIG. 7. A caricature of the effect of the roller, from *The New York Dramatic Mirror* (1890)

—is an event of almost weekly occurrence, cannot some steps be taken by managers, scenic artists, and master carpenters to relegate to the limbo of oblivion that still surviving remnant of Noah's Arkæology the lumbersome, cumbersome act-drop roller? It is expensive to produce and unwieldy to use. It is a source of danger to hats and heads when it descends. It is a 'snapper up of unconsidered trifles' in the shape of hats, cloaks, and swords when it ascends. Even the train of a lady's dress is not safe from its boa constrictor-like clutches; in fact, nothing is sacred to the act-drop roller. At a matinée a few weeks since a lady, while standing with her back turned to the act-drop fiend, had her train taken up in it, and the public witnessed an effect not advertised in the programme. When the roller is down its clumsiness is still in evidence, for when it is moved on one side to allow you to take a call, it bumps against your shins. If a painted act-drop is necessary—which I very much doubt—let it work up and down like an ordinary cloth with a light batten attached.[1] If want of height will not permit this, use tableau falling curtains. For do we not remember the act drops of our youth? They were either confections of draperies, 'where tawdry yellow strove with dirty red', or Turneresque landscapes with a broken Corinthian column and a number of more or less—generally less—dressed nymphs disporting themselves. We have changed all that now; let us have the gracefully-falling, easily-manipulated tableau curtains—not garish in colour, but of a neutral tint which will harmonise with auditorium decorations, on which the eye, satiated with the splendours of the scenery—can rest.

The second reference is to a series of drawings in a number of *The New York Dramatic Mirror* during the year 1890. These form a song without words entitled: '*The Manager's Strategy, an unrehearsed tragedy in five acts—The Sad Fate of the Actor who said the Curtain Should Not Rise unless he got his Salary.*' At a passing glance, we might be forgiven for dismissing their grim burlesque as a groundless exaggeration, but after our foregoing study we realize that there is perhaps more than a grain of truth in their absurdity (Fig. 7).

Concerning the reason for the existence of both flat scenes and drop scenes side by side, we read in a passage directly succeeding the last we quoted from Rees:

Although the drop scenes are the most simple, it is necessary sometimes to have recourse to those scenes which are called flats. . . . The principal use of the flats is where apertures, such as doors, windows, chimney-pieces, &c. are wanted in the scene, which may be opened and shut as required; these are called, in the technology of a theatre, *practicable* doors, &c., because, when not to be used, they may be painted on a drop scene.

The drop scene then is said to be simpler—and of course it obviated the use of grooves with all their attendant possibilities of jamming. But, we notice, the flat was retained beside the drop and one reason at least was that

---

[1] By this time the flying system of working cloths had come into use, but had as yet been applied evidently only to the drop scenes on the stage and not extended to the act drop, in which probably the roller lived to its greatest age.

only in a firmly framed-out flat could one have a practicable door. It is true that today a practicable door can be inserted in a cloth, but only when that cloth is what is called a 'framed cloth'—in which case it is battened out and becomes something like a very large and flimsy single flat, and can no longer be rolled. But apart from this, no firm practicable opening can be made in a cloth. (Of course a cave-entrance or an architectural arch can be cut out of a cloth, but these have no moving doors or window-flaps hinged to them.) Practicable doors demand a firm frame around the opening to which the leaf may be hinged. If the door is not practicable, that is if it does not open, then, in Rees's somewhat elliptic phrase, it 'may be painted on a drop scene'.

It will therefore follow that one may hazard a rough guess that the flats would be the special medium for interior scenes and the cloth would be more likely to be reserved for exteriors—for landscapes and gardens. We shall in fact find evidence that such a division was to some extent the practice.

Concerning this distinction between the use of flats and drops, Benwell informs us on much the same lines (and with much the same curious constructions in his English as before) that flats

are used when a practicable door or window is required in a scene which has closed in on the back scene, and where, for this reason, a drop scene is of no use. They can be used on any part of the stage, but are generally pushed on from the second entrance. In some pieces these would again be drawn off, bringing into view another set of flats, which would, perhaps, also be drawn off, and expose a fresh back 'cloth', which has been set during the interval the two former were in use. 'Flats' can, of course, be used also as back scenes; in fact, interiors consist mainly of these. Interiors are seldom painted on 'cloths', excepting for corridors, passages, etc., where doors and windows are not required. Pantomime and burlesque interiors, such as kitchens, with all the different utensils painted in, attics and caves, are as a rule, painted on 'cloths'. It is very effective when sliding flats suddenly and rapidly open and discover another scene behind, especially if the latter be a bright and sparkling picture.

As we have come so far out of our chronological period through having had to illustrate the Restoration drop with Victorian examples, we might note an odd passage from a book on *Stage Effects* by Edward Mayhew (duo., London, 1840). He makes three main divisions of scenery, but differs somewhat from Rees in that he appears to include cut flats under the head of *flats* and for his third category brings in *set scenes*, which Rees elected to relegate to the subsidiary head of '*pieces*' and which lead to a territory we have still to examine. But after this division Mayhew makes a remarkable statement; his passage runs:

There are but three different kinds of scenery; known by the terms *drops*, or cloths, flats and set scenes. The rest, as wings and side pieces . . . being adjuncts. Formerly the chief part of all stock scenery consisted of *drops*, as is still the case in most country theatres; but these are now seldom used in London, flats having superseded them; except close to the proscenium, where they are lowered when any extraordinary space is required to display the scene which is to follow.

Further from the footlights than the middle of the stage, *flats* are seldom used, the remaining half being devoted to set scenes . . .

and there we leave him for the moment.

The above would seem to assert the cloths are older than flats, which we believe is not the case, and that the chief use of cloths was latterly near the front of the stage only, so that they left a considerable depth behind in which 'discovery scenes' might be set. Mayhew also limits the utility of flats to the space in front of the mid-point of stage depth.

There may be some grain of truth in this, but it needs to be carefully winnowed from the accompanying chaff with all the experience we may gain by subsequent study.

The drop came into the story and came to stay. So surely has it stayed that it is still with us and in as lively a state of health and employment as it has ever been (or almost so: for some schools begin to despise the drop). For this very reason we cannot complete its history; that is still being written. We have therefore contented ourselves, in examining the drop scene, with a short summary covering the theories of its birth and the one characteristic of it that has gone out into the historical past and become a museum piece offering itself for research—namely, the roller.

The principle of the drop has gone on unimpaired and has sloughed off its old associations with the idea of the flat scene and so it passes outside our present province. Whether, today, it has the prospect of as long a future as it has a past is not so certainly to be affirmed. Some schools among the moderns decry cloths as a relic of painted scenery and therefore, they say, an artificial monstrosity, ill suited to associate with the three-dimensional actor, and as their theories take us out of history and into the present, and as they involve us in opinionated controversy instead of collected research, we relinquish the story of the drop and return to that of its erstwhile companions among the flat scenes, taking up the tale where the seventeenth century merges into the eighteenth.

28. Model reconstruction by the author of Wren's drawing for a Play House, showing Restoration proscenium doors (*c.* 1674)

29. Sir James Thornhill's drawing for 'The 1st Great flat Scene'

THORNHILL, HOGARTH, FIELDING, AND THE EARLY EIGHTEENTH CENTURY

✻

Thornhill's 'Great Flat Scene' c. 1705—An unidentified water-colour— Wings on Powel's Puppet Stage, 1709—Hogarth's Sensino print, 1723— Groove and flats in Hogarth's 'Indian Emperor' painting, 1731—Bottom flats in Fielding's 'Tumble-down Dick', 1736—Clouds in 'The Rival Theatres', 1737—The information of the Covent Garden Inventory, 1743 —Tate Wilkinson, 1747—Grooves in Coffey's 'The Devil to Pay', 1748

✻

WE open our study of the eighteenth century with evidence in the form of a drawing. The drawing is ascribed to Sir James Thornhill (1675–1734) and is now in the Art Institute of Chicago. It is reproduced, with the very kind permission of the Art Institute, in Pl. 29. A slight pencil sketch for this drawing is in Thornhill's sketchbook in the British Museum, folio 50 recto.

It is inscribed 'The 1st Great flat Scene' in pencil above, and it bears a scale below. The scale has an oddness about it, its description would appear to be as follows: it consists of a pencil line some 6 in. long marked into eight divisions with ink dots; the first two divisions are subdivided again into thirds and sixths, and the first of these thirds is marked again into quarters. This would appear to be a scale of 24 ft. at $\frac{1}{4}$ in. to 1 ft., marked off in eight 3-ft. intervals, six of which are plain while two are subdivided into feet and half-feet, with the first foot subdivided again into four 3-in. intervals; all of which might be perfectly understandable. But the oddness comes in the pencil figures showing very faintly above the scale; here, over the *first* main division is marked '6' (where we should expect a '3'), above the third '12', above the fifth '18', and above the seventh '24'. The eighth and last appears to be unmarked but should, as one would suppose, have the '24' over it. If the scale is really a record of 4 ft. to 1 in., then each figure above has been displaced by one main division to the left and should, to stay in this position, read 3, 9, 15, 21, (24) respectively; alternatively the numerals themselves should remain unaltered but each be shifted in position one main division to the right, when they would correctly read '6', '12', '18', '24'. It appears a curious mistake for a draughtsman of Thornhill's experience in decoration to make, but it seems we must accept it as a mistake since below the scale is written in almost illegible pencil '24 f? Sc . . .' (the obscure letter after the *f* appears a capital H but might be a double *tt* or a *t* with a flourish). The indications suggest very strongly that what is intended is '24 ft Scale' or '24 ft Scene'.

When, now, we compare the scale with the drawing we find that its length is exactly the same as the width of the design inside the stone arch. If then this drawing does represent a flat scene, and one which is 24 ft. wide, then the flanking Corinthian columns, together with the vertical sides of the masonry arch against which they stand, are to be assumed as designed to be painted on separate wings.

We examine further features of the drawing for dimensions and note that the caryatid figures will be above life-size on this reading of the scale and will be each exactly 9 ft. high.

Next our eye rises to the most notable feature of the whole design, namely the horizontal line ruled across it 20 ft. above the ground. This might be read as the metal tie-bar to the arch. It is, I believe, more significant than this.

We start from the information in the inscription that this is a 'flat scene'. We have read of flat scenes in the preceding chapters; here now is a labelled picture of one. It is not inscribed a 'curtain', and therefore we have every right to believe that all or part of what is shown in the drawing was painted on a pair of shutters to open and close in the usual manner of a flat scene. That backscenes designed for such a division down the centre were known to Thornhill is clear from his drawings for the scenery of the opera *Arsinoe*, for in two of these the division is clearly indicated. This division-line is, however, rarely seen either in pictures of a scene on the stage or in drawings for scenery, firstly since it was a disfiguring feature, and secondly since its position was clearly known to any stage carpenter as central and thus had no need of indication. We deduce, then, that we have here a pair of shutters running in grooves; of the nature of the grooves we can only say that they would either have been of a similar pattern to those in Jones's *Salmacida Spolia* or of a more or less different pattern about which no evidence whatever has, as far as we yet know, survived to us today. The supposition that there would be one groove at the bottom and another at the top is, I believe, reasonable (cf. Pl. 2).

The next question is whereabouts would these top grooves come? A point is needed at which the design could be cut across at an arbitrary, horizontal line; no indefinite arched edge could run safely in grooves.

It is just this arbitrary, horizontal line which is present in the drawing, as we have remarked, 20 ft. up. If now this marks the top of a normal backscene, what is the nature of the rest of the picture which appears above the line?

Let us notice here two points. First, that the proportion of the design considered only up as far as the horizontal line is a proportion very acceptable to practical experience of backscenes. It happens to be 24 ft. wide and 20 ft. high. This is not unreasonable for a normal, smallish backscene. Nor is it outside the bounds of carpentry to make a framework 12 ft. wide and 20 ft. high for each of the halves of such a backscene, and make it so that it was reasonably light to handle but not impossibly flimsy. But, on the other hand, a framework 12 ft. wide and 29 ft. 6 in. high (which is the dimension of this drawing up to the arch-crown) *is* likely to be either unwieldily heavy or unwieldily flimsy; and thus we come to the second point to be noticed—this design is not inscribed as a normal flat scene but as one of the 'Great' flat scenes. It is therefore to be supposed as something possibly intended to work in the normal grooves of a theatre, but having a different and 'greater' effect. It may then be a special flat scene.

All this is leading to a specific conclusion: that flat scenes in the Restoration theatre could be of two sorts presenting very different proportions to the eye. The first sort would be the normal, horizontal rectangle of the 'landscape' picture—that is, appreciably wider than it was high. The second—and this is perhaps unexpected to orthodox views—would have what the painter calls 'portrait' proportions, and be noticeably higher than it was wide.

A 'vertical' scene-design is, on the whole, a new idea to the theatre student. But there is no reason against such a thing; we have already remarked the proportions of Jones's drawing ascribed to *The Queen of Arragon* (see p. 65), and we have noted that the great effect-scene in *Salmacida Spolia* was 14 ft. wide by 26 ft. high at the back. We shall moreover see when we come to have enough information to reconstruct the working of the groove system in a model that such a scene-proportion was, indeed, almost inevitably suggested by the arrangement. Yet blind acceptance of the practice of theatre today has forced us to consider a vertical scene-design to be impossible from the practical point of view.

If now we accept the implication in Thornhill's drawing that such a thing was possible, we have to ask, How was it worked?

In the first place we must take some step to raise the normal border line across the top of the scene. Unless this is done the summit of our vertical backscene will be hidden. Merely to raise the borders so that they part from the wing-tops clearly cannot be done, but the problem as well as the solution was already well known to Jones. In fact he designed special side pieces of upper scenery to maintain this connexion with the wings below (and 'whereby ye grooues aboue were hidden & also ye howse behind them'), yet do it in such a way as to permit him to raise the central portion of the borders as high as the amazing figure of 29 ft. clear. In other words the solution is to use an arch-border, that is to say a very deep border whose ends hang down to the wings but whose centre is cut out in a more or less high arch. It is exactly this type of design which Thornhill indicates in his drawing.

We are now left, in imagination, with a normal-height 'horizontal' backscene flanked by normal wings, but masked above by high-arched borders. Such masking is, however, at the moment, inadequate. We can now see up under the borders and over the top of the backscene. The next step, then, is to drop a special upper backscene above the first backscene to increase its height and close this gap—and then to continue the design of the lower scene upwards on to the addition. With this idea, again, the Thornhill drawing is entirely consistent.

What authority have we for the existence and practical working of such an upper piece? Exact and categorical evidence is in the Jones plans. There (see Pl. 2) the 'upper back shutters which were also hung in grooues and changed as ye others did' are clearly marked and resemble (as we have seen) a very deep up-stage border directly against the shutters. We have then proof that such a system was used in the masques, and we now conclude it was carried over into the public theatre of the Restoration. Substantiating evidence is available in such references as that of Dryden's to the 'Upper Part of the House, as well as the Side Scenes' being involved in a scene-change, and we shall find further evidence as late as 1736.

This upper backshutter of Thornhill's was, we suppose, divided down the centre as was the lower backshutter, and consisted of two frames each bearing a projecting flange along the top, which flange ran in a special, high groove and enabled the pieces to hang just in front of those of the scene below; the whole forming, save for a line of shadow, approximately one big surface.

The effect of the revelation of such a scene in its tall grandeur after the lower scenes of the normal method must have been truly impressive, especially if it took place under one's eyes.

Most frequently, we suppose, the upper backshutters bore (owing to their position) painting of clouds. They then might come to be termed cloudings; and if they hung as they did, then we may feel little surprise to find, as we shall in 1743, that a Covent Garden inventory lists a 'hook to draw off the cloudings'.

Note further that the very subject shown in that part of Thornhill's drawing which we take to be the upper shutters is the appearance of a deity in glory in the clouds. There is no indication that any actual revelation of this detail was intended in this scene, but the indication is clear that here the method was at hand when such a revelation-effect was needed (as it often was, on the evidence of stage-directions). Clearly it would be very easy to duplicate the working groove that held these upper backshutters so that a second pair of shutters could be hung directly in front at need, to be drawn so as to discover the farther pair, and thus change the aspect of the 'sky' independently of the landscape below it.

One technical point is worth making. If these upper backshutters were indeed drawn off to the sides, then the groove which held them would have to be a very long object—for instance, to hold Thornhill's upper shutters when they were withdrawn, the groove would have to be 48 ft. long and proportionately thick. The groove below, holding the tops of the lower shutters, had perhaps no need to be so long since, when a lower shutter was withdrawn, it would still be safely supported on the stage if only a quarter or a fifth of its upper edge were left in the groove (like a book part-drawn from a shelf), but the upper shutters could not rest their weight on bottom grooves as the lower shutters could—they depended solely for support on the single top groove from which they hung. Had they been pulled part-way out of a shorter groove so that they projected beyond its support, they would tend to sag and thus to jam. So the upper-shutter grooves had to be very long and were presumably continuous across almost the whole stage.

As we shall see, when we come shortly to consider a painting of Hogarth's, it is very likely that the grooves which held the tops of the lower shutters were also, in this early period, pretty long, heavy, and continuous, though their continuity would have presented a grave difficulty, as is suggested in the next paragraph.

If such a two-storied backscene could be arranged at intermediate positions on the stage as well as at the back, we come upon this problem; that when all the shutters were open and arch-borders used, the empty top grooves of the lower shutters would span the stage picture, as we observed concerning the drawing for *The Queen of Arragon*. It is, moreover, clear that in such a design as this of Thornhill's, the old method of hiding the grooves with ranks of clouds might be illogical, and so we see ourselves soon to be faced with the need to find a way of moving the centre portion of these grooves out of the way when the space was needed. We shall shortly find proof of the existence of such a method, but of the date of its introduction we are not yet sure. One supposes it would have been needed from the opening of the first scenic theatre, but as yet we have no indication of it.

A further point to be deduced from this drawing is that, although wing-heights in Inigo Jones's designs (and also on the rough sketch of scenery shown on the stage of Wren's sectional drawing presumed for Drury Lane (1674)) decreased in perspective as they went back up the stage, yet it is likely that with the introduction of scenic machinery to the regular public theatre the height of wings would soon be standardized, since shutter-groove heights are somewhat dependent upon wing-groove heights, and if these vary, then the heights of stock shutters must vary also and each pair is then limited to run in one position only on the stage—a limitation that would clearly be a nuisance. For instance, a stock garden-scene that was lower than a stock street-scene and thus had always to be set farther up-stage would be useless when one wanted to arrange a 'discovery' in the street by opening the garden upon it, since the garden could only be set behind the street.

A further puzzling point arises concerning the borders across the top of the stage; when these were changed, did they part centrally like the upper backshutters and draw off sideways? Or were they raised upwards out of sight as ours are today? It appears at first glance very obvious that they must have been raised, since to draw off sideways the two halves of a border near the stage-front (where borders would be longest) must entail the use of a tremendously long groove, and would seem impossible. Yet we have the certainty (according to the Covent Garden Inventory of 1743 soon to be discussed) that *cloudings* at any rate were 'drawn off' with the help of a hook. On this matter there is, however, a further curious point: namely, that cloudings seem sometimes to be spoken of in *pairs*—there is, for instance, in the inventory an item of '6 borders and 6 pair of cloudings fixt to battens. . . .' Were then, the borders separate, shorter, central things, and the cloudings in the nature of two outer 'legs' which hung at the ends of the borders and dropped down to cover the wing-tops? Such an arrangement is exactly what we found in Inigo Jones's plans. If they were so, when did the modern, continuous border first come into existence and how were —even in the earliest days—*arch borders* constructed? One scarcely imagines them in three parts.

Even now, if we allow that the 'cloudings' might have been drawn off sideways in upper grooves, we have still to seek the method by which the central border-piece was changed. Jones offers us no help here.

We may note finally that the ordinal '1st' in the inscription '1st . . . flat scene' suggests that the piece was intended to come in the first grooves, or near the front of the stage.

Concerning this matter of the two-story backscene, it seems very likely that a splendid example reposes unrecognized in a certain water-colour drawing at the British Museum. The drawing I refer to is still one of our great theatrical puzzles; it is undated, it is anonymous, it is not certainly ascribable to any theatre nor to any play. Furthermore, that it refers even to English work at all is not firmly established. There are, however, certain hints on all these points which while taken alone are all too frail to build any structure upon, yet put side by side they add up to a possible inter-pretation that is remarkable in itself yet inconsistent in no detail with what we have learnt of the intricacies of our subject so far.

The drawing is reproduced in the frontispiece. Let us begin with the one point about which we may claim some certainty. This point is that there is undoubtedly a line in the drawing beginning at the bottom of the backscene and running up uninterruptedly to a point about the centre of the arch in the upper story. Above this point it is not visible. This line appears most likely to represent the join between a pair of flats.

If now we consider the wings which flank the backscene, and look at their tops, we notice a row of upstanding urns; were these urns cut out in profile and attached to the top edge of the wings, their projection upwards would interfere with the smooth running of the tops of the wings in their grooves. Therefore the wings must end higher than the architecture and their upper portions must have part of the sky painted on them as well as the urns. If now we follow this level back in perspective to the backscene we find it agrees exactly with the level of a line across at the spring of the arch in that backscene. This line also runs along the top of the moulding just under the balustrades in the side features flanking the upper story. Here, then, it appears the cut between the upper and lower flats of the backscene came. The remainder of the architecture above would be painted on a deep border or upon a pair of upper flats—which, we cannot decide—but no central dividing line is shown.

Turning now to the more tenuous conclusions latent in the drawing. The first is based on the relatively small number of wings—only three pairs are shown (apart from the pair in front about which we wish to speak later). The design is therefore not ruled out of possibility for an English theatre whose stages commonly used shallower sets than those on the Continent.

If these wings, now, were considered as being masked at the top by normal straight borders, it is very clear that the deepest border would cut right across the upper story of the backscene and quite obscure it. This is unthinkable: the scene in the drawing cannot be one of the 'horizontal' sort; it must be of a different make-up. If the borders were arched sky borders, then the upper backscene might be revealed as shown, and the whole scheme becomes reasonable to stage.

Next, let us turn to the front of the drawing at the top. The proscenium opening is shown as having a large three-centred arch, with a thickness decorated with built or painted coffering. Behind it hangs just the sort of swagged proscenium border that we shall see in Hogarth's painting, later to be considered and reproduced in Pl. 30. Before the arch is a very remarkable feature which appears to be a sort of 'glory' surrounding figures upholding a coat of arms with reasonably complicated quartering where, upon the lower, dexter quarter, a harp is very strongly suggested. This whole feature projects markedly below the proscenium arch at its centre.

One theatre in London had a very similar proscenium arch with a curved head, a decorated thickness and a feature in front projecting down below the arch at its centre, portraying a glory with figures supporting a coat of arms with complicated quartering including the Irish harp of the royal arms. This theatre was Vanbrugh's Opera House. A reference to this new theatre will form the subject of our next item of evidence to be noted as soon as we have finished with the present drawing. In the meantime we may say that Vanbrugh's Opera House, built in 1705, has possibly the most obscure history of all contemporary theatres so far as its interior disposition went. It was frequently altered. Such prints as we have of it date from 1792 (see *The Carlton House Magazine* for 1st February), when we have a somewhat crude engraving which, however, shows a proscenium head remarkably like the one in the drawing.

Yet an inscribed water-colour signed William Capon, in a private collection, and marked as showing the Opera House as it was in 1785, shows a quite different proscenium opening with a square head. It adds that this building was burnt in 1789. Therefore we suppose the Opera House had a square-headed opening for some period just before 1789 but that after 1792, at least, it had an arch resembling that in the water-colour we are discussing. It may be that the water-colour belongs to this late date, yet its style scarcely suggests this, and we have no other evidence of two-storied backscenes after 1736. This drawing sorts better, we feel, with early eighteenth-century styles of work. Does it then represent the Opera House in a form before it was altered by Novosielski in 1785, and in a form which, oddly enough, *was returned to* later after the fire—even so closely as to revive the encroaching 'glory' above?

If so (and it is admittedly a stiff condition), then this may be a scene in the Haymarket Opera House.

But the most notable feature of the drawing and, if it is proved, the most revealing, lies in the nearest pair of wings. We have confidently spoken of the arched head of the proscenium opening above, but the careful reader will have observed by now that this nearest pair of wings *comes in front of the proscenium*. The detail on the wings matches generally that on the deeper wings, but the tone is heavier and there are two marked differences:

first, that the nearest wings have no upper feature crowned with urns, second, that unlike the rest they bear each a projecting statue.

Can there be found in English theatre records any justification for the placing of wings outside the scene and before the proscenium sides? Remarkably enough, there can. On at least two occasions we find the same curious phrase in the opening stage-directions of an opera; the one is in the 1674 edition of *The Tempest; or, The Enchanted Island*, produced at Dorset Garden, and the other in Dryden's *Albion and Albanius*, produced in 1685 and also at Dorset Garden. In the former we read: 'The front of the Stage is open'd, and the Band of 24 Violins, with the Harpsicals and Theorbo's which accompany the Voices, are plac'd between the Pit and the Stage. While the Overture is playing, the Curtain rises, and discovers a new Frontispiece, joyn'd to the great Pylasters, on each side of the Stage.' Interesting as is the reference to the placing of the orchestra here, it is the last sentence which concerns us most. This is almost exactly echoed in the later extract (from *Albion and Albanius*), which reads: 'The Frontispiece. The Curtain rises, and a new Frontispiece is seen, joyn'd to the great Pylasters which are on each side of the Stage.'

Just what did these frontispieces look like, and how were they joined to the great pilasters? What the great pilasters were is pretty certain to those who remember the proscenium of Dorset Garden theatre as shown in the illustrations to *The Empress of Morocco*; they stood either side of the proscenium opening, flat against the side-walls, and were possibly repeated (as in Wren's 'Drury Lane' section) between the proscenium doors in the sides.

The appearance of the frontispiece in *The Tempest* is described in the direction thus:

This Frontispiece is a noble Arch, supported by large wreathed Columns of the Corinthian Order; the wreathings of the Columns are beautifi'd with Roses wound round them, and several Cupids flying about them. On the Cornice, just over the Capitals, sits on either side a Figure, with a Trumpet in one hand, and a Palm in the other, representing Fame. A little farther on the same Cornice, on each side of a Compass-pediment, lie a Lion and a Unicorn, the Supporters of the Royal Arms of England. In the middle of the Arch are several Angels, holding the King's Arms, as if they were placing them in the midst of that Compass-pediment.

Now this is not an exact description of what we see in the unidentified water-colour at the British Museum, but it is so remarkably similar in general that one is very much inclined to consider seriously whether we may not have in the latter an illustration of one of these special, temporary frontispieces. The differences are that in the British Museum drawing the front wings match those of the set and are not an independent frame, and that they seem not to be part of a complete arch but only to supply the sides, with the existing arch of the theatre appearing over their heads. (But this may be a painted border and so throw down our whole ascription to the Opera House while yet increasing the belief that this is a special frontispiece.) Yet we may remember that in early scenery there often was to be found a tendency to ally a scene with the architecture of the auditorium on occasion rather than attempt to distinguish between them. This function the arrangement in the drawing would well perform.

Further: if these frontispiece sides were arranged not against the most distant pair of pilasters flanking the deep Restoration forestage, but against either of the nearer pairs, they would then serve to mask the proscenium doors. Now, proscenium doors are not generally needed in opera—being rather a characteristic of the dramatic stage—and both the shows we have quoted above were operas, and the theatre to which we have tentatively ascribed the British Museum drawing was an opera house. Moreover, it was an opera house which did not consistently succeed in its policy of presenting opera and frequently, after the opening, had recourse to dramatic presentations. These would need the proscenium doors, and such doors were at some time built in Vanbrugh's house. When they were there, the arrangement of such a temporary frontispiece as we have been considering would hide them admirably and restore the opera atmosphere in any return to original policy.

If it in fact masked the dramatic doors (which would still be available for entrances through the wings), such a temporary frontispiece, joined to the great pilasters, would fully enable the whole of the deep forestage to be used in the presentation of the spectacle without the singers being forced to 'come forward out of the picture'. This playing upon the threshold of the picture instead of within it was reserved for actors in the dramatic stage where the spectacle was far less significant than in opera, and where the personal player with all his fine nuances of expression and character in close contact with the audience was of great significance.

The theatre student may object to the above theory, saying that the frontispiece sides in this arrangement would only mask the doors from the centre seats—from the sides the audience would look across and glimpse them clearly (again, though possibly only by chance, a perfect illustration of the point is to be found in Hogarth's painting in Pl. 30). But we shall have occasion to show that such discontinuity in side-masking seems to have been a feature of early stages, and apparently disconcerted the spectators not one whit.

There is one oddity in the two above quotations concerning special frontispieces—namely, that they are said not to be revealed till the curtain rose. The curtain, then, hid them. How could this be since we know the curtain position was normally *behind* the proscenium (and its pilasters) altogether? An obvious solution is that the curtain, for operatic occasions, might be moved and brought forward. If it was of that system of working in which the ascension is performed by gathering it on vertical lines in bunches up to the top (sometimes called a 'french valance' or 'festoon' system), and not by any method of rolling or 'flying', then this system could as perfectly well be worked if the curtain were hung to the front of the forestage as it could were the curtain at the back.

By such an arrangement a dramatic stage with its deeper forestage and its essential, Elizabethan public-theatre tradition could be easily and effectively transformed into a stage of the entirely opposite category—a 'picture stage' of the masque type with the whole scene close to the audience and framed in a special frontispiece. All intervening doors and boxes would be hidden.

Thus would be achieved an adaptability of stage that theatre-planners of today are racking their brains to bring forth—to answer the terms of an identical problem!

Finally, a word on the two figures projecting from the nearest wings. Proscenium statues were a curious but characteristic feature of certain early-eighteenth-century theatres in England. We find a number of examples of them—one of the best is in Pl. 35. It will be seen that these characteristic figures are *closely associated with the proscenium* rather than with the scene.

A profound and intriguing problem is offered us in the working of early stages. It seems that we must, in the present state of our knowledge, be content with the awareness that it may have been considerably different both from what we commonly suppose and from our own methods; we must therefore seek for every indication in later evidence that can throw any light backwards upon early technique.

It seems, too, that this is a matter where the brave research-worker must go on and, following the example of illustrious predecessors, risk blunders. The field is too large for him always to keep his mouth shut until knowledge is certain, for then he holds up the research of others who may see where he fails and can build from his puzzles. We must be content with an unfinished picture across whose obscurities we have, as yet, too often to write 'We do not know'.

The new London theatre or opera house was built by Vanbrugh in the Haymarket in 1705, making (as far as we know) the third theatre with Drury Lane and Lincoln's Inn Fields open to the playgoers of the metropolis in the first decades of the eighteenth century (Dorset Gardens was largely abandoned by now, and Sadler's Wells was as yet not more than a music house).

To this opera house in the Haymarket, Steele makes reference in our next note which comes from the 14th *Spectator*, 1709. His reflection concerns the looseness of handling of wings in scene-changes and is in the form of a compliment to Powel's marvellous Puppet Stage, of which he says: 'As to the mechanism and scenery, every thing indeed was uniform, and of a piece, and the scenes were managed very dexterously; which calls on me to take notice, that at the Haymarket, the undertakers forgetting to change the side scenes, we were presented with a prospect of the ocean in the middle of a delightful grove; . . .'

That one might in a professional theatre *forget* to change one's wings is a remarkable reflection.

But Powel's famous puppet show has another claim to a place in our review. A print of it has been left us and—what is especially significant—left in two forms where, though one seems clearly pirated from the other, the evidence conveyed in each is of strikingly different value. Both show the stage and the same scene set upon it, but one (see Pl. 28) gives the kind of representation of stage scenery which is far too often made, and where no detail of the make-up of the setting is recognizable but the whole thing faked to look unlike scenery. In especial is the space at the top utterly un-communicative; it would seem to promise to an investigator that no such theatrical realities as borders were ever used. This print is reproduced in Duchartre's *The Italian Comedy*, 1929, but no source is given.

The other print (which is from *A Second Tale of a Tub*, 1709), superficially similar though reversed from left to right, is of an entirely different school of honesty (see Pl. 27); here the typical appearance of the upper part of a stage scene is shown in faithfulness and the print becomes a document of its time.

It is remarkable to think that many of the other prints we now possess may owe their lack of clarity as technical evidence to a whim to prettify actualities and improve upon the true appearance of the stage, and may at one time have existed in a more detailed rendering which would have told us far more of the story but which was suppressed by a publisher in the interests of the picturesque. These two prints are evidence that we may often find the essentials left out of stage records.

Examining the puppet-stage print which shows us the borders in detail we find four things of importance to note in it. Firstly, it proves the use of footlights in 1709 quite unmistakably. Secondly, it shows a set of four pairs of wings bearing statues in niches and the first pair crowned with a balus-trade while the tops of the rest are hidden by a set of four cloud borders with cut edges. (The curious truncated wings of the other print are now explained; they appear to leave off indefinitely in the air, while in truth they disappeared behind the clouds.) Thirdly, concerning these borders, we have a clear example of the traditional clouds dragged in to mask the top of a scene of architecture with little regard for naturalism. Lastly, we see a simple flat scene at the back representing a wall with niches.

Some surprise may be felt at the use of borders (at any rate in such number) on a stage designed for marionettes where, it seems, they would interfere with the freedom of movement of the puppets. In this connexion Mr. George Speaight has made (in *Puppetry*, 1944–5) an ingenious interpretation of their positions based on evidence suggested in the print, which does largely away with this difficulty and allows for the puppeteer's bridges.

A somewhat similar example of the suppression of evidence to that in the Powel print comes in a caricature of Hogarth's from 1723. It is of considerable importance, even in its 'improved' state, as a record of a typical scene of its time. But when we come to consider another print from the same plate, now in the British Museum and representing an earlier state of the engraving, we find that Hogarth's uncompromising faithfulness was originally even better exemplified—for the first state shows the join between the two halves of the flat scene. In the later state this line is burnished out! The print is a caricature of the singer Senesino, and others, performing foreign opera in London, and in its representation both of typical scenery and typical stage costume is of high significance (see Pl. 32).

Typical stock wings bearing columns are shown, and in the background appears a large arch in front with a back arch beyond and farthest of all a landscape. It is quite possible that such a scene would be represented in three distinct planes, for the Covent Garden Inventory of 1743 lists both the 'arch' and the 'back arch' of the same palace scene as different flats, and then suggests the existence of a backing to stand behind these. Compare the example in Fig. 5 showing a similar arch and backing.

Hogarth's strict truth of statement makes him an excellent source of evidence. In turning to our next reference—a picture of 1731—we shall see that the evidence may turn out to be the earliest actual representation of grooves we possess after the Restoration. We may, however, only guardedly apply the evidence to the public theatre, for the picture in question records a children's performance in a private house. There is, however, much to show that on some other counts the presenters of this little show kept surprisingly close to professional technique, and thus it may well be that the evidence of the picture has application also to the public theatre—and if so, it offers an important piece of new information.

The picture is William Hogarth's painting of the performance by young Lord Sempster, Lady Caroline Lennox, Lady Sophia Fermor, and Miss Conduit (prompted by Dr. Desaguliers) of a play of Dryden's; the painting was engraved in 1792, when the title was *The Indian Emperor, Or the*

Conquest of Mexico; Act 4. Scene 4. As performed in the year 1731, at Mr. Conduit's, Master of the Mint, before the Duke of Cumberland &c. From the original Picture in the Collection of Lord Holland. The painting itself is now darkened with age, but the engraving preserves many delicate details —among them a piece of information of the first importance concerning backscenes. See Pl. 30 and the especially significant detail enlarged in Pl. 31.

We see a very low, simple platform arranged at one end of a private room and faced by a group of adults and children watching the performance. Upon the stage are four children playing in costume, a prompter, and a collection of scenery.

It is clear at once that we may rely in this picture upon Hogarth's well-attested accuracy of portrayal. He makes no attempt (unlike the print publishers) to improve the scene upon the stage or to make it look like a real prison instead of a set of painted pieces. Further, since this is an informal occasion and takes place in a normal dwelling-room not specially equipped, certain theatrical elements have been left aside as unnecessary; among these being, most fortunately for us, the masking elements at the top. Again, Hogarth makes no attempt to hide any inadequacy, but portrays for us with candid care all the usually hidden features of the tops of the scenery; and among these one that especially concerns us.

The backscene consists of an interior wall in a prison or castle. Its centre is occupied by a door surmounted by an arched and grilled opening and flanked by stone piers. These piers rise to the top of the scene. Above the top of the scenery the frieze and cornice of the normal decoration of the actual room beyond may be clearly seen. But the stone pier beside the prison door does not reach as far as this frieze. There intervenes an extremely curious, horizontal, dark band running across at the level of the top of the backscene, but apparently (from the evidence of what appears to be pretty careful drawing) running in a plane *intermediate between the farthest wing and the backscene.* The end of the band is hidden behind the wing, but the backscene appears to be cut off at its top by the band. It is highly unlikely that the band is some painted feature of the prison wall, since the thicknesses of the painted pier and arch are cut by it, yet no attempt is made to suggest any set-back of edge as the band traverses these 'steps' in surface, nor to cut off the thicknesses with a perspective line to simulate where they reach the undercut face of a projecting band.

Every other object in this carefully observed and very literal picture is understandable after study save only this one dark band, but it, I believe, is wholly incapable of explanation unless upon the following lines:

It will be seen that the dark band is associated with a wider grey band above it; the lower, darker band stands to the upper in exactly the same relation as the receding lower edge of a horizontal beam to its upright frontal face.

The suggestion here advanced is that this is, in fact, a beam, bearing along its lower face a set of grooves, and that it is temporarily placed here so as to support the backscene whose upper edge runs in this groove, and that its presence was essential to enable the backscene to be changed since no other means existed of changing such a scene than by sliding its two halves apart sideways like the shutters of the masques.

Certain criticisms of this suggestion will now have to be met; the first is that the beam appears unnecessarily massive. But it has a very considerable span to cover; it must not be supported save near its ends else when the scene is opened the supports would show; and it must not in the slightest degree sag, or the scene would jam and not slide freely. Further, it is to be presumed, I think, that such an elaborate setting as is shown here would not have been specially made for one single children's performance but is likely to have been hired or borrowed from a theatre. If, on the other hand, this is not true and the scene was specially built, then it is likely to have been entrusted to an experienced stage carpenter rather than to have been made the subject of especial invention and design by a novice. Hence it would most likely have followed normal stage procedure. If in point of fact it came from a theatre, then, as we already know, early upper grooves might be called upon not only to sustain the tops of backscenes but also upon occasion to support the considerable weight of the front edge of an *upper stage* serving as the floor to a glimpse into heaven or some other elevated playing-place (see above, Pl. 5). Thus such a groove would have to be cut in timber of pretty considerable dimensions. The size of the timber is then not disproportionate.

A further objection might be raised that it is all very well to argue that this is a groove in which the two halves of the backscene might slide apart, but where is the space into which the drawn-back pieces could slide, since the walls of the room appear so close? A consistent reply is, however, forthcoming even to this, for we shall see later that various shifts were resorted to when the narrowness of wing-space forbade the full drawing of the scenes. One of these, used a century later at Ipswich, was to cut the backscene not into halves but into four vertical parts giving a set of narrow pieces much more like our own flats of today, and enabling the scenes to be carried much more easily when on tour. Sometimes, also, a pair of flats was built purposely narrow, and then its width was made up by the addition of matching 'close-ins' when that scene was used on a wider stage. But if this were so we ought to be able to trace signs of such subdivisions in Hogarth's painting. The remarkable thing is that there they undoubtedly are—one just to the spectator's right of the left-hand hoop of candles, the other running up a little to the left of the centre of the same hoop. These lines are unbroken and cut arbitrarily through all the features of the painting—they clearly represent joins and not details of the painted architecture.

In further corroboration we may anticipate again to say that we shall find an identical arrangement to this in all respects with signs of its presence surviving to within my own memory (and possibly to today but for bombing) in the Prince's Theatre, Bristol, as we shall note on p. 395. At Bristol the arrangement might appear a latter-day invention which never found much favour, but the fact now stands out that it was a technique resembling in every essential that used in the time of Hogarth on this private stage in Mr. Conduit's house.

Finally, it might be objected that no similar beam or piece of timber is suggested at the heads of any of the wings as would be expected were the normal groove-system to have been used as in the later court masques. I reply to this that we know for certain that very frequently even the masques were presented in such a way that the side-scenes or wings—scenically less important elements—remained set throughout the show and only the back-scene suffered change. Indeed, a comparable changing of wings was rare and elaborate. One may well imagine a children's performance being content with standing wings and reserving its scene-changes to the essential opening of the backscenes.

On the whole it seems that the above suggestion, that Hogarth has given us in this painting the first pictorial representation of the English groove known to us, is not ill founded. We may now take a final step: granted the correctness of the identification, the following new item in the history of the English groove is confirmed and may be stated in the following way.

For reasons which we shall see later the groove during much the greater part of its career was a bipartite thing, existing as two separate ends with a gap in the centre between them. In point of fact, the present is the only pictorial reference to a continuous, upper, backscene groove that I am able to make (except for earlier references in the masque plans, which are all concerned with continuous grooves). Since all subsequent references will be to *pairs* of grooves—that is to their being divided in the centre by a gap —it would seem that a continuous groove may have been known in the early Restoration theatre like that of the masques but that this continuous groove went out sometime after 1731.

The objection to a continuous groove spanning the stage at the level of the top of the normal backscenes is that upon the occasion of the use of a high set with arch-borders (like that of Thornhill's at the beginning of this chapter) the empty groove would stretch across the stage like a bare perch across a bird-cage. How such an objectionable intrusion came to be avoided we shall see later.

Another point in the present picture which is shown very clearly indeed is what was (owing to an apparent over-punctilious modesty) burnished out of the Hogarth caricature of Senesino of 1723—namely, the join down the centre of the backscene. In Pl. 31 it is recorded very clearly indeed (a record almost unique in English theatre iconography) running down behind the left-hand candle of the group jutting into the right side of the detail. This crack appears to be shown in such uncompromising fidelity that even its variations in thickness are visible—variations between the thickness immediately above the door, where the stiles of the flats may have warped, and the thickness between the two leaves of the door itself, which would be two separate hinged pieces and thus offer a different edge from that of the flat itself. In this sort of 'human' inequality there is an authenticity that will go straight to the heart of anyone who has ever dealt directly with scenery.

The engraving does not stop even here in its faithfulness. An enlarged photograph shows what was not immediately apparent even in the original print: namely, how the cut-canvas 'iron' bars above the door were held in place—and the method is exactly what we would use today over two centuries later—by glueing 'invisible' net behind. We are thus informed that this grilled lunette is cut out, or 'open', and that a light in the corridor outside could be seen through when it was in use on the stage. We may even notice that the lit 'thickness' to the top of this arch was not a real thickness-piece but only painted on the flat—for the net which supports the bars does not stretch across this lighter passage of stonework.

Much else of first interest remains in the print (and possibly more in the original painting): the profile proscenium-statues, the rich, cut-drapery border above, the ingenuities of the perspective on the wings—and we know not how much more which lack of knowledge prevents our recognizing.

There is important material for our history of the flat scene in the skit of Henry Fielding's called *Tumble-Down Dick; or, Phaeton in the Suds*, performed in 1736 at the New, French, or Little Theatre in the Haymarket (opened opposite the opera house in 1720). Here to begin with we find an announcement of the play, ending with a satiric flourish: 'And the Scenes painted by the Prodigious Mynheer Van Bottom-flat.'

This brings a group of very interesting suggestions to our notice. The first is the mention of the scene-painter at all. Today the name of the scene-painter is scarcely ever mentioned even upon the programmes, let alone in the preliminary flourishes to a play. We may have a more or less considerable acknowledgement of the scene-designer, but never now of the man who put the designs on scene canvas and made them pieces of theatre. The scene-painter today marches with the labourers or the contractors, while the designer of the scenery may never lay brush to flat in the whole course of the show's preparation. In those days the scene-painter was both designer and executant.

But in this satiric puff of Fielding's there is more to be found in the name which he gives to his scene-painter than in the fact that he mentions a name at all.

To begin with he makes him a Dutchman—or gives him a foreign name at least, alluding to the number of continental painters then at work in England—thereafter he bestows the surname upon him of Flat and finally adds the specific first-name of Bottom—Mynheer Van Bottom-flat.

Whatever the finer significances in this name, one fact stands out strongly as relevant to our present interest. We are to presume that the noun *flat* had at length come into its own in the theatre. Here is the painter and he is named after what he paints—the flat. And from this occasion I date the earliest use of the word *flat* as a special technical noun at present known to me.

It is with some relief that I welcome the entrance of this noun into the story, for before this date a conscientiously scientific historian ought to have avoided using the word, since it was not hitherto in current use. Yet it is so essential an item of any theatre technician's vocabulary that he gets on ill without it; and it may slip in before its date to the most careful of essays, for the noun *flat* is the only name really to give to these successors of Jones's shutters. To call them 'that variety of flat scene which parted in the middle', or 'which was not a drop' is impossibly cumbersome; no term can properly designate what is indicated here save the term *flat* or perhaps *pair of flats*. The flat is the essence of the anatomy of scenery.

But what are we to deduce from the curious adjective that forms the first name of this fictitious scene-painter?

After the evidence offered above on the use of two-story backscenes in the early English theatre I believe it is quite likely that Fielding's *Bottom Flat* was something more than a fancy name. Moreover, if this theory of the continuation into the public Restoration theatre of Inigo Jones's system of upper and lower backshutters, or flats, be correct, then it can be well understood that the appellation of a scene-painter would be more likely to allude to the bottom flats than to the top flats, since of their nature the top flats would most likely be mere examples of simple cloud painting (though in special scenes there is, of course, no end to the possibilities of what they might represent), while the lower pair of flats would be the proper province of the showy painter—they would bear the chief design.

The interest of *Tumble-Down Dick* is not, however, exhausted at this point. There is this very pertinent passage in which *Machine* is speaking to *Prompter*:

Mach: Are all the Rakes and Whores ready at *King's* Coffee-House?

Promp: They are ready, Sir.

Mach: Then draw the scene. Pray, let the Carpenters take care that all the Scenes be drawn in exact Time and Tune, that I may have no bungling in the Tricks; for a Trick is no Trick, if not perform'd with great Dexterity. Mr. *Fustian*, in Tragedies and Comedies, and such sort of things, the Audiences will make great Allowances; but they expect more from an Entertainment; here, if the least thing be out of Order, they never pass it by.

Fust: Very true, Sir, Tragedies do not depend so much upon the Carpenters as you do.

(Whereas 'Painting and Carpentry'—sneered Ben Jonson—'are the soule of Masque'.)

There is much worth pondering in the above passage. Noteworthy is the instance it gives of the Great Scenic Controversy in its distinction between the two types of show, dramatic 'tragedies and comedies' on the one hand, and the contemporary pantomime on the other. In the former, tricks and scenic effects were held in low regard and actually with jealous loathing: the latter depended 'upon the carpenters'.

It should be noted that even the drawing of the scenes was a matter for nice timing, and was as prejudicial to the show if ill-judged as a badly timed curtain is with us today. It is not clearly enough realized by literary commentators on the Restoration and eighteenth-century drama, who decry the technique of presentation—and especially the stage-directions and the systems of entrances and discoveries and of visible scene-change—as puerile and undeveloped, that the whole arrangement of the setting of shows not only admitted, but was designed to exploit, a nicely-thought-out and long-traditioned system of staging that offered much to dramatic effect; but that is not surprising for few beside technicians of the theatre realize today the exactly parallel value to a scene of the timing of the curtain. It 'may be of the subtlest value to a show, or may make just as subtle mischief if over-looked or bungled. . . . Here is a point of which the non-critical mind rarely sees the importance. He will sit back as the lights go up and say "My! that was a fine scene!" And that is all you want him to say. It may none the less be true that what contributed the final touch to his enthusiasm was a faultlessly-timed curtain closing at exactly the right speed, and to a heart's beat at exactly the right moment.' (Richard Southern, *Stage Setting*, Faber, 1937, p. 104.)

Just this element of true theatre could reside also in the drawing of scenes 'in exact time and tune'. It is a very pertinent injunction, and one obviously from a man who understood the theatre. It is technically as important to

[195]

stage-managers as Hamlet's speech to the players is to actors. And the need for this timing in the eighteenth century was greater even than today, for then the 'scenes' closed so much more frequently than the modern curtain, and so much more patently, and, instead of being in one unit, they were in two independently controlled halves.

But the final shaft of interest from *Tumble-Down Dick* is towards the end of the play. There we have full confirmation of at least one of the points we made on the name, Van Bottom-flat. We find that the noun *flat* was undoubtedly used, alone, and in the singular, to denote the parting back-scene. The passage runs:

> *Fust*: But pray how is *Phaeton* fall'n all this time?
>
> *Mach*: Why you saw him fall, did not you? And there he lies; and I think it's the first time I ever saw him fall upon any Stage. But I fancy he has lain there so long, that he would be glad to get up again by this time; so pray draw the first Flat over him. . . .

Here then is the word in indisputable use—established at last. Its application is clearly not yet the same one that it has today, but it is now certain that some time in the half-century between *Guzman* (1669) and Fielding (1736) the phrase *flat scene* was shortened into the word *flat* and that this *flat* descended to us today, suffering changes in the passage admittedly, but becoming the label of one of our basic pieces of scenery.

The quotation above also corroborates our deduction that flats were used at the front of the stage as well as at the back, for it contains the request to 'draw the *first* flat over him', that is, to close a flat scene at a part of the stage nearest to the audience, so hiding the larger area upon the centre of which poor Phaeton lay spread. The *first* flat is the *front* flat.

A little sidelight upon stage clouds (and seas) comes in 1737. It is pertinent here because of the curious attitude towards the top-masking of the scene which it implies; we see how nearly clouds and interior borders might be dismissed as the same thing—and thus we are closely reminded of the Powel print in Pl. 27. The reference is in an anonymous 'Tragi-Comi-Farcical Ballad Opera' called *The Rival Theatres; or a Playhouse to be Lett*, produced in 1737 at the Aungier Street Theatre, Dublin, and printed in that year and in that city. In one of the scenes representing the theatre two Managers speak with a Wardrobe-Keeper:

> *1st Man*: Here Wardrobe-Keeper, bring the Book of Accounts with you— Now Brother, you shall see how large our expenses are.
>
> *2nd Man*: Read the Articles.
>
> *W. Keeper*: Imprimis—a Cloud and a half, with the three odd waves.
>
> *1st Man*: What necessity could there be for them?
>
> *W. Keeper*: O dear Sirs, Clouds are the most useful things we can have; for they

must always appear to an Audience, tho' the Scene lay in a Bed-chamber; and with the Addition of the three odd Waves, we had now enough Waves to make a Sea.

The remark 'they must always appear to an Audience' suggests there was a popular appeal in stage clouds, and that at that time the theatrical sky was one of the fascinations in a visit to the theatre, promising spectacular effects and surprising disclosures. They still harked back to the romance of the novel cloud of John Ross in 1574. They *must* appear to an audience.

Our next reference brings us again to the grooves and belongs to the year 1743. Our last direct evidence of the groove was in the references to court shows between 1674 and 1690 (see p. 159). What follows is the first direct evidence of the use of grooves in the regular professional scenic theatre since its opening in 1661, and we have had to wait for eighty-two years after that date for confirmation of our theory. In the year 1743 John Rich, manager of Covent Garden (the Covent Garden that opened in 1732), assigned the original lease to a Martha Launder as security for a mortgage of £1,200, and in the papers is an inventory of scenic material on the premises at the time.

This Covent Garden Inventory of 1743 is at once one of the most important and the most baffling documents in the history of English scenery. It has been printed in full by H. Saxe Wyndham in *The Annals of Covent Garden Theatre from 1732 to 1897* (2 vols., 1906) as an Appendix in vol. ii, p. 309. (Though not without certain small textual errors, the commonest of which is the printing of 'hill' for 'hell' and 'tint' for 'tent'.) The document is unfortunately too long to reproduce in detail here, though the total of its intriguing items forms as fascinating a puzzle picture as any theatre student could wish to find, but several details must be referred to as of great importance to our review.

We will take first the three references to grooves which are to be found in the inventory. Among the properties listed as being in the 'First Flies'— that is, the first or lower fly-floor; large theatres might have more than one of these galleries each side the stage—are

12 top grooves with 6 iron braces and ropes.

In the first place this is final evidence that grooves were used in public theatres; they become unassailably a part of English professional theatre-craft. Now let us examine this item in detail.

The grooves mentioned are *top* grooves (we shall find bottom grooves later in the inventory), that is, they were suspended above, presumably groove-surface downwards, and held the tops of the scenes. They are mentioned as being 'in the First Flies'—the description is not confined to suggesting that they were merely stored there; they were presumably fixed there permanently as their proper position. How they were fixed we have no detailed evidence for the moment.

There are twelve of them; presumably therefore there were six a side on Covent Garden stage—which is a bigger number than is shown on any of Jones's plans: there the limit was four a side. Hence Covent Garden could stage scenes with six pairs of wings which is a reasonably large number for an early English theatre. We rarely use as many as six a side today—but today it must be remembered we can set them at a more economical angle and so save on their number—and further, we use them wider now than they used to do, as I shall show later. In confirmation of the above, we find elsewhere in the inventory mentions of sets of twelve wings, that is six pairs in each set.

When we come to the six iron braces we are puzzled. Presumably the braces were used to help suspend the twelve sets of grooves, but why are there only six? Were the grooves so big that they stretched right across the stage, and one brace could support two grooves? Were half the grooves of a different nature from the other half, heavier in character and so needing more support? Either may be possible but they are only guesses.

We have here to call attention to a terminological difficulty that we shall have to meet more than once; was the term 'groove' used to cover one groove only or a number of grooves connected in one group, or was a 'set' of grooves the whole collection of groups of grooves needed for a given stage? For instance, in this item under consideration, does one single, so-called 'groove' of the twelve consist of a composite piece bearing more than one actual groove—such as the multiple piece we shall find later in the Bristol Theatre Royal, illustrated in Pl. 37? Or was there now only one groove in each position? If the former, how many grooves constituted each unit at Covent Garden? Was the number different in different units? Were there more or fewer down-stage than up-stage, that is to say in the front or nearer sets than in the more distant? Were wing-grooves different from backscene-grooves? To which class did these belong—or were they composite? These questions it is useless to attempt to study without fuller information to be gleaned from later methods, but they raise points we must bear in mind.

Though we have not at present enough data to answer these queries, we must bear in mind that possibilities are open for one of a number of answers in each case. We have a lot to learn before the groove system becomes perfectly clear. It has elaborate complications.

The second item in the inventory concerning grooves informs us that on the stage itself were to be found—

30 bottom grooves of different sizes.

At first this seems to be a staggering number. If there were only twelve top grooves, what point could there be in no less than thirty bottom grooves? And what can 'of different sizes' imply?

If I am to venture any explanation of this I shall have to anticipate for a moment. We shall learn later that in at least one theatre in England—the Theatre Royal, Plymouth—it is certain that the top grooves were connected in sets making a series of multiple units each of the same sort as the unit at Bristol, but that those below on the stage, although arranged in sets to correspond, had certain of the individual grooves built separately and removable from their neighbours. The reason for this we shall see later.

If this were also true of Covent Garden in 1743, then we may perhaps be forgiven for making the following pure guess: There are said to be twelve top sets—that is six a side. Each set may contain one or more individual grooves. But if the bottom grooves were, each groove, separate, then we can understand that there might be thirty individual grooves (not sets) below. That means fifteen a side. If the first three positions either side had two grooves each, lying together and making a unit, that would leave eighteen grooves to be divided up among the up-stage three pairs—that is to say three to each position.

Turning now to the last mention of grooves in the inventory, we find that here we meet something different in nature; we read:

A barrel, groove and wts to trees in Orpheus . . . an old woman and grooves in Faustus, a trophy, a rock and grooves, rape . . .

These are all classified under 'Properties, &c., contained in the Cellar'. Here we have the word 'groove' in the singular; this may offer warning that what we have now may be different from what we have just discussed. Nothing in the cellar under the stage is of any use to a show unless it has some connexion with what goes on above on the stage—either by rising to it or by some other action. A groove below the stage suggests a means of moving something up to that stage. This vertical employment of groove technique is not new to our study; in our earliest reference we decided we had an indication of a single groove as a railway for a moving (perhaps rising) cloud at Elizabeth's court. Again, in the legends upon the plans for *Salmacida Spolia* we have encountered vertical grooves which held a 'crosse peece of tymber to which ye seate was fastened'. Here at Covent Garden we have presumably something of the same sort—a vertical groove in which an object rose, and for this object we have not far to seek; in the first item it was 'trees in Orpheus'. We know that in the pantomime of *Orpheus and Eurydice* at Covent Garden one of the effects consisted in the magical rising of trees by degrees from the earth. This then is a definitely specialized groove employed for a certain effect; we are led to imagine that what we have here is the ancestor of that intriguing accessory, the *sloat*, or *slote*, or slot, by which rising scenery was worked in the Victorian period.

Associated with this groove and the tree-pieces are two other articles— a 'barrel' and 'wts'. These presumably were part of a counterweight system.

The second of this group of items is perhaps the most picturesque of all— 'an old woman and grooves in Faustus'. *Dr. Faustus* was always a spectacular show, lending itself to rising visions—here is one of them. But it has an added interest; if indeed the 'old woman' is truly a vision of an aged female and not a pet-name for some piece of apparatus, then it follows that in the vision where she appears no real woman was raised by a trap as we might suppose, but a cut-out, profile figure afterwards stored with the other scenery. There are other indications that all the figures seen on the Restoration stage (and indeed up to Victorian times) were not flesh and blood ones, and that frequently recourse was had to painting for special characters. Sabbattini has an amusing chapter on raising a painted, expandable ghost through the stage floor (Book 2, chap. 56).

He comes to mind again when we review the third item above—'a rock and grooves, rape'. This would appear to be an effect of a rising mountain in *The Rape of Proserpine*, a well-known piece of the time popularized by Rich. Maybe the manipulation had some reference to Sabbattini's in his Book 2, chap. 25.

We now turn to a matter in the inventory which demands a description of the way the items are listed. When we consider the document as a whole we find it is broken up so as to list various kinds of scene-piece in separate groups. This in itself is instructive; we find that the items of the full scenic investiture of a theatre's store were divisible into the following six categories, which are given below with a list of the parts of the theatre in which they were, on that particular occasion, to be found.

Flats

>Flats in the Scene Room
>Flats in the Top Flies
>Flats in the Shop

Back flats

>Back flats in Scene Room
>Back flats in Great Room
>Ditto in the Top Flies

Wings

>Wings in the Scene Room
>Wings in Great Room
>Do. in Painters Room
>Do. in the Shop

Pieces

Painted pieces in the Scene Room
Do. in Great Room
Do. in Yard
Painted peices in the first flies
Do. in the Top Flies
Do. in painting Room
Do. in Shop

Properties

Propertys in Scene Room
Properties in Great Room
Do. in the Yard
Do. in the first flies
Do. in Top flies
Do. in Roof
Properties in Painting Room
Do. in the Shop
Do., &c., contained in the Cellar
Do., &c., on the Stage

Stuff

Stuff in the Yard
Do. in Rope Room
In the flies
The Green Room
Candle Room
Properties continued

The categories then are Flats, Back Flats, Wings, Pieces, Properties, and —if it has any particular theatrical significance—Stuff. *Wings* we know (and may be interested to find here listed under that name and not any longer as 'side scenes'). *Pieces* we shall later learn from Rees are any odd bits of scenery that do not fit into the principal categories, for instance— '2 pieces transparent Hell, a balcony, old garden wall, . . . pedestall, front of gallery in Ariodante, a small palace border in do. . . . 7 open country peices, 4 orange trees in potts . . .', and so on and so forth. Borders and cloudings seem to be listed indiscriminately in this category or the next. *Properties* are usually well understood; they are generally items of portable odds-and-ends including almost anything beyond flat, painted scenery, for example— 'key and collar to the fly in Perseus, the scroll of 1000 crowns a month, 6 handles and 12 brackets for the sea . . . the great machine Jupiter and Europa, the curtain bell and line, a hook to draw off the cloudings, three lighting sticks . . . 7 waves not coverd, the cutt chariot in Sorcerer, a large modell of the Stage not finished, the thunder bell and line . . . 6 borders and 6 pair of cloudings fixt to battens with barrels, wts. and ropes . . . three frogs, one toad, one snail . . . 2 boars one stufft . . . Minerva's shield, 6 dancers chairs . . . 2 green lawyers bags, a stufft ham, the shield in Perseus of looking glass . . .', etc., etc., etc. *Stuff* seems to refer to items such as lamp-posts, swivels, muffle ropes, weights, and the like.

Thus we are left with the subjects of the first two categories to define—*Flats* and *Back Flats*; what is the distinction between them? It is pretty clear that some deliberate distinction is made, and perhaps the best way to approach a solution of the query is to list the items in these categories. This we may do as follows:

Flats in the Scene Room.
1. Cottage and long village.
2. Medusa's cave and 3 pieces Grotto that change to Country house.
3. Inside of Merlin's Cave.
4. outside of ditto.
5. dairy.
6. Hermitage.
7. Clock Chamber.
8. Farm Yard.
9. Country House.
10. Church.
11. town.
12. chimney chamber.
13. fort.
14. Rialto.
15. Harvey's hall.
16. Othello's new Hall.
17. Hell transparent and 2 peices.
18. Inn Yard.
19. Arch to Waterfall.
20. Back of Timber Yard.
21. Short Village.
22. Second Hell.
23. front of timber yard.
24. garden.
25. Short wood.

Flat in the Top Flies.
26. Ship Flat.

Flats in the Shop.
27. A large pallace arch.
28. an old low flat of a tower and church.
29. an open flat with cloudings on one side, and palace on the other.

Back flats in Scene room.
30. Harvey's palace.
31. Bishop's garden.

32. Waterfall.
33. long village.
34. long wood.
35. corn fields.
36. the arch of Harvey's palace.
37. back Arch of Ariodante's pallace.
38. a canal.
39. a sea port.

Back Flats in Great Room.
40. The flat to the arch and groves.
41. open country cloth.

Ditto in the Top flies.
42. The Sea back cloth.
43. the King's Arms curtain.

If now we seek to find what was the difference between a 'flat' and a 'back flat', we may begin by glancing through the lists and then considering, in the light of our knowledge of the make-up of a typical scene gained so far in our study, what element of normal scenery is omitted if we try to make up a scene with flats, wings, and pieces only.

It seems very clear that what would be missing (let us, for instance, consider such a scene as that in Hogarth's caricature of Senesino in Pl. 32) is that particular element which goes behind any large, single opening in the flats and so forms a backing—such as the landscape in the print just mentioned which shows beyond the back arch. This may well be what was termed a 'back flat' or backing flat. If this is a true reading of the matter, then the *flats* would generally be large surfaces in two parts, while *back flats* would generally be smaller surfaces probably in one part and made to back an opening in the flats—we can, for example, well imagine that the 'canal' and the 'sea port' in items 38 and 39 would fit perfectly into this definition and see them in Hogarth's scene in place of the landscape.

Some very slight confirmation of this theory is afforded by a couple of entries in another, much later, inventory from the Theatre Royal, Bristol, referring to about 1829. Here we find among many other items a pair of tent flats whose overall measurement is fortunately given; it is 16 ft. high by 19 ft. wide across the pair (the general dimensions of pairs of flats throughout the list is 16 ft. high and either 19 ft. or 20 ft. wide), but near to the item of the tent flats is an item of an unusual measurement, 14 ft. by 13 ft. This would clearly not fit into the grooves, and it is called '1 Star Piece to back the Tents'—perhaps, then, it was a 'back flat' in a single piece made to go with a pair of cut flats, and bearing a night sky.

If now we assume this theory of the nature of a back flat, let us examine the items of the Flat lists and Back Flat lists of the Covent Garden Inventory one by one.

Item 1. *Cottage and long village.* This adjective is still something of a puzzle. We have supposed a long scene to be one which stretched back into a recess behind the back grooves and having something in common with Jones's scenes of relieve. But here we find a long village listed as if all its parts were contained in one piece not—as we should most expect—consisting of a, possibly cut, flat with a row behind of painted pieces. But the accuracy of such an inventory is not beyond listing a flat as is done here and yet for that flat to need the addition of a series of pieces behind before it could be complete on the stage. It is difficult to see how flats in any interpretation could have been associated with a 'long scene' unless they were profiled or open flats (like those in Fig. 5). This may of course be the case here.

This is the only item of the whole twenty-nine concerning *flats* proper in which the word 'long' appears. The other examples of the adjective are in items 33 and 34, under *back flats.* The only supposition that will fit the theory is that here we have a pair of flats, partly occupied by a cottage, and partly cut away, which went in one of the front five sets of grooves and were designed to show a vista of village beyond, reaching to the depth of the stage.

But beyond this we must not lose sight of the fact that the classification in these lists may not be faultless. For it is clear that, however careful the compiler was, his system was occasionally abandoned, and items belonging properly to one category of scene-piece would get into the list belonging to another category. As instance of this we have at least two definite groups of *pieces* included in the first *flats* list: namely the '3 pieces Grotto that change to Country house' in item No. 2, and the '2 peices' mentioned with the Hell transparent in item 17. These could not have been *flats* if they were (as they are said to be) *pieces.* Similarly, later in the inventory we find *wings* and *borders* mentioned among the *Painted-pieces* lists, although wings at least have a set of lists to themselves later in the inventory, and borders even occur under the head of 'Properties'.

So we must bear in mind that it is not impossible that parts, at least, of the 'long village' may be wrongly classified here, and may belong properly to the 'pieces' lists.

Item 2. *Medusa's cave and 3 pieces Grotto that change to Country house.* Here is a most interesting item. It is, so far as my present knowledge goes, the only item of which we can by any stretch of imagination conceive the actual appearance. This we may do in the following way.

In 1730 Rich produced at Lincoln's Inn Fields (the forerunner of this Covent Garden) a pantomime called *Perseus and Andromeda.* The book of this pantomime was printed in 1738 with a pair of illustrations, possibly by Hogarth. One of these shows Medusa's cave, and before the entrance to the cave is a reasonably solid *piece*, or cut-out of scenery, against which is reclining the headless body of Medusa, while Pegasus flies aloft, presumably upon a machine.

It may well be that here we have a representation based on the actual scene-pieces mentioned in this inventory of 1743. That such a scene might have been brought with other scenes and properties from the old theatre to the new Covent Garden when Rich made his great transfer in 1732 is proved by the item in the list of *Properties in the Cellar* of '6 old iron rings and chains for branches brought from Lincoln's Inn'. This move was a great event, and was caricatured in both poem and cartoon at the time.

But why Medusa's cave should have, bracketed with it in the same item, this '3 pieces grotto that change to Country house' is not so simple a problem. As it is, we can but make a likely guess that here is itemized a piece of trick scenery, which stood as a threefold screen, and by means of hinged flaps suddenly transformed itself at a cue into a residence in the country. The working of such a piece it is not beyond our means to guess at, but is a little outside our study of orthodox scenery at the moment.

Items 3 and 4. The *Inside of Merlin's Cave* and the *outside of ditto*. These very definitely suggest two related pairs of flats, one a cut, rock-arch flat, and the other the backing to it. They may very well belong to *The Royal Chace; or, Merlin's Cave*, a pantomime produced at Covent Garden on 19 February 1736. Presumably the opening was fairly large and needed more than a single back flat to mask it—thus involving a full pair of flats.

Items 5 to 11. These next seven items contain little enough for us to expand upon. We can, at the moment, do nothing more than suppose them all to have been typical pairs of stock flats.

Item 12 is interesting in view of what we found in *Sir Patient Fancy*, since it is a chamber scene specifically designated a *chimney chamber*, and therefore reminding us of the cut chimney scenes, from the fireplace opening of which figures, having taken a hasty refuge, might peep forth with faces 'blackt'. Perhaps the *Clock Chamber* of item 7 was so called to distinguish it from the chimney chamber.

In this connexion we must note that if we were right in supposing that, as early as 1669, the flat scenes of *Guzman* were called flat to distinguish them from the scenes in several planes, then here we must allow an extension of the term to its more general, later use as any scene made of two framed pieces joining in the centre, whether they were 'cut' or not. The distinction is now not between—

plain flat scenes and {(a) cut flat scenes
                          with also
                          (b) relieves or 'long' scenes

as it seems to have been then, but between—

(*a*) plain flat scenes *with also* (*b*) cut flat scenes	and	relieves or 'long' scenes (that is, any scenes not composed primarily of a pair of flats).

Items 13 and 14 tell us little; we suppose them, in default of more information, plain painted flats.

Item 15 is interesting as exemplifying a custom that obtained at least up to 1880 (we shall find it in a log book of the Prince's Theatre, Bristol), namely that of labelling a scene by the name of its painter. *Harvey's Hall* is almost certainly a pair of flats representing a hall and painted by Harvey. Of Harvey we do not know a great deal, but among the information we have is a note in *The Daily Journal* for 18 September 1732 concerning the immediately prospective opening of the then new Covent Garden Theatre: 'We hear that Mr. Harvey and Mr. Lambert have been employed some time in painting the scenes for the new Theatre in Covent Garden', and E. L. Blanchard, in a review of *Scenery and Scene Painting* published in *The Era Almanack* for 1871, says (also of the new Covent Garden): 'Harvey, a landscape-painter, and Amiconi . . . executed the decoration of the proscenium, an allegory of Shakespeare, Apollo, and the Muses.'

Item 16 shows us another form of nicknaming: here the flats are labelled by the name of the play for which they were originally painted, not that of the artist who executed them: *Othello's new Hall*.

Item 17 (which Saxe Wyndham transcribes as '*Hill* transparent and 2 peices') is easy to guess at: presumably the flats showed something like what is seen in the later print of *Harlequin Everywhere*, 1779, also a pantomime of Rich's at Covent Garden, and the two 'peices' are two small cutouts that stood in front of it. The word 'transparent' pretty certainly indicates that a passage of the scene was cut away and filled in with translucent material, such as varnished silk, so that a light might be exhibited behind it for more dramatic effect. One imagines the passage might have shown flames.

I am not sure that all early theatrical uses of the word *transparent* signify the presence of this effect—a *transparency* as we should call it today. Often in the masques one is tempted to suppose that the significance of this word is merely *pierced*, or *with cut-out passages*.

Concerning the Georgian transparencies which were in point of fact passages of scenery rendered transparent (or more strictly 'translucent') by the insertion of areas of material such as varnished silk, reference may be made to the very detailed description of a 'transparent scene' by its designer, Thomas Lediard, which was quoted in an article by the present writer entitled 'Lediard and early 18th century Scene Design' in *Theatre Notebook*, vol. ii, p. 52. The occasion was a presentation at the Haymarket in 1732 of Lediard's *Britannia* (see Pl. 33). This strange Englishman, most of whose work was carried out in the Hamburg Opera, forms a landmark in the mostly undocumented period of the British seventeen-thirties. He was only recently rediscovered, and this particular number of *Theatre Notebook* was chiefly given to recording his rediscovery and discussing the nature of his work. His was, however, scene-design of an elaborate and unusual nature—not especially informative of everyday methods of normal stage procedure. An earlier transparency scene is apparently alluded to in the Warrants for Work on the Cockpit in Court for 25 January 1674/5: 'To make a Temple in the Cloudes with sceenes of Varnished silke & places for lights for ye same.' (See Boswell's *The Restoration Court Stage*, p. 236.)

Item 18, the *Inn Yard*, tells us nothing more than its name conveys.

Item 19, however, an *Arch to Waterfall*, is interesting in that one inclines to connect it with the item 32 in the list of *Back flats in the Scene Room*, and to picture a verdurous arch of trees or rocks, with possibly a pool below, set in one of the nearer sets of grooves, and cut out to disclose a glimpse beyond of the waterfall proper on another pair of flats in the back grooves. A perfect illustration is shown in Fig. 49 of M. J. Moynet's *L'Envers du Théâtre* (1873) where, though the item is dated as late as about 1834, it is styled as a 'décor anglais'.

Item 20 is presumably again a pair of backing flats, and since it is not in the lists of *Back flats*, we may imagine that though it was designed to back the cut-out item 23, *front of timber yard*, yet the latter was so widely cut out that it needed a full pair of flats for a backing.

Item 21, the *Short Village*. Here is a problem. It might have been simply a plain pair of flats with a village scene painted upon them, and have been called 'short' to distinguish it from the other village (item 33) composed of several pieces and reaching far back in a vista up the stage. Or it may have been such a pair of flats with an accompanying set of similar pieces, but the whole only designed to cover the space of a few groove-sets.

Item 22, the *Second Hell*, was probably a simpler version of item 17.

Item 23, see item 20.

Item 24, probably a straightforward pair of plain garden flats.

Item 25, *A Short wood*: similar remarks apply here as in item 21.

Up in the *Top Flies* was a *Ship Flat* (item 26). Why was it itemized in the singular? Possibly merely for shortness. I do not think there is any reason not to suppose the whole item consisted of a pair of flats as usual. Fielding used the word in the singular to express the pair forming a backscene, see above, p. 196. But what a pair of flats is doing in the top fly gallery, or how they got there, is more than I can guess.

Of the *Flats in the Shop* one might legitimately suppose (presuming this 'shop' to be the carpenter's) that they had gone for some structural reason, and were there for prospective extension, adaptation, or repair, and in fact we find:

Item 27 is *A large pallace arch*, and so may possibly be there to be cut down.

Item 28 is the opposite—*an old low flat of a tower and church*. This, equally possibly, might be there to undergo 'topping-up', so as to fit it to the normal groove-height. This use of the word 'low' is interesting in suggesting that there are no grounds for supposing that the term 'short scene' (as some might have supposed) meant a scene of little height, for the term here used to designate that quality is 'low' not 'short'.

Item 29—*an open flat with cloudings on one side, and palace on the other*— is perhaps a simple pair of cut flats, showing a palace towards the left or right side, and having the remainder occupied with profile clouds. On the whole it is, I think, not likely that the palace was on the back and the clouds on the front. Double-sided flats are known today, but they are very unsatisfactory, and are only to be found on very impoverished stages; and the difficulties of a double-sided open flat are greater still.

We now turn to the three lists of *Back Flats*.

The first, relating to those in the *Scene room*, begins with

Item 30, *Harvey's palace*; for Harvey, see item 15. This may well have been such a backing as was shown in Pl. 32.

Item 31, *Bishop's garden*, might be again a reference to a scene painter, though I have not been able to find one of that name at this date, or it might be the garden of an episcopal character in some play.

Item 32, see item 19.

Item 33, see item 21.

Item 34, see items 25 and 21.

Item 35, *corn fields*, tells us little beyond the name.

Item 36, *the arch of Harvey's palace*. Perhaps this would seem an exception to the theory that back flats were backings, for one can fall into the trap of supposing a palace arch must inevitably be large and on a full pair of flats, but here note that we have both *Harvey's palace* and *the arch of Harvey's palace* listed among back flats, but it is not impossible that there was a second, or back, arch in Harvey's palace (perhaps associated with item 15) having a backing behind it as in the quoted Hogarth print, and as is suggested by the next item:

Item 37, the *back Arch of Ariodante's pallace*, fits in well with the theory; it was presumably a cut flat to be set behind a larger and nearer arch no longer in the theatre's store, with a view of more distant parts of the palace beyond.

Ariodante was an opera of Handel's which, when it was 'put on again' on 8 January 1735, had the dancer Mme Sallé as a performer (according to Saxe Wyndham, vol. i, p. 45, but he gives no date of the first performance).

Items 38 and 39, *a canal* and *a sea port*, have been commented on briefly above.

The first item of the two *Back Flats in Great Room*, item 40, is puzzling; we have *The flat to the arch and groves*. One might be tempted to read *grooves* for *groves*, but one is little enlightened. And until one can gather which is *the arch*, it is a little dangerous to enlarge on what *the flat to* it might be.

Item 41 is, by comparison, both clear and interesting. It is not a pair of flats but a drop. It is called an *open country cloth*, and so seems sufficiently to define itself. Both this and the other two 'cloths' mentioned below are classed as Back Flats (they would perhaps be more strictly described as *flat scenes*). Some of the 'back flats' were clearly cloths, but I see no reason to suppose many were other than simple, single, framed flats.

Both the 'back flats' *in the Top flies* are presumably drops. Item 42 is *The Sea back cloth* (did it back a cut-out *ship flat*, such as item 26 might have been? And could it be crowned with pacific clouds in the upper flat-grooves above and then have these parted to reveal the rack of a tearing storm as the act developed . . .?) And item 43 is the somewhat puzzling *King's Arms curtain*; whether a royal coat or a public-house scene we may never know, but I am far more inclined to spurn the lower interpretation and suppose it heraldic—possibly a throne, or alcove, backing.

One thing is clear: we may now realize an amazing variety in the scenery of an early-eighteenth-century theatre—a variety not only in the subject of the scenes but in their form as well. Those who suppose all early theatres to have been cruder and less varied than ours are proved mistaken; here was variety enough, a very galaxy of shifting scenes and different dispositions.

When we consider the inventory for information on wings we are straightway furnished with a hint that bears out our theory of the different regard in which wings were originally held. One might have expected, after the very long list of flats which we have already considered, that the sets of wings would be roughly equal in number, but this is very definitely not so. We find that this theatre, though carrying no less than forty-three backscenes in its stock, yet could boast no more than nineteen sets of wings, to which we may add four more items included among the 'painted pieces' lists. Moreover, there is nothing like the speciality of character to be found in the labelling of the wings; almost every item is dismissed with a mere single word of description. Here they are extracted from the inventory and set in a list:

Wings in the Scene Room

1. 4 Ariodante's Pallace
2. 12 Harvey's Pallace
3. do. rock
4. do. wood
5. do. Atalanta's Garden
6.   teem (?)
7.   town
8.   tent
9.   Ceres
10.   Garden
11. 6 vault
12. do. Hell
13. do. Inn Yard
14. do. fine chamber
15. do. plain chamber

Wings in Great Room

16. 8 Moonlight

Wings in Painter's Room

17. 2 of Ariodante's pallace but one rubbed out and not painted

Wings in the Shop

18. 2 tapestry
19. 2 old rock.

Among the Painted Pieces in the Scene Room, '2 wings' are mentioned; among those in the Top Flies are '3 old wings', and among those in the Yard are '2 wings and 1 border to the back machine' and '8 wings to great machine in rape'.

Little comment seems necessary; we may notice that only in three items is there any mention at all that the sets of wings are connected with any special scene—these are items 1, 2, and 5 where the wings are expressly stated to be for Ariodante's palace, for Harvey's palace, and for Atalanta's garden respectively. Two wings for the Ariodante palace (item 17) have found their way to the painter's room presumably because they were 'rubbed out' and needed retouching.

If those two rubbed wings were put along with their four fellows in item 1, then we should have six scenes for which three pairs of wings were provided—namely (1) Ariodante's palace, (11) vault, (12) Hell, (13) Inn Yard, (14) fine chamber, (15) plain chamber—and four scenes for which six pairs of wings were provided—namely, (2) Harvey's palace, (3) rock,

(4) wood, (5) Atalanta's garden. Five items bear no indication of the number. Two items (18 and 19) have only one pair—tapestry and 'old rock'. One item (16) has four pairs—the 'moonlight' wings.

Among the information to be gained from the above is confirmation of our deduction from the study of the grooves that this Covent Garden of 1732 had provision for a maximum of six wings a side. Also that it could use shallow scenes on occasion needing no more than one pair of wings.

Generally speaking, we may suppose that those subjects with the greater number of wings were capable of showing the deepest scenes, but we must not forget that in the case, for instance, of Ariodante's palace, though we can only muster three pairs of wings, yet at the back of this particular scene, as item 37 in the Flats List told us, there was an arch and there may have been means to provide a deep vista behind this arch. So, fewness of wings does not necessarily mean a shallow set, though certainly those scenes such as Harvey's palace with the greater number of wings would have offered a deeper acting-area.

I do not know the reason for the omission of any number from items 6 to 10. I am inclined to suppose the compiler of the list has merely dropped out the 'do.', and that these wings were each in sets of twelve.

It is perhaps possible that 'teem' in item 6 is a mistranscription for 'tree', since a set of stock tree wings would be essential for such a theatre and none is elsewhere mentioned. Tent wings (item 8) were popular for battle scenes. (Items 6, 7, and 8 are omitted from Saxe Wyndham's transcription of the inventory.) 'Ceres' I take to be cornfield wings unless the word is wrongly read. Moonlight wings (16) are possibly dark, garden wings with silver high-lights on the hedges, such as those painted by Louis Jean Desprez for the firework scene in Kellgren's *Queen Christina of Sweden* (1785) now preserved in their original form at Drottningholm Castle in Sweden.

The other four wing items which come under the head of Painted Pieces are somewhat cryptic. It is very hard to find a reason why the first two of these were not listed under Wings—save that one might hazard a pure guess that they may have come from the old theatre in Lincoln's Inn, and been too short for the grooves of the new theatre. The last two items do, however, convey a glimmer of something intriguing. They are '2 wings and 1 border to the back machine' and '8 wings to great machine in rape'. The details are a mystery, but the picture that rises to mind is of a sort of miniature scene within the scene showing through an opening in trees, or a temple-arch, or flanked by clouds through a hole in heaven.

Two small further references may finish our chapter up to the year 1750. First is Tate Wilkinson's pleasant memory of a scene remembered by him from some forty years before, thus setting the date about 1747: 'It has wings and a flat of Spanish figures at full length and two folding doors in the middle. I never see those wings slide on, but I feel as if seeing my old acquaintance unexpectedly.' Whether we are to read 'Spanish figures' as further evidence for people painted on the scene or regard it as a reference to a Spanish style of decoration, the fact remains that the mention of recognition at seeing 'those wings slide on' is as clear as could be wished and, beside vividly instancing the spectacle of visible scene-change, it emphasizes the 'stock' nature of certain early scenery.

And lastly, in 1748 there was printed an edition of Coffey's play *The Devil to Pay*. There is a copy in the British Museum (643g, 7–11) endorsed *Francis Waldron*; scene iv of this play is laid in 'the open country', and there is at this point a marginal inscription: 'Wood, 1st grove ...' This is to be taken for a misspelling of the word 'groove', and the note is interesting as the first indication so far that in English procedure the grooves gave the principle to a system of naming the areas of the stage. A scene might be set in the first grooves, or in the second grooves, and so forth, thus indicating its position, and later, as we shall see, a cloth or drop might also be said to fall in the second or fourth grooves (for instance), despite the fact that it worked quite independently of the grooves and only had reference to them in so far as its position was concerned.

II

THIRD INTERLUDE
CHETWOOD'S INNOVATION

———————————————— ★ ————————————————

THERE is a certain outstanding point arising from the study of scene-changing which must be considered before we may proceed farther and which deserves an interlude chapter. We have noticed a few scattered and mysterious references indicating that the wings were occasionally *moved by machinery*. Of what sort might this machinery be? And what indications are there of its use in England?

Possibly the first hint of the existence of a machine for this purpose is in the Account for the Revels at Court. We saw on p. 160 that a certain reference there to a rope might or might not mean that such a machine was then in use. But the first positive evidence comes in a mid-eighteenth-century book by William Rufus Chetwood, and it is of sufficient importance to study in some detail.

Chetwood's book appeared at Dublin, published by E. Rider in 1749. Its full title was: *A General History of the Stage (more particularly the Irish Theatre) . . . with notes, antient, modern, foreign, domestic, serious, comic, moral, merry, historical and geographical, containing many theatrical anecdotes. . . .* The passage which interests us appears on p. 73 and reads as follows:

When I came first from *England*, in the Year 1741 [to Dublin] I brought over an experienc'd *Machinist*, who alter'd the Stage after the Manner of the Theatres in *France* and *England*, and formed a Machine to move the Scenes regularly all together; but it is since laid aside, as well as the Flies above, which were made as convenient as the Theatre would admit.

We would give a great deal to know more about what is referred to in this passage, and to have details of this machine which moved the scenes regularly all together, and which, we appear to be informed, was after the manner of something used generally in the theatres of France and England. Note that not only wings alone are moved by this machine, but the 'scenes' are moved 'all together', thus, we are to suppose, including the backscenes.

Perhaps equally surprising with the statement of the construction of such a machine is the suggestion that it was in common use in theatres in England

[213]

at and before that time, and furthermore that *it was also the French method*. We have discovered heretofore next to nothing of the existence—let alone the nature—of any such machine in England. Was it used in place of the grooves or in concert with them? In the latter case it could hardly be a method used in France, since the French adopted no groove system. And if this machine replaced the grooves, how was it that the grooves survived, and—though difficult indeed to trace—may be discovered to have an apparently continuous history from the origin of the theatre to Irving's day? Were the grooves occasionally ousted by another method of scene-moving? Did the grooves have a rival? It appears from Chetwood that they must have had; and then the question immediately arises, What was the nature of this rival?

What was Chetwood's innovation? Chetwood's own statement contains no information save that this machine, introduced about 1741, was by 1749 (the year of the publication of his book) 'laid aside'. The innovation then would seem to have proved unsuccessful; it was, for the time at any rate, abandoned.

This innovation of Chetwood's at Dublin is also recorded by another chronicler, some few years later, who gives us slightly more information. In Hitchcock's *History of the Irish Stage* (1788) (vol. i, p. 116) we learn that when Chetwood went to Dublin to lend assistance to Duval of Smock Alley Theatre:

> To his advice and experience the Dublin stage owed many improvements. By his direction a machinist from one of the London theatres was engaged, who first worked the wings by means of a barrel underneath, which moved them together at the same time with the scenes. This was publicly boasted of as a master-piece of mechanism; at present (1788) it is well understood and constantly practised.

So it appears that the nature of the innovation was the harnessing of wings and backscene by ropes to a common shaft under the stage which was turned by means of a barrel or drum, and thus synchronization of movement was achieved. The concluding remark suggests that this innovation had by 1788 been widely adopted, and it is a little difficult to reconcile with Chetwood's own statement that by 1749 it had been 'laid aside'. It seems then that it was brought into use again after Chetwood's departure.

We have a newspaper reference to the use of this machine in the year of its introduction, in *Reilly's Dublin Newsletter* of 14 November 1741:

> There is now in Rehearsal and will be performed in a few days at the theatre in Smock Alley, a Comedy never acted in this Kingdom, call'd Teague O'Divelly or the Lancashire Witches; with all the Musick, Songs, Sinkings, Flyings and other decorations suitable thereto. There is prepar'd two new Flyings for the Witches to fly with and also the Wings and Scenes on the stage made to move and

change in a moment, by an engine obtained at a Great Expence; the Stage entirely new Painted and illuminated in a beautiful manner.

So Chetwood's innovation received a preliminary puff before its first night; and the wings and scenes were promised to move and change in a moment, by an engine.

An apparently conflicting statement on the subject of 'scene-changing machines' comes from 1758, in *Faulkner's Journal* for 31 January–4 February, describing the imminent opening of another Dublin theatre—that at Crow Street. We read: 'The Stage is framed in such a Manner as to admit Machinery never attempted in this Kingdom, and is to be finished with 20 different views of Scenes, which may be shifted in less than one minute by one Man only.'

It is difficult to suppose, for all the claim of originality here, that this is not a version of the barrel and shaft system. But whether or no the *Journal* went beyond the truth in claiming originality for the idea, it appears unescapable that a scene-changing machine was in use at several places in the mid-eighteenth century.

If in fact the above-quoted claim for originality is not so well founded, then we have to ask what indication earlier still may point to the previous employment of such a machine. To begin with, since Chetwood had been prompter at Drury Lane before his visit to Dublin, and since he refers to the system as in use in theatres in England, it is possible that it may have been employed at the Drury Lane of about 1730.

Again, bearing in mind the connexion mentioned above with French technique, certain authorities have supposed that the engine for scene-moving may be understood to have been already in use even as early as *c.* 1673 at the Duke's Theatre, on the basis that Betterton (see Lowe's *Life of Betterton*, p. 113) 'invented new machines and otherwise developed materially the spectacular resources of the stage. He is said to have visited Paris by the special command of the King in order to observe how the English theatre could be improved in the matter of scenery and decoration', and, it is fairly reasonable to suppose, he would include machines in his field of study.

To go farther still: remembering that the Duke's Theatre was Davenant's house and that Davenant was referring (in his Prologue to the Second Part of *The Siege of Rhodes*) to the movement of scenes by *Engines* as early as 1661, there is nothing to suggest that though his remark most likely referred to grooves it yet was impossible that some anticipation of Chetwood's 'barrel' may have been present then.

So the engine for scene-change may in some form go back to 1661. In what form we have at present no shred of evidence at all. What we can do is study in detail the French method of a later period, and—from

Chetwood's remark on its similarity with the method used in England—deduce at least the principles of this use of harnessing scenes to a barrel.

Fortunately, of the French method there is a great deal of evidence. Diderot includes detailed engravings in his *Encyclopaedia*, and many writers up to Moynet in his *Trucs et Décors* of 1893 and Pierre Sonrel in *Traité de Scénographie*, 1947, have given illustrations and descriptions allowing us to form a pretty clear idea of the development of the scheme throughout the years.

The main feature of the French system, and that in which it most differs from the English, is that the wing is not stood on the stage but hung on a frame or pole, which projects up through a slit in the stage and which rests, at its lower end, on a wheeled carriage running on rails in the cellar. Two or more of these carriages exist at each wing-position, and once having created this elaborate machinery, it is an almost obvious step to harness one carriage from each position to a central roller passing through the cellar from front to back, then, by means of a return rope fixed to the off-stage end of the carriage, running thence through a pulley on the side-wall of the cellar and back again to the roller, but winding round it in the opposite direction, one is enabled by turning the roller one way to draw all the relevant carriages on-stage simultaneously, while by turning it the other way all the carriages are simultaneously withdrawn. One has only then to harness the second carriages of each position in a similar way but with ropes turning round the roller in the reverse direction to the previous ropes, and then one turning of the roller will not only withdraw the unwanted carriages with their poles and the wings attached thereto, but draw on a fresh set into position at one and the same time.

A diagram in the article in Rees's *Cyclopaedia* shows this method adapted to English procedure in 1811 (see Fig. 8).

But how the backscene was brought into the working of the system is still uncertain—at any rate in Britain, though in France we have evidence. But unfortunately the French *ferme* was very different in principle from our pair of flats; the French had no system of dividing scenes centrally but, instead, brought their *fermes* up through a cut in the stage by means of a system of sliding *cassettes*, which closely resemble the English *sloats*. It appears to be certain that the backscene was included in this scene-changing machine from the remarks in *Faulkner's Magazine* and from Chetwood. But whether such backscenes were of a new form or were the old English pairs of flats we entirely lack evidence at present to decide.

The odd thing about the whole business, so far as Britain is concerned, is that direct references to this elaborate and surely somewhat marvellous arrangement are so sparse that even in two centuries one may find no more occasions than might be enumerated on the fingers of one hand.

And during the whole of that period references to grooves are also to be found. Now, as will be seen, the carriage-and-pole system and the groove system appear to be mutually exclusive. One would suppose that where one existed the other would not be present. It is then something of a puzzle to find, contemporary with mentions of the grooves, certain still rarer references to the existence of the opposite system of carriage and pole.

It would seem that the carriage-and-pole system was toyed with, probably introduced on several occasions, but that after each, in a more or less short time, this standard continental method was 'laid aside', in Chetwood's phrase, in favour of a return to the old grooves.

Even in 1863 when the great innovations of Fechter at the Lyceum were signalled with so much *éclat* in an article in *All The Year Round*, we have only to go a few years farther to 1881 to find that Irving was concerned again to. do what one might have supposed Fechter had done thoroughly already —namely to remove the grooves. Evidently for all Fechter's experiments, the grooves had found their way back and the innovation had been discarded.

Irving, it is interesting to note, did not, after discarding the grooves, adopt the carriage-and-pole system as many of the preceding innovators had done, but instead he formed the modern system of 'free plantation' (to adapt a French term) where the scene-pieces were arranged at any desired position and angle on the stage and supported by braces. It then followed that for a scene-shift the curtain had to be dropped, and an army of highly drilled carpenters invaded the boards to *strike* the old pieces and set those of the new scene.

When we turn to the article in *All The Year Round* we shall see in detail how the writer describes the so-called innovation at the Lyceum and see that it closely resembled what, so far as we can tell, Rees, Chetwood, and possibly even Davenant, had referred to many years before. Also we may see how, as might be supposed, the adoption of the carriage-and-pole system on an ordinary English stage involves a very considerable amount of complicated structural alteration. The relevant passages are these (referring to Fechter in 1863):

Now, as far as this country is concerned, it must be reluctantly confessed that stage machinery has hitherto not advanced as other things have advanced; and it is, therefore, with the greater satisfaction that we now put it on record that at length a plan for working the machinery of the stage, the efficaciousness of which has been for years tested at the principal Parisian theatres, has at length found its way (with improvements suggested by experience) over here, where it seems more than probable that it will speedily become naturalised. . . .

In plain English, Mr. Fechter has recently caused to be constructed in Great Britain, and out of materials supplied by the British timber-merchant, a stage upon a principle entirely different from any previously tried in this country.

. . . and just as it has been fitted together like the pieces in a child's puzzle, so it could be taken to pieces again, and removed with perfect ease, did occasion require it. . . .

Beneath the stage is another stage, at a distance of about seven feet, and beneath this again, at about the same distance, is the lowest floor of the theatre, or in other words the excavated ground. . . .

It is, however, between the first and second stages, between the real stage on which the play is acted, and the second stage, that the more important part of the machinery for working the scenes is to be found. . . .

We must keep at present to the main-deck—the stage that is visible to the public when a play is acted. The first thing that strikes you in examining this, is, that it is traversed completely from side to side by certain narrow slits, through which you can see down into the second stage below. There are two dozen of these slits in parallel lines. Having observed them, and wondered what they are for, you notice a number of strong upright poles rising out of the stage, where the wings are ordinarily placed; going up to one of them you see, on examination, that though it is a pole above the stage, it has a broader lower member—part and parcel of it—which descends through one of those slits already described, into the 'between-decks' below. Descending a companion-ladder, you post off to see what becomes of it after it has passed through the slit, and then one glance reveals the simple plan by which the scenes are pushed backwards or forwards to their positions on the stage. That broad flat piece is received in a travelling crane below, which runs on wheels along an iron tramway, and moves so easily that a child might move it with but little exertion. These iron tramways are laid along the floor of the second stage, exactly underneath the slits above; it will be obvious that the pole which descends through the slit may, by means of the travelling crane which runs along the tramway, be pushed to any part of the stage where it (the pole) is wanted.

Here, then, is the formidable operation of scene-shifting reduced to the most simple of proceedings. Formerly, all that will now be done under the stage was done *on* the stage. There were grooves—raised grooves on the stage . . .

At this point there follows the description of the old groove system which we wish to reserve for discussion in its proper chronological place in Chapter 17. That description leads up to an objection against the bottom grooves because of their projection above the floor of the stage, which forbids their extending far out from the wings because actors might trip over them, and at the conclusion of the objection we resume:

Now this is not the case, according to the new system. Slits, unlike raised grooves, can be carried completely across the stage, and, accordingly, any scene or piece of a scene can be pushed anywhere. It may be mentioned, by the way, that those slits, or portions of slits, which are not required for any particular performance, are filled up with wooden slides prepared for the purpose, so that no flaw whatever appears on the stage's surface.

So, in spite of the persistence of the groove system to the end of the nineteenth century, we have found these references in theatrical history to occasional and apparently unsuccessful attempts to introduce another method of scene movement which, though it appears never to have had wide acceptance in British procedure, yet was the standard method in France for nearly three centuries.

The references to this rival of grooves may be summarized as follows—and probably research will add more:

First. The uncertain conclusions based on the visit of Betterton to France to obtain news of possible improvements to scenic systems, 1673.

Second. The obscure note on 'putting new ropes to them', in the Account for Work at Whitehall, may as we saw on p. 160 refer to a system of mechanically moving the scenes, 1681.

Third. The above-quoted remarks of Chetwood, 1741.

Fourth. The above-quoted reference in *Faulkner's Journal*, 1758.

Fifth. Rees's writer's statement, concerning wings, that : 'In some large theatres they are moved by machinery, in others by manual labour' added to which is his not altogether satisfactory diagram, Pl. X, Fig. 1, which is reproduced below with the relevant extract from his text (*c.* 1803).

Sixth. The query about 'stage machinery for the wings' raised in *The Theatrical Looker-on*, 1822; see p. 311.

Seventh. The above-mentioned innovation of Fechter's at the Lyceum in 1863.

Eighth. Two drawings in the Soane Collection, giving cross-sections through the stage of Wyatt's Drury Lane, and clearly illustrating the use of wing carriages at that theatre during part of its career.

Ninth. A set of diagrams in Edwin O. Sachs's *Modern Opera Houses and Theatres* shows that Walter Dando's Royal English Opera House, Shaftesbury Avenue, 1891, was equipped with wing carriages.

And on nearly every occasion we see the method hailed as a great innovation. And after every occasion it was 'laid aside'.

The long and detailed passage in Rees's *Cyclopaedia* is a typical example and, since it is not easy to come by, may be quoted in full to conclude this Interlude. (The references to figures have been kept as in the original. What is there called '*Plate X, Fig. 1*' is reproduced as the present Fig. 8; '*Fig. 2*' as our Fig. 9; and '*Plate XI, Figs. 1 and 2*' as our Fig. 10 and Fig. 11 respectively.)

The plan of moving the wings of the late theatre of Covent Garden, and that of the Theatre Royal of Glasgow, invented by the writer of this article, are represented in *Plate X*.

Fig. 1, is a transverse elevated section of the stage cellar, and stage of a theatre, where the wings are moved by a cylinder, or barrel under the stage, as was done at Covent Garden. D, D, are the side walls of the house; at A is a strong horizontal beam of wood, such as builders generally call *sleepers*, laid upon the floor of the cellar under the stage. Of these there must be a sufficient number to serve as railways for the frames of all the wings to run upon: four of these frames are represented and distinguished by the letters B B, C C. The frames B, B, are in front of those marked C, C. Each frame runs upon two small wheels, to diminish

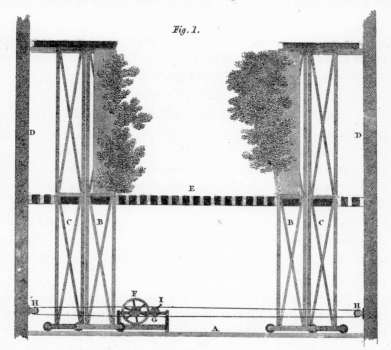

Fig. 1.

FIG. 8. The working of an English stage about 1803, from Rees's *Cyclopaedia*, Plate X, Fig. 1

the friction, and all passing through longitudinal apertures in the stage, which serve as guides, rise to a sufficient height above the stage to support the wings which are attached to them in front, so as to be quickly removed, and others substituted. The line of the stage is represented at E. Two frames at each side of the stage only were used for each set of wings. At F is a long cylinder, or barrel of wood, revolving upon iron axles, and extending from the front to nearly the back of the stage, so as to move all the wings at once. It will appear, by inspecting the plate, that the cords, or endless lines, passing from each frame round the barrel F, and over the directing pulley H back to the same frame, are so disposed that when the upper part of the barrel is moved towards the right, the front frames B, B, will move forward upon the stage, and the back frames C, C, will be withdrawn. In this state they are represented in the figure. When the motion of the barrel is reversed, that of the frames will also be inverted; the back frames will advance, and the front ones will recede. When a change of scenery is requisite, the wings are taken off the frames which are out of the view of the spectators, and those fixed on which are to be next displayed. Upon the barrel F is a wheel, moved by a pinion G, by means of the handle I, to give motion to the barrel, and increase the power. A horizontal fly wheel, like that of a jack, was also added, but in so short a motion it is not probable that it could be of great advantage.

Fig. 2, is an elevation of the machinery by means of which the wings of the new subscription Theatre Royal of Glasgow are moved, and is the only plan of the kind hitherto attempted. It may be thought strange that any deviation should have been made in this theatre, from the plans adopted in the Theatres Royal in

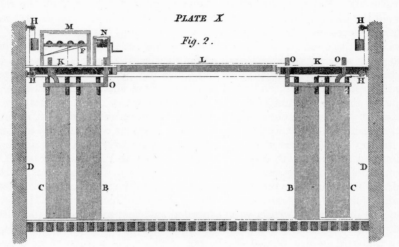

FIG. 9. A system for moving hanging wings, from Rees's *Cyclopaedia*, Plate X, Fig. 2

London: the reasons are the following. Before plans for moving the machinery had been procured, the architectural part of the house was finished, and three apartments upon each side under the stage having been fitted up for dressing-rooms, there did not remain sufficient room to construct the barrel and apparatus to advantage in the stage cellar, which was sufficiently occupied by the footlights and trap framings already described. It became necessary, therefore, either to alter the house, or to abandon the idea of working the wings by machinery, unless another place could be found where the machinery might be placed to advantage, without interfering with that space behind the scenes allotted to the performers and servants of the theatre. In every theatre it is necessary to have platforms at each side above the stage, and between these a temporary flooring, for the purpose of hanging up, taking down, or moving the flat scenery. These side platforms are distinguished by the letters K, K, and the intermediate moveable flooring by L in *fig. 2*. This suggested the idea that the barrels might be placed upon one of these platforms, and the wings moved above instead of below. But had the moving lines been attached to the upper parts of wings resting on their bases, every motion of the barrel must have overturned those wings, or at least have made them totter, and impeded their motion. To obviate this it was thought expedient that the wings, instead of resting upon the stage, should be hung from above, the basis being so near to the stage as to appear to every spectator to rest upon it, although really suspended over it. Upon this general principle arising, as most inventions do, from a case of immediate necessity, the machinery which shall now be described was planned and executed.

Under the platform K were placed horizontal boards upon their edges, $\frac{3}{4}$ of an inch in thickness and seven inches deep; these corresponding to the number of the wings to be used, were separated at each end by square pieces of board, of the same thickness, to keep them asunder; at each end the whole were bound together by a clasp of iron, O, which passing upwards through the platform, was secured by wedges passing through the arms of the clasp; by means of these wedges the clasp, and all the wings suspended from it, could be raised, should the platform yield in any part. The clasps, horizontal boards, and intermediate pieces, were secured by a screw-bolt passing through the whole. The horizontal pieces of board served as rail-ways for the suspended wings to move upon, and were seven feet in length within the clasps; from these the wings were suspended by sheers of iron, in each of which was placed a small friction roller resting upon the board, and the lower part of the sheers was screwed to the wing, so that its base might be nearly an inch clear of the stage. Between the pieces of wood which separate the railways in front were pullies of about six inches diameter, two of which are represented at P P; a cord attached to a staple in the top of the sheers of each wing, and passing over each of these pullies, connected the wing with one of the barrels above at F. When the barrel was turned these cords necessarily pulled forward the wing to which each was attached, and thus the wings were brought forward. To allow the wings to recede, another cord, attached to the sheers, was conducted over the directing pullies H, H; and from the other end a weight was suspended sufficient to overcome the friction and pull the wing back whenever the cords attached to the barrel were slackened. The frame M, which carried the barrels, consisted of upright posts of wood about four inches square, and the horizontal rails for carrying the barrels were of cast iron with brass bushes for receiving the axles or journals of the barrels. The barrels were solid pieces of fir, six inches diameter, and hooped with iron at each end; the longest, which moved six wings on each side of the stage, was divided into three pieces, and the journals connected by coupling boxes. Eight barrels were used, four of which were placed as represented in the figure, and the other four above upon the rail at M; because the barrel, when pulling forward the wings, was obliged to raise all the weights for making them recede; a counterpoise, equal to the sum of all these weights, was placed upon the barrel in an opposite direction. To increase the power each barrel had a wheel and pinion on one end, exactly similar to what is represented at F and G in *fig. 1*; the pinion containing one-third part of the teeth in the wheel of course trebled the power, and thus one man was able to work 12 wings at the same time with sufficient velocity, for the wings always advanced or receded more quickly than the drop scenes could be raised or sunk. The direction of the cords will be very obvious by inspecting the figure, two barrels with the counterpoises being corded.

For raising and lowering the drop-scenes another framing was constructed carrying 12 short barrels, a profile section of which, with one barrel, is represented at N. When the drop-scenes were pulled up the barrel was secured by a ratchet-wheel and catch.

Although this machinery was constructed rather to correct an error in the general construction of the theatre than for any other reason; it appears, after four years trial, to possess some important advantages over the plans of the

London theatres, whilst it is fair to state that it is equally liable to some objections. As it was constructed in a hurried manner, the practical part was not executed so perfectly as might have been wished; all the directing pullies were made of wood, and the grooves to receive the cords by no means sufficiently deep to prevent them from slipping occasionally, which must have frequently interrupted the motion of the wings. For this reason the counterpoise weights were substituted for the double or endless line; and this was more necessary, because the cordage being new, it was perfectly evident that the natural stretch would in a few days render it quite unserviceable in this respect, unless greater care had been taken than is generally to be expected. This machinery, with very little attention, has been found to answer the purpose remarkably well. Its advantages over that used in Covent Garden seem to be the following:

The frames which carry the scenes by the plan *fig. 1*, resting upon the floor of the stage cellar, required a strength of framing to keep them steady, which both renders them heavy to move and involves a very great expence for the timber and workmanship; besides this, many people must be employed to change the wings upon the frames when drawn back, and in this respect no saving of labour can arise, and the only advantage gained by the machinery is regularity of motion. The hanging wings of the Glasgow theatre are greatly lighter, and might be much more so than they are, for the whole frame-work was finished upon the presumption that they must rest upon their bases, as in the case of other wings. But it will at once occur, that a much greater strength of frame-work will be necessary for a scene upwards of 20 feet high, and resting upon its base, than for one suspended from above, where the force of gravitation acts in a contrary way, and which requires no other power than what is necessary to distend the canvas. Add to this, the weight of a framing passing through grooves in the stage and running upon a rail-way nearly 20 feet below, and without exactly measuring the dimensions of the wood, which must always depend upon those of the theatre, the disproportion of the one plan to the other will appear enormous. In the working of the wings according to either of these plans the superiority also evidently rests with the latter. A person or persons under the stage are situated in a most inconvenient place for observing the conduct of the drama, and regulating operations to forward its effect. On a platform above every thing is easily visible, and common attention to what passes below is all that is necessary. In the London theatres, as also in most respectable provincial ones, a whispering tube is placed, to convey sounds from the prompter to those employed above, for their occasional government; this tube is entirely similar to a common speaking trumpet.

The defects of the hanging machinery, as constructed at Glasgow, ought also to be noticed. The rail-ways, upon which the wings move, were found sometimes apt to warp, and had of course some tendency to interrupt the motion of the wing; this might be easily remedied by making the rail-ways of cast-iron, and if the upper edge should be well polished the friction would be very small indeed.

In a provincial theatre, where a certain set of wings are almost constantly used, the plan of screwing the sheers which carry the pullies to the wings may answer very well; it is, however, certainly more desirable that means should be devised for altering the wings with greater speed than can be done by the drawing of screw-nails. Many plans may be contrived to answer this purpose; one, which may do sufficiently well, is represented in *figs. 1* and *2, Plate XI*.

Fig. 1, is a profile elevation of the suspending apparatus and upper part of the wings as in *fig. 2, Plate X*. B is the platform above; A, A, the hanging supporters, with wedges to raise or sink the whole as may be proper. C is the railway which in this instance is supposed to be of cast iron. E is a pair of sheers or clutch of malleable iron, through which is an axle to carry a small friction wheel on each side. F, F, are fractions of the wings, suspended by screws or bolts and cutters, so as to be easily changed. The cordage and barrels may be either as in the former plate, or the endless line may be substituted, if precautions are taken to prevent the cords from slipping off the directing pullies.

Fig. 2, is a transverse elevation of the same apparatus, taken directly behind the wings as they advance or recede, and the various parts are distinguished by the same letters of reference as in *fig. 1*.

PLATE XI.

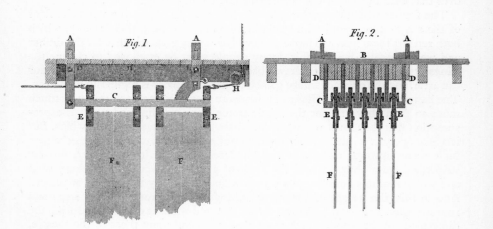

FIG. 10. Elevational detail of hanging wings, from Rees's *Cyclopaedia*, Plate XI, Fig. 1

FIG. 11. Sectional detail of hanging wings, from Rees's *Cyclopaedia*, Plate XI, Fig. 2

The object of this apparatus is, in the first place, to ensure the regularity of the motion of the wings; and in the second to effect this motion by as few servants as possible. The hanging part of all the divisions between the five wings represented may be of cast iron, and the projecting parts under the friction rollers may be either cast as *feathers*, or in separate pieces, and joined by counter-sunk screws. The intermediate pieces to preserve the distances, where the bolt D passes through, may be of well-seasoned plank.

By these means, and the application of the double rollers, an interval is left by which any wing may be speedily removed, without unfixing a single screw or bolt; and the moving cords, being merely hooked to the wing, may be instantly unfixed and placed upon hooks in the suspending apparatus, as represented in *fig. 1*, until a new wing is placed on the railway. At the same time, by using cast iron, the whole may be compressed into so small a space, as to have all the wings, necessary for an evening representation, fitted in their places before the exhibition commences, unless in very extraordinary cases.

However frequently, or to what extent, the continental wing system was

30. Print from Hogarth's painting of a private performance of *The Indian Emperor*, 1731

31. Detail of Pl. 30

32. Hogarth caricature showing typical scenery about 1723

(On this date see Harry R. Beard, 'An Etched Caricature of a Handelian
Opera', *Burlington Magazine*, September 1950, p. 266. The reproduction there given shows clear signs of the burnished-out centre line)

33. Thomas Lediard's design for a 'transparent' scene for *Britannia*,
1732

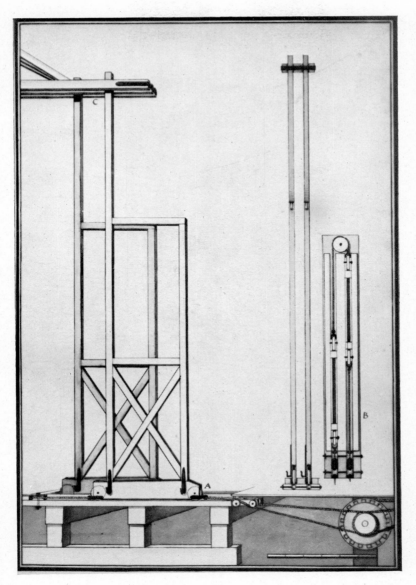

34. A drawing by Jacopo Fabris for working wings in grooves by ropes

35. Riot at a performance of *Artaxerxes*, 1763

introduced in Great Britain remains still a puzzle. It is very clear that it was not unknown. Yet the grooves and the flats persisted through all the innovations and remained the British method until the Reform of Scenery came about.

Postscriptum

After the above chapter had been set up in type, M. René Thomas brought to my attention a most valuable work published in Copenhagen by Dr. Thorben Krogh in 1933. It is a reprint, with introduction, of a manuscript of 1760 by Jacopo Fabris, and is entitled *Instruction in der Teatralischen Architectur und Mechanique*. Included in the introduction to this study of the equipment of theatres is a drawing of Fabris's from the Royal Print Collection at Copenhagen of the very greatest interest to the present study. It offers a complete explanation of how wings running in grooves could have 'ropes put to them' so as to work simultaneously by the action of one man. The drawing is reproduced by kind permission in Pl. 34, and the method there shown is as follows.

The stage at each wing position is cut out into a pair of flush grooves. In these, not the wings, but special frames to carry them, run forward and backward on wheels. Each frame has two hooks on the bottom rail (into which the bottom of the wing is placed) and, at the top, one of its vertical stiles is produced to engage in a horizontal fork above, so keeping it upright.

Each wing-carriage has a rope attached to its off-stage bottom corner (to the spectator's left in the Plate) which turns round a horizontal pulley in the floor at the end of the grooves, and is finally attached in a similar position on the other wing-carriage. To the on-stage end of each carriage a line is also fixed; this, however, passes through the stage-floor bearing between a couple of small vertical pulleys which deflect it. Thence it passes to the centre of the understage space, turns round a shaft and retraces its path through similar deflecting pulleys up through the stage again to be finally attached to the neighbour wing-carriage.

This system connects all the wings on either side of the stage to a common shaft, by revolving which every other carriage may be drawn off and, simultaneously, every alternate carriage drawn on.

Thus may wings be worked all together in grooves with ropes.

Later in this book we shall see that our neighbours the Dutch seem to have been the only other peoples in Europe beside ourselves to develop the groove system. There remains today in Amsterdam a most highly interesting, large, contemporary model of the Stadsschouwburg stage in the Leidscheplein of the late eighteenth century, with many sets of scenery and working details by famous Dutch scene-painters such as F. J. Pfeiffer (1778–1835). In this model a very similar principle of rope arrangement is to be seen to that in Fabris's drawing. The whole model, though it is slightly reconstructed, is one of the most valuable and informative theatre relics and, being so clearly distinct in its working from the general continental chariot-and-pole system, may prove to be a precious source of information upon how the British theatre of the time occasionally worked. The wings stand, and work, obliquely.

The model is in the possession of Jhr. Six van Hillegom, to whose great kindness I owe the pleasure of inspecting it.

12

THE LATER EIGHTEENTH CENTURY
AND THE DISCOVERY AT BRISTOL,
1766

★

Borders in 1760—The size of flats and the price of painting, 1763—Wings in the 'Fitzgiggo' riot print, 1763—The Bristol groove and a model reconstruction, 1766—The scenery of 'The Padlock', 1768—'The Hibernian Magazine', 1771—The Crow Street Inventory, 1776—Wings in 'The School for Scandal' print, 1777—'Harlequin Freemason', 1780—Wings in 'The Heiress' print, 1786—References in Boaden, 1792—Lord Barrymore's grooves at Wargrave, 1792—Grooves in a Kemble prompt-book, 1794

★

TWO or three shorter references precede in date the main item of this chapter; we open a survey of movable scenery in the second half of the eighteenth century with a note which Fitzgerald quotes in *A New History of the English Stage*, vol. ii, p. 234, but for which he does not indicate the source: 'About 1760, an observer pointed out the want of propriety and order in the regulation of the scenes. "The scene-shifters often present us with dull clouds hanging in a lady's dressing-room, trees intermingled with the disunited portions of a portico, a vaulted roof unsupported . . ." '

This cavalier attitude towards the details of scenery seems to us a curious thing. We frequently meet about this time such accusations of unsuitability in the components of a scene. That sky borders should be allowed in an interior, or that tree wings should be crowned with architecture, or that an arch-border should be hung over the stage without the closing-in of proper column wings to support it, appear to us gross errors of management such as would scarcely be countenanced today. Yet there is no doubt they marked the eighteenth century, and we have clear statements of the fact.

A different light on our subject comes from the same period and concerns the size of flats and the price of painting them in Scotland in 1763. Dibdin relates, in his *Annals of the Edinburgh Stage*, that

In the beginning of the month of March, Mr. De la Cour, the scenic artist, considered himself sufficiently aggrieved to make public a complaint against the 'managers', not only for having underpaid him for his work, but for taking on a new man to supplant him. The following are his own words, and they afford us some interesting details regarding the size of the stage and other matters:—

Mr. De la Cour to the Public (*Courant* March 5th.)

'As the managers of the theatre, in order to prejudice me, do now employ another to paint their decorations for both here and Glasgow, spreading about that I have been too dear, the only remedie I could think of to expose this false report and undeceive the public, was by giving an account of my prices, as also in what manner I have been paid. For the front scenes, such as towns, chambers, forests etc. of fifteen feet square each, never above £7. 7. 0; for the wings £1. 1. 0.; and so in proportion for the rest, though those I did for Newcastle were still cheaper. As I received the payment of above only by benefits, the managers, instead of being losers, must have considerably gained, because they were always on such nights as the charges of the house could not otherwise have been cleared. Last year, for instance, they gave me Monday February 1st. as this was a fast day of the Church of England. Had it not been for the goodness of my friends I could not have defrayed expenses, which amounted to £22.

W. De la Cour.'

(The House held about £60 at that time.)

Mr. De la Cour's attempt to minimize the figure of his fees leads us into what may be an unworthy suspicion—for we query his 'front scenes . . . of fifteen feet square each'. They are all very well, but was ever a *front* scene so narrow as fifteen feet? And was ever a front scene *square*? It may be so, but to a student of the flat scene it certainly looks as if a 15-ft. square piece might be only one half of a pair of flats, for the two of which the painter would therefore get £14. 14s. However that may be, this implied dimension of a flat scene is one of our few early records of size; but the point is very uncertain for these 'front scenes' may have been cloths, and in any case early proscenium openings might be very narrow; for instance that at Richmond, Yorkshire, measures only 15 ft. 9 in. across—and so such scenes would have been perfectly suitable there.

The next piece of evidence brings a considerable point of information upon the nature and convention of early scenery. It is the well-known print of the 'Fitzgiggo' riot in 1763 (see Pl. 35). The subject of this rioting was the price of seats at Covent Garden, but the interest of the print for us is in another direction. It shows a scene in the performance of the opera *Artaxerxes*, by the celebrated Dr. Arne, first produced the year before. We see that some at least of the characters are dressed with definite regard for Eastern costume; one actor is, for instance, attired in baggy Persian trousers and a turban, though the actress is apparently clothed almost normally in contemporary English dress. But the scene around the players is very different. We have, clearly represented, three pairs of column wings and a plainish, panelled wall on the backscene. There is no feature of Persian atmosphere in the scenery at all. We are clearly looking at a stock scene. But, beyond this, consideration of the print suggests that we are looking at a stock scene where the wings do not belong to the backscene.

If we suppose the designer of a panelled chamber planning his backscene with the simple but effective design of mouldings shown in this print (and the painting of mouldings is always effective in the hands of a capable scene painter), then it is hard to imagine that he would not extend the same scheme to his treatment of the wings, so making a unity of the set. But the wings here have no point in common with the backscene. They are not inconsistent with it, it is true, but then half the art of a stock-scenery designer lies in producing work which will fit as consistently as possible into the greatest number of variations, and here seems an admirable example of his success; these columns are forthright, clear, and simple. Their subject is admirable for disposition upon a side wing—in fact nothing could more suitably be expressed upon a row of interior wings than a row of columns in a room. It is not until one comes to study these column wings as architectural elements of a saloon interior that one realizes how entirely conventional they are, how carefully interpreted and impressed into the theatrical convention while having, at the same time, no architectural justification at all!

No columns in the world would stand in relation to the panelled walls of a room as these do; yet what more admirable backscene could be imagined than this panelled wall, and what better avenue of framing wings than this stretch of purely conventional paired columns? The connexion, in short, is purely theatrical; it appears logical and satisfying yet in fact it is a theatrical convention of the rankest, and no whit a planned unity of correctly related elements of architecture—but it is, we believe, an example of scenery typical of the time, and we shall have to discuss some interesting implications in the use of stock scenery in a later interlude.

What to take as our next reference in order of chronology is not quite certain. It may be an actual and veritable set of grooves in all its concrete reality—at least the remnant thereof. The Theatre Royal, Bristol, was begun in 1764; it can almost certainly be affirmed that it was equipped straight away with grooves. Were these grooves ever renewed? If not, a certain fragment discovered there is immensely important, for it comes fairly early in chronological order among the sparse sources of information at present available on the English groove in the public theatre—and here is no vague reference, no equivocal sketch, but the thing itself. I believe we are not too sanguine in dating it about the years 1764–6.

In 1939, in company with the manager of the theatre and the curator of the Bristol Museum, I examined the loft of the theatre. This space between the roof and the decorated ceiling of the auditorium has a few ancient partitions, a well-head over the central rose-grille of the ceiling underneath, a highly interesting thunder-run, two modern ventilation shafts, and an accumulation of dust as thick and as soft as the sands of the sea. Otherwise it was empty save for one object in an obscure corner which lay, almost invisible in the dimness, on the floor near the stage-right side of the theatre and against the wall dividing the loft from the flies over the stage. Its form seemed to recall something in the plan and section for *The Siege of Rhodes*, for it had grooves in it. It was lowered to the stage, examined, measured, and photographed.

No one in the theatre recognized it. It did not belong where it was found. It appeared the relic of some turn-out of unwanted lumber. How it reached the loft and became forgotten there no one can tell.

Since this is our first meeting 'in person' as it were with a principal character of this present study, and since it was this discovery which led to much of the study, we may consider the find in detail. We are now to offer some indication of what an English groove was really like and, even, something of how it worked.

The fragment consists in essence of two boards, one longer than the other, battened together edge to edge, with a number of strips fixed to one face of each board, and on the reverse face certain other, less regular, pieces of wood. At one end of the longer board are two strap-hinges now broken away from whatever they held. The whole is considerably worn and shows many signs of breakage.

In Pl. 36 is a photograph of the back surface of the object. The longer member is seen behind and the shorter in front. The two are battened together with cross-pieces of wood in such a way that the back, or upper, surface of the shorter member is 2 in. lower than the longer.

At the right-hand end of the longer piece (itself about 5 ft. 8 in. long and 1 ft. wide) a rectangle of wood projects upwards; it is about 11 in. wide and 9 in. high and a little over an inch thick. Its nearer top corner is broken off. Close beside its base, a piece of 3 in. by 1 in. batten is nailed flat across the piece. Moving to the left, we next come to a thin fillet of wood; this fillet is separated by a space of 3 in. from a thicker cross-piece (about 3 in. by 2 in.), from the side of which three old, hand-made nails project sideways and slightly upwards. Close behind this is the first of the wide cross-pieces which batten the whole together; it is about 6 in. wide. At the other end of the whole is the second cross-piece, this time considerably wider (about 13 in.) and close to the end of the long member. Upon the back surface of this cross-piece is the remains of a batten, probably originally between 3 in. and 4 in. square in section. Under this batten are the flaps of two strap-hinges; the other flaps project, empty, beyond the end of the piece.

The shorter member is about 4 ft. 6 in. long by 7 in. wide; between it and the connecting battens, distance-pieces can be seen intervening so as to cause the member to be sunk 2 in. below the long member. It lies close by the side of the latter in such a way as to project some 4 in. beyond it on the left-hand end and to come within about 1 ft. 5 in. from its right-hand end.

Turning the whole piece over, we are able to study the under surface. Fig. 37 shows this, looked at squarely over its whole extent; and Fig. 38 shows it from one end.

The longer member has six pieces of wood attached along its surface. Two of these (approximately 3 in. by 1 in.) are attached to the side and project, forming a sort of shallow trough. The other four lie in pairs along the bed of this trough: each pair consists of a piece of square timber as long as the trough and about $1\frac{3}{4}$ in. thick, lying close beside a thinner piece on edge, about $1\frac{1}{4}$ in. wide by $\frac{3}{4}$ in. thick. Thus three grooves are formed, approximately $1\frac{3}{4}$ in. deep by $1\frac{1}{2}$ in. wide.

On the face of the shorter member an almost exactly similar arrangement is to be seen, save that the attached pieces of wood are approximately 3 in. wide by 1 in. thick. They are attached along their edges and so form three considerably deeper grooves than those on the long member. This, added to the fact that the short member is already set lower than the other, means that the groove-walls on the shorter member project 3 in. farther than those on the long member.

Finally, on the opposite side of the long member, traces of a further groove may be seen in the form of two pieces of 3 in. by 1 in. timber, separated by a piece 1 in. square. But one side of the groove so made has been broken entirely away. This remnant of a groove lies flush with the hinge-end of the long grooves, but runs beside them only for about 4 ft., ending at a point nearly opposite to the end of the short grooves on the far side.

It is possible that this fragment may have two ages—that part of it, namely the long grooves, is older than the rest. The long grooves are nailed together with hand-made nails, while the short grooves appear to be additions and are now fixed with screws. In view of the lack of means of verification we must not allow ourselves finally to date this example of grooves; part may be 1764, part may be later.

What is perhaps more important is to answer the questions, What does this object mean, where did it go, and how did it work?

The first step we may take is to infer that the short, deep grooves are for wings and the long, shallow grooves (to which an extension was apparently once hinged) are for flats.

Next we remember from our study of Aphra Behn that a wing is likely to stand more or less closely *in front of* the flats it frames; thus we suppose that the short grooves were on the audience side.

Next we realize that from the complicated nature of the back of the object it is not likely to have lain, grooves upwards, on the stage but must have been suspended, grooves down, from above. We know, further, from the Covent Garden Inventory that upper grooves seem to have been connected with (and possibly suspended from) the fly-gallery.

Can we now make a scale model of the fragment and associate it with a skeleton of the relevant section of the Bristol Theatre Royal stage, and essay to fit the one to the other?

The result of such an essay, based not only on information discovered up to this date in our study but also on deductions from what we are still to discuss from later periods, is shown in Pls. 39, 40, and 41.

This model shows a slice, as it were, cut out from across the Bristol stage. It is made approximately to scale—approximately because since it was begun (with the assistance of John Terry, a one-time student of mine now making stage equipment) some ten years ago, subsequent discoveries have given us information that would cause certain minor dimensions to stand revision. (For instance, the recovery in 1950 of an inventory of scenes at the Theatre Royal, though concerning the year *c.* 1829, informs us that flat scenes there were actually 16 ft. high by 9 ft. 6 in. or 10 ft. wide each half. Those in the model were figured at 18 ft. by 12 ft. but in the main the layout stands.)

A strip of the stage floor, some 3 ft. wide by 50 ft. across, is represented with a skeleton indication, at each end, of part of the side-walls. From these side-walls project the fly-galleries, or 'fly-floors', with their 6-ft. high rails; and one of a number of catwalks is shown bridging over the stage between the rails. The whole is viewed from the back of the stage as looking towards the audience. All these features are based on existing structures in the Theatre Royal today (whose dimensions, it is interesting to note, are held by tradition to be almost exactly repeated from those of the Drury Lane of the time—that is Wren's Drury Lane with whatever modifications it had received by 1763).

Next (Pl. 39), to the underside of the left-hand fly-floor (as we look at the print) was attached a replica of the discovered fragment, arranged to project some 4 ft. 6 in. out into the stage space, and braced there in position by a diagonal timber fastened to the railing of the fly-floor. To the hinges at the end of the fragment was attached an extension of the long grooves adding some 5 ft. 6 in. to them, and kept horizontal by a chain (for which we shall find later evidence) from the fly-rail; the extension is capable of being raised at need by a line from a pulley above in the grid. This line is led back to the fly-floor and, for its working, a system has been borrowed in this model from one installed at the Theatre Royal, Plymouth, to be discussed in Chapter 14. The presence of this system here in a model which has certain reference to Bristol is not to be taken as a suggestion that the system was actually used at Bristol; but it is combined with it merely because it enables study to be made of a nearly contemporary method of working grooves and borders, whereas no particular information now remains on this subject at Bristol.

A duplicate of the groove unit was similarly fixed above the other side of the stage.

Next, a pair of flats was made reproducing in detail information, to be discussed later, from Contant's *Parallèle des Théâtres* (see Chapter 15). The type of flats chosen was that showing a practicable double door in the centre with a window low in the left-hand flat and another up in the centre of the right-hand flat (cf. Fig. 31). The former flat is shown in clarity by itself on the left of the model. The opposite flat is shown with two wings visible beyond its outer edge, which must not be confused with the framework of the flat. All details of stiles, rails, and corner-braces in the construction of the flats are reproduced from Contant.

The flats in the model have been specially arranged to show two separate moments in the closing of a pair of flats; that on the right is seen fully closed in position in the centre of the stage, with the 'drawer' standing beside it, his work done. (The details of costume are taken partly from a, possibly unique, print by Antoine Fouré showing a stage-hand at work among machinery. The print is in the Drottningholm Theatre Collection, Stockholm, and belongs to about 1750.) The other half of the flat is shown at a moment a few seconds earlier in the scene-change, with the scene-drawer pushing it along in its grooves.

The bottom edges of the flats are shown also in grooves.

To the right of the stage is seen a third stage-hand who has thrust forward a fresh wing in front and is in the act of withdrawing the wing from the previous scene under cover of the first.

In this model no bottom grooves have been provided for the wings. This is on the assumption that wings and flats would be built all the same height, and because the wing-grooves of the fragment discovered are carefully built-on so as to be an inch or two lower than those for the flats (this may have been a later alteration). It is presumed the flats were raised on the bed of the lower grooves while the wings run on the stage itself. Some confirmation is given to this theory in the recently discovered inventory, since the wings there itemized are shown as 16 ft. high—exactly the same height as the flats.

So much for the use of the groove and for the position it probably occupied on the stage. Now as to the hingeing of the groove-arm or extension—what is the function of that, and what is to be learned from it?

The model shows a scene-change in progress. Above the stage are represented two borders: the nearer is a straight cloud border with a simple cut edge following the shape of the clouds, the other is a deep arch-border. The sky border is shown as being raised up out of its set position; when it is lowered it would descend till it came just in front of the grooves and hid them from sight, neatly masking the tops of the wings and flats. The arch-border is, on the other hand, shown lowered in its set position. The 'legs' of the arch correctly mask the tops of the wings, but it will be very clearly noticed that in this position the hinged extensions of the grooves (which are necessary to support a closed flat-scene) jut out intolerably into the void of the arch and may be allowed to remain in this position only when a straight border is used, but have to be disposed of in some way when an arch-border is used.

Note also that it follows that an arch-border cannot be used with a flat scene unless some species of upper back flat be drawn in above the flat scene to mask the gap at the top. The arch-border can, however, be associated with another kind of scene altogether, composed of elements different from the flats and to whose nature we shall have to devote special study in the next chapter before we close this Second Part of our review and end our survey of the eighteenth century.

Ignoring then, for the moment, the nature of this other type of scene, we return to the model and see the function of the strap-hinges attached to the end of the fragment we discovered. They are there solely to enable the attached groove-arm to be raised up like a 'common draw-bridge' (to anticipate Rees's simile in Chapter 13) and be cleared out of the way so as not to project into the high, arched opening.

A very significant consequence follows from this; in Pl. 40 is shown the model with the straight border lowered and the groove-arms down ready to take the pair of flats which are about to close in to complete the scene, but which are here deliberately drawn back in the wing positions to enable us to note a special point—namely, the particular proportions of the opening left.

Now in Pl. 41 is shown another arrangement; here the straight border is raised, the arch-border is lowered in position, and the groove-arms are hoisted out of the way, so as no longer to intrude into the opening. The flats remain as before. Note now the remarkable difference in the proportions of the opening left; we now see the tall, arched prospect that we had brought to our notice in Thornhill's drawing in Pl. 29. We recall that this drawing could have been for Drury Lane theatre and that Drury Lane theatre was supposed to resemble this at Bristol in main dimensions, and immediately we see how scenes of the proportions of Thornhill's and scenes of the common, shorter and wider proportions more familiar to us today need not be wilful misrepresentations of contemporary artists but could actually have been achieved on the same stage.

The study of the discovery at Bristol is, then, productive of some informative conclusions, once we are able to follow the implications latent in it into some three-dimensional and practical form upon a model.

Two or three final points may be made before we leave the reconstruction. First, we see how, if the groove of the English public theatre were once continuous across the whole stage as it had been in the masques and as seems to be suggested in Hogarth's painting of the children's performance (Pl. 30), then at some time before the middle of the eighteenth century it had developed into two halves, with a gap in the middle and a capability of increasing the size of that gap by a particular mobility of the inward ends of the two remaining parts.

Secondly, the catwalks above were presumably used by actors passing to and from cloud chariots worked from the grid. They also perhaps were called into action if a piece of scenery fouled another in moving, or was caught by the rising arm of a groove (a near-accident of very much this sort can be seen in the cinematograph record of the working of visible scene-changing at Drottningholm Theatre, of which a short version, edited by the present writer, is published by Common Ground Ltd.). At the top right of the model (Pl. 39) a stage-hand is seen mounting the ladder built into the fly-rail to reach the catwalk for this purpose.

Thirdly, at the top left is shown a stage-hand working the borders according to the method employed at Plymouth (cf. Fig. 19).

Finally, upon the stage a 'green-clad man'—a servant in the livery of the theatre—is setting a solitary piece of furniture ready for use by the players in the succeeding flat scene.

Before we leave the Bristol fragment there is one feature that still remains a puzzle. What is the meaning of that curious, additional, short groove, whose wall is now broken away, which we noticed at the up-stage side of the piece—the opposite side to the other short grooves for wings? Presumably, because of its shortness, it was also a wing-groove, but why is it on the other side of the flat-grooves? No conjecture seems useful in clearing up this point.

One of the ambitions of this study is to enable us to form the truest conception possible of what period scenery looked like—of what its actual impression was when seen upon the stage. Our next illustration helps towards this conception more, I think, than any other print I have so far found; it appears to be a most faithful representation of how a scene in a performance would look to a spectator.

It is a print published in 1769 entitled '*Mr. Dibdin in the Character of* MUNGO *in the Celebrated Opera of the* PADLOCK'. It bears a line from the negro's part in that play—'*Me wish to my Heart me was Dead, Dead, Dead!*' It was engraved by B. Clowes (but whether from a painting, and if so by whom, I have not yet discovered) and printed for Carington Bowles, 69 St. Paul's Church Yard (see Pl. 43).

There is an example of the print in the Burney Collection in the British Museum. Mr. Eric Walter White reproduced my photograph of this example in *The Rise of English Opera* (Lehmann, 1951), and I am indebted to his publisher for permission to use the block again here. Mr. White discusses Bickerstaffe's opera, *The Padlock*, produced at Drury Lane, 1768, in his book; here we shall examine only the technical implications in the print.

To begin, its impression of the lighting effect is probably very faithful. In the commercial theatre, economy would enforce a limit to the number of candles and lamps so that, to modern eyes, the eighteenth-century stage would probably be a place of gleam and shadow rather than hold the blaze we know today. In this candlelight something of the richness of the scenery might be a little enhanced, but much would be softened into near-gloom. This character of tone the print excellently suggests.

The solitary figure may be oddly proportioned and his limbs a little stiff, but the truth of a conventional pose is probably here, and the theatrical motley of the dress chimes authentically with the pathos of the character.

The species of illusion which such a stage scene might suggest is pregnantly here; clearly no attempt at normal naturalness, as we make it, would be very successful in these conditions. The illusion is that created not by convincing imitation but by invoking the fantasy of the painted and the artificially lit. The very basket the figure so strangely holds appears to be a painted 'prop' in profile, not an actual basket. Especially do the tree wings carry the conviction of foliage painted with deliberate touches of light and shade upon thin board and cut out with a saw. This foliage sorts perfectly with massed candlelight. The feet of the wings nest unobtrusively, but with a faithfulness of record that is far too rare, in veritable grooves, and no fiction of pretending they grow in earth is offered to beguile us. Thus, most likely, grooves would strike a spectator of the eighteenth-century stage.

But it is in the nature of the backscene that the print stands unique, to my knowledge, among contemporary theatrical records. Here is a backscene of a sort entirely new to our review—a backscene composed of a narrow centre-piece and two sides *set at an angle to it*. We shall not meet the technical phrase 'raking flats' till well on in the next century, but here seems an anticipation of the method beyond all question. The style of architecture is soberly theatrical and in perfect terms of scene-paint; whether the shadow across the back flat is painted or cast is not certain, but one has scarcely any doubt that, in view of the nature of the lighting of the period, it must come from the skill of the painter. But the print leaves us in uncertainty on one point—whether the 'steps' at the foot of the back flat are practicable steps or the separate bases of two dark columns—perhaps the latter.

The plot is laid in Salamanca. The scene represented in the print is Act I, Sc. v of the opera. The direction reads: '*Changes to the Outside of* DON DIEGO'S *House, which appears with Windows bar'd up, and an Iron Grate before an Entry.* DON DIEGO *enters from the House, having first unlocked the Door, and remov'd two or three Bars which assisted in fastening it.*' Later we read that Mungo enters 'with a Hamper' and a little after he 'goes in'. Some business follows, including the locking-in of the characters, '*After which,* LEANDER *enters disguised, and* MUNGO *comes to the Grate.*' Leander is the young hero and has come to serenade Leonora who is left in the charge of her old maid, Ursula. We see something of the reason for the character of the set when we find that, with Mungo at the Grate, first Ursula 'appears at the Window above' (to quote now from a later script of 1815), and then Leonora 'appears at another Window'—a typical comic-opera scene is thus provided, grouping amusingly the three listening characters round the singer in the garden. (The earlier script lacks the inserted directions and simply says at the opening of this section, 'LEONORA, MUNGO, URSULA *above*'.)

It is not uninteresting to add, in view of the great success of this show which was compared with that of *The Beggar's Opera*, that the charm of the scenery seems to have struck another artist some four years later. By now the success was great enough for the characters to be named alone without mentioning the opera (see Pl. 42). In 1773 Robt. Sayer published this almost equally interesting print (*I. Wilson del. et fecit. Robt. Sayer Excudit.*) which was entitled simply *Leonora and Leander*. The relation of the print with *The Padlock* seems clear enough not only because of the names but because of its fitting with the directions, Act I, Sc. i—'*A Garden belonging to* DON DIEGO'S *House* . . . [enter] LEONORA *with a Bird on her Finger which she holds in the other Hand by a String* . . . [*Putting the Bird into the Cage.*]' All the details are here in the print—save that Leander's serenading does not take place in this scene and his appearance seems a piece of print-seller's licence. However that may be, the greatest interest of the print for us is again in the faithfulness with which painted, practical flats, and cut tree wings appear displayed under the candlelight of the stage. Whether the 'grass mat' be also artist's licence or a piece of added evidence we, alas, do not know.

Thanks to these tender pictures we can add to the technical information implied by the Bristol groove something of the atmosphere of the scenes on the stage which were the intimate companions and the dependent masters of those grooves.

As we pass the year 1771, we note an irritable jibe (no doubt deserved) at clumsiness in handling scene-changes—this time from Ireland: in *The Hibernian Magazine* for April 1771, p. 145, we read: 'We would ... advise the person, who has the superintendence of the scenic disposition at Smock Alley, to give a little more attention to propriety; and when he would give us the representation of a merchant's compting house, not to give us in the side scenes a colonnade of enriched pillars interspersed with statues, which decoration we think belongs rather to the gallery of a palace.' Here is inconsistence as well as difference, and beyond all question of doubt. Here are stock wings, whatever was the origin of the 'compting house' backscene, and these stock wings, let us note, bore just that subject of representation which we have already noted on wings that we have come to suspect as stock scenery—namely a colonnade of pillars.

In 1776 we find another inventory, this time of scenes and machines and such-like at Crow Street Theatre, Dublin, quoted in vol. i of Boaden's *Life of J. P. Kemble*. There we find the item: 'Two sets of fly grooves with barrels.'

Again, just what a *set* of grooves implies is not certain; it may mean what we have ourselves called a set of grooves, that is to say, one single, multigrooved group belonging to one position on the stage like that we found at Bristol, or a 'set' may signify all those grooves on one side of the stage—it might be four or six multiple units each bearing their quota of grooves. On the whole it seems that the latter is the more likely interpretation to put upon the word here, since one cannot imagine the inventory of a fully equipped theatre itemizing only two units of grooves. Further, the additional mention of *barrels* rather suggests a number of groups of grooves since the barrels were parts of the machinery for working a number of groups of grooves simultaneously.

Notice that here the reference is limited to *fly-grooves*, that is, presumably to the upper grooves attached to the fly-floor. No mention is made of lower grooves.

Despite the use of the word 'set' here, we shall find it convenient to go on meaning by 'set of grooves' one unified group such as that discovered at Bristol.

The connexion in this reference of barrels with grooves is important.

No information on what the barrels were is given, but we are shortly to find pretty full explanation which we shall then be able to refer back to this earlier article. They were presumably the same things as what we called *shafts* in our account above of the model.

The next step brings us smoothly in our review to one of the most famous of all British theatrical prints, that depicting the performance of Sheridan's *The School for Scandal* at Drury Lane in 1777 (Fig. 12). Here the subject is so well known that one's acceptance of its unity is almost automatic—here, one takes it, is scenery just as we know it today. But let us examine it in detail.

This print shows us, through the proscenium opening of Drury Lane, a backscene on which is painted a window and a vast array of bookshelves well befitting a library. Framing this are two wings on either side, strictly formal and each bearing the painting of a squared Ionic column upon a pedestal, forming the on-stage edge, with a stretch of wall-space, decorated with painted panelling and carving, disappearing off-stage.

From a modern point of view it might, however, be a matter for a certain amount of surprise to see how, upon this notable occasion—the first presentation of *The School for Scandal* at Drury Lane—and with the intriguing subject of a library to be staged, the painter had concentrated the whole of any adjuncts truly stamping the atmosphere of 'library', *upon the back scene only*.

To turn from the richly furnished shelves of volumes that ornament the back to the cold impersonal columns at the side is to experience a disappointment. No attempt has been made to write 'library' here: these might be any walls; elaborate they admittedly are, but they increase the atmosphere of the scene not one whit. There is no doubt they would be just as suitable for a room in a house, for a dressing room, or for a picture gallery! In other words, they would not be out of place in any scene whatever in this particular play.

Can it be that these were 'stock column wings' standing throughout the play, and that a careful management had restricted expense in this scene to the mere provision of a library back? (If indeed that too were not a stock item, for one looks, with disappointment again, for a glimpse in the painted window of some house where might dwell that too curious 'opposite neighbour'; her opportunity for scandalous enjoyment is often forgotten by those producers that place Lady Teazle by that very window before covering her—from the audience but not from the neighbour—with the famous screen.)

However this may be, there is no shred of detail to give foundation to

FIG. 12. The screen scene from *The School for Scandal*, 1777

36. Groove fragment, front and upper surfaces

37. Groove fragment, under surface

38. The groove fragment as it might have appeared
in its original position to a spectator standing under
the L.H. fly gallery and looking up and across the
stage. This groove was discovered by the author at
the Theatre Royal, Bristol

39. Model reconstruction by the author

of the working of the English groove system

40. Model of the groove system showing 'horizontal' scene

41. Model of the groove system showing 'vertical' scene

any theory that these wings were designed to match the backcloth, saving possibly one small point which we may thus consider:

There are various members of a moulding running across the top of the set, visible just underneath the draped curtain at the top of the proscenium, and reaching down to the level of the highest bookshelf. These it may be argued tally sufficiently (though not exactly) with those upon the cornice above the columns to justify the view that they match them. But the cautious spectator will at once see that no evidence exists for supposing these mouldings across the top of the set *to be painted on the backscene*. To mask the top of the scene, the inevitable borders would undoubtedly have been necessary. In which case it is far more likely that these mouldings were painted on a stock border which of course might very well match the stock wings, the whole having been designed as a matching set, than that they have any connexion with the backscene.

We can, however, form this indisputable conclusion: that whether in fact these wings and back were designed together and painted as a unity, or whether either or both came from stock, yet the conception is of a backscene that contains all the essential elements of a library—and in fact is the scenery proper—and a set of wings which particularizes the scene in a far lighter way, having no reference to a library and existing only as a *setting* for the specific statement of the centre backscene.

Whether or not the particular wings had been seen before, we have from another source indisputable evidence that such independent appearances were not uncommon. Only three years after this, a writer in *The Gentleman's Magazine* for 1780, discussing *Harlequin Freemason* at Covent Garden, says: 'The front scene is also a very picturesque representation of the subject it is designed to represent. The side wings have been seen before but the whole of the centre is new and painted with great skill and success.'

No plainer statement of the difference between a wing and its backscene —or between the back scenery and its frame or setting—could be desired.

But we are not to understand that this distinction was invariable. It was no more than a general procedure. Wings to match the backscene are not by any means unknown, as witness the print of a production of *The Heiress*, 1786, in the Burney Collection at the British Museum, where a very different story from the last is told (see Fig. 13).

Here we have one of the best illustrations in existence of the artificial nature of wings when used to represent the side-wall of a simple chamber interior. Here is unequivocal evidence of their existence and effect—and also a good example of a set in which the wings match the backscene. We must beware of supposing that this was never the case, but we are quite prepared to accept this evidence without feeling forced to abandon our

FIG. 13. Scene from *The Heiress*, 1786

theory on the nature of wings in general. Moreover, the print is some confirmation of our conception of the stock nature of much eighteenth-century
scenery.

We see a room with a panelled dado on both back and wings, above which
a close, formal, diamond, all-over pattern stretches to the frieze. Such of
the scene as is visible is strictly non-committal, no feature of any sort showing to break the regular scheme. (We are taking it for granted that the door
belongs to the proscenium and not to the scenery.)

This very regularity and non-committal lack of special feature is (if it be
not a deliberate simplification of the print-maker's to concentrate on the
players) something of an indication that we may here be dealing again with
stock scenery. 'Surely,' one might exclaim, 'a specifically painted scene
must have been made more interesting!' This thought will return to us in
Chapter 16, when we shall have occasion to seek to precise the notions of
wings and stock scenery, but for the moment we simply say that it does not
follow that eighteenth-century scenery was boring, nor even that the use
of stock scenery as a system need lead to boredom. Indeed a review of the
evidence when we have finished examining the references to wings will
lead us, I believe, to an almost opposite point of view.

The century draws to a close with one or two open criticisms of the
system of flats and grooves, and there is an uneasy premonition of the
revolution that is to follow in the next decades and of the attack that is to be
launched on the style of scenery. We find in chapter xiv of Boaden's
Memoirs of Mrs. Siddons a reminder that Boaden tended to be on the side of
those who object to any justification of scenery on its own merits in the
theatre, and that he was in fact a notable contestant in the Great Scenic
Controversy.

Discussing the scenic characteristics of the time as exemplified at the
Opera House (Queen's Theatre) in 1792, he mentions among his objections
'the scoring line where the flats meet each other' and 'the grooves in which
they move'. Both of these notes are important; in the first we have almost
the only frank and clear reference so far found in our study to a feature
of the flat scene which the discerning reader will have felt puzzled about
from the very beginning—that is the crack between the flats. Did it show?
The answer is, it decidedly did, and it annoyed certain people too! Indeed,
it is strange to realize how many, by implication, accepted it, judging by
the rarity of such a remark as the present.

It begins to be apparent that an uneasiness was in the air concerning the
form of stage scenery as a whole. Small as is this remark of Boaden's, it is
the first portent we have received of what we shall later find was the dawn
of a new technique of scenery. It is felt here at the time when the nineteenth

century is about to open. It will carry its troubled development into our own day. The details we shall gather as we progress in our study. Let us for the moment acknowledge the sign as a threat to the life of our groove; what is not so obvious is that it is also a threat—whether intended here or not—against the whole system of visible scene-change, but this will become apparent later; let us now turn again to consider this, as yet, unsuspecting progress. We have many details to uncover before we gain sufficient information fully to appreciate the fine points of objection that arose against flat scenery and the grooves that held it. The ingenuity of a threatened technique often rises to its height just before its collapse in a desperate defence of its own existence.

It is worth while extracting certain other passages from the works of Boaden here, for their evidence of the growing dissatisfaction. Elsewhere in his *Life of Mrs. Siddons*, and referring again to the transfer from old Drury Lane to the Opera House in the Haymarket which took place in 1792, he draws attention to the inadaptiveness of flats for stages of new dimensions: 'In point of scenery little could be done at the Opera House for the accommodation of the English drama; and the small flats of Drury Lane were lost under a roof so towering.'

The same dilemma is similarly described in his *Life of Mrs. Jordan*, vol. i, p. 201:

The Drury Lane company, in the season of 1791–2, removed to the Opera House on the 22nd of Sept. . . . Of all things that could be named, an Italian Opera House was least suited to English play and farce, demanding a constant succession of scenes called flats, run on suddenly for the frequent changes of place, and the small-sized scenes of Old Drury, were, with much difficulty, applied to the grand void devoted to the groups of the French ballet . . . However we were drawn by that stage into a fondness for spectacle, which we could gratify, sooner than a demand for sense; and at length the people themselves preferred the great theatre to the little one.

And again in the same book, p. 254:

The present stage required scenery, certainly, thirty-four feet in height, and about forty-two feet in width, so that an entire suite of new scenes was essential on great occasions, though where *display* was not material, the old pieced flats might be run on still, and the huge gaps between them and the wings, filled up by any other scenes drawn forward, merely 'to keep the wind away'.

This slight picture of the makeshifts and resorts of the carpenters to 'fill up' by thrusting forward any old scene is as interesting as the implication, in the reference just before to the need for 'an entire suite of new scenes', that at this theatre the use of stock scenery was commonly the rule.

Boaden's final smack at the flats is in his *Life of John Phillip Kemble*, where he writes: 'The memory of no very aged persons may present if closely urged, some not very brilliant impressions of the miserable pairs of flats that used to clap together on even the stage trodden by Mr. Garrick.'

To the year 1792 also belongs an interesting item from a sale at Christie's. The catalogue lists the contents of the eccentric Lord Barrymore's short-lived private theatre at Wargrave-on-Thames, and it contains the item: 'All the loose and fixed grooves.'

Here we are given the first confirmation of an anticipation expressed above that we should find that some grooves were removable. For what purpose we shall define after further evidence, but the point is definitely established that at least as early as 1792 some of the grooves were *loose* while others were *fixed*.

Drury Lane had become too small and had to be rebuilt. Mr. Charles Beecher Hogan was kind enough to acquaint me with the last reference for this period which he found in some manuscript memoranda of J. P. Kemble's in the British Museum (Add. MS. 31972–5) concerning the building of the new Drury Lane of 1794. Here the requirement is made of '. . . Grooves all of one Height—five cuts in each Groove'.

The implication that wings of decreasing height were no longer to be used, as they once had been to increase perspective effect, is not unexpected at this period. It is, however, interesting to note that there is a suggestion, in the very fact of this direct specification, that the old perspective decrease in height had obtained sufficiently recently to make it still necessary to state whether the new grooves should all be level or not.

The second half of the reference is especially interesting in providing what I believe is the only indication yet found of a distinguishing name being given to each individual unit in any set of grooves—the unit is here named a 'cut', and each groove unit is specified to contain five cuts—that is to be capable of holding five scene-pieces, though of what nature these were is not indicated, whether all wings, or all flats, or mixed.

PART THREE

THE REVOLUTION
IN CHANGEABLE SCENERY
IN THE PUBLIC THEATRE
OF THE NINETEENTH CENTURY
AND THE RISE OF
'THE ART OF THE THEATRE'

13

FOURTH INTERLUDE

(THE SET SCENE AND THE FLAT SCENE)

————————————————— ★ —————————————————

WITH Part Three of this book we open the study of a century of change. The eighteenth century has seen the consolidation of the system of changeable scenery as part of the spectacle of a show; throughout the nineteenth century changeable scenery will remain as the scenic principle of the time, but towards the end—at the dawn of our present period—it will lose a feature that once was essential to it, for the changes will no longer be visible.

In the last references we made to the eighteenth century there were signs of a certain discontent. The discontent is to grow during the nineteenth century. The system of changeable scenery had created a convention of machinery which seemed admirable for its purpose, but a new demand is to rise as the taste of the times develops, and in answer to it scenery will begin to grow unwieldy for the form of machinery that changed it. The form of machinery will be scrapped. The need to change scenery will remain—indeed, it will become more insistent—but the means to change it visibly, and in the twinkling of an eye almost, will break down. Changing remains, but changing becomes hidden. Scenery becomes a problem: some seek to reduce it from a fascination to a mere furniture, some incontinently push it to an elaboration which demands that an old play must be rearranged to accommodate it and a new play must be specially written to observe very particular limitations, others again rise phoenix-like with a new cry that has not been heard in our review before—that scenery is an 'art of the theatre'. But almost everyone has to accept the doom that scene-changing must be hidden and that performances must now contain intervals in which to effect those hidden changes.

Part Three will also offer us the final evidence in our review and thus enable us to begin to form certain conclusions upon the nature of scenery in the past. Two of these it is convenient to deal with at the opening and—since their references are somewhat scattered in date—to deal with in the freedom of an Interlude-chapter. Both are intimately concerned in the

[249]

revolution that is to take place. The first conclusion concerns the nature of the set scene and the second the full significance of the word 'flat'.

The reason for introducing the former subject here particularly, at the end of the eighteenth century, lies in a sentence in Fitzgerald's *Lives of the Kembles*, referring to the use in 1800 of what he says was, 'I suppose one of the earliest specimens of "set" scenery ' (see below, p. 268). This may or may not be a correct supposition, but it suggests that some development of the set scene as such was, at that period, taking place. Here, then, before we step over into the nineteenth century, we will turn to that form of scenery which was distinct from the flat scene.

This flat scene, which was the common, typical scene for over two centuries, had, as we have found, three constituent parts—the wings, the borders, and the flats themselves. But we have also found that there was a curious other element in the anatomy of scenery which was never incorporated in the flat scene—and which was called the 'piece'. As Rees (whom we shall soon be examining) puts it, there are items which 'may occasionally be placed and displaced, such as the fronts of cottages, cascades, rocks, bridges, and other appendages, requisite in the representation of particular dramas. These are generally called pieces.'

That 'piece' is in fact a technical term we have seen from the Covent Garden Inventory. But what exactly does Rees's passage mean? And what is our reason for introducing this scenic 'piece' into a study headed 'The Set Scene'? The present chapter is to begin by showing the meaning of the set scene and its close connexion with the piece.

Since we have made ourselves more independent of chronological order in our Interlude-chapters, I may begin with a statement made in 1840 by Edward Mayhew in his *Stage Effects*:

Further from the footlights than the middle of the stage, *flats* are seldom used, the remaining half being devoted to set scenes, which, in the painter's and manager's estimation are the first kind; and a piece [i.e. a play] is generally cared for by the theatre in proportion to the number of set scenes bestowed on its production. . . . It was once desirable an author should so construct his plot, that flats and set scenes might alternate one the other; and this for authors not intimate with the theatre is still a good plain rule though the improvement of machinery now enables the carpenter to work *set scenes* consecutively; but it needs some acquaintance with the capabilities of the theatre to do this with effect, and the accidents and delays common on the first nights of pantomimes, are cautions not to be disregarded.

From this it appears (though perhaps somewhat obscurely) that set scenes are, firstly, deep scenes; secondly, they enforce formal restrictions on dramatic structure; and thirdly, they are a kind of scene which their makers and their arrangers estimate especially highly. But the point of primary interest is that flat scenes and set scenes are two different and contrasting types of scene, and that here it is said they should alternate with each other. Wherein did they essentially differ?

It is only when we seek for information to enable us to define the set scene that we realize how much its distinctive qualities have become a thing of the past, and that we need to take some care today before asserting what a set scene was and how far it goes back as a system in history.

The term 'set scene' is not now of very common usage in the theatre; we shall find it is not included in the three latest theatrical glossaries which we shall soon consider. If it is used at all, it is very loosely applied and seems to mean little beyond what the user wishes it to mean—save that perhaps it suggests nowadays something having elements solidly built.

But we find the opposite is true with another modern term, the *set piece*. This is in very frequent use today. It is a convenient term and the carpenter would be hindered without it, and yet when one attempts to define the scope of its application one finds here also, in spite of its frequent use, a considerable element of uncertainty.

Let us, however, note before we go any farther that in this new term *set piece* we have already combined the two main, but apparently unconnected, words mentioned at the opening of this chapter, namely, the technical term 'piece' and the specific adjective of the phrase '*set* scene'.

A 'set piece' in modern usage tends to apply to any piece of subsidiary scenery standing separately in the middle of the stage. The piece may be cut out in profile—as a tree—or be built up in three dimensions—as a mossy bank whereon to recline. I suppose the nearest one can get to the flavour of the word is '*separate* piece', in the sense of its being distinct from the basic wings, backscenes, and borders. It generally bears something of the sense of an addition. But this does not quite cover it, for you may hear talk of 'an elaborate, built set piece' and find that what is intended is a huge detailed construction representing, say, a curved row of full-sized columns, with plinths and cornices, forming the half or more, of a spectacular set, and built for ease of shifting upon a *boat-truck* (a low, wheeled platform), upon which it is slid bodily from the stage into the dock at a scene-change.

Thus, the application of the word is not strict. And it will not become clearly definable until we look at its history. Let me repeat that *set scene* is in very infrequent and loose use on the contemporary stage, and that *set piece* on the other hand is very common, and then let us turn to the *Dictionary* once again to seek enlightenment.

Our first experience on settling the pages of *The Oxford English Dictionary* is a surprise, and a considerable one. Leaving the rarer term aside as less likely to be included we take the commoner first and we find, under the uses of the word *set* in combination, this: 'Set Piece, (*a*) a painting, or a

sculptured group of figures; (*b*) a picture or design composed of fireworks.'
And that is all. It does not mention the theatre; it ends with fireworks!

This essential term of everyday usage in the modern theatre has no
recognition or reference. But directly afterwards we discover a comparatively
long explanation of the other term *set scene* which, as I say, we go a whole
lifetime on the stage and never hear used in current parlance. This is what
it says:

> Set Scene, an apparatus built up and placed in position upon a theatrical stage
> before the rise of the curtain; a collection of side scenes, 'skies', etc. depending
> upon one another for a particular effect; so *set scenery* . . . 1887 *Spectator* 25 June
> 857/2 Theatrical speculators now spend such vast sums on the upholstery of their
> set scenes. 1854 FAIRHOLT *Dict. Terms Art* 382 The scenery . . . was entirely of
> the nature of what is now termed set-scenery, regularly built up by the carpenters
> before the curtain rises, to be taken to pieces again when it falls.

There is a great deal here that needs examination. Let us take the first
part of the definition and make one remark upon it before we pass to the
second. A set scene is said to be an apparatus built up and placed in position
upon a theatrical stage *before the rise of the curtain*. Let us note this well.
We must find out what is the reason for this last phrase. Why is it a set
scene's distinguishing feature that it is set up before the rise of the curtain?

Meanwhile we have the second part of the definition which is even more
puzzling. There a set scene is said to be a collection of side-scenes—we note
in passing the unexpected use, in a 1914 volume of a dictionary, of this
seventeenth-century term for wings—and of 'skies'—a curious substitute,
presumably for borders, and a term I have never heard used in the theatre
in my life—and of other things unspecified, but all *depending upon one
another for a particular effect*. Here again it is the conclusion of the passage
that involves us in the chief puzzle. One is tempted to ask in what circumstances the wings, borders, &c., of any properly arranged scene do *not*
'depend upon each other' for effect—whether 'particular' or not? Surely
in any right-minded, modern scene design, the elements must be mutually
interdependent, and the 'particular effect' of that scene depends upon the
interdependence of the parts and the proper composition through them of
the whole. Yet we seem to be told here that if these parts depend upon one
another for a particular effect, then the scene they make is a set scene. This,
one is apparently given to deduce, in contradistinction to a collection of
parts which are not dependent upon one another for a particular effect, in
which case they do not constitute a set scene! Which seems, of course,
absurd.

Note, further, the scene-parts mentioned (wings, borders) are all general
parts which might belong to any scene; the especial part, as we shall see
later, which is limited only to set scenes and which fundamentally charac-

terizes them, namely, the *piece*, is not mentioned at all. The *piece* is practically inseparable from the set scene, it is part of its very nature and so should surely come first, not be lost completely among the *et ceteras*. But the connexion between the *piece* and the set scene we have still to discover.

In passing we should perhaps in fairness to the *Dictionary* remember that the old flat scenes were often guilty of having parts which did not properly 'depend upon one another' in the sense that they were thrown together from different parts of the stock, and it may be claimed that a set scene on the contrary was distinguished by possessing a set of parts all designed for use together and for use only in one effect. This possibility of interpretation we must keep in mind for confirmation or discarding.

Finally, we have the cryptic rider—'so *set scenery*', which is a term I do not remember ever having heard in normal use, and whose significance is hard to explain. In fact the *Dictionary* does not, at first, offer us any real aid to solving the mystery of the set scene at all. We must seek elsewhere.

In the discussion of the set scene it will be desirable to take full advantage of the latitude we permitted ourselves in Interlude-chapters. It is difficult to make any attempt at first to place the origin of the set scene because it is far harder to arrive at a satisfactory definition of the term itself than when we were concerned with grooves or flats or drops. It will be best here to make a beginning not in the past but in the present, and to concern ourselves with comparing and examining such modern definitions of the term as we can find and then gradually to trace back its usage till we arrive at some point where the circumstances which give rise to it become clear, and the root meaning of it may be extracted.

The latest glossary available to me at the time of publication is *The Glossary of Technical Theatrical Terms*, published in 1947 by the Strand Electric Company. Its reference to the word 'set' is the most modern but also the most removed from its historical significance; we are simply told that *Set* is the 'General term for any complete set of scenery. Thus *Box and Chamber Sets*, Interiors. *Exterior Set: Garden Set. . . .*' No reference to 'set piece' and no specific reference to 'set scene' are included.

Among other recent publications which deal in detail with the technique of stage scenery is the collection of articles by various authors published (after issue in periodical form) in two volumes by Pitman and called *Theatre and Stage*. It includes 'A Dictionary of Stage Terms' by Edward W. Betts, in which we may find the starting-point of our backward progress in search of the basic nature of the set scene, although the term 'set scene' is not itself included. The 'set piece' is, however, noticed and is defined as a 'small piece of scenery used within the scene to represent a garden bank, rocks, etc.; any scenery that stands on the stage is a set piece'.

From the word 'stands' it would seem that the significance of *set* might be to suggest something *stood* or *set* upon the stage. But we shall find reason to question this and to incline towards attaching another sense to the word, or at least another variant of the primal sense. As a definition, the above is not going to take us very far. It tells us that a set piece is 'small', but we have ourselves already noted that the name is today also applied to large and elaborately built units. The phrase 'used within the scene' is not conclusive; presumably it means 'standing in the acting-area on its own, rather than at the side of it and associated with the scenery on its perimeter'. But the ostensibly explanatory sentence at the end—'any scenery that stands on the stage is a set piece'—stultifies the whole; it suggests that any scenery save hanging scenery can be included under the name of set piece—if so, what is the use of the term at all? In point of fact we already well know that much of the scenery that stands on the stage belongs to other categories than that of set piece.

Two references at the beginning of Betts's *Dictionary* lead us to the possible sources of his information. They are to W. G. Fay's *A Short Glossary of Theatrical Terms* (French, 1903), and to a short glossary at the end of C. B. Purdom's *Producing Plays* (Dent, 1930). The former is probably the basis of the first part of Betts's definition, the latter of the second part. If we look up the former reference (in Fay's *Glossary*), we read: 'Set Piece. A small piece of scenery representing a rock, the side of a building, or other object that has to be set within the scene. It is placed there to help the perspective or for practical use as in the case of a garden gate, or a grass bank, etc.'

Here we have the mysterious phrase again, 'set within the scene'—now perhaps a little clearer because of the replacement of 'set' for 'used', since it is now pretty certain that what is meant is 'set inside the usual scenery'. But again the limiting word 'small' is included.

The other source, Purdom, merely has: 'Set-piece. Any piece of scenery that stands on the stage and is not flown', but since this includes all scenery saving hanging stuff, it is of no use whatever save as suggesting the source of the latter part of Betts's definition.

Now let us begin to trail our two hares a little farther back. In Henry L. Benwell's series of articles on 'Practical Scene Painting', in *Amateur Work*, beginning in 1884, we have for the first time a notice of the two terms side by side, and hence a recognition of the separate existence of the *set piece* and the *set scene*. In successive paragraphs we read, firstly:

Set Pieces—Scenes placed obliquely on one side of the stage when it is required to show a cottage, corner of a house, or porch. They are also placed across the stage, just in front of the back cloth, such as palings, low walls, side of ship, bridges, etc.

We seize with interest on the word 'obliquely'—is this the distinctive

[254]

characteristic of the set piece? But no, for immediately beyond we read that the low wall across in front of a backcloth is also a set piece. And regretfully we have to decide that this definition contributes in fact very little more than the earlier ones.

In the immediately following paragraph we have, for the first time since *The Oxford English Dictionary* mentioned it to the exclusion of the term *set piece*, a statement of the *set scene*. And at last we begin to glean something coherent and logical rising in the confusion. We read on:

> Set scenes.—These are very elaborate. Instead of the whole picture being painted on the back-cloth, the distance only is put in, the middle distance and foreground being composed of set-pieces, raking-pieces and ground rows, with strong lights behind each. It requires great skill and experience to paint and arrange a set scene.

Here is positive information. A set scene is said to be one with certain elements painted on separate pieces and stood in front of a backcloth which contains only the farther distance. These separate pieces may be 'set-pieces', 'raking-pieces', or 'ground rows'. What do these terms mean?

The set piece we have already grappled with and, as yet, failed to satisfy ourselves about. The raking piece and the ground-row are, however, new to us. What is known about them? We will finish our consideration of this passage and then discuss them.

A set scene, we are told in the first words, is 'a very elaborate' scene. This is consistent with our initial supposition that it was more rarely used, at any rate in the early days, than 'flat scenes', but was reserved for special effects and for scenes of climax. Presumably the special requirement of skill in painting a set scene depends on the fact that its composing elements are separate and on different planes, consequently demanding a greater care for the control of the paint-tone, and the general unity of the whole scheme even than is demanded in the one-surface painting of a flat scene.

Now, before tracing the definition of *set scene* back into earlier references still, we pause to consider the two terms *raking piece* and *ground-row*, which we may with some justification suppose are elements in the succession of planes which marks the nature of a set scene, that is to say they are sub-varieties of the main group, *set piece*.

The Oxford English Dictionary has 'Raking-piece, (*b*) a low sloping piece of stage-scenery.' But it gives as the example a curious and, I think, non-technical usage: '1898 "P. McGinnis" *Bohem. Girl* 124 The theatre was like a barn, and we had to get to our dressing-room up a raking-piece with ribs nailed across.'

This seems a gangway rather than a piece of scenery. We are better enlightened by a picture. In Frederick Lloyds's *Scene Painting* (1875) a clear diagram with a clear inscription admits of no doubt. Did we need any more, the term is defined verbally in Fay's *Glossary* as 'A triangular piece of scenery painted with a rising road or bank used to mask in a ramp.'

The clarity of the definition would be improved by the insertion of a hyphen after 'mask', for it is fairly certain that what is meant is that the raking piece masks a ramp or covers it from the audience's view, so that it is *masked-in*. A ramp is (according to the same authority) 'A slope made of planks from a rostrum to the stage when steps are not used.' A rostrum is any platform used in a scene. A raking piece then is intended to mask-in the side of one of these ramps.

We should find in actual practice that a triangular piece of this nature, with a profiled hypotenuse, is also used for other reasons than to mask-in a ramp; it may, for instance, be used as a short ground-row to stand at the foot of some vertical piece, say a wing, to lead its foot into the picture.

The other reference to the raking piece that I mentioned is in Betts, and is a word-for-word repetition of Fay, save that the initial 'a' is omitted and the word 'mounting' substituted for 'rising'.

I have used the term *ground-row*, above, as part of my explanation of a raking piece, thereby implying that sufficient evidence is already in the reader's possession to enable him to make some approximation of what a ground-row is. If that be so, then when he comes to turn up *The Oxford English Dictionary* to seek to precise that approximation he will receive a considerable shock. However vague he may be about its details, he will by now be fairly sure that a ground-row is some sort of a piece of scenery. But in the *Dictionary* he will find, under the general use of the word *ground* in combination, merely the laconic phrase; '*g-row*, a row of gas-jets on the floor of a theatre stage.'

It seems almost incredible, but we have to remember that the date of the G-volume of this dictionary is 1901, and perhaps it is not so strange that it should refer to gas-jets on the stage. By 1951 we need almost the abbreviation *arch.* to excuse the solecism as a reference to bygone days. There, however, it stands in its categorical statement, and affairs have changed. Now, few will still imagine gas to be permitted by the Home Office as a method of modern stage-lighting.

But beyond all this, we have sufficient evidence to show that the word *ground-row* is used today, and has been used for years, with a very different meaning. However, further study of the glossaries confirms that at one time the ground-row had a connexion with lights. Before we go on to them, there is a certain unexpected element in the meaning of the term to which familiarity has somewhat blinded us. It is this: in every variety of application of the noun *row* admitted in the *Dictionary*, the sense of *series* is present, as—'a number of persons or things arranged in a straight line'. And it certainly seems odd, once this is realized, that we should find this very collective word used to name a unit of scenery into whose nature the sense of *row* does not come at all—save maybe only in special cases when its visual nature is the representation of a *row* of hills or such like.

And in the face of this inconsistence, we are inclined to see some reason for the *Dictionary's* peculiarity; we may be in the presence of a transferred epithet. What once applied to a *row* of lights along the foot of a backscene might have come to be applied to certain low strips of scenery designed especially to hide those lights. With this possibility in view we turn to the glossaries.

The latest, the Strand *Glossary*, is informative. We read:

Ground Row. Any low piece of scenery running horizontally, usually to complete the scene at the back, such as *Ground Row*, Landscape; *Sea Row*, Seascape; *Horizon Row*, etc. Also electrically, a length of magazine troughing generally placed horizontally behind such scenery. Sometimes, as for cycloramas, lengths are double or treble banked.

We shall later find reason to disagree with the conclusion above that a 'ground row' is so called because it shows the 'ground' in a landscape. We shall go so far as to prove that when it is used as part of a seascape, its proper name is also, paradoxically, 'ground row'. We note with interest the marked connexion with lights, even today.

Betts, the next to date, lands us in nearly as great a confusion as did the *Dictionary*. He says: 'Groundrow. Low pieces of scenery to represent wells, ledges, etc.'

We may pause, completely mystified. He says no more; not a single word in explanation of this extraordinary excursion into the cryptic. Can it be that the assistant editor of *The Era* has passed uncorrected in two places a printer's proof that was originally intended to finish with the words 'walls, hedges, etc.'?

Fay's *Glossary* gives the following under *Ground Row*: 'A painted flat of which the length is greater than the height placed in front of a backcloth to represent a wall, a bank, distant hills, etc. When it is necessary to use a rostrum to get elevation on the stage it is usually concealed behind a ground row.'

Provided we clear our mind of the old definition of the word 'flat' as half a backscene, and read it merely as meaning a framed canvas whose height, in this case, is less than its width, then Fay's definition is clear and useful. But we have something to add: in certain plates published in Contant's *Parallèle des Théâtres* (1859) and illustrating the construction of various type-pieces of English scenery, we shall find two figures associated with those of flats, showing something closely resembling ground-rows. The first of these (see Fig. 30) appears to scale at 33 ft. 3 in. long. It shows a piece made up of three sections, joined together with jointing-plates. It is cut up in this way presumably for ease of moving and packing. Its height varies from 1 ft. 6 in. to 6 ft., and it is described as a *terrain* or 'ground' for setting across the stage to simulate a river-bank or the verge of a declivity, and serving also to mask the opening of a 'cut' in the stage floor, should that be needed to represent the descent into a hollow behind, or the depth of a river, and serving, moreover, to mask a *row* of lights lying along the stage with the function of lighting the bottom of the piece of scenery behind—or, more exactly, of 'killing' the shadow of the ground-row itself that would else be cast by the footlights in front, upon that piece of scenery behind.

It is highly interesting that we should find the apparently strange definition of the *Dictionary* confirmed to this extent that in 1859 a ground-row was intended, among other things, to hide a strip of lights.

In Contant's second diagram (see Fig. 31) is a cut-out piece designed to mask the front of a row of rostrums, placed to give a hill or mound effect at the back of the stage. The piece is 33 ft. 2 in. long and is in three sections. Its height varies from 5 ft. to 12 ft. 6 in. As a type of scenic piece it is distinguishable in no way from the one we have just discussed, save that it forms a higher wall. A modern carpenter would unhesitatingly class them both as ground-rows.

But I am not so sure that the carpenter who made them nearly a century ago would have used that name for them. The term is not an old one and it is not easy to state what name he would have used, but we may bring in in this connexion the following rather interesting observations.

In the toy-theatre prints of Redington (worked 1850–76) and of Pollock (1856–1937), his successor, which offer us, with those of other contemporary publishers, a fund of unexpected information on contemporary scenery, we shall not find the term *ground-row* at all. The type of scene-piece to which we should expect the name to have been applied is not absent from the prints, it is exemplified in Sheet No. 1, Sc. 1 of Pollock's *The Blind Boy* series, where it is simply labelled 'to be placed at the back, 1st distance', or in Sheet No. 4, Sc. 3 of *The Forty Thieves*—'to be set across the stage, 3rd. wing'. But no specific name is given to the pieces.

For some indication of a probable name we turn to a highly interesting sheet from Redington's *Baron Munchausen* (No. 11). It represents a street with a wall covered with advertisements; these include some for Redington's own wares. There is, for example, one announcing '*Redington's* ½*d*, 1*d*, 2*d*, & 4*d stage fronts, Plain and Beautifully Color'd*'. But what is of chief interest to us at the moment is another announcement, in the form of a list of miscellaneous sheets obtainable, mentioning '*Drop Scenes, Top Drops*', and '*Foot Pieces*'. A definition of the latter two terms is possible by reference, for the first, to a sheet entitled '*Pollock's Top Drops to Paul Clifford or any other play. No.* 1', where a *top drop* is seen to be equivalent to our border; while for the second (our immediate concern) we may refer to '*Pollock's Top Drops and Foot Pieces in the Silver Palace*', where a *foot piece* is seen to be exactly that kind of low strip which we have defined as a ground-row.

We have then to table, for testing when opportunity occurs, the opinion that the early name for our modern ground-row was *foot piece*. It is a term capable of some variation; for instance, on Sheets No. 10 and 11 of *The Miller and His Men*, we find '1*st and* 2*nd ground pieces*'.

The adjective *ground* must not be taken to mean—on the evidence, for instance, of Contant's *terrain*—that these 'ground-rows' were so called because they represented ground; the word merely signifies 'set along the ground or floor'; *ground* piece equals *foot* piece. And in fact some ground-rows actually represent water, or sea.

One comes across such terms as 'water row', 'sea row', 'mountain row', and such-like, but I think we should do wrong to add to this list, as if it were merely another variant, the term 'ground-row' on the supposition that, since the former bear their names because they represent streams, sea, or mountains respectively, so the latter is named because it represents *ground*. Rather is 'ground-row' the generic term classifying and including all these strips of scenery *because they stretch along the ground*, or stage, and some of them may be—quite logically—further particularized by the use of both adjectives, the generic and the specific or descriptive—indeed, one occasionally hears such a full term used on the stage (in such a case one may be so struck by the apparent anomaly of the name as to dismiss it as a freak of carpenter's carelessness rather than treasure it as a relic of genuine tradition), as for instance *sea ground-row*. This would seem now to be a perfectly correct expression.

But possibly the most romantic term of all for such an amphibious piece is that given at the opening of the book to Pollock's *The Miller and His Men*, where the various succession of 'rows', representing the stream by that celebrated mill, are together most euphoniously referred to as '*set waters*'.

So at length, then, we come back to our word *set* again. Now, we may add to the terms *set piece, set scene, set portico* and *set steps*, the new *set waters* of Grindoff, the brigand miller, and his rascal band.

We are reminded we have still to seek the meaning and origin of this strange adjective, which has so extensively pervaded the technology of scenery, and we return now to the process of unwinding the meaning of the term *set scene* from more and more distant references in the past.

About 1875 a copy of *Scene Painting* by Frederick Lloyds was purchased by a certain enthusiast named Mr. H. R. Eyre. This Mr. Eyre enriched his copy with an addition of the highest value; he had it rebound with some

152 blank pages at the end. In these blank pages he stuck a long series of cuttings, relative to scenery, from a contemporary journal, or journals, and added thereto some very detailed notes and excursions in manuscript, based on the comments of an acquaintance of his, W. J. Burgess, the then manager and scene-painter of the Theatre Royal, Ipswich. The many comments, and their accompanying illustrations in actual scene-paint upon scraps of paper carefully inserted, form a monograph upon the contemporary scene-painter's method too valuable to be discussed in detail here, since the whole subject of English scene-painters and the peculiarly distinctive form of scene-painting practised in England is important enough to have a study on its own, wherein Burgess's life-knowledge would more aptly fit. But from this wealth of unique information I take the following five passages, directly relevant to our story:

Firstly, in one of the newspaper cuttings (possibly from a series of articles by Henry Lancaster in *The Furniture Gazette*), the author, enumerating the scenic elements of a theatre, sweetly concludes: 'Then there are set pieces to represent cottages, bridges, water pieces, rocks, etc., all used to add to the general effect and beauty of the scene.'

But later he is more informative:

Set Scenes—In these you can have recourse to furniture, and it is also usual to employ real ivy or artificial flowers, trained up house fronts, covering ruins, or climbing the trunks of old trees; grass embankments are sometimes covered with green velvet. The projecting irregular outlines of boughs from trees are made with *papier-mâché*, which being modelled to the required shape, is stuck on them, and then painted to add to the effect. Roofs of houses are often built out; and in many other ways readily enough suggested by the author's descriptions in the play, ingenious tricks and dodges may be adopted to add to the general effect and reality of the mimic scenes.

From the same source we have: 'Set pieces, for transformation scenes, are often very numerous. Sometimes as many as eighty or ninety pieces are used in the building up of a single scene.'

In Mr. Eyre's manuscript notes of Burgess's comments we find: 'In all set scenes it is necessary where practicable to have gas behind each piece, not only to light up the piece that is behind, but to prevent the shadows of the pieces falling on the back scene.'

And lastly, in a further newspaper cutting describing the painting of various types of subject for scenery, we read under 'street scenes', firstly, a passage dealing with the painting of a street scene upon a pair of flats (suggesting that street scenes destined to be used in the first grooves are preferably designed to show a row of house façades *across* the stage, while perspective views down the length of streets are more consistently reserved for painting on more distant flats), and then we have the following highly interesting passage:

[260]

Street scenes can be made very effective, and particularly so by using set pieces leading up to the scene. . . . In set scenes you can introduce many realistic effects, such as balconies built out from the houses, set portico pieces over the doors with set steps, made by the carpenter, leading to the doors etc., all of which add to the effect and apparent reality of the scene.

Before examining these five passages in detail let us pause for a moment to remark the vividness with which the last recalls that 'long street' scene which we found in Aphra Behn's *Sir Patient Fancy*, above p. 151, and to notice what confirmation it seems to give of the theory we there proposed that this 'long' street was an arrangement of receding, separate pieces of scenery leading right to the back of the stage.

It seems that here in 1875 we have an echo of an old tradition for street-scenes dating back to the beginning of our theatre, in which, beside the usual one-surface presentation upon a pair of flats, another method was available, making a 'particularly effective' result, 'by using set pieces leading up to the scene'. That is by putting only the farthest distance upon the back canvas, and leading up thereto by a succession of cut-out pieces, bearing the houses and so on of the foreground and middle distance. Thus we find our first, albeit as yet tenuous, link between the *set scene* of the Victorians and the *long scene* of the Restoration. We have to see if this link is capable of any reinforcement.

To turn to the examination in detail of these five passages: ignoring the first as contributing little new information, we find an interesting point at the beginning of the second, and something that is completely new to us—namely, that in a set scene 'you can have recourse to furniture'. Just what lies behind this novel and unexpected announcement?

Again our study of Aphra Behn's stage-directions puts us on the way to part at least of an explanation. We noticed that the chief piece of furniture in her *Sir Patient Fancy*, namely the big bed, had given her some trouble since it was a 'discovery' and had to be in place before the opening of the scene—further, she had to resort to a momentary closing of a pair of flats in order to conceal its removal. Would then that bedroom scene have been termed, by the early-Victorian stage-carpenter, a 'set scene', despite its consisting (as we presume) of a pair of flats behind, and on the score of its containing furniture?

We have now uncovered a complete new problem in the history of theatrical scenery—the problem of the placing and disposal of stage furniture in the early days of visible scene-change; and indeed there is also the problem—to what extent was furniture used at all in the first two centuries of our theatre? But avoiding the second problem for a moment, and considering that Aphra Behn has proved already that furniture was used, if only very rarely, how did it get on to the stage? Was every scene involving the use of a chair, inevitably and by that very fact, a discovery scene? Could no furniture be used in a front scene? How was the furniture ever set in place and removed?

W. J. Lawrence contributed a neat little article to *Ireland's Saturday Night* for 16 July 1923, in which he traced the setting of furniture back to Elizabethan days as the work of special, liveried servants of the theatre, and brought the persistence of the convention almost to the present with his conclusion, 'As I can personally testify, the furniture remover was still at work in the provincial theatres in the early 'eighties'.

For the period of the early nineteenth century he has a pleasant extract from *The Belfast News-Letter* of 24 December 1813, wherein we read:

Two boys in livery are in constant attendance to bring in and remove chairs, tables and other articles necessary to a change of scene. They are a genteel appendage seen in the London and Dublin theatres, and since there must be persons to execute this office . . . it is pleasing to see these well-dressed boys, in lieu of . . . a ragged little being, whom we have formerly seen obtrude himself for the purpose.

Either this method of liveried servant, or 'greenback', was used or, as we have noted in our first chapter, Fitzgerald actually claims that furniture was shifted in visible scene changes by the pulling of an attached string!

Such methods will suggest that the use of furniture in any but set scenes would be reduced to a minimum. Nothing, or perhaps a single chair, would be the rule. Occasionally the playwright noted, as did Aphra Behn, 'A Table and six Chairs'—and said no more about the setting.

In retrospect the 'furniture remover' seems a most remarkable and highly artificial convention—one almost reminiscent of that most artificial of all theatrical conventions in the world, the 'invisible' property man of the Chinese stage.

Thus far from our prime subject of the set scene have the first words of Mr. Eyre's carefully clipped-out newspaper article led us. Or rather, I should say thus deeply into our prime subject, for though set scene and furniture are separate things, yet there is a province in which they quite overlap and the knowledge of the former cannot be complete without an acquaintance with the conventions concerning the latter. But we return to our examination of the article.

After our initial discovery, we are not surprised to hear that 'real ivy or artificial flowers' are also in usual employ for set scenes. There seems never to have been fixed any limit to the possibilities of their decorative bedizenment. Modelled boughs may grow from their trees, built-out roofs crown their houses. In short, any 'ingenious trick and dodge' that the 'author's description in the play' suggests may have its fling in the field of the set scene.

In the fourth passage, from Burgess's own lips, comes an emphasis on the use of gas in set scenes.

The interesting point in the last of the passages (beyond the already discussed reminiscence of the Restoration 'long street') is the emphasis on *built* elements in set scenes, and the application of the adjective 'set' to describe such elements—as *set portico piece*, or *set steps*. It is presumably from this characteristic of the set scene that there has sprung one modern use of the term *set piece* to describe any three-dimensional, built piece— that is, one not painted on the flat, but more or less self-contained in its character, and forming an addition to the ordinary painted scenery of the scene.

We have still to add information before discovering the root meaning of the word *set* in the term *set piece*. Let us, in our search for this root meaning, turn now from specific definitions of the terms *set piece* and *set scene* and try to gather some impression of the general character of a set scene as it appeared on the stage about the time when those definitions were penned.

We shall find one such impression in Vandenhoff's *Leaves from an Actor's Note Book; or, Anecdotes of the Green Room and the Stage*, 1860. In speaking of Planché's comedy of *The Knights of the Round Table* he says: 'The piece was admirably put upon the stage; and the final scene of the fifth act, a view of London from Hampstead Heath, a hundred years back, was an elaborate "set"; and, as was universally admitted, was so admirably painted and arranged, and the light so skilfully disposed as to form a most perfect landscape, equal to one of Cooper's or Moreland's.'

Something of the elaborate nature of the set scene is to be gathered here. It is also interesting to note the calling of this scene an 'elaborate "set"'; we use the noun *set* today to describe the whole assembly of scenery for any scene, not only for one particular variety of scene. A *set* is a *scene*. Perhaps the reader might have been inclined to relate the word with its sense of 'collection', and hence to suppose that we called a set a 'set' because it is a collection, or set, of scenery, just as we speak of a *suite* of furniture or a *suit* of clothes. But it is rather to be supposed now that the word originates in the term *set scene*, which was formerly a special and a rare type of scene—a contrast to the commoner *flat scene*.

How then, we may pause to ask, did our term 'setting' come to be? Is it a mere development of *set*, or does it trace back to such a phrase as the 'orderly setting foorthe' of the masques that we find used as early as 1571? Today the theatrical setting of shows is understood to cover every branch and variety of scene and scenery. The root meaning, however, was more specific and we must return again to it.

A *set*, we have established, was originally a *set scene* as distinct from a *flat scene*, and in that sense it is, of course, applicable still to any scene save a one-surface painting—which means today a scene painted wholly on a cloth. And so we come to the truth hidden behind one of the first definitions we examined which said that a set piece is 'any piece of scenery that stands on the stage and is not flown'. As it reads it is meaningless, but transpose its terms a little farther back in time, and relate it to a period when the old pairs of flats had just been done away with in favour of the cloth or drop scene, and finally replace the word 'piece' by 'scene', and the definition becomes true, though relating now to ways long left behind; it would, with these amendments, read: a set *scene* is any *scene* that stands on the stage and is not flown, that is to say, any scene that is not a drop scene, and that, in its turn, is to say that is not a flat scene, since when flats were abandoned the drop was the sole surviving form of the flat scene. And so the definition now states that a set scene is any scene that is not a flat scene, and thereupon comes into agreement with one of our first discoveries about the set scene.

So we find that, if we examine historically what is now nonsense, we uncover an idea that was once true, but has since, in the progress of time, become so garbled and corrupt in its usage as to lose any meaning at all.

In much the same sense as Vandenhoff's is Professor Morley's use of the words *set scene* in his *Journal of a London Playgoer*, where under date 6 August 1864 he tells us, of *The Streets of London* at the Princess's Theatre, that 'It has two set scenes, a set scene of Charing Cross and Trafalgar Square as seen from the corner of Hemming's row, and a scene of the house on fire, which take the place of literature to secure a long run for the drama'. Here again the term means an elaborate scene of several elements (not a one-surface painting on a drop or a pair of flats), and probably with several of these elements built out in three dimensions.

It was the inconsistence of alternating built scenes with one-surface painting that aroused much of the anger of those who criticized the elaborate Victorian set scene. For instance, Edward F. Spence very clearly presents his objection, in *The Artist* for December 1887, writing of Miss May Anderson's presentation of *A Winter's Tale* at the Lyceum:

. . . Now what is the cause of all this cruel cutting? [of the script] . . . The employment of elaborate scenery in order to produce the four 'tableaux' referred to in the bill and book of the words (but not mentioned by Shakespeare). The waits have to be very many and long. . . . Consequently the cuts must be made or the elaborate scenery must be sacrificed. . . . For no play ought to be elaborately mounted if there be a change of scene in the middle of an act. The consequence of neglecting this law is disastrous. At the Lyceum we first have a mere drop scene with everything obviously painted and unsubstantial, then a set scene in which everything is (more or less) real and solid. What can be more inartistic than this violent succession of different conventions—than this alternation of

[264]

sham and substance? It may be answered that to some extent it is necessary—
that to keep changing the background of flats is cumbersome; but anything is
better than 'swopping horses in crossing a stream'—than changing conventions
during a play. Even if the system of drop and set scenes is necessary then let it
be borne in mind that the less elaborate—the less real and solid the set the more
congruous is it with the drop and so the more harmonious. Apart from the dramatic view of the question there is another objection; if the carpenter and scene-
painter are employed to produce realistic pictures then this change from drop to
set is to the last degree a hindrance to their success. . . .

Drop scene and set scene are antitheses. More than that: they are here
pointed out to be artistically irreconcilable one with the other—or recon-
cilable only if the set scene be free of 'real' or solid elements. There may be
much to be said for this point of view. The idea of keeping the conventions
of the scenery consistent throughout a show is, of course, deserving of
respect. But for us the main point is that the set scene of this period was
developing, in the manner so clearly described above, away from the old
flat scene with which it was, apparently, always a contrast, but has here
become an inconsistence.

The objection to set scenes was also voiced by Fitzgerald in *The World
behind the Scenes* (1881); there, on page 7, he says: 'Of course it may be
said that mere spectacular display is all that is now desired, and a brilliant
gaudy show; but if *illusion* be sought, it can only be repeated that too
much light, too much colour, and the principles of "set scenes" are destructive of it.'

Many critics at this time were greatly exercised about the elaboration of
the contemporary set scene. It would seem that had the elaboration been
merely in the realm of painting, and had it been confined to cloths and
flats, with the set scene used much more rarely and more restrainedly (as
it had once been), many of the bitter attacks on the extravagance of scenery
would never have come into being.

Fitzgerald does not, at this place, define his term 'set scene', but a little
before the passage quoted, he was exclaiming: 'How conventional a thing
scenery is', and instancing 'The arrangement of those profile banks, with
the tree in the foreground, as it were cut out in cardboard, and whose
trunk does not effect to be round or solid! These layers, placed one behind
the other, are regarded by the painter as the foundation of his illusive
craft. . . .' And this we may take as being descriptive of one type at least
of contemporary set scene. The 'layers, placed one behind the other' are
clearly descriptive of the multiplane nature of the set scene.

He has more to say on the subject. We quoted (above, p. 21) a passage
of his objecting to the 'clatter' and 'labour' involved in changing elaborate
and built-up scenery as against the ease of 'the old system, where a simple
"cloth" quietly glided down'. And immediately after this passage, he goes

on to state exactly the criticism made by Spence of May Anderson's *A Winter's Tale*:

> In Shakespearian plays, where there are many scenes in each act, the 'cloth' or painted scene has to be frequently used when there is a large set scene behind, filling nearly the whole stage, and which must be removed. But to the eye accustomed to the 'built up' scene, this sudden introduction is discordant. . . .

Later, on p. 221 of the same book, Fitzgerald speaks of a poverty-stricken theatre which had only two cloths in its stock, so that one had an alternation of these, instead of being—and these are his words—'bewildered with elaborate and tedious "set scenes", as I believe they are called'. And so he makes the necessity of an impoverished stage a virtue in that it relieves the audience of the set scene.

Again and again we find the set scene blamed for distracting from, or hindering, the show. As for instance, again, in James R. Anderson's *Seven Decades of an Actor's Life*, where, speaking of the presentation of his own play, *The Three Great Worthies*, at the Standard Theatre in October 1866, he uses the words: 'The scenery by that clever young and rising painter Richard Douglass was admirable but the time the "sets" took up would have "damned" a better play.'

A. B. Walkley, under the pen-name 'Spectator', sounded the note of the coming change in *The Star* for 2nd August 1890. There, writing of a performance given for the benefit of the widow of the outstanding scene-painter William Beverley, he produced the following very significant passage (speaking of the painters of the earlier part of the century):

> Their work was genuine painting on the flat: the foundation of it was a picture on a back-cloth. In our day the art has to work in space of three dimensions; it has ceased to be pictorial and has become plastic. The back-cloth has been superseded by the solid set, the scene-painter by the scene-sculptor, or, rather, modeller. And the more you multiply the solid elements of your scene, the nearer you get to abolishing your back-cloth, for the simple reason that where the two are in juxtaposition there you get the contrast of true and false perspective. . . . The contrast between the two passed unnoticed under the old conventional system of acting, when the players spoke from the footlights and made all their entrances and exits from the wings. [And still more, we would interpose, when, before that again, they made their entrances by special doors in front of the scenery and giving direct on to the forestage.] But under the present realistic system the players have to speak and conduct the business of the scene 'up stage' as well as down, and once your actor is brought into close proximity with the back-cloth the whole thing is thrown out of proportion. You see men as trees walking.

His conclusion, after an uncertain attempt to visualize the future, is: 'But this, as I have said, means the disappearance of scene-*painting*, in the strict sense of the term. We shall have no more Beverleys.'

We must notice, however, that not all set scenes were clumsily changed or slovenly put up; some made history by the ingenuity of their mechanism. But even these proved, by the very necessity for that high ingenuity, what strain the set scene imposed on a stage, especially when—as is instanced in the next reference—it took place directly after another set scene, with no intervening act-curtain or carpenter's scene to afford time for its building up. Still, for a set scene that did change satisfactorily we turn to John Hollingshead's *Gaiety Chronicles* (1898, p. 106), where, concerning a production of *Uncle Dick's Darling* at the Gaiety in 1869, we read this quotation from *The Daily News*:

The final change from the blacksmith's shop—a very elaborate and picturesque scene—to the old village green, and the dreaming hawker still asleep on the cart-shafts, is perhaps one of the most marvellous performances of stage mechanism yet achieved. Time was, when inexperienced authors were warned against expecting one heavy set scene to follow another; and even now the most experienced are not able to escape the clumsy contrivances known as 'carpenters' scenes'—that is, scenes painted on a mere curtain, brought near to the footlights, for the purpose of giving time for building more elaborate scenery behind. But if changes such as those effected in the last act of *Uncle Dick* are possible, it is certainly difficult to understand why these rude devices should be permitted to flourish.

And so we see that the trouble about the elaborate set scene was that it *could* be made to work on occasion and in certain types of play, and that its success was, occasionally, so unqualified that it threw the poor, old, one-surface scene quite in the shade and created the appetite for further essays in elaborate ingenuity; but for another type of play and production, whose presenter did not care to spend elaborate ingenuity on his scenery, the set scene was a sore thorn in the flesh.

However that may be, the student would like to ask, in passing, what was the principle behind this marvellously efficient scene change in *Uncle Dick's Darling*. And a manuscript note of W. J. Lawrence's suggests an answer: 'I think the innovation was a "rise and sink". At any rate there was a "rise and sink" in the play, and one night in Dublin when Toole was acting in it, it stuck badly.' What exactly constitutes a *rise-and-sink* is a matter more suitably left for discussion under trick scenery and special effects, and how much of an 'innovation' it was at this period is a question for debate; but, broadly speaking, it can be likened to a pair of flats that divided horizontally not vertically, part rising to the flies and part sinking through a cut in the stage.

So much for a general picture of the set scene with its merits and demerits in the late nineteenth century. To pursue its history farther back is not easy. We must content ourselves with the following sparse and inconclusive references.

Firstly, for a possible example of a set scene in the transition from the eighteenth century, we read in Fitzgerald's *Lives of the Kembles*, vol. ii, p. 19, concerning Joanna Baillie's *De Montfort* at Drury Lane on 29 April 1800: 'The carpenters, however, exhibited a prodigy of skill which might rival the ambitious efforts of our own day: "a church of the fourteenth century, with its nave, choir, and side aisles, magnificently decorated, and consisting of seven places in succession". I suppose one of the earliest specimens of "set" scenery.'

The quoted passage in the above reference is presumably from Boaden's *Life of J. P. Kemble* where, at vol. ii, p. 257, we find an exactly similar passage beginning: 'Capon painted a very unusual pile of scenery, representing a church of the 14th. century with its nave, choir and side aisles, magnificently decorated; consisting of seven planes in succession. In width this extraordinary elevation was about 56 feet, 52 in depth and 37 feet in height. It was positively a building.'

There is no definite information here that this *was* a set scene, though Fitzgerald seems satisfied to give it that name. It is, however, very useful to find that the careless and unmeaning word 'places' in Fitzgerald's quotation was in reality 'planes' in Boaden's original. On the whole it seems likely that the term 'set scene' was justified, but it must be remembered that neither here nor in any earlier reference that I have been able to find is there a direct use of the phrase. The kind of scene which the phrase was later used to designate seems pretty certainly to be found before this, but the name itself is still to seek at so early a period.

We have two other, even less conclusive, earlier references and then we must try to draw these loose threads together and establish upon the evidence some sort of definition of the term *set*.

The first of these references appears at the outset so valuable, and then upon examination is seen to possess no substantiation. It purports to state the origin or invention of the set scene (though still contributing little concerning its nature). It is in Dutton Cook's *A Book of the Play*, chap. 14, and it states of the late-eighteenth-century scene-painter, De Loutherbourg, that 'He found the scene a mere "flat" of strained canvas extending over the whole stage. He was the first to use "set scenes" and "raking pieces". He also invented transparent scenes. . . .'

The second relates to an earlier period still and is, I think, pretty well unique in its suggestion. It is in Robert W. Lowe's *Life of Betterton*, chap. 2, where, in quoting the stage-directions of the last scene of Dryden's *Albion and Albanius*, he speaks of their interest for us in showing that 'elaborate "set-pieces", row behind row, were used in these productions'.

And now, before we can judge these last two references we must come to some conclusion on the evidence collected regarding what the set scene fundamentally was, and what particular characteristics made it a set scene, and gave it that name.

No term has so developed, and spread, in the technology of the stage as the term *set*, but we can, I think, begin to come nearest to its original meaning if we note, above all, that a set scene is the antithesis of a flat scene. The character of a flat scene is such that merely closing the pair of flats, or lowering the drop (with perhaps an adjustment of wings and borders), is sufficient to put the new scene ready for immediate use. It is essentially a type of scenery that does not call for furnishing or detailed arrangement. It slips on almost—one might say—of its own accord, sufficient unto itself and its scene, and upon the cue at the scene's end it slips off or is closed in by another. It can take place on any part of the stage where there are grooves to accommodate its elements. It is essentially mobile, and wrapped up with the idea of visible scene-change. It is light. It is (generally) a one-surface painting.

A set scene is none of these things. It is the antithesis of the flat scene. It stands where the flat scene cannot go. 'Further from the footlights than the middle of the stage, flats are seldom used, the remaining half being devoted to set scenes.' It is compact of many parts, and its painting is distributed over many planes. Set scenes are 'in the painter's and manager's estimation the first kind' or most important kind of scene. In set scenes 'you can have recourse to furniture'. In set scenes only is found that fourth element of scenery, that irregular, ill-defined element, not a frame like the wings, nor a top-mask like the borders, nor a backing like the flat scene, but an 'appendage', an adjunct, something that 'may occasionally be placed and displaced', that goes in no special place but just 'stands on the stage', that element of so many variant forms, that element of which there are over 113 examples, or sets of examples, listed in the Covent Garden inventory, namely, the mysterious, all-sufficient, multiform element, with so simple, so modest, so uninformative a name—the scenic *piece*, the *set* piece.

Taking now all these characteristics of the two types of scene, set scene and flat scene, into consideration, there arises one prime distinction: the flat scene is mobile, the set scene is static; and upon this distinction, and bearing in mind the visible nature of all early scene shifting, we are at length in a position to essay a final, basic definition of the set scene which shall explain the terms of its title:

If a *flat* scene is one that can be shifted and placed in position completely, before the audience's eyes, then a set scene is essentially one that can, because of the nature of its elements, only be placed in position previous to its being disclosed to the audience's eyes; or shifted away piecemeal after it has been concealed by a curtain or has had a flat scene drawn over in front of it. A set scene is a *pre-set* scene.

And in every single characteristic, the set scene is analogous to the 'scene of relieve' of Inigo Jones, just as in almost every characteristic the flat scene is analogous to his 'shutter scenes'.

Both set scenes and relieve scenes are composed of separate planes, are reserved for the back of the stage behind the province of the flats, are the more elaborate type of scene, and are disclosures, or 'discovery' scenes, that is, are set up in place before the moment of their use and are disclosed by opening the scene in front. They must, indeed, be so discovered because of the number of small pieces which constitute them, and which by their especial complexity make both set scene and relieve scene specifically scenes of special effect, of climax, or of points of high spectacle in the show.

Both relieves and set scenes demand the sandwiching between of scenes of a more mobile construction, otherwise there are needed the most elaborate ingenuities of folding parts and trick lines and hinges if the steady progress of the show from scene to scene is not to be hindered or subject to intervals.

If now we take the principle of the Stuart relieve scene as being that from which the Victorian set scene sprang, what evidence can we find to justify a continuance of the tradition between the two periods?

Our first link is the 'long scene' noticed in Aphra Behn, that kind of scene which, the evidence seems to tell us, extended back into the deepest part of the stage beyond the region of the flat scenes.

Our second link is the existence in so many early theatre plans of a special back annexe, or recess, behind the stage proper, into which the wing-and-flat system did not reach, and which, in one plan at least (that of Green's Newcastle Theatre), is specifically shown as available for pageants and special processions. In Wren's Drury Lane section, 1674, in the Bristol Theatre Royal, 1766, in the Theatre Royal, Plymouth, 1811, in Green's Newcastle Theatre, 1836, in all Contant's theatre plans, 1859, we notice this back recess to the stage. And this, there seems sufficient reason to suppose, was, or could be used as, the province of the set scene. For though a set scene could, of course, be set immediately behind the front pair of flats, yet its quality was such that only with the type of scenery it alone comprised could the complete depth of the stage be used and the nearly interminable vista of marvellous visions, so dear to the eyes of all early lovers of the theatrical-picturesque, be opened up to the unending gaze.

Our third link is Lowe's opinion that such plays as Dryden's *Albion and Albanius* could not, in some scenes, be staged without a succession of cut-out planes such as were used for Davenant's masques and were presumably brought along also, by Davenant, to his great new scenic public theatre. And—though this is but an opinion—it seems on the face of it very likely

[270]

indeed that successors to the relieve scenes, or antecedents of the set scenes, were used in the Restoration theatre.

And so when we read in Dutton Cook that De Loutherbourg introduced set scenes in the eighteenth century, we not only take the statement as confirmation of their existence at that time, along with the unquestionable evidence of certain of De Loutherbourg's own scene designs and models still remaining to us, but we rather extend the claim to read not that De Loutherbourg invented set scenes, but that he developed the already existing relieve scene, or its successor.

Of the existence of the set scene in the nineteenth century we have plenty of evidence, and of its development to a degree almost out of the carpenter's power to control. And yet, it is interesting to note, when the set scene so blossomed into almost limitless elaboration it did not therefore blow and wither, and die of its own fullness; instead it parasitically drew extra substance from the unoffending flat scene with its principle of visible scene change, and killed it and devoured the remains, to become not only the recognized type of *all* scenes today, but to give its very specific name '*set*' to any scene whatever.

We pay the price for the loss of the old flat scene by the presence of intervals in our stage shows. For a change of *set* is now accomplished not behind a carpenter's scene—that last relic of what was once the standard flat scene—but behind a blank curtain, on the other side of which the audience must wait. Though there is still a tradition in the theatre that all heavy scene-changes should be arranged if possible to come at an act-wait, and not at the junction between the scenes within an act, should the act contain, now, more than one scene. And still the principle maintains, to some extent, of arranging, at any rate within the act, to alternate shallow scene with deep scene. But the old, apt system, so well designed, it seems, to speed the show is nearly forgotten: true a 'carpenter's scene' is occasionally present in review and pantomime, but stage setting today is almost wholly a matter of what once would be called, but with a different meaning, *sets*.

And so at length we may return to the *Dictionary*, and find, after all, that in spite of its misleading whole, there was a part of that definition of *set scene* which pointed to the essence of its nature, namely, the statement that a set scene's elements are 'placed in position upon a theatrical stage before the rise of the curtain'. At least it is true to say that a set scene's elements are such that it is a 'discovery' scene, and not one that closes in before the audience's eyes and so belongs to the family of *mobile* scenes which alone have made possible the system of visible scene-change. These 'mobile' scenes were essentially composed of flats, and now to complete the study of the two main varieties of scene we must take the step forward into the next century to find there the final information that will enable us to build a complementary review of the flat scene—the antithesis of the set scene.

We now reach the period when Rees's *Cyclopaedia* was published, and it will be a fitting opening to the significant century of changes which leads us into our own day to consult in detail this publication whose matter links the eighteenth century to the nineteenth. The information we shall find is so closely related to the study of flats that we shall take the opportunity of extending what Rees says about flats to sum up our own considerations upon the history of the word and what it signified.

Between the years 1803 and 1819 this encyclopaedia was published in various parts and editions. It was arranged as far as I can ascertain by a certain Dr. Abraham Rees. Its full name is *Cyclopaedia, or universal Dictionary of Arts, Sciences and Literature, illustrated with numerous engravings.* Here is to be found not only the first article known to us in English on Dramatic Machinery, but the first English diagrams of theatrical mechanisms, saving only those plans of Jones.

The article headed 'DRAMATIC *Machinery*' in vol. xii occupies some ten columns of closely printed matter and is, thus, a relatively lengthy study. An analysis of it in full detail would occupy a larger space than can be afforded in this book, also many passages are relevant to different parts of our review and have been quoted, or will be quoted, in those contexts, and so, though we devote a special study to it here, we shall only include a selection from the text.

The subheadings of the article are as follows: '*Construction of the Stage*', a general note of nearly a column on stage-rake and its relation to inclination of pit and thus to slope of galleries and height of theatre; '*Apertures of the Stage*' deals with traps and is quoted from in our Chapter 14 on the theatre at Plymouth. This is followed by '*Framing of the Traps*' and then by '*Disposition of the Stage Lights*', and finally come six columns on the '*Disposition of the Scenery*'. We have quoted a substantial part of this section at the end of Chapter 11 in our discussion of Chetwood's innovation. Some of the remaining, opening portion we must consider now and especially from the point of view of the information it gives of the Regency conception of the flat scene.

Rees's writer opens this section with a long passage of major importance which we quote in full:

Disposition of the Scenery

The scenery of a theatre consists of the flat scenes which form the termination of the perspective across the stage, and the side scenes, or wings, which are disposed upon each side of the stage so as to be shifted as often as may be necessary, and to afford opportunities for the actors to come upon the stage, or quit it, at any of the intervals between the respective sets. Besides these, there are scenes which may be occasionally placed and displaced, such as the fronts of cottages, cascades, rocks, bridges, and other appendages, requisite in the representation of particular dramas. These are generally called pieces.

The flat scenes are of three kinds: the first of these are drops, or curtains, where the canvas is furled or unfurled upon a roller, placed either at the top or bottom of the scene. A difference of opinion exists as to the placing of the roller, which, as it is a mere matter of taste, may probably never be determined—both ways are used in the London theatres. The rollers, in either case, are made to revolve by means of cords tightened or slackened as may be necessary; and when the scenes are large it is usual to wind them up by means of a cylinder and a winch, as in the trap machinery.

Although the drop scenes are the most simple, it is necessary sometimes to have recourse to those scenes which are called flats. In these the canvas is stretched upon wooden frames, which are generally constructed in two pieces, so as to meet in the middle of the stage, the junction being in a perpendicular direction. The sides frames are moved in grooves, composed of parallel pieces of wood fixed upon the stage, and so constructed that they may be removed with facility from one place to another. The upper part of the framing is also confined by a groove, to retain the perpendicular position of the flat scene. These are sometimes constructed, to save room, upon joints, by which they may either be lowered to the horizontal position, or drawn up to the side walls. In this respect their construction is pretty similar to that of a common draw-bridge. This plan was used in the late Theatre Royal, Covent Garden, where they were called flys. The principal use of the flats is where apertures, such as doors, windows, chimney-pieces, &c. are wanted in the scene, which may be opened and shut as required; these are called, in the technology of a theatre, *practicable* doors, &c., because, when not to be used, they may be painted on a drop scene. A third kind of scene is the profiled or open *flat*. This is used for woods, gateways of castles, and such purposes: it is framed exactly like the other, and the only difference consists in parts of the scene being left open to shew another behind, which terminates the view.

A very important part of the scenery of a theatre is the wings. These also are stretched upon wooden frames, and slide in grooves fixed to the stage. In some large theatres they are moved by machinery, in others by manual labour. The disposition of the grooves will be seen at the letters K, K, in *fig. 1*. In this figure are nine sets of wings, the front only of which are marked by the reference letter. The wings, like the flats, whether moved by the hand or by the aid of machinery, usually stand upon the stage. The plan of moving the wings of the late theatre of Covent Garden, and that of the Theatre Royal of Glasgow, invented by the writer of this article, are represented in *Plate X*.

We break off at this point because the next long passage of the section has already been quoted in full at the end of Chapter 11, to which the interested reader is referred for the continuation of Rees's article. After this long passage on the mechanical movement of scenery, the article concludes with a brief and somewhat less informative allusion to 'occasional engines

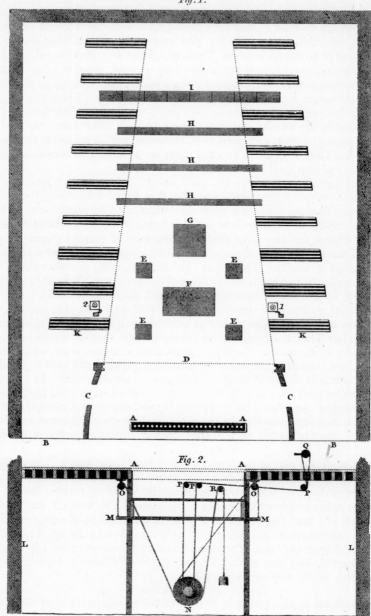

Fig. 1.

Fig. 2.

FIG. 14. Plan and cross-section of an English stage about 1803, from Rees's
Cyclopaedia, Plate IX, Figs. 1 and 2. (See also p. 284.)

. . . to suit particular pieces. The limits of this article will not admit of going much into detail respecting these; nor is it necessary.'

Research may establish the name of the author of this account, from the statement that 'the plan of moving the wings of the late theatre of Covent Garden, and that of the Theatre Royal of Glasgow' were 'invented by the writer of this article'.

Let us, however, examine his words in detail, grateful to extract all the information we can from them even though their writer may remain for the present anonymous.

The first point is the meaning of this word 'flat'. To begin with we should be quite clear that the word 'flat' used today so widely in the theatre has not quite the meaning employed here. No flat today is, of course, connected in any way with grooves. The flats of the *Cyclopaedia* were canvased frames as ours are, but they were much wider, amounting in fact to half the back-scene; such a thing is virtually unknown to us now. They were used, says the article, as alternatives to 'drop scenes'—that is to say, to 'cloths'.

The reference to 'side frames' a little lower in the article may be puzzling for a moment. It is a curious phrase for its purpose; it really means the two halves of the backscene just described. Wings, as will be seen, come under consideration farther on.

Concerning the grooves themselves we learn with great interest that they might be 'removed with facility from one place to another'. These, then, are the loose grooves of the Christie catalogue. The reference is to the lower grooves—somewhat different mobility is described for the upper grooves a few lines later—so we may conclude that 'loose' grooves were only to be found among the lower grooves down upon the stage. Presumably the purpose of this removability was to leave the floor clear of what must have been very incommodious ridges, when there was no need for them. How they were fixed, however, we must note as being still to seek.

We must not allow the modern shade of meaning of the word 'remove' as 'to take right away' to blind our eyes to the older meaning that may be all that is implied here—namely, to move from one place and put in another. Perhaps there were not enough flat-grooves supplied to fill every position where a flat scene might need to be drawn and so they were made to be moved to whatever place they were needed when the occasion arose.

When we come to the upper grooves which were built on this 'draw-bridge' principle a very surprising point arises—one indeed that we would almost be prepared to question, so unexpected is it—in that, upon the installation of jointed upper grooves at Covent Garden, 'they were called flys'. It may be that 'flies' is a somewhat elastic term today, but it is certainly not one that we should have traced back from its modern use to these jointed grooves. Nevertheless the above passage gives us our justification for the completion of the Bristol fragment in our model reconstruction.

The reference at the end of the quotation to a system of machinery for moving the wings in a scene-change is one that we have already examined in our chapter on Chetwood's innovation.

When we turn to the diagram described as Fig. 1 in the article (see Fig. 14) it must be confessed that we are rather puzzled than enlightened. One fact, however, that it does clearly show is that at this date the groove-sets on either side the stage still converged towards the back to give enhancement to perspective vista effects. The first three sets have three grooves apiece; the remaining six, only two. It may be said that nine wings a side seems a great number for a normal English stage. There is no indication—though we greatly need it—of the loose grooves for the flat scenes. It strikes one somehow as being a half-hearted diagram, and when one sees in the text that the walls are said not to be represented in their proper relation with the rest (see p. 284), one wonders whether one can depend on it at all.

So much for the main technical points concerning flats and grooves in the above-quoted passage; let us now consider the variety of scene-parts which the writer distinguishes. We said at the outset that the items of scenery used in a theatre were to be divided into backscenes, wing pieces, borders, and there was the hint of a fourth category, the piece. If we turn to Rees's writer we find he follows exactly this division, save that he omits the comparatively less important category of borders, but he adds some new information in his description of the details.

The three elements of which 'the scenery of a theatre consists' are (1) *'the flat scenes* which form the termination of the perspective across the stage'; (2) *'the side scenes,* or wings'; and (3) the 'scenes which may be occasionally placed or displaced. . . . These are generally called *pieces*'.

Here is a usage of the word *scene* which is a little different from our own. A scene is not the whole stage picture, or complete collection of elements in their designed unity, but it is each or any of those elements taken separately: the 'back piece' is a 'scene', a wing is a 'scene', a 'piece' is a 'scene'. A scene then is an individual piece of scenery.

Upon reference to the *Dictionary* we find this usage is exactly defined. There are six separate theatrical shades of meaning given for the word *scene*: (1) the stage of a Greek or Roman theatre (1638); (2) 'the stage or theatre as standing for either the dramatic art or the histrionic profession. Now *arch.* 1682'; (3) A stage performance *obs.*; (4) 'The place in which the action of a play, or part of a play, is supposed to occur . . . 1592'; (5) a subdivision of an act of a play . . . 1540; and lastly something which we must quote in full: 'Scene. 6. The material apparatus, consisting chiefly of painted hangings, slides, etc., set at the back and sides of the stage, and intended to give the illusion of a real view of the *local* in which the action of a play takes place; the view thus presented to the spectators at any time during the action of a play. Also, any one of the painted hangings, slides, etc. used for this purpose.' Then follows some quarter of a column of examples, beginning (rather doubtfully) at 1540 and finishing at 1904. Among these, three are especially useful to note; the first is to the directions in *The Masque of Blacknesse* (1605) which we have already quoted in Chapter 3; the second is '1719 YOUNG *Busiris* iv (stage-dir.), The back scene opens. *Ibid.*, Scene shuts on them.' And the last is Pope's famous line from '1731 *Hor. Ep.* II. 315. Back fly the scenes, and enter foot and horse.'

Now this sixth meaning of the word *scene* brings, as other references to the dictionary have brought, a sense of surprise. It is to be wondered what the modern general reader will make, in this book of reference dated 1914, of the inclusion of the word *slides* among the scenery of a theatre. He will not find any illumination under the head of 'slide' itself if he turns the word up, for the dictionary, though using the word here with a specific theatrical meaning, gives no specific theatrical definition under 'slide', nor any indication whatever of the use or application of the word upon the stage at all. And if the general reader turns to his theatrical friends he will gain no more light, for I do not suppose one person in a thousand has heard the word 'slide' used to designate a piece of scenery upon the modern stage. In fact the general reader will be told the word is not known. He may perchance find a knowledgeable old carpenter who can tell him that certain sections of the stage floor with a specific design and function are called 'sliders', but they are definitely not scenery in any sense of the word. And that is as far as he will get, unless he turn to the forgotten past. But we have collected at least one piece of definite information from the reference, namely, that a 'scene' may be 'any one of the painted hangings, slides, etc.' of a stage, and was used in such a sense as early as 1540.

We may set out Rees's three constituents of scenery as follows:

1. *Flat scenes* in three sub-varieties—
   (a) *Drops*
   (b) *Flats*
   (c) *'Profiled or open Flats'*
2. *Wings*
3. *'Pieces'*

We see that the backscene had three variant forms and that the term 'flat scene' is a generic name for all three forms. But of the flat scene's three sub-varieties one is itself labelled 'flats'. It seems to be suggested therefore that there is more in the word 'flat' perhaps than meets the eye.

It is interesting because it seems to suggest that a 'flat scene' was not so called because it was made of flats, as might be supposed by a modern reader, but rather that flats were so named because they were part of a flat scene. For we are told that if a scene had a *drop* (or hanging, painted 'cloth', or canvas, on rollers) at the back, it would still be termed a 'flat scene', though it had no 'flats' in it. Yet if a 'cloth' were not used, and if the flat scene were framed-out in two separate rigid halves, then these two parts were called *Flats*.

We venture to refresh the reader's memory of what we said in definition of a modern flat. A flat is probably the commonest article of stage technique. It is today a piece of scenery consisting of a canvased frame. It is tall, reaching up to the top of the set. It is comparatively narrow, ranging generally between 1 ft. and 6 ft. in width. It and the great hanging 'cloth' are the two basic forms from which most scenes (other than 'built scenes') are made.

A modern flat can stand separately at the side of the stage as a wing, or it can be joined with others to form a row making up the back wall, or the side-wall, of a stage room.

A flat may be plain or 'profiled' (that is, provided with a cut edge). It may contain a door, window, or other opening. It may be separate or hinged to another to form a 'booked flat' for use as an angled wing. It may be rectangular in basic shape, or irregular.

Rees's article uses the word 'flat' in two capacities, as a qualifying adjective in the phrase 'flat scene' ('The scenery of a theatre consists of the flat scenes which form . . .', &c.) and as a noun in its own right ('It is necessary sometimes to have recourse to those scenes which are called "flats" ').

Let us begin with the adjective.

Reference to the dictionary meets with complete disappointment. *The Oxford English Dictionary* makes no mention that I can find of the existence of any such term as 'flat scene'. There is, however, one thing that we may deduce from this: that the term is not, after all, a special term, with a technical significance in the word 'flat', as we might have been inclined to suppose, but that, in the phrase, the usages of both words are clear, simple, and direct; they are used in their normal sense. The term merely means a scene that is flat. This is some confirmation of what seemed to be indicated in Rees's writer's usage—namely, that the technical noun 'flat' is derived from the normal term 'flat scene', not that the term 'flat scene' is compounded from some original noun 'flat' with a particular meaning.

When we turn, however, to the substantive use of the word in the dictionary we do find a definition. A flat is recognized as a definite, technical term; we read: 'Flat C.11. *Theat.* A part of a scene mounted on a wooden

frame which is pushed in horizontally or lowered on to the stage. 1807
Director II, 331 The entire assemblage of wings and drops and flat. 1836–9
DICKENS *Sk. Boz* (1850) 259/1 A strange jumble of flats, flies, wings [etc.].'

The first part of this definition is consistent with the modern usage
explained above—it says 'a part of a scene mounted on a wooden frame',
but it needs qualification; this it receives in the second part but in terms
that may surprise and confuse a modern stage student, for this frame is
'pushed in horizontally or lowered to the stage'.

Now it is true that the *running* of a flat from its pack in the wing-space
to its place on the set can be termed 'pushing in horizontally', but the
phrase has an odd over-emphasis. In a text so economical of words as the
dictionary, the presence of this 'horizontally' suggests a more specific
action than that familiar to us. We can guess perhaps from what we have
learnt about grooves that, in fact, this emphasis is not so much out of
place as out of date. It does not apply to 'running' the flat at all but to an
old system of movement no longer in practice. In fact the dictionary is over
half a century behind the times; since, however, the F-volume was published in 1901, this is inevitable.

When we come to the last phrase of the definition—'or lowered on to the
stage'—we may well confess ourselves puzzled indeed. But the tangle can
be sorted out. This last is, to a modern, an unexpected particularization
and one moreover that is not accurate. No flat as such is, or to my knowledge
ever has been, lowered on to the stage (save on exceptional occasions such
as in clearing a stage preparatory to storing or removing the scenery, or
when a repair is necessary).

In fact there is only one occasion known to me today when a flat suffers
vertical movement at all, and then it is in a special arrangement, which is as
follows: when a row of flats, set across the stage as a backscene, has to be
quickly struck, or removed, in a scene-change, the separate flats of the row
may be bolted together behind with long battens of wood into a solid wall,
and the whole is then attached in the manner of a backcloth to a set of lines,
and 'flown' or lifted into the 'flies'. These battened pieces are called col-
lectively a *French flat*. But, to my knowledge, only a 'French flat', and not
a flat pure and simple (and there is a considerable difference between the
two), is ever regularly flown. Therefore there are two objections to the
dictionary's phrase: firstly, a flat is never moved vertically, and secondly,
it is not a *flat* but a *French flat* that is 'lowered on to the stage', and taken up
again when done with.

But if we reconsider the dictionary definition in the light of what we
read in Rees, we begin to see how the confusion arises. We had expected a
modern dictionary to have a modern interpretation of a word widely in
modern use. Granted it is a technical word in this case, yet it is a very old

one, and the dictionary professes to include a group of '*Theat.*' expressions. To a certain extent the dictionary fulfils our expectation when it defines a flat (as it should be defined today) as a part of a scene on a wooden frame; but thereafter it lapses into an historical mood without our recognizing the fact. The second half of the definition is not applicable to any modern flat at all *but it is applicable to the flat scene whose varieties were set out in Rees in 1803,* and of which the first variety, the 'drop', is 'lowered on to the stage', while the second and third varieties are 'pushed in horizontally'. The confusion has arisen from our failure to distinguish the noun 'flat' from the adjectival use 'flat scene'. 'Flat scene', however, is an obsolete term now, and should not today have any of its shades of meaning included in a modern definition without a note of the fact, especially when that meaning follows a description of a flat as having a *wooden frame,* for this no normal drop yet possessed, since it is no more than a loose hanging canvas, and yet *only* a drop is lowered to the stage.

Briefly, it is the *flat* which is 'part of a scene mounted on a wooden frame', but it is only the obsolete *flat scene* which can be described as either 'pushed in horizontally or lowered on to the stage'. Applied to the modern flat the words are nonsense.

Before we leave the definition in the dictionary we have two other points to raise. First, it offers us no means of distinguishing between a ground-row and a flat, or between a set piece and a flat; and second, the date given for the earliest use of the word—1870—is surprisingly late. We found a use of the word in 1743 in the inventory of Covent Garden and in Fielding's burlesque in 1736. Earlier than that I have not yet found it in the sub-stantive form—but in the adjectival sense we may trace the words 'flat scene' right back to 1669, and this I believe to be the earliest use known at present.

This precedence of the adjectival form over the noun is the final proof that the latter was derived from the former—that a *flat* is, or was originally, so called because it was an element of a *flat scene,* not that a flat scene was so called because it consisted of flats.

And now summarizing what we have learnt about what were once the two essential forms of scenery, it appears that their story is something like this.

In the beginning the masques had (*a*) scenes in one plane made only with shutters and (*b*) scenes of relieve, some made with shutters and some without, but all in several planes. Note that the distinction is that of being either in one plane or in more than one plane; the distinction is, apparently, *not* between shutter scenes and relieve scenes—because, on occasion, a shutter might be cut to reveal another behind it as a backing. It was then called a relieve despite its being made of shutters.

In the Restoration this distinction was (again apparently) made clear, and a scene in one plane was called by the new and very logical name of *flat scene*. But, in our present knowledge, we suppose a scene with a fire-place in it, or with intervals cut out between tree-trunks, was not called a flat scene—for the simple reason that the scene was *not* flat. It is possible that the scene in a number of planes was called a 'long scene'.

Then the term 'flat scene' becomes shortened to 'flat'; we find such usages as 'draw the first flat over him'. Once the word becomes a noun we find it applied to all framed canvases forming backscenes, and the Covent Garden Inventory lists *both* plain frames and cut frames as *flats*. In other words, cut flat scenes, which seem once to have been classed with scenes in relief, seem later to become classed, instead, as flat scenes along with the plain flats.

Once this happens the distinction grows between the developing *set scene* with its multitude of *pieces* on the one hand, and the scene painted mostly on one surface (which now comes to include *drops*) on the other. At first drops were rare, and pairs of flats very common. Then in the nine-teenth century drops increase in number.

Then the 'pair of flats' makes some attempt to emulate the three-dimensional nature of the set scene. For instance, the pair becomes a trio with the two outer members set at an angle as in *The Padlock*. Later still (as we shall see) interior scenes are made of a back flat and two *raking flats* at the sides. Thence it is but a step to the Box *Set* (note the word *set*), which reproduces three walls of a room in their actual relation and is composed of elements still called (though with a forgotten reason) *flats*, which are the descendants of the old, great frames, but now are used as part of a *set*—that is to say, of a kind of scene which cannot be changed before the audience but is complicated in parts and must be built up and changed behind a curtain.

Thus the original distinction is quite lost, and we may today say un-challenged that a *set* is something made up of *flats*, and yet, once, the *flat* scene and the *set* scene were the opposite ends of the scenic world and mutually exclusive.

14

FOULSTON'S DESIGNS FOR THE
THEATRE ROYAL, PLYMOUTH, 1811

★

Foulston and Rees—Foulston's grooves—Use of long grooves—Faulty masking—Dimensions of backscenes—Number of wings—Loose and fixed grooves—The cross-section of the theatre—The upper grooves—A special problem—The working of the borders

★

OUR picture now widens. So far the scraps of information upon stage machinery have been sparse enough. By dint of careful examination of each scrap and the interrelation of all the items of information, we arrived at some picture of the sort of thing a groove was in itself. Now we are to have an opportunity of studying a full stage, and of relating the grooves to the whole of which they were a part. Our next piece of evidence is a set of plans showing the full arrangement of a complete system of grooves on a specific stage, and in relation to other contemporary machines.

Mr. Edward Carrick called my attention to a volume entitled *The Public Buildings in the West of England as designed by John Foulston F.R.I.B.A., printed for the author and published by John Williams, library of the Fine Arts, 100 Great Russell St., London*, MDCCCXXXVIII. This volume includes seventeen plates of the details of the stage of the Theatre Royal, Plymouth, whose foundation was laid in 1811. The discovery of the book had a double interest for me, for, beside the information in the plates, I knew the theatre and had played there and had painted upon its paint-frame.

There seemed a golden opportunity to compare the original plan of an old theatre with the existing structure. But before I could return to Plymouth after seeing the book, the theatre was demolished.

It was not nearly as old a house as the Theatre Royal, Bristol, but the original plans of Bristol (in spite of tantalizing suggestions in various books) have never come to light, and so Plymouth had seemed to offer a unique opportunity to compare plans with actual building. The opportunity now no longer exists, and one must fall back on memory.

The shell of the theatre had remained virtually the same as when it was built. Interior alterations had been made in the course of its existence, and the original machinery had been removed, but much of the form remained, and the paint-frame on which I worked in 1928 was probably the same one that Foulston had put in. It was at any rate in the original position and worked in the same way as is shown on his plans.

Among my memories of the fly-floors of theatres, the pleasantest is of those at Plymouth with dusty sunbeams coming through the paint-room windows and lighting a mass of cordage with accents and shadows. It is these easy, 13-ft.-wide fly-floors that are a notable feature of the plans. Below them the grooves, which are detailed in the plans, once worked.

The plans form a far better series of illustrations to the nearly contemporary article in Rees's *Cyclopaedia* than those poor diagrams which the writer himself included, and we may at this point turn to the article and read its details on the planning of the stage with some enlightenment since we have these plans of Plymouth at hand for exemplification of its points.

We will begin with the stage floor, first reading Rees and then referring to Plymouth for illustration.

The writer in the *Cyclopaedia* gives us a general description of the floor of a typical stage, and introduces us to some useful technical terms. He begins by discussing the stage rake, or the slope given to the floor of a stage, and goes on to consider the carpentry of the floor itself, concerning which he says: 'In constructing the joints and framing, the architect must in the first place consider the number of apertures which ought to be made for the purpose of conducting the business of the stage with propriety.'

In this mention of certain 'apertures' in the stage floor we have something that is considered as a vital means of scenic effect and of scene-change. The immediately succeeding passage shows their importance in this respect and indicates, as well, that developments of scenic method were at this period often made. It is another portent of the revolution that was to sweep grooves away. The Figure referred to below is reproduced as our Fig. 14 above. The architect should consider, we are told,

the dimensions and disposition of these apertures; and the easiest and most economical way of forming others to suit that succession of novelty which seems to be the prevalent taste of the present day. In adapting his jointing and framework to answer these purposes, will consist his chief difficulty. The constant changes and improvements which take place, render it impossible to ascertain any precise mode of doing this, but the general way will be considered under the section of this article; *Apertures of the stage*, comprising the foot-lights, traps, flaps, and sliders—to these we now proceed.

Apertures of the Stage

The first aperture in the stage immediately behind the orchestra, and in front of the proscenium and curtain, is that for raising and lowering the foot-lights, both for the purposes of trimming the lamps, and of darkening the stage when required. It is marked by the letters A, A, *fig. 1, Plate IX. Miscellany*, which is a horizontal plan of a stage 60 feet in length, and 25 feet in breadth at the curtain line. In this plan, the lines which represent the side walls of the theatre are too much contracted, for it is necessary to give at least eight or ten feet of additional room for the performers and scene-shifters, behind each wing. The letters B,B, denote the line which forms the front of the stage behind the orchestra.

The next apertures are the side traps, of which any convenient number may be constructed. Four of these are exhibited in the plan, and are distinguished by the letters E,E,E,E. In the middle are two larger traps. The first, at F, is of an oblong form from six to seven feet in length, and from three to four feet in breadth. It is most frequently used for the grave scene in Shakespeare's tragedy of Hamlet.

The trap marked by the letter G is generally square, and is chiefly used for the sinking of the cauldron in the tragedy of Macbeth. Behind these, in larger theatres where many changes of scenery are frequently required, there are a number of longitudinal apertures across the stage, which are covered by planks moveable upon hinges, so that by throwing them back, the stage may be opened in a moment. The use of these is to allow the flat scenes to sink through the stage, when required. Three of these will be found in the plan, at the letters H,H,H, and are known by the name of *flaps*.

In the late Theatre Royal of Covent Garden, much of the scenery, not in immediate use, was kept in the cellar under the stage. For the purpose of raising and lowering these scenes with facility, other apertures were made, and closed with square or rectangular pieces of wood, which could be placed or displaced in a few minutes: these were called sliders, and a plan of one is given at the letter I.

There follows a description of the working of the footlights trap and the observation is made that in contradistinction to the mechanism usually associated with some of the traps—'no machinery whatever is permanently attached to the flaps or sliders, for as these apertures serve generally for the passage of the flat scenes through the stage, the machinery must depend upon the particular effect which it is necessary to produce. The flat scenery is generally raised by a crane, unless a very rapid ascent or descent be required, when it may be done by the application of a counterpoise.'

We have, then, apertures in the stage of six different types: First, the *footlight trap*; second, the square *side traps*; third, the longer, oblong *grave trap* farther back; fourth, the *cauldron trap*; fifth, the long, narrow, apertures called, after the manner of closing them, *flaps*; and lastly, a similar but wider opening, not here specifically named, but covered with sections called *sliders* instead of with hinged flaps.

Concerning these flaps, we are informed that flat scenes can slide up through them from below and sink back again, as an occasional alternative to the more usual sideways movement.

As for these varieties of openings, we note the suggestion that there is no fixed rule governing their arrangement, and a given stage may possess only a few of them, but we shall find that the names and general principle remain similar.

We may now return to the plans of the stage of the Plymouth Theatre Royal. A brief note on the building together with four of the plates was reproduced in the present writer's *The Georgian Playhouse* (Pleiades, 1948).

This stage in 1811 was about 44 ft. deep from front to back wall (see

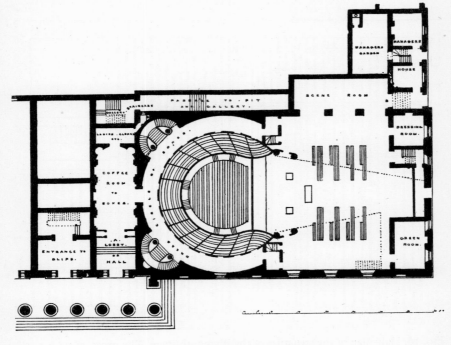

Published by John Williams 106 Gt Russell Street Bloomsbury Sqᵗ London.

FIG. 15. Plan of the Theatre Royal, Plymouth, 1811, from Foulston's *The Public Buildings in the West of England*

Fig. 15), with the addition in the back wall of a sort of smaller, farther stage, situate centrally, some 12 ft. deep by 20 ft. wide. The whole stage was 58 ft. wide, and the proscenium opening at its narrowest part was 24 ft. across, leaving the magnificent spread of 17 ft. each side for wing-space; although on these points the plans are not entirely consistent, those of the whole theatre showing, for instance, a 3-ft. wider opening for the proscenium than those of the stage details.

The openings in the floor are as follows: there is no footlight trap, but in the front of the stage are two side traps, each 2 ft. 6 in. long by 2 ft. 2 in. wide. These come, it is interesting to note, in front of the proscenium line, that is to say they are on the forestage and would not be hidden at the fall of the curtain. Next comes a central grave trap but no cauldron trap.

Beyond this we have three cuts in the stage floor, indicated in Fig. 16, which are closed by sliders, and which are: the front one 3 ft. 3¼ in. wide, the second 2 ft. 10 in., and the third 2 ft. 7½ in. In length they are 25 ft., 24 ft., and 22 ft. respectively.

Fig. 16 also shows a trap at the back of the stage within the small recess, measuring 7 ft. 4 in. long by 5 ft. 6 in. wide. This is situated over the car-

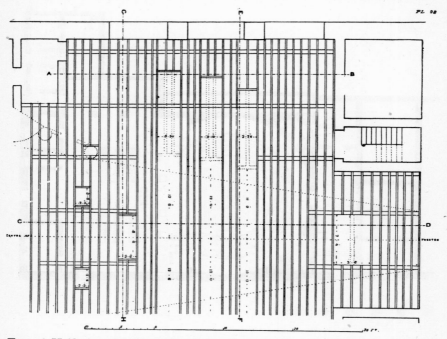

FIG. 16. Half-plan of the structure of the Plymouth stage. The proscenium is to the left. (From Foulston, op. cit.)

penter's shop and, since it is not shown upon the section of the stage floor, it may be that it was principally used, not for effects, but for the convenient getting-up of stuff from the shop to the stage. No mechanism is shown beneath it, though no doubt it could have been arranged should occasion arise.

Next, we are able to look at the actual placing of a complete system of grooves upon a stage. This set of plans and sections will together enable us to visualize the principle behind the whole system. The plans of the stage floor which we are now considering open our subject by showing us the 'lower grooves for scenes'. Not only does Fig. 15 show us clearly the disposition of these, but we have, in Figs. 17 and 18, what is up to now unexampled in theatrical histories—detailed, large-scale drawings showing the exact measurements and the method of fixing these grooves.

The grooves are in eight groups, four on either side of the stage. Each individual group consists of two parts: firstly a number of short grooves,

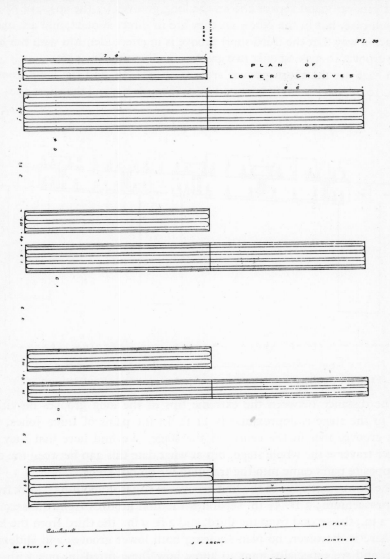

FIG. 17. Plan of lower grooves on the left-hand side of Plymouth stage. The proscenium would be at the top of the plan. (From Foulston, op. cit.)

and secondly, immediately up-stage of them in each group a number of longer grooves.

There are three short grooves in each set, but the long grooves vary; in No. 1 set, nearest the front of the stage, there are five; in No. 2 set, four;

in No. 3 set, three; and in No. 4 set, three. But the No. 4 set has a peculiarity which differentiates it from the others: in the Nos. 1, 2, and 3 sets the short grooves stand separate from the long grooves by the space of 6½ in. in each case, but in the No. 4 set they are in direct contact, and are made in such a way that the third short groove is in effect identical with the first long groove, so making only five grooves in all in the No. 4 set.

In each set the short grooves are 7 ft. 4 in. long, and the long grooves 13 ft. 10 in., having a 6 ft. 6 in. extension inwards beyond the short ones.

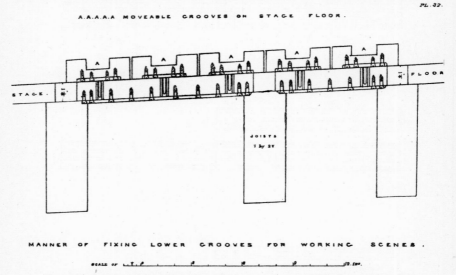

FIG. 18. Section through one set of lower grooves. (Foulston, op. cit.)

The distance between the extreme tips of the long grooves on either side of the stage is approximately 11 ft. In the plans of Inigo Jones, the long grooves met in the centre of the stage. We find here that they no longer traverse the whole stage, but at what date this gap between the tips of opposite pairs came into the tradition we do not know.

The downstage edge of the first grooves is situated about 6 ft. back from the proscenium; 3 ft. 5¼ in. separates the first grooves from the second; 3 ft. 2 in., the second from the third, and 2 ft. 9 in., the third from the last.

There is, however, no plan showing both lower grooves and sliders at once, and we especially want to know how these fitted in, one with the other.

We have then to make our own drawing of the stage combining the information and attempting to set the grooves and the sliders together. As soon as we attempt to do this we have borne in upon us very strongly the fact that in these prints there is sometimes considerable discrepancy between the figures marked on the plans and the scale shown on the same

[288]

plate. We are put to a good deal of calculation and, in the end, to an occasional, inevitable approximation.

Grooves and Openings. First we find that the lower grooves are arranged to come almost exactly in the spaces between the slider openings. We presume, however, that, since the long grooves were for flat scenes, when the flats were drawn together at any position no use could be made of the cut behind. On occasions when a cut was used, then, no scenery would come at that position, and the grooves could be therefore removed.

Use of Long Grooves. We notice the long groove sets are all in two sections, one part exactly like the short, wing sets, the other an extension at its on-stage end so that we have, in effect, a stage provided with eight groups of grooves either side, each 7 ft. 4 in. long, but the second, fourth, sixth, and eighth groups having a 6 ft. 6 in. extension, making the full length of these particular groups 13 ft. 10 in. Such a stage as this could present flat scenes at any of four varieties of depth.

Greatest Number of Flat-grooves in Front of Stage. We noticed that the flat-grooves vary in number in the different sets and that the set with the greatest number came at the front of the stage behind the first wing-grooves, where there are five grooves in the set. This should be emphasized. We are thus led to suppose that the most frequent use of the flat scenes had now come to be for shallow scenes at the front of the stage (not as with Jones, where they were exclusively used at the back).

We are reminded of the various modern systems of setting to be seen, for instance, in the music-hall, the revue, and in many revivals of Elizabethan plays, where shallow front scenes are frequently interspersed with deeper scenes, so that the action of the play may continue on the front of the stage while the scenery is changed behind for a succeeding deeper set. This system of alternating shallow and deep scenes is of great importance to the speed and continuity of a show. The deep scenes may contain an elaborate arrangement of scene-pieces and furniture; all may be set in position easily and unhurriedly without the exercise of forced ingenuities of trick-strings or raising machinery that might have had to be called into use otherwise. Upon the conclusion of the deep scene, the closing of a pair of flats in the first grooves would cover it again and enable its elements to be as discreetly 'struck' as they had been set, whilst the show proceeded again before the front scene. With four sets of grooves for flats—one set at each wing-position—clearly a great variety of scenes could be presented on the lines of the above system.

Wider Entrances Down-stage. The space of stage between the front wing of one group and that of the next has not received a distinct name in English procedure. On the French stage the terminology was more distinct, and each stage was said to be divided into so many *plans*, and each *plan* was subdivided in its turn into three elements, the *rue*, the *trapillon*, and the *costière*.

Exact analogy between the two systems, French and English, is not possible since the working was different, and the French did not use grooves, but, allowing for these differences, the *rue* corresponded to the space through which the actor walked on to the stage; perhaps the nearest English equivalent is the word *entrance* used in the sense of the old directions in melodrama texts—for example, R.U.E. or Right Upper Entrance, meaning the space between the stage-right deepest wing and the next downstage. But I can find no equivalent in the English language for the French word *plan*, the main unit of division. It is very easy to specify its meaning as the area of stage between the front wing of one set and the front wing of the next adjacent set. Perhaps we may employ the word *section* to designate this space. If so, the point to notice is that the 'sections' at Plymouth were of varying depths. The first section is, in effect, a blind section, extending between the proscenium and the first wing-groove. It measures approximately 6 ft.; the second section (from the front of the first set of wing-grooves to the front of the second) is 6 ft. 4 in. wide, and the third section is 5 ft. 10 in., and the fourth 5 ft.

A curious anomaly now arises from this decrease in section-depth as we go up-stage. On the one hand, it satisfies one of the perspective demands for the shrinking of remoter distances, but, on the other, it lays the stage open to the fault of masking least efficiently at the point where the sight-line demands are greatest, that is, at the nearer part of the stage. There, so sight-line science tells us, wings ought to be closer together to mask: they may be farther apart the farther they go up-stage. Yet apparently the point was ignored on this stage in favour of the opposite, perspective demand that, to obtain consistent effect in a vanishing row of wings, the more distant should be closer together than the nearer.

Tips of Grooves Parallel, not Convergent. This regard for perspective is, on another point, reversed, and we find somewhat to our surprise that although the adjacent wing-sets are closer together up-stage, yet the central avenue between the opposite pairs of grooves is parallel, and not, as we might expect, convergent. And this despite the fact that in several of the plates a side sight-line is shown clearly drawn from the outermost seat in the auditorium, past the corner of the first wing-grooves. The other wing-grooves are not made to touch that line.

Maybe we have not far to seek for the reason; perhaps it would have narrowed the deeper part of the acting-area too much to have had the wing-lines converge as they did on older stages.

Faulty Masking. Perhaps the most surprising point in regard to the position of the wing-grooves is the great distance between the proscenium and the first set. For any student of sight-lines it will be clear at once that to be wide enough to mask in this position the first wing would have to be approximately 18 ft. wide, and that is an impossible size.

By no rearrangement or juggling of the parts can any possible solution be found to this problem of masking save this; that a pair of extra proscenium wings, painted in some neutral design, that would suit any scene, be added and set either side between the first wing-grooves and the proscenium. If that were in fact the case, we should suppose such wings to be a permanent accessory of the proscenium opening and therefore, since they suffered no change with the change of scenes, they were not run in grooves but were probably simply a pair of self-supporting 'booked wings' (that is, wings in two parts hinged up the centre like a two-leaved screen) whose descendants have come down to our own day and are still to be found in some provincial theatres. Such wings are sometimes seen supported at the top in forks, but concerning 'forks' we must wait for information belonging to a later part of the story.

Whatever solution was found to this problem by the nineteenth-century stage-carpenters, and presumably by those of the eighteenth century just before them, there is one virtual certainty, that something must have been used to mask the down-stage entrance. Without this something, the masking of the stage under the conditions shown on the plan would have been quite impossible.

Proof that such a use of booked proscenium wings was known is to be found in a plan of the stage of the Theatre Royal, Ipswich, a building belonging to roughly the same period as the Plymouth theatre. (The plan is reproduced in *The Architectural Review* for August 1946, p. 41, fig. 4.) Here the distance between the proscenium and the first grooves is even greater, scaling some 9 ft., but in the interval between the two a pair of booked proscenium wings is indicated beyond all doubt, and the design of those wings is shown in a drawing accompanying the original plan.

But we have not done with this difficulty of masking, for an application of sight-lines to the next entrance (that between the first set of wing-grooves and the second) shows that here too there are considerable difficulties to be faced, and here we can offer no such simple solution as the interposition of an extra piece of scenery. This question of the wings 'masking' properly we meet again and again, until we have finally to admit the only conclusion possible—one which is fortunately borne out by evidence—that in the eighteenth and nineteenth centuries masking was held in little account.

Dimensions of Backscenes. When we come to examine the section of the stage, we shall see that the distance between the lower grooves and their corresponding upper grooves is constant whether they are at the front or the back of the stage; furthermore that the height of the flats is the same as that of the wings. Therefore—as regards height at least—the wings and flats in the scene-store are capable of use in any position on the stage and their height is constant. What, now, was the width of the flats which had to work in the grooves?

The evidence is slender; let us first consider the flats. We can set a limit for the width of each member of a pair of flats by halving the distance from the centre-line of the stage to the side-wall. Clearly a flat could not be wider than that or it could not be completely withdrawn. But we have a further limitation. Were we to take that as the actual measurement, we should be in the unfortunate position of having all our flats, when they were withdrawn, completely blocking the wing-spaces, and allowing no passage for actors to their entrances. This we cannot allow. There must be left at least 3 ft. between the edge of a withdrawn flat and the side-wall of the stage. Under these conditions, the maximum width of an individual flat on this particular stage must be 13 ft., and therefore the width of a complete backscene should be 26 ft. Can we verify this? We have a very important piece of evidence in the dimensions of the paint-frame built into this theatre by the architect, and presumably, therefore, designed to take exactly the size of scenery necessary upon its stage. This paint-frame measures exactly 26 ft. in width, and the cut in which it sinks is only 27 ft. long, giving 6 in. of clearance either end; we may therefore take it that no pair of shutters were together wider than 26 ft. Were they wider, each half would have had to be painted separately, and that would raise the difficulty of matching the paint at the join. The pair were presumably set side by side on the frame and painted as one surface. A further point concerning the width of flats is raised by the scene-dock at the side of the stage. This dock is in the form of a bay opening out of the stage-right side-wall, and measuring approximately 35 ft. long by 14 ft. deep.

But this depth is reduced in effect by the presence of two 2 ft. 6 in. square columns supporting the top of the opening. These columns cut down the clear depth of the recess to 11 ft. 6 in.

The problem arises of the movement and storage of a pair of flats. There is, as far as I know, no evidence to show how flats were handled on the passage from store to grooves, and so one is forced to suppose, as the only apparent possible method, that they were, despite their huge size, 'run' or slid upright on their lower edge, just as are the much narrower flats of our own day.

If this be so, the most economical way of storing a collection of flats would be to run them from the grooves direct into the store in much the same position as one pushes a book into a bookshelf. In that case, these flats would not go completely into the dock, but would reach from the back wall to encroach on the space between the two columns. This, however, would be a good arrangement, for the columns would act as divisions between the packs of flats, thus helping to keep the various packs upright.

It is interesting to note that, although the flats belonging to the stage-right side of the scene could be pushed into their grooves direct from the store, by entering them at the off-stage end of the groove and pushing them along, yet the flats of the other side would have to be entered from the on-stage end of their grooves, since insufficient space existed for them to be manœuvred off-stage on the left. Furthermore, a certain amount of what the modern carpenter calls 'playing chess' would have to take place were a flat from the up-stage end of the dock needed for use in one of the down-stage grooves; it would have, presumably, to be run on-stage at the back and shunted down to its position and entered from the on-stage end of the groove, or tilted back at the top—a dangerous job with so large a piece—and juggled under the intervening grooves till it could be inserted in its proper position. Or else advantage would have to be taken of the mobility of the top grooves, and they would be lifted out of the way like the halves of the Tower Bridge at the approach of a steamer, and dropped again to trap the top of the positioned flat. Therefore flats once in their grooves could not be taken out and replaced by others during the course of a performance.

Number of Wings. It is interesting to inquire why there are three wing-grooves in each set. We have hinted at an explanation of the variability in number of the flat-grooves in different sets, but what conditions the fixity of number in the case of the wings?

Concerning this point we have to inquire how the wings were moved at a scene-change. The simple system would seem to be to have had two grooves at each position, one to take the wing of the current scene, the other to take the drawn-back wing of the previous scene, which after use could be completely slid out of the grooves and packed against the side-wall of the stage, while the wing for the third scene was entered in its place ready for pushing on at the next change, and so on. But if such was in fact the procedure, what was the use of the third groove?

An immediate answer might seem to be: in order to accommodate a third wing to save time or trouble. But just how it can be shown that a third groove would save time or trouble (provided the above system of handling be used) I do not clearly see. And if it can be shown, why does the advantage stop at three grooves—why not four or more?

It looks on the face of it as if the above theory of handling is not correct, and that wings were never in fact completely withdrawn from the grooves and packed during a show—at least at this period. Instead it would seem that all the wings were posted in position for the performance and each remained in its grooves—either pushed on or drawn back—till curtain-fall.

But this of course leads us to the conclusion that, whatever the show and however elaborate the nature of its backscenes, only three sets of wings were available. This may indeed have been the case if we allow for the somewhat different conception of the function of wings in the stage picture which certain later evidence will show appears to have obtained in the eighteenth and nineteenth centuries. But if it is true, then we should note that we have facilities for using a maximum of fourteen backscenes in any show, but are allowed a choice out of only three sets of wings to mask their sides.

The arrangement of the upper mechanism of the theatre goes some way to support this theory, for in the flies there are four shafts, or barrels (see Figs. 19 and 21), upon which lines are wound or unwound for the raising or lowering of stuff, and, since one of these shafts is specifically reserved for raising and lowering part of the upper groove mechanism, we are left with facilities for only three sets of borders. Moreover, in the text accompanying the plate three types of borders are mentioned: arch-borders, sky-borders, and ceiling-borders. The three barrels are apportioned one for each type of border.

A temporary conclusion then is that, though wings might, if the show demanded, be provided to a greater number than three sets, yet it is not immediately apparent how more than three sets of borders could have been made available to suit them and so it may be that it was the usage to limit the wings, where possible, also to three sets, and hence arose the three wing-grooves in each position.

We cannot decide whether this rule of three was a current convention or the limitation of one particular theatre. We can only say that our discovery at Bristol shows the same three grooves for wings.

In the illustrations to Pierce Egan's *The Life of an Actor* which we shall shortly be considering, the representations of the wing-grooves are very sketchy, and offer us little to go upon, but they have one point which is difficult to fit in with the above theory that the grooves were the repositories of their wings throughout a show, and that point is that in no instance is more than one wing shown at a time in any set of grooves. On the other hand, there is a vague indication in the darkness of the wing-space in Pl. 49 of wings packed against the side-walls—whether merely because they were not needed for that show and there was nowhere else to store them, or because they belonged to preceding or succeeding scenes, and would only be placed in their grooves for such scenes, we cannot decide. A rough study of the mechanical arrangements for working the borders is shown in the sketch in Fig. 19. The fourth of the four counterweighted shafts shown was reserved for working the lines attached to the loose arms of the upper grooves. It was upon this evidence that the system shown in the model of the Bristol grooves was based.

The Loose and Fixed Grooves. Continuing our examination, we have next to consider one of the most important pieces of new information conveyed to us in these plans. It shows not only that parts of the lower grooves were removable but also the method by which they were fixed on the stage at need.

Pl. 32 of the plans (reproduced in our Fig. 18) is entitled 'Manner of

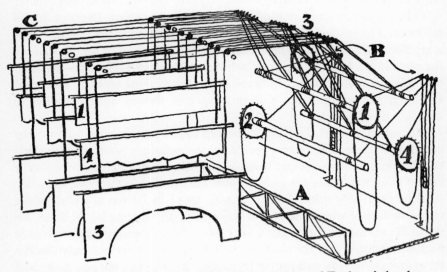

FIG. 19. Reconstruction by the author of the working of Foulston's borders.

fixing lower grooves for working scenes', and consists of a cross-section through the stage floor and through one set of grooves. We are not told specifically through which set of grooves, but since there are five grooves shown in the set, and these are at equal intervals, it is to be presumed that we are dealing either with the composite set of wing- and flat-grooves at the back of the stage, or, as is more likely, with the group of five flat-grooves only, from the No. 1 set. No other set offers us five grooves at equal intervals.

Of these two alternatives it would be interesting to know with how much certainty we could lean towards the latter, for, with this confirmed, we should have presumptive evidence that only the flat-grooves were movable, while the wing-grooves remained fixed. Moreover we are inclined to suppose that, of the flat-grooves, only that part projecting on-stage beyond the wing-groove end would be movable. Our reasons would be that in all the plans a line is drawn across the flat-grooves at a level with the wing-groove ends, suggesting a bisection; further, as we shall see, the only movable part of the upper grooves hanging from the flies was that part of each that similarly projected beyond the wing-grooves; and lastly the wing-grooves themselves in the stage floor, coming so close to the feet of essential pieces of scenery, would not be such obstacles to the movement of actors as the longer projecting arms of the flat-grooves that would only contain a flat occasionally.

What, then, really needed removal, when not in use, was simply that 'arm' of the flat-grooves which encroached so far into the normal stage space.

This reasoning does not of course supply anything like conclusive evidence. The system of mobility may have applied to every groove on the stage floor. We are offered little illumination in the line of text describing the plate in the body of the book, which merely reads: 'Plate 32—Manner of fixing moveable Grooves in Stage Floor, for working scenes.' Though if anything, the wording has a slightly specific flavour as if referring to certain only of the grooves.

The principle of their fixing according to the plate was as follows: the boards of the stage floor were provided in the necessary positions with slots, whether in the form of round holes or long slits is not clear, but one slot or line of slots was made for each groove. Each individual groove was constructed separately in the form of a 4 in. by $1\frac{1}{4}$ in. batten of wood, in the upper surface of which the groove was cut, $1\frac{1}{2}$ in. wide and $\frac{1}{2}$ in. deep. To the under surface of the batten was screwed a plate bearing a peg or line of pegs which fitted into the slots on the stage floor. Hence not only could a set of grooves be removed simply by picking it up at will, but one individual groove of a set could be removed or dropped into place independently of its fellows.

Back and Side Passages. It is interesting to note on this plan that though there is shown a passage about 3 ft. or 3 ft. 6 in. wide in the wing-space for the movement of actors when the flats were drawn back (which is no excessive amount), yet at the back of the stage beyond the back set of flats we have a clear space of 9 ft. Not only so, but beyond again is the recess in the back wall adding another 12 ft. What is the purpose of this generous depth of space at the back of the scenery? Why was not part at least utilized for another set of grooves? On this matter we have no information, but the dotted lines on the plans, showing the range and limit of the side spectators' view, traverse these spaces, going right back to the far wall of the recess; it is therefore to be presumed that these spaces were included, upon occasion, in the spectators' range of vision of the stage and were included as part of the scene. Is it too much to suppose that here we have a deep extension of the acting-area, capable of being revealed occasionally by the withdrawing of the back flats, and of bearing within itself a set scene of some depth, effect, and elaboration?

We are clearly facing so similar an arrangement to Inigo Jones's deeper stage, where his special scenes were set behind the shutters, that, given any evidence for the use of this space at all for scenery, we cannot avoid supposing a general identity of function between the two.

The Cross-section. When we turn from the ground-plan to look for a complete, related, vertical section of this stage we meet with disappointment. No drawing of any dependable accuracy in the series gives us an indication of the proscenium height or of the height of the fly-floors above the stage, and there are many minor discrepancies in detail measurements.

True, there is in one plate of the book a tiny longitudinal section through the complete theatre incidental to a small-scale section of the whole block of buildings of which the theatre formed a part (see *The Georgian Playhouse*, Fig. 23), but the arrangement of details here is not exactly the same as shown in the larger-scale sections of parts of the stage among the plates we are considering.

There are sections in the plates through the stage floor and through the parts under the floor, and there are sections through the stage roof and the working floor under the roof, but there is no section of the space between these two extremities of floor and roof; we have only one slender fact upon which to base a guess at the intervening space and so at the height of the fly-floor, as follows:

Since we found that the presumed width of a pair of flats was 26 ft., and then had confirmation of this point in the discovery that the paint-frame, designed to carry them while they were painted, was exactly 26 ft. wide, we may not be wrong perhaps in supposing that the height of that frame, which is 17 ft. 6 in., represents the height of the flats.

If we are right, then the distance of the fly-floor above the stage was 17 ft. 6 in. (or an inch or so more to allow for the beds of the grooves), since the upper grooves are fixed directly to the underside of the fly-floor which is raked parallel with the stage. The small section of the theatre seems to show exactly 20 ft. for this height, but as in other points it does not exactly tally with the larger sections, we may perhaps tend rather to fix the height of the floor at the smaller figure.

Immediately we begin to set out the upper grooves at this height above the lower grooves, we find an interesting fact. The overall width of each set in the upper series is less than that of the corresponding set below. These measurements are given in plain figures, so we have here no aberration of scale or reproduction. Each set of lower wing-grooves is marked 10½ in. wide over all, but each set of upper wing-grooves is only 8 in. wide. Fig. 17 shows the bottom grooves and Fig. 20 the top.

The first set of flat-grooves is 1 ft. 5¾ in. wide below and 1 ft. 5 in. above. The second set is 1 ft. 2 in. below and 1 ft. 1 in. above. The third 10 in.

below and 9½ in. above. The fourth, composite, set is 1 ft. 5¾ in. below and
1 ft. 5 in. above. The small interval between wing-groove groups and flat-
groove groups in each set is constant, above and below, 6½ in.

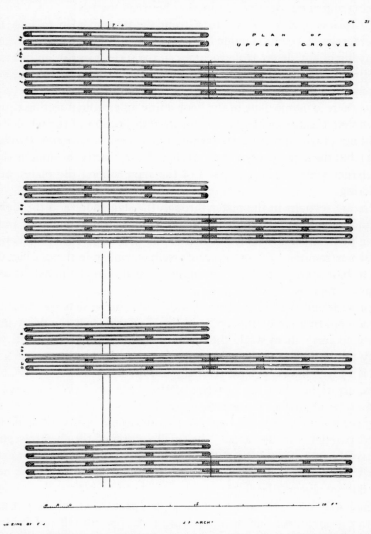

FIG. 20. Plan, looking up, of upper grooves on the right-hand side of Plymouth
stage. The proscenium would be at the top of the plan. (Foulston, op. cit.)

The fact that the ratios of these reductions is not constant in the various
sets of grooves is puzzling, but the main facts suggest that it may have been
that these flats and wings were made (as are some of ours today), not out
of wood of a regular thickness, but with tapering stiles (or uprights) so that

they were a fraction of an inch thinner at the top than at the bottom—which is a great help to balancing them easily on the run.

We note that there is no perspective drop in the height of the upper grooves (as for instance was markedly present in Jones's section). Instead they follow the level of the stage and hence the back grooves are actually higher from the horizontal plane than the front ones.

Any attempt to guess the relative positions of borders and wings is doomed to disappointment. We can only say that, according to any height of proscenium that is allowed by the inconsistent drawings, the masking of the top of the first wings of the set is extremely difficult and could only be achieved by two 6-ft. proscenium borders and one scene border. Yet the ends of the shafts or barrels upon which the border-lines were wound are too far back from the proscenium to include lines for the hanging of the first two of these, and (failing the introduction of further systems of lines from the grid, not shown in the drawings) we have to suppose the upper masking to have been held in even less regard than the side masking at the front.

The Upper Grooves. When we come to examine the incidental drawings of the upper machinery in this theatre, we find an explanation of one of the points made in our earlier study of grooves. In the article in Rees's *Cyclopaedia* we read that the upper grooves 'are sometimes constructed to save room, upon joints, by which they may either be lowered to the horizontal position, or drawn up to the side walls. In this respect their construction is pretty similar to a common draw-bridge.'

These plans of the Theatre Royal, Plymouth, give us much evidence on this point. In Fig. 20 is a 'Plan of Upper Grooves, hung to the Flys, to an enlarged scale'.

This plate shows that the upper grooves were built on a lighter principle than the lower ones, and were made in an open formation of thin strips of wood, edge-down, and separated by distance-pieces. Each of the sets of wing-grooves is built in one, but each set of flat-grooves is divided across its length into two parts. The off-stage part is fixed, like the wing-grooves, to the underside of the fly-floor, but the part projecting on-stage is, as we see in Fig. 21, hinged to the end of the other and can be raised by lines, in a way 'pretty similar to that of a common draw-bridge', into a perpendicular position (see also *The Georgian Playhouse*, Figs. 24 and 25).

But what is the purpose of this displacement? We have seen in the Bristol model that it is to allow the use of tall scenes with arch-borders. We know from the heading to the plates in the text of the Plymouth Theatre notes that arch-borders were among the three types provided for in the flies. It is therefore to be supposed that this ability to raise the grooves owed its motive to a need to clear the upper space for high or arched scenes.

If this is the case we might have supposed that the groove-arms would have been kept permanently raised, save when they were needed to take a pair of closing flats, and that then only the one necessary set of groove-arms would be lowered. But against this there is the remarkable fact that all these groove-arms are attached by lines and pulleys to one barrel on the fly-floor, and so presumably had all to be raised or lowered simultaneously. In this case, it is to be supposed that the usual position of the groove-arms

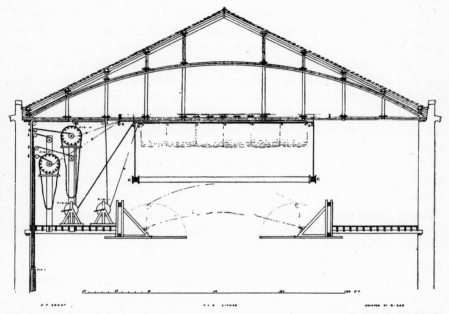

Fig. 21. Cross-section of flies at Plymouth, looking towards the proscenium. (Foulston, op. cit.)

was down, and that they were only raised (and all in concert) upon the occasion of a high scene, which would be both an infrequent occurrence and a very special one. But we should anticipate enough to say here that the evidence from Contant, to be considered shortly, will show that in the scheme he represents each arm could be raised independently.

A Special Problem. The problems of the groove system are manifold, and one stands out among the others in Foulston's plans. It concerns the working of flats in the bottom grooves, and it can be approached in the following question: Was the typical bottom-groove, before this time, a single piece with its own walls and its own bed, or was it a pair of separate strips fixed on the stage, an inch or so apart, to form the walls, while the bed was supplied by the actual surface of the stage itself?

Until the reference we are considering at present, we had not sufficient evidence to attempt an answer, except in one limited instance: we were, exceptionally, able to say that Inigo Jones in his *Salmacida Spolia* section shows the bottom grooves to be a conglomerate whole, having three grooves, one for each scene, and hence four walls, and each groove had its own bed raised by the thickness of the wood above the stage surface. Upon these beds the bottom edges of his scenes slid.

The shutter-grooves, then, had to extend right across the stage so that this raised bed to the groove should be continuous to the point where each half-shutter met its fellow. The wing-sets, of course, only had to be long enough to take a wing drawn back and a wing pushed forward; that is, their length was twice the width of the wing.

Beyond this one reference we have no direct information upon the existence of a bed to the groove till the present instance. And here, in Foulston's plate reproduced as Fig. 18, is the large-scale cross-section of a set showing clearly that each groove was a separate unity possessing its own walls and bed in one piece. In this respect the set almost exactly resembles the sets shown in *Salmacida Spolia*.

But here our difficulty arises; it concerns the origin of the central gap in the lower flat-grooves, and whether, after the introduction of that gap, the grooves all retained the raised bed on which the scenery ran. Suppose that the bed is retained and that these flat-grooves, unlike those of Inigo Jones, do not extend across the stage. When now the flats were closed together, their off-stage extremities would still be held in the groove all right but their on-stage extremities would overhang in mid-air—with an inch or so's gap between the bottom edge and the stage. This fact is to be clearly noticed when one begins to work the model reconstruction based on the Bristol groove. One is immediately impressed with the thought that if, by a miscalculation, the groove were made too short, then the flat, when pushed on in that groove, would at a given point overhang so much as to overbalance and tip its leading corner down on to the stage—thus endangering its whole mobility.

Does the problem arise anywhere else in the whole set of references that I have been able to collect and present here? Apart from the Jones drawing already quoted, there is only indirect mention. For instance, the Covent Garden Inventory specified thirty lower grooves of different sizes. It seems rather more likely from this that the grooves were, like Foulston's, provided with their own beds; but were they, unlike his, continuous across the stage?

Again, the Christie's catalogue mentions the loose and fixed grooves. The loose grooves again, it seems more reasonable to suppose, were unities like Foulston's. But did they reach right across the stage? If not, the same problem is present again.

Rees's writer seems rather to be thinking of the other possibility. He says that the lower grooves are 'composed of parallel pieces of wood fixed upon the stage, and so constructed that they may be removed with facility from one place to another'. In 'parallel pieces of wood' the suggestion is that each so-called 'groove' was composed of two strips, forming the separating walls, while the stage supplied the connecting bed between.

Now Foulston comes and assures us in black and white that his grooves had their own beds, but also *did not* stretch over the full stage—and we are back again at our difficulty.

But (to anticipate a reference later in date) when we come to Contant we find, indisputably represented in a diagram, the system suggested by Rees, of separate strips with no beds.

There are several references, of course, to the fact that the groove-sides occasioned ridges, but these need not necessarily mean any more than that the walls themselves projected up from the stage surface. We have nothing to say whether the *beds* of the grooves were raised, except this isolated and curious diagram of Foulston's.

It must be noted that, as we have shown, there are other mentions that are indefinite enough to be read either way, and there are mentions that clearly and unequivocally state the opposite—that the grooves did not supply their own beds. But Foulston has the only (apparently) unequivocal statement since Inigo Jones that grooves *did* provide their own beds.

Clearly, different details might be favoured by different carpenters, and different forms will succeed each other as evolution develops them—there is not the point. The puzzle is how was it possible, in Foulston's own particular grooves here, or any others that prove in the end to have had their own beds, to close the flats properly if the grooves themselves did not stretch wholly across the stage? Calculation and experiment with the model show it is a critical matter of dimension; each individual flat here is 13 ft. wide and the distance between the groove-tips is about 11 ft. Therefore the closed flats would project each 5 ft. 6 in. beyond its bed and leave 7 ft. 6 in. still nested in the groove. Thus they would still be balanced, having 2 ft. on the right side, but their on-stage ends would certainly be clear of the stage and leave a gap beneath. It follows that the flat-grooves have only to be 18 in. shorter and then the flats on closing would overbalance and almost certainly jam; and the whole system of changing would be ruined.

15

DEVELOPMENTS UP TO 1860

———————————————★———————————————

Flats at Astley's, 1806—Grooves left in place, 1816—'Joining the flats'—
Extant flats at Oxford, c. 1820—'Grievious' scenery, 1821—Bad wing-
changing, 1822—Wing-sizes in Foote's 'Companion to the Theatres', 1829—
Illustrations in 'The Life of an Actor', 1824—Collapses of scenery, 1821—John
and B. Green's stage plans, 1836—Extant grooves at Leicester, 1836—
Knight's 'Penny Cyclopaedia', 1842—Flats in Charles Dickens, 1846—Bad
Haymarket scenery in 1847—The arrangement in the Ipswich manuscript,
c. 1850—Flats in Kean's revivals, 1853—'The Sailor of France', 1854—
Contant's 'Parallèle des Théâtres, 1859

———————————————★———————————————

W E return to our review, in chronological order, of items of evidence about the development of changeable scenery, and we have in this chapter to assemble and study material of the nineteenth century up to 1860.

The opening note is slight, but it brings a hint both of the ingenuities achieved with groove-scenery and of the implied limitations of a system which demanded such ingenuity. The oddment comes from *The Monthly Mirror* of September 1806, p. 199, in a note on the reopening of the New Olympic Pavilion by Astley. The first pantomime there was *The Indian Chief*, and concerning the flats in that show we read: 'In consequence of being narrow in their limits, the scenes that meet are produced on one side, and then joined, but it is managed with such skill as not to be very destructive of effect'—a curious dodge of which the details are not at all clear, but which suggests that narrow wing-space on one side of the stage forced the scene-drawers to work both flats from the other side.

Another limitation is interestingly pointed out in an extract from *Carrick's Morning Post*, 3 February 1816: 'We observed the scene slides were not left on the stage during the opera (*The Beggar's Opera*); but in the after-piece they were left as usual, both in the groves, parlours and so forth.'

This would appear to be a reference to the lower flat-grooves under a new name—'scene slides'—and the point made about them is suggestive; in the less important of the two pieces presented that night the carpenters seem to have been careless, the *loose* grooves (in the words of the Christie sale-catalogue) were not removed as they ought to have been from the floor of the stage when they were not in use, but remained to present, as we may easily imagine, an awkward series of ridges that the actors had, whenever they crossed them, to avoid as carefully as a porter stepping over railway lines.

We remark the flavour of criticism creeping into the mention of grooves. The technique of handling them and the scene-system they imposed were not keeping up with the times. They were allowed to obtrude themselves upon the smooth running of the show—they were beginning to be old-fashioned and a nuisance.

Thus W. Clark Russell in *Representative Actors*, 1869, p. 296, while describing an undated show at the Coburg Theatre, gives another example of the ill-use of grooves: 'On one occasion the scenes stuck in the grooves, and the gods were much offended at beholding the halves of a house with an interstice of a yard or so between them. At length a sweep called out, "Ve don't expect no good grammar here, but, *hang it*, you *might* close the scenes".' This cry of the sweep has, it seems, been transmuted into immortal verse and passed into theatrical tradition, for in my own experience I have heard a stage-hand say, when the flats (modern flats now, of course, forming the back wall of a box set and innocent of grooves) were ill-cleated together, and showed a crack of light between—

> *We don't expect no grammar,*
> *But for God's sake join your flats!*

—so may tradition maintain a chance phrase when the objects it concerned have passed away.

We may pause here at a curiosity. *The Oxford English Dictionary* has no reference to a *flat scene*; it has a theatrical definition of the word *flat* (which we have quoted in Chap. 13). If, now, one turns to the *Supplement* to the *Dictionary*, published in 1933, with the hope of finding further definition of either word one is at first disappointed, and then one makes a curious discovery which it seems very significant to quote here after this reference to the cry of the sweep at the Coburg.

The *Supplement* gives at the end of its study of the word *flat* the following: 'Flat, 11, Phr. *To join the flats*, to make into a consistent whole, to give unity. 1901 *Daily Chron.* 21 Aug. 3/4 The "flats" of her career, so to speak, are not quite joined. 1908 *Ibid.* 29 Apr. 3/3 The "flats" of the new edition are not very well "joined".'

No indication of a theatrical origin is suggested—indeed any source for

42. Leonora and Leander in *The Padlock*, 1773

43. Dibdin as Mungo in *The Padlock*, 1769

44. A surviving backcloth (*c*. 1820)

45. Part of a set of wings to match Pl. 44

46. A surviving 'pair of flats', each in two parts

47. Wheel under bottom rail near join in pair of flats (the metal plate with two screws is a modern precaution to keep the door closed)

48. A small provincial stage showing groove above first wing. From Theodore Lane's illustrations to *The Life of an Actor*, 1824

49. View across stage showing wings and grooves end-on. From Theodore Lane's illustrations to *The Life of an Actor*

the phrase is left unmentioned; but one is very tempted to suppose that if such a phrase was current in the first decade of the twentieth century, it must have sprung from just such an historic occasion as when the halves of a house had the 'interstice of a yard or so between them'. The very fact that the word 'joined' is in quotation-marks in the second example suggests the same unity of phrase which I heard from my carpenter many years before I read the reference in the *Dictionary*.

The next reference is to an object which still exists, and it raises the question: What pieces of stage scenery surviving today may claim the title of the oldest in England? The question has so rarely been posed before that we have practically a virgin field. This present account may bring forth other candidates, but the pieces here to be described constitute the most likely claimants yet brought to my notice for this title.

The remnant of a collection exists today in which we may still count four backcloths and a number of wings and flats. Some of the latter prove upon examination to have unusual features.

The story of this collection of scenery is in itself a valuable footnote to the country life of the nineteenth century and moreover it contains all that remains of evidence upon which to date the pieces. The details were given me by the kindness of the present owner, Mr. Herbert Hinkins of Oxford, the possessor of one of the finest collections of Juvenile Theatre prints. In 1866, as certain existing records show, the decorating and carpentry firm of Hinkins possessed a fairly numerous stock of items let out for hire for the equipment of stages. This stock was added to from time to time by the members of the firm, but it appears that certain pieces were in the possession of the business at a much earlier date.

We may go back to the time of a certain George Rivers Higgins, who settled in Royston (which was then partly in Cambridgeshire) and there founded a decorator's business in the year 1818. He was assisted, and later succeeded in business, by William Hinkins, who thus brought the business into the ownership of the present family. Before 1818 Higgins had been an actor and scene-painter in a company of travelling players. After 1818 he still maintained his connexion with the stage as one of the leading spirits in the local dramatic society under the name of George Rivers. Another member of the society played under the name of Williams and is said to have been William Hinkins, once of His Majesty's Servants at Norwich, and to have played frequently at the Barnwell Theatre, Cambridge, between about 1810 and 1820. It is George Rivers Higgins who is supposed to have brought the nucleus of this store of scenery to Royston, and the older items are reputed to date back to his time. If this is true, then we may well be about to consider some pieces that go back in the history of English scene-painting as far as 1818. Two scenes that appear to be quite reasonably assignable to this early date are the Wood Scene and the Armoury Scene, illustrated in Pls. 44 and 46.

An inventory and notebook of the scenery exists containing references beginning about 1881. The entries are abbreviated and often cryptic, but some picture can be made from them and a few extracts will be given here so as to be with the scenery to which they refer, though the notes belong to a period possibly half a century later than the scenery.

We find three main categories of scene—backscenes, wings, and separate smaller details used in association with certain scenes. We find that the backscenes are of two sorts called 'Back drop Scenes' and 'Framed Back Scenes'. The first worked on rollers and hung from above and the second stood on the stage. The inventory mentions five of the drop scenes, which—since most of the pieces in the collection are painted on both sides—means ten different scenes. They are as follows:

1 and *2*, 'Blue Drawing Room with fire' (area of canvas, 13 ft. 1½ in. wide; 10 ft. 2½ in. high). This shows a plain wall having a painted skirting with a line of decoration immediately above, and a frieze-line towards the top of the cloth. In the centre is a nice example of period fire-place and above it hangs a framed picture. The whole is competently painted, displays strongly marked cast shadows, and is a not ineffective piece of scenery.

The reverse side of the cloth, however, is especially interesting. Here is a 'Forest' (Pl. 44). This bears all the marks of belonging to the earliest period of the scenery. The design is executed in a firm and competent style. There is no weakness of brush-stroke or daubing of effect. The handling is crisp and the tone-contrasts in the foliage are distinct and deliberate. Its colour is sober but effective. Considering its history it is surprisingly well preserved. It shows signs of retouching, but still has character. With this forest back-scene are associated a set of wings as mentioned later.

3 and *4*, 'Cut Palace with vases flowers'. This is a far less attractive design and seems to belong to a later date. It shows a wall with frieze and dado pierced by a central, cut opening flanked by curious columns, and then again by flowers in vases upon pedestals. The chief interest of the cloth is that upon its reverse side there is painted a 'Cut Kitchen with plate shelves or windows and plants'. This curious description applies to a plain wall with panelled dado and a window either side; but the centre, owing to the opening between the columns of the scene on the back, is cut away. The cut may be concealed by setting in front one of two 'pieces', the first representing plate-shelves and painted on a loose roll of canvas to be suspended from above, the other a 'framed Kitchen window' to stand in front of the opening and for which there is listed a separate small piece as follows: 'Piece drab panelled dado for framed Kitchen window 3 ft. 6" long (Roll)' to hang from the window-sill to the stage and conceal the opening beneath. This cloth still exists.

5 and *6*, 'Lake Dungeon (Roll)'. Of this cloth we have apparently no trace.

7 and *8*, 'Act drop'. The act drop is unique among the pieces in not being painted in distemper direct upon the canvas. It consists of a large paper picture laid down upon the fabric of the cloth with paste or glue. The design upon the paper, is, however, of considerable interest and charm. It consists of an Indian landscape with trees and native figures, taking back one's mind almost to the days of Oroonoko and the noble savage.

On the reverse side, the drop is painted in the ordinary way in distemper and shows a stock street scene with a seventeenth-century flavour. The work is a little hard and the perspective somewhat unsure, but on the whole the painting is competent. This drop still exists.

9 and *10* is noted in the inventory as a roll cloth with 'Clouds' on one side and a 'workshop' on the other. Unfortunately the drop is now not to be found and the interesting question as to the nature of the cloud scene must remain unanswered except for a guess that it might have been like these 'sky cloths' or 'horizon cloths' sometimes obtainable among the sheets of the Juvenile Theatre.

The second category of backscenes, the 'Framed Back Scenes', has two items, one of which has apparently not survived, but the other of which is of very considerable interest. It is entered as: 'Back Scene of 4 frames, Armoury & Cedar R. with folding doors in centre.' The scene now lost was: 'Set Back Scene of 7 pieces being Green R. with Bay 1.1. window & flat 1.1. window in No: 2 L. Wing from front.' The former scene is shown as 14 ft. 1 in. wide and the latter 12 ft. 8⅝ in. The letters '1.1.' signify 'leaded light'.

The 'Armoury' (upon whose reverse is painted the 'Cedar R[oom]') is, in its class, a notable piece of painting (Pl. 46); it is severely simple and consists of nothing but a plain wall with pseudo-Gothic panelling below and a frieze above, but the handling is direct and firm and the tone of the cast shadows accurate and put in with delicately thin paint. (In none of these pieces are any signs present of unskilful mixing of size in the distemper; no cracking is anywhere observable, the canvas is still flexible and the only blemishes are a slight fading, considerable rubbing—especially where battens come under the canvas—and damp-stains.)

The Cedar Room upon the reverse is a less pleasing and, by its style, probably a later piece of work.

The great interest of these pieces lies in the fact that they constitute the only surviving examples yet discovered during the writer's twenty years' study of theatrical history of a divided flat-scene.

Peter Paterson in his confessions of a strolling player, published in 1864 and entitled *Glimpses of Real Life as seen in the Theatrical World and in Bohemia*, begins a heart-rending story of the fiasco of his first attempt to play Hamlet in public, with the words: 'When the stony ramparts of Elsineur drew asunder, and the audience beheld "*Scene II—A Room of State in the Castle*"' ... These parts of the Armoury which we illustrate in Pl. 46 must often have been seen to draw asunder in just this way. It is this drawing asunder that lies behind the design of the Armoury doors. They are so framed-up that the crack between the two leaves of the door is carried up through the wall above so that the whole backscene may be 'drawn asunder'. If further proof were wanting, we have but to turn the scene on its side and look at its lower edge. There we find, what is never to be found on such a piece of scenery today, a wheel set into the bottom rail to assist the pieces to slide easily (see Pl. 47).

In circumstances where scenery had to be taken out of the theatre and toured, the 'pair' of flats was often subdivided—as here—into more sections than two for convenience in handling.

The inventory continues with a short list of separate subordinate pieces, all of which are now lost. We see such items as 'Chimney piece, fitting into Armoury doorway', 'Dwarf Stone Wall—18 ft. long × 4 ft 5 high', 'Triangular panelwork for side of stairs'.

Next, Wings are listed and the first list is, interestingly, one devoted to 'Roll Wings', thus suggesting loose canvases that hung from above. They are all double-sided and generally vary from 3 ft. 4 in. wide to 4 ft. 6 in.; though two are marked as much as 6 ft. 11 in. wide. There are three 'Dungeon Wings', six 'Blue Room', four 'Clouds', one 'Green Interior', four 'Workshop', and four to match the Armoury scene above.

A second list of wings is headed 'List of framed Set Backs and Wings'; thus it contains not loose rolled canvases but framed-up pieces. Eight trees are listed (these exist and match the 'Wood Cloth'; see Pl. 45 for a selection), four Armoury, six 'Cedar R', and other items. The significance of a 'Set Back' is not quite clear. No example appears to survive. It may have signified a 'set' backscene, that is, one revealed by the opening of a 'pair of flats' but not itself openable; or, most probably, a return bay with its sides set at an angle like the backscene in *The Padlock*.

The notebook's information is, we repeat, later than the possible date of the earliest scenery, but it gives notes of the dimensions of various halls in which it was customary to fit up the stage, and of difficulties to be guarded against in each. Then follow a number of pages devoted to the Stage Fittings. Here, alas, there is much that is obscure. Generally it would appear that four 'fly ladders' as they are here called were erected at the corners of the stage. Between the two front ladders and the two back, some sort of top batten seems to have been hung, which is, however, occasionally referred to also as a fly-ladder. Across the stage, between these latter pieces, were hung 'fly laths' to take borders. More than one fit-up was in use and that called 'No 2' possessed—

3 pieces white & gold panelwork
3 crimson baize frames
1 Maroon distd: upper frame which is screwed on the horizontal crimson baize frame before latter is taken up into position
2 front posts,
2 Back do:, with 2 large 1 [iron] stays to beam
2 Side frames or ladders for wings & flies,
2 cord stays from back posts to windows.
6 Papered Pros: frs:
2 Distd: grooved cornices
2 Distd green drapery side boards
Skirting, Cornices, grooves.

The last item, the grooves, appears to have been a form of the traditional horizontal upper groove in which the heads of the scene-pieces slid and were supported as they moved, but later in the notes, under date 12 April 1893, we find mention of another system of 'iron wing forks'.

We find brief descriptions of at least two proscenium fronts made to fold and to travel with the scenery. One of these is pleasantly called 'Mr. B's crimson frames' and tradition has it that Mr. B. was a Mr. John Beaumont, a gentleman interested in amateur theatricals, living near Royston and whose material later came into the possession of the Hinkins family.

Many other details of the stage of the English Victorian country-side are present in the notebook. We read of a 'Total length of Pfn Footlights, complete 13ft 9'—and we may almost smell again the 'pfn' or paraffin which lit the dramatic occasions. This was in 1881; in 1887 we read also of 'The gas service laying on stage floor' for use with footlights.

Again a passing note of dimensions conjures up a picture of the bustle and preparation for those festive nights. For instance, it is noted for reference that 'Beaumont's green Curtain before alteration by us was 15' 6" *total* width of Baize but only 12' 3" when lapped at ends as originally fitted up to suit battens'. And again: 'Our old carpet (all made up in 1 square) is 11' 10" × 6ft.' And 'John St: *Winter Gardens* total depth of Orchestra for Pfte: and 11 other Pfrs, and conductor—5' 9" from panelled front of Stage, but 6' 0" would have been far better'. A thumb-nail sketch-plan appended shows the crowded pianoforte wedged behind 'Plant tiers'.

Careful 'Conditions for Letting Stage Materials' are listed. The 'Revised Charges' noted in 1895 are:

Making up platform, fixing & hire of largest stage fittings . . . removal after entertainment, leaving platform in original condition or otherwise to satisfaction of Institute Manager,—attendance of stage Carpenter and necessary Assistants at Performance and at one rehearsal if desired.

(Memo: at the Rehearsal we do only sufficient shifting to enable the Performers & ourselves to understand the evenings arrangements.)

Foregoing includes gas foot-lights, 3 rows fly lights, & side lights, all shifting, management of green baize curtains, also assisting Stage Manager with arrangement of Properties, etc (and fire engine) £3. 2. 0.

To this price must be added the cost price of 2 copies of *each* play for cutting up into our 'Stage Manager's book'.

Each roll or framed backscene was charged 2s. 6d., and each roll or framed wing 1s., and each double-width roll or framed wing 2s.

'Lamp lit on table' was one shilling extra and 'Our old carpet' cost a shilling for hire, including laying. The Second Night (if any) was charged '¼th that of 1st—but, if not consecutive, ⅓ or ½ according to circumstances'.

Wigs and details of costume, including 'Courtier's suits' and 'slashed coats', were to be hired for about a shilling apiece.

Among the final pages is a list of 'materials generally wanted for Out-town Theatrical fitting up'. It rounds off our picture of the times very well. Among things to be remembered were the 'glasses' for the footlights, and the paraffin, 'black and tinned tacks', 'wing fillets', cut clasp nails, ordinary nails, screws, wire, cord and twine, L-plates, filling-can and funnel, carpet, painter's box, dusting brush, 'Fire Engine & 2 pails', 'Bell', 'Benzoline lamp', 'Baize Curtains' and a 'Looking glass'.

We have, in order to include our study of the notebook connected with this early scenery, had to pass out of the first two decades of the century and glance at affairs of the eighties. Now we return to 1821.

The reference is once more highly critical, and is the more interesting in that it roundly condemns work which came from the hand of one of the great scene-painting names of the period. Even the masters were indicted. *The Dublin Theatrical Observer* for April 1821, speaking of the opera of *The Devil's Bridge* at the Theatre Royal says:

As to the scenery, we have to commend the manager's modesty for saying nothing of it, as has been usual, in the bills, for certainly nothing could be worse— we had the old Scotch Fisherman's hut changed to an Alpine Cottage, and when we expected to see the Alps frowning above us, we were presented with a beautiful Italian view, and an Inn where *Guido* had refreshed on his way to *Mirandola*— not a pine or a fir could be recognized in the side wings, but the old elms, which answer for every Country from the North Pole to the Southern Pacific, and in the prison where *Belino* sang of '*Vaulted Roofs*' we had rustic beams, entwined with straw. What are the *Messrs. Grieve* about?—the absence of their brush in appropriate scenery upon this occasion was indeed grievous.

One is not made quite clear about whether the complaint against the Grieves was for painting unsuitable scenery or for failing to paint scenery at all so that the settings had to be drawn from stock. But the critical attitude against unsuitability of details is very clear. The old haphazardness was not to be tolerated.

In 1822 we have a very outspoken demand that a reform should be contrived. *The Theatrical Looker-on*, a diminutive weekly published at Birmingham, apostrophizes Mr. Bunn, lessee of a local theatre, in its second number dated 3 June:

MR. BUNN. In the farce of *Bombastes Furioso* on Friday last, the wing of a Palace was left during an entire scene in a cottage. Pray when are we to expect that the stage machinery for the wings will be used; and how long are we to see the dirty fingers of your scene shifters pushing them along the grooves, frequently without being able to move them in time? CENSOR.

This is an interesting note. Though it deals with the theatre in the provinces, it shows a weakness of the groove system that we have already realized—namely the difficulty of getting the scene-shifters to move their pieces in synchrony. But especially to our point is this picture of the scene-shifter who forgot one wing altogether and left a piece of a palace throughout a scene in a cottage! Had a mechanical system been adopted whereby the movement of all the wings had been controlled by a central machine, this overlooking of one could not have occurred. Clearly this was one of the many theatres where the scenes were shifted by manual labour. The writer seems to refer to 'the stage machinery for the wings' as something he well knew and felt a right in demanding.

The question offers itself, How could the hands of scene-shifters be seen when pushing the wings along the grooves? The next reference provides some answer. It should be understood that were a scene-shifter to put his hand on the off-stage edge of a wing today, that hand would be invisible from any seat, owing to the placing of the wings. A properly arranged wing is so angled and of such a width that it fully masks behind the one in front, and a standard wing today is 6 ft., or more, wide. But now if we turn to Horace Foote's *A Companion to the Theatres*, 1829, we note that the wings of even Covent Garden were only 4 ft. wide (though they were actually 21 ft. high) and the flats were 14 ft. wide, each half. To find a wing only 4 ft. wide in a large theatre today would be next to impossible. We have had indication before that earlier wings were narrower than ours and thus that they masked less jealously and permitted glimpses between them which must often have included the dusty hands of the scene-shifter ready to draw them off.

Our next authority is a pair of pictures (see Pls. 48 and 49) from the series drawn and engraved by Theodore Lane for Pierce Egan's amusing book, *The Life of an Actor*, 1824. Here under the title of '*A Beggarly Account of Empty Boxes*, PROTEUS *losing by his Benefit. No joke in* THEATRICALS' is a grim picture of a tiny theatre with a glimpse of the stage with the far-side wings and a fragment of the backscene. The Number One Wing, or that nearest the audience, is not adequately masked at the top or side, and we are allowed a glimpse of a curious, apparent 'capping' to the wing; it might be supposed a sort of cornice, but such a cornice would not show on the back as well as the front, and thus it is to be supposed that here we are looking at a groove. We turn the pages and find a second illustration; this gives a cross-view of the stage in which the far-side wings are presented edge on. If we look at the top edges of the two wings shown, we see they have the same flat cappings to them; but we are now offered an additional point of detail, for here the bottom of the fly-floor is vaguely visible in the shadows and we see not only that they bear approximately the same spatial relation to the underside of this gallery as did the sets of grooves in Foulston's plans but that the second one seems here to be situated lower than the first, thereby recalling the grading down of wing-height which prevailed in the old perspective system of scenery, in which the back wings were shorter than the front; though this point may be due only to a looseness of drawing.

In this second illustration, which seemed at first to offer little, we find the final piece of confirmation; a magnifying glass will show that the undersides of these so-called cappings are marked with additional lines—in this second picture the artist has indicated the grooves in the lower faces of the pieces.

Two points occur to the mind about which we desire more information. Firstly we look for some such corresponding grooves on the stage floor beneath to take the bottom edge of the wing. But we are disappointed. In neither of these two illustrations is any indication given of lower grooves. Have they been overlooked by the artist or are they, in fact, by now beginning to be abandoned? If this last is true, as seems to be the case, one feels the position of the wings must have been very precarious; an accidental kick at the lower edge might displace it an inch or two, and that might well be sufficient to dislodge the upper edge from the grooves and start the whole scene collapsing like a pack of cards. And in study we find not only records that the scenery often jammed and stuck in these grooves, but several accounts of complete collapse. For instance, in the *Dublin Theatrical Observer* for 2 November 1821 we read, concerning a presentation of *The Witch of Derencleuch* at the Theatre Royal:

The next good thing we have to notice is a piece of excellence merely in scenery. A prison is represented which is attacked by the smugglers and its destruction presents a custom house on fire, a splendid spectacle truly. . . . The effect however was somewhat injured by an accident or act of neglectfulness on the part of the carpenters which caused the prostration of an entire scene.

Again, Fitzgerald (*The World Behind the Scenes*, p. 75) quotes the 'facetious Raymond's' narrative of events on the night of Elliston's arrival at Buxton for *The Castle Spectre*, telling us how Muley, in a too-ingenious attempt at economy, performed both the part of an actor on the stage and that of the musician outside to whom he was listening, by sticking his head and shoulders through a small window in the scene, simultaneously continuing his lines and playing a fiddle with his hidden hands:

But, alas! just at this moment, when in the act of a second time pulling in his body from the narrow aperture, the exertion necessary to the operation, together with the fragile state of the antique scenery, produced a most awful crash; the whole side of Osmond's castle-wall, with Muley sticking in the window frame, like a rat caught by his neck, fell inward on the stage, disclosing at one view a heterogeneous state of things beyond, beggaring all powers of description.

On the very next page of Fitzgerald's book there is another example:

At the Surrey Theatre, in a play called 'The Burning Bridge', there was a striking scene called 'The Orange Grove', in which the painter Tomkins had exhausted his art. After a little interval for a duet, says the author, 'Mr. P. Honey was in the piece, "Take, oh take this golden fruit". Henry Kemble had to rush into the orange grove as a sorcerer or a tyrant; in doing so, his long costly robes becoming entangled in a set piece, pulled down with it, the orange trees excepted, every morsel of scenery on the stage, discovering only bare walls and flooring.' The delight of the audience may be conceived, which was added to by the speech of the stage manager, who began, 'Ladies and gentlemen, the scenery has fallen down!' (Roars of laughter.)

Such stories clearly suggest a weakness in the groove system and they lead one to suspect that the doing-away with the lower grooves may well have already begun.

Secondly it occurs to one to ask if any method existed of raising or lowering these grooves. Without this power of movement, they would impose a very rigid condition on the makers of scenery; for a touring company would have to see that the height of the grooves in each theatre they proposed to visit was exactly the same, and that the height of the wings they intended to carry with them just corresponded. This means in fact that touring scenery would have to be standardized in height. If so, can we find any indication of the standard height of each wing? If, moreover, the wings were in fact (as the drawing seems to suggest) graded down in height as they went up-stage, what a great complication is laid upon the long-suffering carpenters and what exactitude must have governed their work.

So lacking are we in any evidence for supposing that wing-height was thus rigidly standardized that we may consider for a moment an alternative possibility—that we have here a very real reason for the use of stock wings. For a travelling company might perhaps happily carry its own backcloths, but the host-theatre would be depended upon to provide a reasonable choice of wings of its own, designed to fit the heights of its own sets of grooves. The question of stock scenes we must consider in its place.

Perhaps, then, there is some very pertinent reason in the former of these two illustrations to *The Life of an Actor*, behind the coldly impersonal intrusion, between the first house wing and the house backscene, of an incongruous column and curtain. Maybe the host-theatre had no other pair of house wings, and 'pushed on' the nearest to hand.

But against this suggestion that touring companies did not travel their own wings we have at least one obstacle. There is a famous print of Hogarth's of a company of strolling players dressing among an untidy conglomeration of scenic details. Among these pieces are two or three wings. If these are strolling players and the wings belonged to them our theory falls, or at any rate fails to apply to that earlier period, but if they belonged not to the players but to the theatre, we may hold it again.

Next we turn again to the evidence of a plan. In 1836–7 two architects named John and B. Green prepared plans for the present Theatre Royal, Newcastle. About the same time they also planned another theatre called by them 'Le Goût du Temps' but otherwise unidentified, and upon the ground-plan and section of the stage in the latter scheme they indicated the position of the grooves.

Their indications are especially interesting for they give us an introduction to a novel arrangement of groove-plan to be seen in certain later theatres. This formation is characterized by an oddly cryptic quality. After the fullness with which Foulston indicated his grooves on the plans for Plymouth it occurs to one to wonder at first if some later architects drew the groove-positions on their plans with a definitely more casual and less explanatory pencil—as if to say to the carpenter—'Those groove-things come hereabout—you are always arguing on the exact details of them, build them as you like. I only indicate where they may go. The details I leave to you.'

Either this or we are beginning to come on a development of groove layout that should be noted as a most important step in their history.

For the Greens' indications in the plan are simply a series of sets of short lines either side the stage showing no distinction between long grooves and short. They are lettered for explanation, but the accompanying legends shed a confused light on what is intended:

(*a*) Six Cuts or Grooves 4 for wings and one for Flat Scenes [*sic*]
(*b*) Five do. do.
(*c*) Five do. do.

(*d*) Three do. do.

(*e*) Wing Ladders & Gas Lights.

These explanations are puzzling. At (*a*) there is presumably intended a statement that the down-stage set contained six grooves in all, and that some of these were to take wings and some flat scenes, but there is nothing to show whether the architects supposed that there was no difference between the sizes of grooves for wings and those for flats, or whether (which is an interesting possibility) all grooves were made initially the same size and fixed firmly on the stage, but that some, or any, of them could be transformed at need into flat-grooves by the addition of a loose 'arm' or extension.

But if that were the case, why should some of the grooves in the Greens' sets be specified for flats and some for wings? Possibly because only some had the slots in the stage at their extremities designed to take the dropped-in pegs of extensions?

But there is a further possibility. Were the lower grooves gradually coming to be found unnecessary? Had part of them at least—the part we have hitherto thought of as a movable extension—been removed so often that it had occurred to some carpenter, either a sloth or an innovator, that a pair of flats could be nearly as easily closed if he did not take the trouble to put the lower groove-extensions back? For, provided the flats were run smoothly along the right line, the top grooves (if they were deep enough) would keep them upright, and the lower grooves were always only a guide, never, like the upper ones, a support. The lower flat-grooves would then be identical in shape and size with the lower wing-grooves. This possibility seems indicated on the plan and we have to see in what follows whether the innovation was adopted and—as it might well be—extended.

How this matter was settled in the upper grooves remains entirely obscure.

However that may be, the puzzle of the legend is still not cleared away, for there is, I think, no arithmetic to be found to explain how Six grooves can be divided in Four and One and yet leave none unaccounted for. The method of wording the legend is itself cryptic, but we presume in the lack of more certain knowledge that it was intended to read either: 'Six cuts or grooves, (of these) four (are) for wings and *two* for flat scenes', or 'Five for wings and one for flat scenes'. Or it might have been 'Six grooves for' (and the 'four' repeated in error from dictation) 'wings and one for flat scenes'. And this, in spite of its oddity, seems to accord best with the drawings where some *seven* pieces in all seem to be represented, apart from the farthest, eighth piece which we read as a 'wing ladder for gas lights' and not as a piece of scenery.

After this uncertainty the exact significance of the abbreviation 'do. do.'

for the (*b*), (*c*), and (*d*) sets of grooves is still more obscure. It would appear to mean that of the numbers of grooves specified in each case all but one were for wings and the remaining one for flats.

'(e) Wing Ladders & Gas Lights' signifies fixed actual ladders behind each set of grooves on which were hung a vertical strip of light points.

It seems pretty clear from this that the Greens made no distinction in shape or size between wing-grooves and flat-grooves. Whether the carpenter who equipped the stage went further than this and gave us the sort of arrangement with which we are more familiar, having long and short grooves, we cannot tell.

The chain of facts is tangled and obscure, the evidence is as incomplete as in the best murder mystery—indeed it may be that that is what it is; that we see here the first movement of an attack upon the grooves, which was in time to eat them away bit by bit, lopping off section after section, till in the end it needed but one determined attack to wrench the last remnant of a two-century-old tradition out of its position and cast it, a corpse, upon the waste heap.

Why are the Greens' grooves so summarily shown after the fullness of Foulston's?

Had we a plan of the Greens' stage at the level of the upper grooves we might be much nearer to a solution. For then we could answer the question, Were there any groove extensions to the upper grooves? If we could learn that there were, then we could take the omission of the lower extensions as a definite move to reduce the groove mechanism. For the omission of the lower groove extensions would then pretty certainly be judged as intentional.

If, on the other hand, the upper grooves were found to have no extensions represented, then we would be in a dilemma: either they were omitted at both levels through ignorance or to save time, but would be, in practice, installed, at top and bottom, just on the Foulston principle, or, if the omission were intentional and we are faced with an actual development in the system whereby the length of the flat-grooves was reduced until they were identical with the wing-grooves, then how was a closed pair of flats supported in an upright position? For now only the very outward extremities of the top edge of the pair would be held in grooves, and with pieces of such a great size this would be an insufficient support.

So far as the inadequate facts go, there is only one logical conclusion. It is that the Greens' omission of the lower grooves is intentional, that the lower edges of flats were no longer confined save at the off-stage extremities but instead ran free upon the stage, and that in addition to this the upper grooves remained in their old form with the long, probably still movable, extensions to guide the upper edges of the flats and hold them upright.

We suppose finally, then, that the innovation on the Green plan was deliberate and that, by 1837, the gradual elimination of the groove had set in and had begun by the reduction in length of the lower flat-sets—in short, by the removal for ever of the 'loose' grooves. Their very mobility betrayed them. Their projection in ridges was a nuisance. They were taken up and not put back.

At this point we reach the period where we may best include a discovery by an ex-student of mine, Mr. Richard Leacroft, at Leicester. This concerns the existence in 1948 at the old Theatre Royal of a pair of working grooves belonging possibly to about 1836. But these grooves are today clearly no more than relics and are never used for their original purpose; moreover there is every likelihood that they are not now in their original positions, for though they are attached still to the fly-floor yet it is demonstrable that the present fly-floor is an alteration of the original and dates from a reconstruction in 1880.

There are probably other rare survivals of similar grooves, or their remnants, in other out-of-the-way corners of provincial theatres; but as a rule such things have vanished long ago and any such survival is a matter of interest. One theatre known to the writer where a similar discovery was made is that at the Alexandra Palace, Wood Green. The collection of such pieces of evidence as these may well throw further light on the history of grooves, though we must take care to remember that such survivals as are left are probably adapted for other uses, or removed from their original position. A brief review of the Leicester grooves will give some idea of a typical situation. (A short note by the present writer, illustrated with valuable and detailed diagrams by Richard Leacroft, on the stage mechanism at Leicester appeared in *Wood* for August, 1948.)

Pls. 50, 51, and 52 show the prompt-side grooves at Leicester in their present position. The grooves are to be seen a little above, and a little to the side of, the proscenium opening. They appear as a jointed horizontal arm projecting from the bottom end of a pair of uprights attached to the railing of the fly-floor and braced from these uprights by diagonal stays.

The alteration from their original position amounts probably to no more than a shifting outwards away from the proscenium edge when the fly-floor was narrowed in 1880. The floor appears originally to have stretched nearly to the side of the proscenium opening. The tips of the opposite groove-arms would then originally have been not 12 ft. 6 in. apart in the centre as they are now, but only some 5 ft. 6 in. apart. Otherwise their general situation seems substantially the same.

Pls. 50 and 51 show the prompt-side grooves raised. The hinge is at a point just in front of the junction with the diagonal stay. They will be seen to be in the light form of open construction (presumably later than Bristol) with no solid connecting bed, but only a series of distance-pieces dove-tailed into the individual groove-strips. Originally there were three grooves formed by four strips, but the fourth strip has been removed save on the outermost, fixed part of the groove. A chain still checks the fall of the arm at its horizontal position. Two intrusive vertical pieces of timber have been inserted later between the strips at the outer end, no doubt to serve as forks for the support of a pair of proscenium wings whose height did not accord with the level of the grooves, and which modern procedure requires fre-quently to be set at an angle, rather than parallel with the footlights—as the grooves would force them to be.

Pl. 52 shows the groove with its arm in the lowered position. No specific means of working this arm is apparent and it may have been raised simply by pulling on the support-chain and engaging the nearest convenient link to the hook of origin.

An interesting feature clearly shown in the plates is that the whole object can be made to slide up or down, for occasional adjustment, by means of a line over a pulley-block situated under the edge of the second fly-floor above.

No special short grooves for wings are apparent.

Presumably this isolated pair was once part of a set of probably four pairs spaced along the stage side like those at Plymouth. Of the remainder there is no trace.

As was said above, Mr. Leacroft's informative drawings of the mechanism of this stage have already been published in *Wood*, and the reader is referred to these for further detail. It may, however, be useful at this point to add, in illustration of the elaborate nature of the working of a stage at this period, certain engravings which appeared in *Engineering*, 28 February 1896. These diagrams accompanied the first serial publication by E. O. Sachs of material that was later to form part of his monumental *Modern Opera Houses and Theatres*, to be referred to again on p. 388.

First, the nature of the stage floor used with the groove machinery: Figs. 22 and 23 show Sachs's plans of a typical English wooden stage, the former at stage level and the latter just below at what is called the 'mezza-nine' floor. The width of the stage was divided into three areas; the two side areas were fixed, the central was highly mobile. The central area was divided into a number of sections, and the floor of each was cut down the centre line so that the left and right halves of each section could be drawn aside under the fixed area of floor at the side in order to open a *cut*, or provide space for the working of a *sloat* or of a *bridge*.

At the front of the stage just inside the proscenium opening are two square *corner traps*. Their purpose was to assist a figure to rise through the stage upon a counterweighted platform running in vertical guides. It was into the corner traps that there could be fitted, upon occasion, that internationally famous variant of trap-door, called the English *star-trap* (Fig. 24). Next beyond the corner traps, and situated in the middle of the stage, comes a larger oblong trap—the *grave trap*. Of this the general use was in being lowered so as to provide a pit in the stage, traditionally instanced in the grave in *Hamlet*.

Beyond these the nature of the openings differs somewhat. There

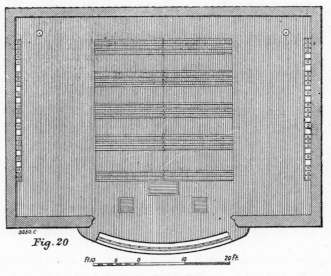

PLAN OF STAGE FLOOR.

FIG. 22. Plan of old-style stage floor. From E. O. Sachs, 'Modern Theatre Stages', *Engineering*, 1896

follows a close series of adjacent *cuts* or long, narrow openings extending completely across the acting-area of the stage. The cuts are of two sorts and the varieties are alternated in a fairly regular succession. Those of the first variety are only about a foot wide; they are called the *sloat cuts*, from the machine which worked underneath them and which will be discussed below. The second variety are some 3 ft. wide and are called *bridge cuts* since in them are worked the *bridges* or long, falling and rising platforms, upon which posed groups of players could be brought up to the stage.

The succession of cuts is more or less the same in all theatres though with occasional individual variations; usually two or three sloat cuts follow immediately after the traps, next a single bridge cut, then a similar group of sloat cuts repeated and a further bridge cut, and the sequence thus repeated again till the back of the acting-area is reached—involving, usually, from three to five repetitions of the unit. Leicester is a little unusual in having two sloat cuts between the corner and grave traps, and then three between grave trap and first bridge. Beyond that the normal succession picks up of two sloat cuts and one bridge.

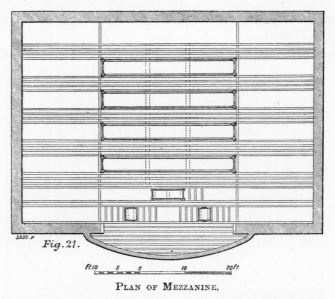

3350.F

Fig. 21.

ft:10   5   0   10   20ft.

PLAN OF MEZZANINE.

FIG. 23. Construction of old-style stage floor. (From Sachs, op. cit.)

The means of opening such cuts is interesting and of long tradition. Each cut is framed below by the floor-joists (see Fig. 25). Running along the centre of the top of each joist is a wooden *fillet,* the same thickness as the boards of the flooring. Between the fillets on any two adjacent joists lies

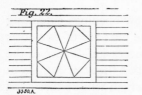

Fig. 22.

3350.A.

FIG. 24. Plan of English star trap. (From Sachs, op. cit.)

the relative section of flooring resting on the remaining part of the top of the joists. This section of flooring is not fixed, but can slide along the joists, and each section bears the name of *a slider.* The sliders, then, run in beds on the top of the joists.

But towards the side of the acting-area—some 5 ft. before the fixed part of the stage is reached—these beds begin to be cut away in a sloping channel running down the inner cheeks of the joists and continued under the fixed floor to the side-walls of the stage itself. The outer end of each slider is normally prevented from dropping into this channel by a lever-system, in which a vertical handle, pivoted in metal stirrups, under the side of the acting-area, raises it to a horizontal position (see Fig. 25). When this handle is tripped, the support is removed and the end of the slider is

50. Surviving grooves at Theatre Royal, Leicester, in raised position

51. Surviving grooves part-lowered and supported by chain

52. Surviving grooves lowered. These grooves are now preserved by the Leicester Museum

53. Reconstruction by the author of Frederick Lloyds's model of a set scene, from *Scene Painting*, 1875

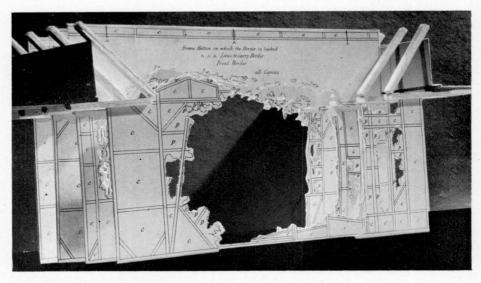

54. Back view of Lloyds's model with backcloth and ground-row removed

55. View from stage of Richmond Theatre, Surrey, dated 1896, showing grooves

56. Presentation plate from *The Graphic*, 1880

57. View from prompt-side fly-floor of Prince's Theatre, Bristol (now demolished), showing vertical groove posts

58. From a drawing by William Telbin, Jnr., showing the working of a stage typical of *c.* 1859. From *The Magazine of Art*, 1889

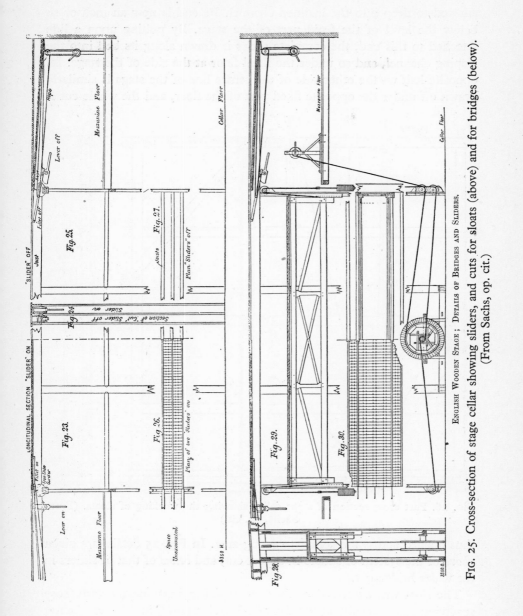

ENGLISH WOODEN STAGE; DETAILS OF BRIDGES AND SLIDERS.

FIG. 25. Cross-section of stage cellar showing sliders, and cuts for sloats (above) and for bridges (below).
(From Sachs, op. cit.)

allowed to drop into the inclined channel. Its end is now an inch or so below the level of the fixed part of the stage. By pulling upon a line attached to this end, the complete slider is drawn along its bed into the sloping channel, and so under the fixed floor at the side of the stage. Its opposite half on the other side of the centre line of the stage is similarly drawn off under the opposite fixed part of the floor, and the whole cut is

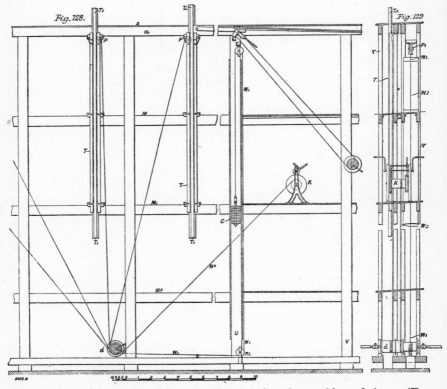

FIG. 26. Part cross-section of stage cellar showing the working of sloats. (From Sachs, op. cit.)

thus opened across the complete acting-area. In Fig. 25 details are given *above* of the system of sliders in a sloat cut, and *below* of that of sliders in the wider bridge cut.

The sloat was described by the present writer, in connexion with those surviving until recently at the Theatre Royal, Bristol, in *Life and Letters To-day* (September 1939). The word is also sometimes spelled 'slote'. In brief, the sloat is a vertical groove containing a sliding tongue (see Fig. 26, T and T_1). Two or more of these were bolted to the floor-joists and the mezzanine joists below any sloat cut. By means of a rope from each sloat, working together upon a small windlass, the tongues could be drawn up simultaneously. Their use was to raise a long, low piece of scenery (of the sort we call a ground-row) to the stage in a transformation scene. The lower edge of the ground-row was supported in metal brackets at the base of the tongues and the top of the piece was nailed through to the tongues at a convenient place.

What is now remarkable to realize is that the whole reason and purpose of all this great elaboration of traditional machinery on the English stage from 1660 to about 1900 lay in the convention of visible scene-change. In changing the simpler kind of scene the two halves of the backscene were slid apart in their grooves by paper-hatted stage carpenters and a further scene was revealed straightway behind. It might be that the borders and wings would often remain in position, but on occasion these too worked— the wings moving off sideways to reveal a fresh group behind, and the borders rising to the grid and revealing others in their place.

But this was only a part of normal procedure. Let us suppose a change to a complicated set scene. Now the whole stage is put in action; the wings begin to slide off to the side, the normal straight borders to rise, and the backscene to open. The new borders descending from the grid may be high arch-borders. Each groove-arm has then to be raised out of the way as soon as the flats are freed, and lifted to the up-reared position against the fly-rail. Simultaneously with all this, further details of the new scene are beginning to be visible upon the stage; firstly, sliders part to either side and through the cuts there rise up on their sloats the successive ground-rows running across the floor of the scene and giving the retreating planes of distance. Beyond these, through the opening flats at the back, are appearing still further vistas of successive set-pieces running away to the distant sky-cloth hung against the very wall of the theatre. And now to perfect the spectacle, the great bridges below begin to work, and into the dazzling picture growing before our eyes there rise grouped ranges of fairies and, last of all—a transcendent echo to their appearance—there descends from the skies a cloud-machine with an array of the celestial deities themselves.

It is not without wonder that one reflects how the relatively small provincial theatres of the period were designed and equipped to act as tools for such a specialized and ambitious usage of the resources of theatrical tradition—the apogee of the act of changing scenery.

Another cyclopaedia (though of a more modest sort) appeared in 1842, entitled *The Penny Cyclopaedia of the Society for the Diffusion of Useful Knowledge*, published by Charles Knight and Company, of 22 Ludgate Street. In it just over two columns were given to a note on scene-painting. After an opening passage on the history of the subject it goes on—most aptly following upon the study of the Leicester technicalities:

Of . . . the quantity of hidden machinery requisite for expeditiously changing the scenes, as well as for effecting more complex displays in pieces of *spectacle*, we shall not here speak, but confine our remarks to the painted scenery alone. . . . These consist of the narrow upright pieces called *side scenes* or *wings*, of the narrow horizontal ones (*hanging-scenes* or *soffits*, painted to imitate a sky or ceiling, but chiefly intended to screen the space over the stage), and of the *back scene*. Backs again are of two kinds, viz. *rolling* scenes, which are let down from above, and *flats*, which are formed of two sliding scenes strained upon framing, like the wings, and meeting each other and uniting in the centre. These are employed when what are termed *practicable* scenes are required, that is, with doors, windows, &c. which admit of being used as real doors, &c.; or else when there is occasion that the 'flat' should suddenly open and discover another scene behind it. In addition to these, there are what are termed *open* flats, which are scenes cut out in places so that both the background is seen and the actors can pass through them. They are commonly used for the representation of groves or forests, but sometimes for interiors with open arches. There are besides what are technically known as *pieces*, narrow scenes placed obliquely on one side of the stage when it is wanted to show a cottage or corner of a house, with a *practicable* door in it. Lastly, there is *set scenery*, as it is termed, a species of stage decoration very recently introduced, where—

(And we pause here to interject a warning to the reader that what is to come is especially interesting and—after what we have studied concerning the set scene—makes a perhaps unexpectedly close link between the set scene of the 1840's and the origin of our *box set*. To resume:)

instead of the usual wings ranged one behind the other, there is a single scene on each side extending from front to back, so that the stage is completely enclosed. By this means a more perfect representation of a room can be obtained than where wings are employed.

In fact side-scenes or wings can be regarded as little better than so many detached screens absolutely necessary to shut out from view the space on each side of the stage, since in themselves they rather detract from than at all aid illusion and effect; more especially in interiors, where what should represent a continuous wall or surface on either side is broken into several pieces, which are besides placed parallel to the back scene or flat, instead of being at right angles to it. If the scenery be viewed exactly from the centre and from the true perspective distance, the defect thus occasioned is not very striking or offensive; but if the spectator be near to the stage, or placed on one side of the house, the whole becomes more or less distorted, and the wings only so many disjointed fragments, so that all scenic illusion is destroyed, and should the back scene be at a considerable distance, no part of it will be visible to those in the boxes next the proscenium, but merely the range of wings on one side, and the gaps between them.

Charles Dickens himself penned a delightful simile which ought to be left out of no history of visible scene-changing. In his *Pictures from Italy*, at the chapter on Rome, written about 1846, we read: The Pope's Swiss Guard 'carry halberds like those which are usually shouldered by those theatrical supernumeraries, who never *can* get off the stage fast enough, and who may be generally observed to linger in the enemy's camp after the open country, held by the opposite forces, has been slit up the middle by a convulsion of Nature'.

The reference is vivid, albeit slightly quizzical. The quiz rises to abuse in the following, where in *The Theatrical Times* of 25 September 1847 we read, in connexion with the Haymarket Theatre:

'the scenery is miserable. . . . The same side 'wings' are used in representing the Park, (Beggar on Horseback), a tea garden (Fortune Hunter), the mountain woods in 'Guy Mannering', and the forest in the 'Invisible Prince', &c. &c. The same street is used in the 'Rivals', and every modern comedy in which there is a street scene. . . . The scenery does not come nearly up to the roof, but the space is agreeably filled up with wooden rack work, and filthy drop scenes, sky, trees, curtains, and ceilings all jumbled together. . . . We have seen almost everything that has been brought out at this theatre for some time past, but we never saw any competent scenery. Besides this error, the scene shifting is performed as if one man had to do the work on both sides of the stage, and it is wonderful if we are not gratified with two sets of wings in making up one apartment.

Thus, although stock wings are here proved up to the hilt, yet definite exception is being taken against them. On the one hand, the same set of wings was used too often; on the other, sometimes a mixture of sets was used in one scene.

It is fair to add that the critic here also mentions other theatres of the time (generally the lesser ones) where scene-handling is ordered much better, but he gives few details of these; his information is only communicative when he is destructive.

We turn to a quieter, more professional atmosphere for our next reference. Taken as a whole, it and the source to which it belongs form, I believe, the most valuable single fund of information yet discovered in Great Britain about the intimate workings of a nineteenth-century theatre. Miss Sybil Rosenfeld drew my attention to the existence at the Ipswich Public Library of a manuscript scrap-book by a figure whom we have already met—H. R. Eyre. It is entitled *Interesting Matter Relating to the Scenery, Decoration, etc. of the Theatre Royal Tacket Street, Ipswich*. The reference reminds us of one at the opening of the present chapter, which alluded to 'scene slides' on the stage, for it relates to a sort of 'occasional' bottom groove. Among what appear to be rejected preliminary notes for the body of the book, inserted at the end, we find this somewhat unusual piece of information:

The old stage during the latter part of Smith's time & up to the purchase by Charles Gill of the Theatre, was very uneven so a board or grove had to be placed across the stage before a flat could be run on. The board or grove was made in two so a piece was pushed on from each side & had a pin in each end which drop'd into a square hole in the stage to keep the grove steady. This arrangement kept the end of the flat off the stage some $1\frac{1}{2}$ inch so enabled the hinged part to swing. The each half of the flat being in those days made in two one half or part being hinged to the other so as to pack for travelling.

Gill took over the theatre in 1855 and Smith can be traced as a manager about 1843, so that we may date the reference at or just before the middle of the century.

When we remember that scene-changes took place under the eyes of the audience we shall no doubt experience a feeling of curiosity as to what these strange grooved boards must have looked like being pushed on from the side in snake-fashion by concealed stage-hands in the wings and then, one feels certain, being checked and manœuvred till their pins dropped in the square holes cut for them in the stage. One wonders how long the operation took and by how many seconds the closing of the flats themselves was anticipated by these creeping forerunners, and if they caused any injury in this way to the concentration of the dramatic climax of the scene?

That this measure was said to have been imposed specifically by the unevenness of the stage rather suggests that by that time bottom grooves were not normally used for flats. (The support of the tops at this theatre we shall consider below.) A problem that is not solved in the reference is: upon what did the flats stand when they were drawn back in the wings?— upon the stage itself? Or upon further grooved boards like the first but independent of them, thus avoiding the tricky lift-up of $1\frac{1}{2}$ in. that would else have been necessary to enter the foot of the flat into the groove?

It is interesting to note that the two grooves did not meet in the middle of the stage. A central gap was left so enabling 'the hinged part [of the flats] to swing'. Just what the significance of this action is is not clear unless the pair of flats contained a door in the centre, in which case a gap would of course have been essential at the part of the groove where the door came so as to free its foot and allow it to open. In any case a consequence of this central gap must have been that a horizontal crevice appeared under the middle of the backscene through which the pitites would almost certainly have glimpsed the boots of the actors and stage staff behind—that is, if the lighting had been sufficient.

Presumably, when the flat scene was drawn open once more, the grooves had to be lifted clear of their pin-holes and pulled off into the wings again so as to leave no obstruction to the actors' movements upon the scene; and all this under the eyes of the audience.

We may, for a moment, turn aside here to notice the unusual system of wing-changing that went with these early Ipswich grooves. The wings— to the number of four at each entrance—once hung round a revolving mast, much on the principle of a postcard stand on the counter of a village shop. But in 1857 these old wings were, we read, 'converted into the modern style'. No details are given in the text, but elsewhere in the book we find two pages of diagrams of the closest relevance to our subject which indicate what this 'modern style' was. It seems to have been a variant of the groove system, but it was very 'modern' indeed for it brings almost the only example yet found in the whole length of groove-history of any considerable deviation from the traditional details. We see in the diagrams that—though the main timbers are much as usual in arrangement—the familiar

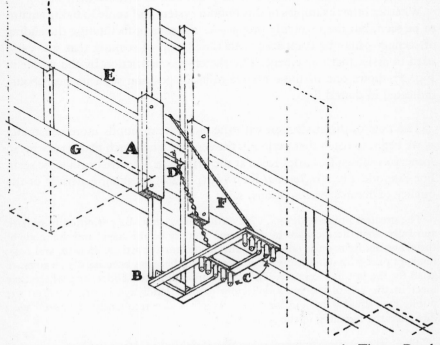

FIG. 27. Reconstruction by the author of the groove system at the Theatre Royal, Ipswich (1857)

grooves are replaced by revolving bobbins. (The diagrams are reproduced in *The Architectural Review* for August 1946.)

The only other example which I have found of such a departure is in the very latest survival of grooves which winds up their story today—a reference in The Hall Manufacturing Company's *Catalogue* for 1931 which will be alluded to on p. 393. The illustration shown there may be compared with these Ipswich diagrams.

In the Ipswich groove system of 1857 there were four pairs of 'grooves' (see Fig. 27). Each member of a pair consisted of a vertical frame clamped against the fly-rail and presumably capable of sliding up and down if the need for adjustment arose. To the bottom of this frame is hinged a similar frame held at right angles to the first by means of a chain. Across the lower face of this second frame are two rows of revolving, downward-projecting bobbins, one row across the end nearest the stage and the other about half-way back. There are five bobbins in each row; consequently four 'grooves' are formed between them for the sliding of wings—and presumably of flat scenes. No indication whatever in any part of the book is made of bottom grooves at this period, so—again presumably—a newly laid stage sufficed for the smooth manipulation of the scenes without their help.

Whether other examples of this bobbin system will come to light remains to be seen, but the revolving prongs—as a means of facilitating the sliding of scenery—may be compared with the system of soaping that was early used to assist that movement. The sketch-reconstruction by the writer in Fig. 27 shows one of these groove-units in position with its neighbours indicated in dotted lines.

The note of dissatisfaction with the old system sounds more insistently as we begin to reach that period in the century when such major reforms in scenery as those of Charles Kean at the Princess's Theatre begin to be seen. For example *The Art Journal* for 1853 (p. 228), speaking generally of the quality of Kean's presentations, said:

The greatest praise is due. . . . Nevertheless we must be permitted to remark generally, that the mechanism of placing scenery on the stage, and the mode of throwing the light on it are still highly inefficient for artistic illusion, and have not kept pace with other improvements; indeed there has been hardly an advance at all for the last half century. The scenes are still in two slides, and where they meet in the centre the most delicately painted landscape is presented to the public eye, divided by a cutting line, which is also frequently disfigured with dirt from the handling of the sceneshifters.

The 'other improvements' were presumably the details of 'archeological accuracy' which were beginning now to be manifest in the work of the arts generally at this time, and for the use of which Kean stood notable with his title of Fellow of the Society of Antiquaries. But the median join with dirty finger-marks upon it began to be an irritation.

To this period also belongs one of the first specific records of the technique we noticed in *The Padlock*, and had brought up again by Knight's *Penny Cyclopaedia*—a technique which showed that the flats themselves were proving more adaptable than their grooves. The evidence is in the form of such a stage-direction as this from J. B. Johnstone's *A Sailor of France* (Surrey Theatre, 1854), where we read in Lacy's *Sixpenny Acting Edition*: 'Sc. 1. *The Private Office of the Deputy-President. Raking flats from the two first entrances forming enclosed room, on L. side a large window, on the R. the door of entrance.*' Raking flats were flats set along the sides of the stage from the front to the back, and joining the back flats to form the three sides of a room. They could of course contain practical doors and 'large windows' built into their framework, and so serve as a step on from the old wing and cloth to the modern box set.

In this position they generally ignored the grooves and became supported either by forks or by braces, and once this happened the obvious development was to cut their great width—so awkward to handle in a change—into several separate sections, joining the parts together with some fastening such as the modern line and cleat. Thence it was a small step to the sort of set used in *The Grip of Iron* (Surrey Theatre, 1887) where the old flats are no longer recognizable and a primitive form of the stage interior of today is clearly seen, with the breaks forward and back in the walls which are so common with modern designers seeking to lend variety to three bare walls.

Wings, as the means of representing the side-walls of an interior, receive more and more criticism. The note in *The Art Journal* goes on to say: 'The wings . . . if applicable to perspective, are so stationed as to shock by the falsity of the lines, and are often disfigured by coarse masses of red, meant as a continuation of curtain drapery to reduce the height of the proscenium.' As the article crisply announced—No advance 'for the last half century'. The passage has more than one interest; it refers to the difficulty of reconciling a wing-and-flat layout with the demands of linear perspective painting whose complications are sufficient even on a plane surface, but it also refers to a custom of painting red drapery on the wings. This painting was presumably limited to those wings near the front of the stage, since the drapery is said to be meant as a continuation of the proscenium border—that deep pelmet so necessary in most theatres to reduce the disproportionately high proscenium arch, which custom has come to expect in a playhouse, to something near the practical 16 ft. so that normal 18-ft. scenery may be used behind it. This elaborate painted drapery was always a feature of scenery since early Georgian times, and its use around the proscenium opening is a celebrated feature of the theatre; in France it has the pleasant name of *Manteau d'Arlequin*. It is a very practical means of varying the size of the opening, within certain limits, to accommodate different sizes of scene, and is an aid of considerable importance to the stage carpenter.

We close our study of the first half of the nineteenth century by consulting a monumental work published in France. The work is one we have alluded to before under the name of its author, Contant, and it is entitled *Parallèle des principaux Théâtres modernes de l'Europe et des machines théâtrales françaises, allemandes et anglaises*. 'Dessins par Clément Contant, architecte, ancien machiniste en chef de l'Académie Royale de Musique, texte par Joseph de Filippi.' The 1859 edition was published in two forms —the first in thirty parts and the second in two volumes. An earlier edition containing less information was published in 1840–2 in twelve parts, and Georges Moynet in his *Trucs et décors* gives the date 1838 to the work. The 1859 edition (on which the following study is based) contains plans of Covent Garden as rebuilt in 1857–8 and thus contains up-to-date information.

The two plates of Contant's vol. i, reproduced here in Figs. 28 and 29, are almost certainly the most exhaustive studies of the English groove that we have. The first plate shows a vertical section across a complete stage from side to side and gives the position of the grooves in relation to the rest of the machinery, and the second plate gives large-scale details of the grooves.

The former is entitled *Coupe transversale, équipe d'un vol tournant, des trapillons et des châssis et fermes. Système anglais*. Rendering this in English as nearly as possible, it signifies: 'Transverse section, showing the arrangement of a machine for circular flights, the sliders, wings and flats. English system.'

The lettered details in this plate which concern the grooves are explained as follows in the accompanying text.

A. Coulisseau mobile guidant la tête des châssis et demi-fermes du fond, mis en état pour le changement.
A*. Position du même coulisseau avant sa mise en état.
a. Tasseaux en saillie sur le plancher de la scène entre lesquels glissent les patins des châssis et des demi-fermes.
B. Ferme de fond en deux parties réunies au milieu et maintenues jointes par des taquets contrariés hors parement.
C. Coulisses ordinaires ou châssis d'aile.

A rough English equivalent might be made as follows:

A. Movable groove, guiding the tops of the wings and the half-flats of the backscene, arranged for a change (of flat scene).
A.* Position of the same groove before coming into position.
a. Raised fillets on the stage floor between which slide the bases of the wings and of the halves of flat scenes.
B. Backscene in two halves, joining in the middle and kept together by alternating joining cleats.
C. Ordinary side-scenes or wing-pieces.

When we turn to study the details of these arrangements we find we have before us, without any doubt, the subtlest, most ingenious, flexible, and advanced refinement of groove-working that we have discovered yet. Here are grooves at their zenith.

The fly-floor shown on this engraving is some 23 ft. 6 in. above the stage. The grooves take scenes approximately 21 ft. high. (These measurements are according to the scale of *pieds anglais* given in the drawing.) Therefore the upper grooves must be stayed downwards by the space of 2 ft. 6 in. from the underside of the fly-gallery. This is achieved by means of a cross-

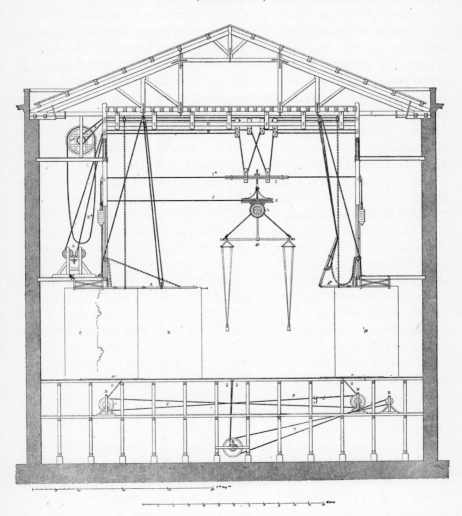

COUPE TRANSVERSALE, EQUIPE D'UN VOL TOURNANT, DES TRAPILLONS ET DES CHASSIS ET FERMES
(SYSTÈME ANGLAIS)

Pl.27

FIG. 28. Full cross-section of an English stage showing grooves, wings, and flats.
From Contant, *Parallèle des Théâtres*, 1859

braced, side-stayed, intermediate frame. The fixed part of the grooves is 9 ft. long: to this is attached not one mobile groove-arm but two, successively, the first hinged on the end of the fixed part and about 6 ft. 6 in. long, and the other hinged to the end of that again and having the amazing

[331]

length of 12 ft. So the whole of this Gargantuan machine is approximately 27 ft. 6 in. long! The distance between the extended tips of a pair of opposite grooves is about 15 ft. 6 in., and the overall width of this large stage is 85 ft.

These are far higher figures than we have yet seen in our story. There is no indication whether this plate reproduces the proportions of any specific theatre or whether it gives a composite of many features of the English system, but in either case we have here an indication that England, a century ago, had stages to be compared with the largest of ours today. (Though it was never our tradition to build stages as large as many on the Continent.) *Who's Who in the Theatre*, 10th edition, 1947, gives only three London theatres reaching this width, namely, the London Coliseum (sloping, 85 ft. to 133 ft.), the Stoll (85 ft.), and the Victoria Palace (94 ft.); Covent Garden is only 82 ft. and Drury Lane 77 ft. 3 in. wide.

The working of these mammoth grooves is interesting in the extreme. Of the three sections of each set, the first or fixed section is braced immovably under the fly-floor, the second or intermediate section hinged to the first is slung by a 40 ft. chain from the grid. Why a chain? Because a chain can stand a considerable tensile strain—and a jerk—without stretching, while a rope will lengthen not only with strain but with atmospheric changes. And, of course, to allow the upper grooves to drop even half an inch would mean that the scenery must jam in them. The third, or inmost, section is supported by a second chain, but this time a much shorter one, attached to the rail of the first fly-floor. Just at its attachment there is to be seen a perforated strip, presumably of metal, descending from the fly-rail to near the end of the fixed section of the grooves. The purpose of this is obscure. It may afford a means of adjusting the groove to meet changes in the height of scenery resulting from differences in atmospheric humidity and other causes, or it may be a ladder to give access to the groove in cases of jamming.

But the third section of the grooves has another attachment. This is the working-line. The working-line is here no simple rope going, in company with others from other sets of grooves, to a common operating shaft, but originates in the first place from a block in the grid, whence it runs down to the sheave of a block attached to the grooves; from here it turns aloft again, circles the sheave of the first block, and descends finally to a cleat on the inside of the fly-rail.

Observe the ingenuity of the working. If this line be heaved in from the fly-floor, the third section of the grooves will lift, bringing the pulley with it, so that the line goes progressively from the diagonal to the perpendicular; when the perpendicular is reached, the fly-man jerks his line and then immediately slackens his pull slightly. This has the effect of bringing the reared-up end of the grooves beyond the perpendicular. Now at this stage it strikes the line which pulled it up—and, were this maintained taut, would go no farther; to keep it in this upright position the line would have to be securely tied off to a cleat. But if the momentary slackening is permitted, the rearing groove, upon striking the vertical rope, will not only strike it but push it back. The groove now passes the vertical and its centre of gravity is transferred to the other side; its tendency is to fold back on itself. Now the fly-man gently checks the yielding lines again, and they become a support for the leaning-back groove-arm. Ease them till they and the arm-tip touch the long chain supporting the second section and they will stay in position without further support.

Take the line again and tug it slightly; it will tighten and straighten, kicking the arm across and past the vertical position again. Check the line immediately this occurs and then proceed to ease it out slowly, and the groove-arm steadily descends to the horizontal again.

A sufficiently ingenious arrangement as must be admitted. But we have not reached the end of the story.

Lift the groove-arm again. This time, when it reaches the vertical, do not jerk nor slacken the line, but continue to pull on it steadily. You will now begin to exert a lifting pressure upon the *second* section of the groove. This too will rise until it achieves the vertical and lies in a straight line with its fellow above. You have but to tie off each groove in this position and the whole space is then clear from the fly-rail on one side of the stage to that on the other.

On the stage below is shown at *a*, as we have seen, the bottom grooves, represented only 14 ft. long, but no information is vouchsafed as to whether these were loose or fixed.

They are worth noting carefully for they solve one of our earlier problems. It is interesting to see that these comparatively short and simple lower 'grooves' are not true grooves but merely a row of raised strips on the stage. They thus show a transition between the earlier full lower grooves of the Plymouth theatre (whose beds lifted the scenery above the stage) and the complete abolition of the lower grooves that we find indicated in other references towards the end of our story. And they present no 'bed-difficulty' for the running of flats.

Turning now to the second of these plates we see details of the grooves to a larger scale.

The descriptive notes are:

DÉTAILS DE LA CONSTRUCTION DES CONDUCTEURS, ou coulisseaux mobiles, châssis et fermes du cintre.

A. Plancher du gril.

B. Plancher du premier corridor.

C. Chevalet ou bâti de prolongement des coulisseaux mobiles sous les corridors latéraux du cintre.

D. Partie mobile du coulisseau mis en état pour le mouvement d'une ferme. Les lignes ponctuées indiquent la position du coulisseau lorsqu'il ne sert qu'à manœuvrer le châssis d'aile.

E. Cheville de retraite en échelle pour pratiquer sur le coulisseau.

F. Fil à la main pour baisser ou lever le coulisseau.

G. Chaîne en fer ou support fixe.

G★. Chaîne mobile pour maintenir de niveau l'extrémité du coulisseau.

Fig. 2e. Coupe des planchers et assemblages de chevalets sous les corridors.

Fig. 3e. Plan général du coulisseau.

Fig. 4e, 5e, 6e, Détails d'exécution ou profils, plan et coupe d'un coulisseau.

An approximate English version would run:

A. Grid floor.

B. Lower fly-floor.

C. Stay or distance framework of the movable grooves under the fly-floors.

D. Movable part of the grooves put in readiness for the sliding-in of a flat. The dotted lines show the position of the groove when it is used only to take a wing-piece.

E. Cleat for fixing the groove.

F. Hand line for lowering or lifting the grooves.

G. Iron chain or check-support.

G★. Moving chain to maintain the level of the extremity of the groove.

Fig. 2. Section of the fly-floors and the arrangements of stays beneath them.

Fig. 3. General plan of the groove.

Figs. 4, 5, 6. Working details, or side elevation, plan, and end elevation of a groove.

What is principally to be noted here is that in order to ensure all possible lightness in this comparatively huge machine, the whole thing is built, not solid, but in an open-work assembly of thin battens with distance-pieces between them.

It will be noticed that four grooves are shown in this set, though there is no indication whether or not this number was standard in all the sets on this stage. There is, however, an interesting suggestion contained in the wording to the sign-letter D, which leads us to suppose that any of these four grooves could be used indiscriminately for flats or for wings, and that there was now no distinct pattern of grooves for the two purposes. It is also stated that the groove-arms were kept in the 'up' position till a pair of flats had to be closed, when they were lowered on to the tops thereof.

When a pair of flats was closed it is interesting to see that 7 ft. 6 in. of each would be pushed out beyond the supporting upper grooves, leaving them held in those grooves only by the remaining 7 ft. of their top edge. It is astonishing to note that the lower edges of the same flats *would be clear of the lower grooves altogether.*

[334]

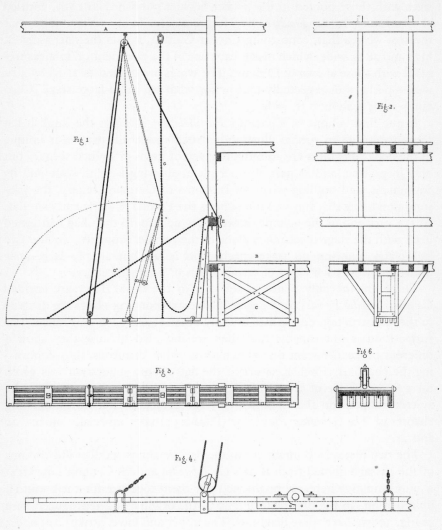

FIG. 29. Details of grooves for wings and flats. (From Contant, op. cit.)

With regard to these dimensions, it is not uninteresting to compare the sizes with those quoted in the pocket booklet published in 1829, entitled *A Companion to the Theatres* by Horace Foote. In its review of various theatres we see that, concerning Covent Garden, it lists the *flats* as 21 ft. high and 28 ft. wide, which makes each one of the pair identical in measurement with those shown in Contant. The wings are quoted as 21 ft. by 4 ft. wide—perhaps unexpectedly narrow for what we call a large stage (Contant's wing is about 7 ft. wide).

In the first volume of Contant's *Parallèle des Théâtres* the English flat scene is also given special illustration. Such special illustration is unique in the book; diagrams are admittedly given of items of French scenery but only in passing, and as part of other plates showing the full stage and its equipment, and nothing whatever is shown of German scenery, the presumption being that this was the same as the French or sufficiently similar. At the very end of the volume, however, which up till then had concerned itself with the stage mechanism alone of the various countries, we find two full plates showing no stage mechanism at all but simply large-scale drawings of the back views of certain items of English scenery.

These are the only plates of the sort in the book. They are entitled *Construction des Fermes (syst. anglais)*. No corresponding plates are devoted to the 'construction des fermes' for any other country—even France. The supposition is unescapable that they are included because they show a different procedure from that obtaining in other countries, thus confirming the peculiarly English nature of the flats. Some suggestion was given for the preference of the British theatre for this arrangement over the system adopted on the Continent, by the present writer in the opening chapter of *The Georgian Playhouse* (Pleiades, 1948), especially on pp. 20 and 21.

The two plates in Contant are in themselves almost perfect illustrations of the passage quoted from Rees's *Cyclopaedia* and, as Contant's own text is uninformative here, we might well put them together for their mutual illumination. In the first plate (Pl. 40 in the original and reproduced here as Fig. 30) we have three diagrams. The upper and lower strike us at once; the one is a very clear drawing of the back of a pair of 'profiled or open' flats, and the other of the back of a pair of plain flats. Between these figures is shown what the modern stage carpenter would unhesitatingly class as a ground-row.

In the second plate (see Fig. 31) we have the representation of a pair of 'open' flats representing arches, below this is another, slightly higher, ground-row, and below this again a pair of flats with practicable double-doors and windows, the door coming in the centre of the pair of flats. In the descriptions of the plates among the text of the book we read:

[336]

Système anglais
PLANCHE 40 [see present Fig. 30]
Construction des fermes

Fig. 1re. Fermes d'arbres isolés traversant la scène dans une décoration de forêts, jardins, etc.

Fig. 2e. Ferme pleine ou de fond, pour une décoration d'intérieur, de site pittoresque, etc.

Fig. 3e. Terrain traversant la scène, bordant une rivière ou une vallée et servant également à dissimuler l'ouverture du plancher et à éclairer les décorations.

PLANCHE 41 [see present Fig. 31]
Suite de la construction des fermes

Fig. 1re. Paire de châssis ouverts.

Fig. 2e. Châssis portant des feuilles de décoration chantournées, pour praticables, etc.

Fig. 3e. Paire de châssis fermés avec portes et fenêtres.

[The numbers in the middle and bottom figures of *Planche 40* are thus transposed in the original.]

The English equivalent of the above is approximately as follows:

English System
PLATE 40
Construction of Flat Pieces

Fig. 1. Cut flat of trees to run across the stage in forest scenes, garden scenes, etc.

Fig. 2. Plain or back flats for an interior scene, a 'picturesque view', etc.

Fig. 3. Ground piece crossing the stage, forming the bank of a river or valley, and serving also to hide an opening in the stage and the lighting of the scene. [The last phrase is curiously elliptic. One takes it to mean 'serving both to mask an opening in the stage floor and to mask a row or *length* of lights lying either in the opening or on the stage behind for the purpose of lighting up a farther piece of scenery'.]

PLATE 41
Continuation of Construction of Flat Pieces

Fig. 1. A pair of 'open' [or arch] flats.

Fig. 2. Framework for cut-out pieces of scenery intended for masking the fronts of rostrums, etc.

Fig. 3. A pair of 'closed' flats with doors and windows.

The phrase *châssis fermés* for the last figure is interesting in that it is evidently intended as a contrast with the *châssis ouverts*, or 'cut-out flats' of Fig. 1 of the same plate. We should unhesitatingly have translated *châssis fermés* as 'plain flats', which is a normal English term, rather than the bastard 'closed flats', save that no modern English carpenter would call a flat with a door in it a plain flat. To him a plain flat is one with an unbroken surface; a door flat is a 'door flat' and never a 'plain flat'. We are therefore precluded from using what seemed so natural a translation of *châssis fermés*.

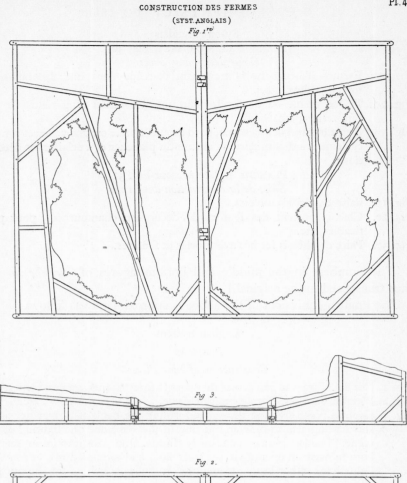

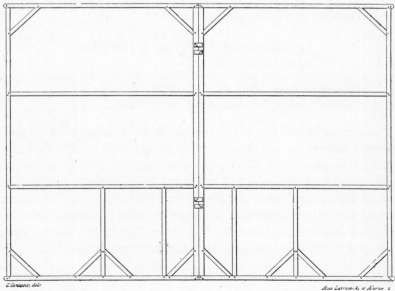

Pl. 40.

CONSTRUCTION DES FERMES
(SYST. ANGLAIS)
Fig. 1re

Fig. 3.

Fig. 2.

C. Contant, del.

Alex Latreuxski & Masson 2

FIG. 30. Construction of flats and ground-rows. (From Contant, op. cit.)

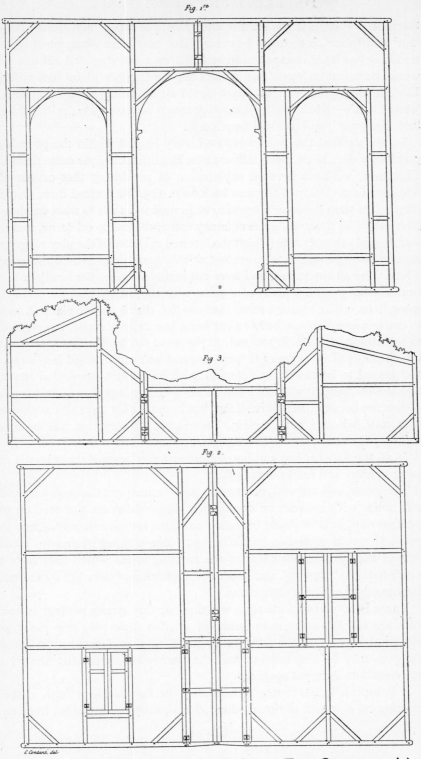

FIG. 31. Construction of flats and ground-rows. (From Contant, op. cit.)

But as the French terms are the equivalents of 'open' and 'shut', not of 'cut' and 'plain', it seems to be evident that only a flat whose opening had no filling (such for instance as an arch flat, or a gateway, or a cut tree flat) would be called an 'open' flat, while both the English 'plain' flats and the English 'door' and 'window' flats would all be called, on the Continent, 'closed flats'—*châssis fermés*—for which words we have no technical equivalent, since our 'plain flats' is inapplicable.

I have stressed this point because it may be just within the bounds of possibility that, since much influence on English technique came from the Continent, we have here an explanation of something that caught our attention in the study of *Guzman* back on p. 145. We noticed there that the then infant term *flat scene* seemed to be limited in its use to what we should later call *plain flats*, while the chimney scene, the cut wood scene, and the astrological cabinet scene (which the internal evidence of the play suggested also had an opening in it) were not at that early date termed *flat scenes*. These were all cut scenes, and were not included under the head *flat scene* until a later period. This is of a piece with the theory that the term *flat scene*, in its origin, meant a scene that was flat, that is, in one plane. A scene in two or more planes, whether a cut scene or a 'relieve' scene, was regarded as something separate. It was not till the word *flat* became associated with the elements of the scenery themselves, and was transformed into a noun, and ceased to be clearly an adjective with its normal sense, that the cut scenes were lumped with the plain scenes and all called *flat* scenes together —now not because they were all flat, but because they were all constructed with *flats*, whether cut or plain. This is pure theory, but the evidence certainly seems to point in that direction.

In all the flats the top and bottom rails project beyond the frame at the outer corners and are rounded off.

The joints, one suspects, are mortise-and-tenons, and the stage carpenter will notice with interest, no doubt, that toggle-shoes are not used on the internal rails, as they would be today, but these rails are all jointed into the stiles. It would of course be likely that scene-shifting in grooves would subject flats to somewhat less of the twisting strain which they have to suffer today in 'running', and hence the weakening of the stiles by mortise-cutting might not be so dangerous.

There is no certain indication whether the tiny circles present on each joint are screws or the more practical wooden draw-pins that today are often put in without the joint being glued, so that if necessity demands the pins may be knocked out and the framework of the flat altered to accommodate different openings.

It is especially interesting to note that the flats are kept flush at their meeting by a system of 'interlocking cleats', or 'joining plates', fixed two on each stile, so as to project by half their length beyond the edge and so lock the faces flush at their meeting.

Furthermore, it should be noted that the two leaves of the central double-door in Fig. 31 have been specially cut at the lower edge to allow them to open on a raked stage. Here is further proof that whatever may have been the nature of the lower grooves, they did not, like the flats, meet in the middle of the stage—had they done so this door would have been impracticable.

In the two upper figures the solid part between the framework would presumably have been of canvas and the shaped parts projecting into the cuts beyond the battens would be in 'profile' board, sawn to shape.

16

LAST INTERLUDE

(ON THE ANGLE OF WINGS AND THE NATURE OF STOCK SCENERY)

———————————————— ⋆ ————————————————

IN the references to wings which we have so far discussed in this review two features have arisen about their general nature which I should like now to elaborate. The first relates to the angle at which wings were set, the second concerns the regard in which wings were held from the point of view of the scenic picture. To the second it will be convenient to add certain special reflections on the nature of stock scenery. I have made this an Interlude-chapter to be free from strict chronological sequence, but we may begin the first part of it (on the angle of wings) with a reference that is closely in step with the advance of our review.

It is of special interest to find a diagram published in 1884 purporting to show the layout of a typical stage and clearly labelling the grooves, yet which at the same time shows the wings set diagonally.

The diagram accompanied a series of thirty-one articles published in *Amateur Work* from the pen of Henry L. Benwell entitled 'Practical Scene-painting for Amateurs' and beginning in December 1884. It is reproduced, with the relative elucidation of initials, in Fig. 32.

Though the text of the articles contains some sort of explanation of technical terms, no allusion is made to this diagram, and the puzzle of seeing grooves clearly indicated yet at the same time seeing the wings set at an angle receives no light.

One possible explanation is that by this period wings were no longer run in grooves, and that only certain backscenes required grooves. The text is clear in stating that pairs of flats were used, though it also indicates as clearly that cloths were equally common. Normal grooves must presumably therefore have been present to take the flat scenes, but the wings were either supported as they are today by separate braces from the stage or they might perhaps have worked in a system of *forks*. For an explanation of these forks we must await the next chapter, but on this matter of the angle of wings we have some reflections to make.

Up to this date we have seen no plan in British theatre history which shows diagonal wings. There are certain early Italian plans which show them, but they were soon abandoned.

When we turn from the clear evidence of plans to that of pictorial prints we are on less certain ground. We find one or two eighteenth-century English prints which seem to show wings at an angle, but we have to remember

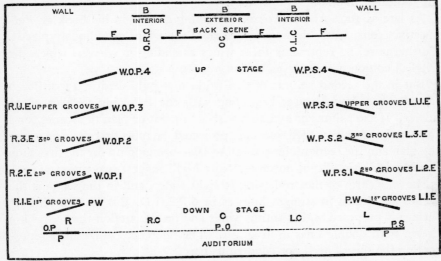

FIG. 41.—DIAGRAM EXHIBITING GROUND PLAN OF STAGE.

P.O., Proscenium Opening.	R.1.E., Right First Entrance.	L.1.E., Left First Entrance.	W.P.S., 1, 2, 3, and 4, Wings and Prompt Side of the Stage.
P., Proscenium.	R.2.E., Right Second Entrance.	L.2.E., Left Second Entrance.	
P.W., Proscenium Wings.	R.3.E., Right Third Entrance.	L.3.E., Left Third Entrance.	W.O.P., 1, 2, 3, and 4, Wings Opposite Prompt Side of Stage.
O.P., Opposite Prompt.	R.U.E., Right Upper Entrance.	L.U.E., Left Upper Entrance.	
P.S., Prompt Side.	O.R.C., Opening Right Centre.	O.L.C., Opening Left Centre.	
C., Centre.	O.C., Centre Opening.	B.B.B., Backings, Exterior and Interiors as may be required.	F.F.F.F., Flats constituting Back Scene.
R.C., Right Centre.	L.C., Left Centre.		
R., Right.	L., Left.		

FIG. 32. Plan of stage with description. From Benwell's 'Practical Scene-painting for Amateurs', *Amateur Work*, 1884

that the perspective painting upon a straight wing was generally especially designed to appear to be vanishing at an angle. Thus the print-maker may give us the *effect* of the wing only, and even deliberately suppress any sign that the wing was straight since this fact cut across the simulation of the painted design as a whole.

There is a dilemma here. Critics strongly objected against the rigid parallelism of wings. Our own sense today of proper masking makes us set every wing diagonally. Why, if wings were originally set diagonally, did they ever come to suffer this change to the less practical straight position, and maintain that position so long and against such opposition? Is it in fact quite true to say that they did maintain this position? There is some evidence to suggest they did not, but it is oddly rare and uncertain.

[343]

Let us begin by considering the early slanting wing and discover the objections against it.

In *The Mask*, vol. 12 *bis*, no. iv, 1927, Edward Carrick published a collection of early Italian theatre plans belonging to the second half of the seventeenth century. Upon some of these plans the position of side wings upon the stage is indicated. In every one of the five such plans the wings are indicated in an oblique position.

As late as 1692 Andrea Pozzo, describing a stage in his book on Perspective, consistently draws and describes the wings as obliquely placed. Furthermore, he represents these wings as sliding in *canales*, which the English edition of 1707 translates as *grooves*.

But in the second volume of this work, first published in 1700, Pozzo introduces a new feature: beginning with the following very excellent advice, 'If the painter or architect wishes to paint or plan the scenes for a theatre already built, or for one only projected, he must first draw on paper the plan and the section', he goes on to say—bringing up for the first time in his work a significant novelty—'Now I will suggest two variants; in A is shown a form of theatre having straight wings, and in the sections the scenes are drawn in straight lines as in 6,P,8,C,D. But in B a kind of theatre is proposed with slanting wings and on the section the scenes are drawn with double lines as in Q. . . .' (The references to the lines representing the scenes need not concern us here.)

The oblique wing position is, then, frequently found in early Italian procedure. But this sound and natural arrangement, obviously the best in the eyes of the early designers since they adopted it, seems to have suffered a setback. Pozzo in his second volume admits the alternative of the straight wing, and we should find in Ferdinando Bibiena's *Direzione ai giovanni studenti nel designo dell' architettura civile*, 1745, no sign that any but straight wings had ever been thought of, and indeed we shall need to pass over many years of history before we find an indisputably oblique wing again; the position was generally abandoned till practically the eve of our own day.

Speaking of the same theatre plans mentioned above, and in the same number of *The Mask*, Dr. W. J. Lawrence says: 'The system of oblique wings to be noted in several of the plans was, I think, peculiarly Italian. . . . It never reached England.'

And Professor Nicoll says, in *The Development of the Theatre* (1st ed., p. 145):

The secret of side wings and flats run in grooves had by this time [late seventeenth century] been fully learned, and numerous changes of setting could be easily secured in the course of one play. In 1671 the *Dario* of Beverini had no fewer than fifteen different scenes, and this example can be paralleled by scores of others. These side-wings, first placed obliquely on the stage, were soon set in their accustomed modern position, parallel to the front of the stage. . . .

A transition from oblique to straight is thus recognized in his statement, but the professor is completely in error in supposing the straight wing to have persisted to our day. Today we have returned—in England at least—to the oblique wing.

There seem to have been two objections to the practical, oblique wing which characterized all the very early stages. The first is that these stages sprang up in an age of rabid perspective which claimed all the exclusive attention of a new toy, and the second that they began to develop in a theatrical era marked by overriding demands for a mechanical system that would allow their scenery to be changed in sight of the audience and without holding up the progress of the show.

Concerning the first condition, we must picture a painter standing before a set of scenes on which he is to depict the vanishing lines of his essential perspective. There is still one especial obstacle before him—that his wings are oblique. Where now can their vanishing-point be found? Most laws of pictorial perspective are framed on the assumption of a picture-surface parallel to the spectator, but for the representation of perspective on an oblique surface some modification of the laws is required. Further, if part of the same perspective scheme is to be depicted on the regular plane surface of the backscene and another upon other surfaces to the side of, and at an angle to, the first (that is to say on the wings), then an ingenious commingling of two sets of rules is required for the adequate representation of a unified subject.

The objection is not impassable. One of the charms of Pozzo's first volume is the ingenuousness with which he frames rules connected with the achievement of false vanishing-points for oblique surfaces, and in the end the observation of three separate vanishing-points upon the horizon is required—not merely of one. Though we must observe that he explains the matter badly in this first book and only expounds a workable solution in the second.

But a further factor weighed in the balance. In the equally exacting search for methods of changing these perspective scenes in full view, a constant drawing on and off of wings was entailed. Now to draw a wing off-stage in an oblique line and, maintaining that line, take it out of sight into the side space is possible, but it is likely to interfere with the straight, hanging borders above, and it raises a very difficult problem indeed when one attempts to combine the movement with two other factors forming intensely important features of the theatre of the time: firstly, when the stage is raked or sloping (in answer again to the call of perspective), and secondly, when the increasing number of scene-changes makes it impossible to have a separate groove for each wing in a show. For the above-quoted *Dario* the number of changes was fifteen; suppose each scene to have had six wings a side, this would involve some 180 grooves! Furthermore, the fact that these changes were visible required that the wings should move neatly and in unison. Sabbattini had clearly had in 1638 some sad experience of the task of making a number of independent stage-hands achieve a movement of perfect unison, and now there was clearly a necessity to perfect a mechanical means by some gearing of all these wings together.

The solution was achieved (maybe first by Torelli) by replacing the groove with a slit clean through the stage, and supplying beneath this slit or cut a carriage whose wheels ran on a rail in the basement, and from which a mast or a framework projected up through the cut above the stage, upon which the wing might be hung and fastened. The upper grooves could then be dispensed with. With two such carriages at each wing-position, one pushed on bearing the wing for the current scene, the other pushed back with the wing for the next, one could achieve an infinite number of wing-changes, replacing the withdrawn wing every time by its successor on the frame which was then back and out of sight. All wing-carriages could be worked by ropes to one great shaft. This is, in principle, the modern continental wing-system.

But couple the fact of a raked stage with such an action of carriages and with oblique wings, and it will be seen at once that an almost impossible ingenuity is demanded to prevent jamming and numerous accidents. There was no way out. The wings had to be straight. The oblique position became a feature of the past.

But the painter's difficulties were not over with the straight wing position. One old difficulty remained, for, though his surface was now flat with regard to him, he still had to paint retreating walls upon it, and if a house in perspective is to be represented on a parallel wing, the vanishing lines, in order to obey the laws of perspective, must converge towards the inner side of the wing. Hence—however neatly the design may be fitted to the rectangle of the wing in other respects—there must always be a narrow triangle unoccupied at top and bottom, whose apex lies at the off-stage corner of the wing and whose short base reaches an inch or two along the on-stage side. The painted contents of this 'left' triangle have always been a problem to painters. In the 1707 translation of Andrea Pozzo's book we are naively told: 'What remains on the Frame, beyond these lines, is to be reckon'd as nothing; but you may paint there Air, or what you please.'

It may well be that in certain of the doubtful English prints that we mentioned the engraver has allowed himself to ignore the existence of this triangle—which was possibly painted so as to be nearly indistinguishable in colour from the stage floor—and that those perspective houses were in reality painted upon wings parallel to the edge of the stage, though their base line seems to be diagonal.

But we have already established that in this parallel position the wings do not mask so well and that the arrangement entails wider wings if indeed it does not make necessary an increase in their number—or else it means inadequate masking. No doubt stage managers of those days were as capable of seeing the disadvantages of the parallel position as we are, yet it seems that some compulsion was laid upon them to adopt it in spite of its disadvantage.

It might at first sight be supposed that the grooves in Britain would not be subjected to the same strict rule of parallelism as was the continental wing-system, and that once the grooves were established it would be a very simple matter to build a stage whereon the wing-grooves were set at an angle and the flat-grooves were dissociated and separated from them far enough to enable the backscenes to be run on, in contradistinction, parallel with the footlights. Such a layout is the logical and economical way of setting a stage, and in it the wings can occupy the position where they are of most use in masking the side spaces flanking the stage.

But the problem of such an arrangement is gravely complicated by the fact that the stage floors were pretty sharply sloped or raked. If, now, a wing be stood on a sloping stage in a position facing the footlights and the direction of the slope, then that wing can be stood exactly upright with little difficulty. (The fact that it will not rise dead perpendicular with the stage surface if viewed from the side is of little account.)

But if the wing be turned to face diagonally across to the opposite front corner of the stage, then one of two things must follow—either it must lean slightly forward or, if it is leaned back to the true vertical, then it will tip outwards towards the top. The inclination may be slight, but it will be sufficient quite to upset any vista of vertical columns designed to be carried on unbroken from the wings into the painting on the backscene.

Again, if the diagonal wing is allowed to slope forward its pressure on one side of the upper grooves will be increased and the whole will need special bracing; or if the wing is tilted upright, then every thrusting of it on-stage in a scene-change will be, in effect, a slight thrusting uphill and entail not only special care in the alinement of the upper grooves but unusual precautions in the bracing of the framework of the flat itself—so as to prevent its being forced out of true rectangularity and thus seriously risking jamming.

A possible solution of the difficulty (pointed out to me by Mr. George Devine) would be to cut the bottom grooves not out of straightforward rectangular blocks but out of blocks worked into an irregular wedge shape —their outer ends being thicker than their inner ends, and with the underside of the block cut away at an angle to accommodate the rake of the stage when the groove-block was set diagonally upon it. The bed of the groove would be then quite horizontal and the scenes could run easily in it. The outer corners of the oblique scene-pieces would be a little higher above the stage than the inner corners, but all would be level with regard to the horizontal.

Now it is interesting that Mr. Devine can claim the evidence of a print

THE LONDON THEATRES. *PLATE. III*.

The Citizen, Act. 2. Scene. 1. as perform'd at Covent-Garden Theatre by Mr. Shuter, Mr. Woodward & Mr. Dyer
published according to Act of Parliament, by J. Payne in Paternoster Row. March 31. 1767.

FIG. 33. Scene from *The Citizen*, 1767

of a performance of *The Citizen* in support of his suggestion (see Fig. 33). Here it does certainly appear that the block at the foot of the wing would be wedge-shaped if the boundary of the drawing were to reveal it further.

This is in many ways a most remarkable print. There seems to be no possibility here that the suggestion of oblique wing-position can be the misrepresentation of an engraver. The evidence (whatever it is worth) is categorical. But the wing itself is a remarkable piece and looks almost as if it were back to front, showing the framework on which it was built. Nothing whatever seems to be painted upon the scenery! There would appear to be unequivocal statement of a centre-back opening to the scene. Finally there comes this most notable suggestion that, though what is shown to us of the groove at the foot of the wing is tantalizingly little, it yet has a thickness that is slightly tapering. So far as my knowledge goes this evidence is unique, but it is so slight that it cannot be final.

Wings began, then, diagonally; changed to straight in the seventeenth century, and became diagonal again at the end of the nineteenth. But there are obscure hints in the eighteenth century of a foreshadowing of such a return to obliqueness.

Turning now to the second inquiry of this Interlude—about the regard in which wings were held as parts of the scenic picture—we may take as our text a slogan upon a toy-theatre maker's sheets. It is a slogan which links with something that events have hinted at before—the subject of 'stock scenery', which existed in all periods we have yet studied, and will remain present during the one we are now exploring.

Though the two chief illustrated books on the Juvenile Theatre have between them some 125 plates, yet neither A. E. Wilson's well-pictured *Penny Plain Two Pence Coloured* (1932) nor George Speaight's valuable *Juvenile Drama* (1946) has a single reproduction of a sheet of wings. This is something of an omission.

The last of the publishers of playsheets to pursue the business was Benjamin Pollock, who died in August 1937. If we take a random collection of his sheets we shall find a great number of reproductions of wings, which also bear something else that might at first seem either a mystery or no more than the *naïveté* of a toy-maker, but which upon examination will probably teach us more about the nature of the early English wing and the relation it bore to the English scene than any other evidence that can be brought on the subject through all our study.

The arrangement of a set of sheets for any play of Pollock's follows a system of numbering as follows: On the book of words that goes with each set there runs a classified summary of the sheets in that set. For instance, if we take that for *Whittington and his Cat, or Harlequin, Lord Mayor of London,* we read on the cover: 8 *plates characters,* 13 *scenes,* 3 *tricks,* 4 *wings. Total* 28 *plates.*

But there is a slight extension of this summary when we come to look at the first of the sheets of characters which—as all leading sheets of characters from Pollock's house—bears a decorative title within a special pictorial design. Below this title in *Whittington* we read: *8 plates of characters, 13 plates of scenes, 3 Pl. of Tricks, 4 Pl. Wings, No. 6, 19, 28, 30.*

It is with these figures which follow the word 'wings' that we are interested. When we turn over the sheets of the play we find each one duly labelled and numbered; each has the name of the play and its proper figure in its series, every character sheet, every scene sheet, and every sheet of tricks—*excepting only the sheets of wings*. The sheets of wings bear what seem purely arbitrary numbers, each in this case having one of the four numbers quoted in the above sheet-title.

Of the four sheets, the first—that numbered 6—bears two pairs of cottage exterior wings; the second, numbered 10, has two pairs of ornate, palace wings with the bases of columns, draped and fringed curtains, and an urn with a plant in it; the third, numbered 28, has two pairs of kitchen interior wings; and the last, numbered 30, bears two pairs of tree wings.

But the most noticeable feature—more surprising than the non-sequence of the numbers—is the legend at the top of these sheets. It now no longer reads *Whittington and his Cat* as it did on every single one of the other sheets, but, instead: *Pollock's Side Wings to suit Any Play*. This is certainly an astounding claim! Has it any justification whatever?

My own collection of Pollock's prints is not by any means complete, but it includes forty-one sheets containing wings only. Very few of these wing-sheets were separately bought, but most came together with one or other of the sets of plays to which they made complement.

Of these forty-one, eight only bear any indication that they are related with a given play. Of the remaining thirty-three sheets, six bear short titles of their own such as *Pollock's Dungeon Wings* or *Pollock's New Gothic Wings*, but make no reference to any play, and the other twenty-seven sheets are labelled *Pollock's Wings to suit Any Play*.

This remarkable generalization of the wings is a puzzling point. It is true that one also finds—though very rarely indeed—that a sheet for a backscene bears not the title of the play with which it was bought and in which it makes part of the set, but the name of another play for which it was originally printed. But since it existed and was sufficiently suitable for a later play, it has been adopted here as well and a pencilled cancellation is usually made on the heading, noting this duplication, and deleting the old ascription. As an instance: the ninth scene sheet in my set of *Aladdin* bears the title *Pollock's Scenes in the Forty Thieves. No. 12.*, but there is written in manuscript in the margin *Also. Scene 10. No. 9. in 'Aladdin'*.

But this device is rare and occurs only a few times in the collection, and in no case is it said of any backscene that it *suits any play*.

The reason for this catholic attitude towards the wings, and the wings only, is not at first clear, but upon reflection it seems so out of the ordinary that it must surely be the outcome of some necessity or some convention.

It is undoubtedly not to be ascribed to the print-publisher himself as some form of work-saving system, since the opportunity to design, print, and sell a set of wings specifically for each backscene was clearly a promise of extra income for him.

And it cannot be an attempt to simplify the changing of scenes for juvenile hands, for some of the ingenuities demanded of those hands in the working of the tricks, far surpass that needed for a mere change of wings—and the wings must often be changed with the backscene in any case.

[350]

Nor is it to be attributed to a form of idleness by which little regard was paid to what wings were used with any particular backscene, for in the first place the variety of sheets of wings is very great, and in the second place, when any backscene of an unusual nature was designed, such as the deck of a ship or a view across a bridge in London that was a topographical representation of a recognizable place, wings were, in fact, specially designed to match, but these, unlike the drawings for the backscenes which proudly bear the name of the show for which they were specially designed, frequently have at the top the same generous claim 'to suit any play'— in spite of their clear origin and intention which was specifically to match and accompany a certain backsheet in a definite show.

Few wings are designed in this special way. The majority are compositions apart—they are 'farm wings', 'dungeon wings', 'tree wings', 'palace wings', 'street wings', 'parlour wings', 'kitchen wings', 'New Curtain Wings', &c., having a separate conception and an individual existence, not matching any backcloth.

In fact it would not be too much to say that Pollock's business may be held to consist of two departments: one for the production of complete sets of sheets of characters and backscenes (and upon occasion ground-rows and set-pieces and tricks), each set to suit one play and one play only, and, secondly, an almost independent department for the production of designs for theatrical wings, whose only connexion is that they are got up in the same style and to the same scale. They are not designed and labelled for a given play. They differ from all the rest of the sheets in that the wings are to suit any play.

So unexpected is the state of affairs viewed in this light that one turns to ask whether, in fact, any reason in the theatre could be raised to justify it.

It is a state of affairs in which the wings are viewed as separate stock adjuncts to a theatre, and only the backscene—and possibly a few *et ceteras* —is designed and specially prepared for the specific scenes of a given play or show.

Having received a pointer in this direction let us see if a study of the available evidence on the use of wings and their relation to stock scenery on the English stage will offer anything to bear out this apparently strange attitude of the toy-maker.

Let us begin by recalling the print of *The Heiress* (see Fig. 13) and inquire what follows from the implication of stock scenery arising from this and other references. What does the use of 'stock stuff' mean to the point of view governing the setting of a show? What justifies its very frequent use in the early theatre? Have the circumstances changed today that we regard stock scenery in a deprecating light? How can the use of it be consistent with vivid and living theatre? And how can scenery 'suit any play'?

It was argued on p. 243 that in *The Heiress* illustration the 'very regularity and non-committal lack of any special feature' might be suggestive that the scene was a stock scene, and we imagined the opinion—'a specifically-painted scene must have been made more interesting'. Let us now, however, consider this remark in closer detail, and see if a broader light may not be thrown on what is the source of 'interest' in a scene.

The implication is that if you put a designer to create, instead of stock scenery, an interior in which one clearly specified set of events is to take place, and an interior which bears a character endowed upon it by circumstances detailed in a script, then his task will involve a quality of specific characterization and this in itself is capable of producing 'interest' in his result. On the other hand, it would appear that if you ask him to design a set of interior scenery to go into stock and become a settled part of your general theatrical furniture, a different problem arises; he must inevitably sink into hack-work or lose inspiration. He has now no special character to achieve, no given atmosphere to embody conferring life and interest on his result—hence his task must appear *less interesting*. But let us examine his task to see if this is in fact the case.

What has the designer of a stock set to bear in mind? First of all the stock set must not err too much on the side of one type of room or it will not be widely useful stock. Yet it must contain an element of acceptability, of satisfyingness, in another direction else it will neither be a good investment theatrically nor the willing product of any artist. This 'satisfyingness' must, however, rest elsewhere than in the suitability of representation and characterization to a given occasion. That is to say, any closely representational quality must yield to some other quality of design, or pattern, or effect, which instead will endow it with interest as an element of the theatre rather than as the portrayal of a particular place in a play. For all elements of theatre must have their interest if the theatre is to hold its audience, and anyone who knows the delicate task of holding an audience will confirm that no risk of losing a fraction of that interest must be permitted. The root of theatre lies here.

So it is a pertinent and important question to ask what is this 'other quality of design, pattern or effect' in stock scenery.

We have now reached a point of momentous significance in the subject we are discussing. We have in fact distinguished something occasionally suggested before, namely the opposition between pure representationalism as the quality of a setting on the one hand, and on the other something else which we have here loosely named a quality for satisfying the interest—that is, something to make the act of attention a grateful and a co-operative one. And we are brought to the vital controversy that exercises not only the theatre but the whole of the art world—the controversy between naturalism and something artificially fancied and treated, between realism in the narrow sense and idealism in the full sense. In other places in this book we have noticed that some authors have met this problem in discussing the thing they name 'scenic illusion'.

We return to our designer faced with providing a set of scenery whose interest and theatrical quality shall lie, not in the characterization of some given room—whether it be a vivid, personal, and shrewd characterization or a faithful, meticulous transcription—but in evolving something that shall become general theatrical stock and, for the maximum number of times, answer a call from its owners to supply a satisfying and theatrical addition to the scene played before it, without being a fixed, narrow, too-recognizable type. His problem shifts into another sphere than representationalism and becomes a work of original composition and something needing the skill of a trained and specialized craftsman—the creation of a whole which in its own qualities, not in its subject, will contain that which is required of scenery. First in his mind, then, there will be not a room, with his task merely the generalization of a chosen type, but the stage, and the adequate provision upon it of a theatrically satisfying setting. He will work from the setting, and not the scenery, end. Theatre will come paramount, and theatrical effectiveness, against the play and the demand for this or that accuracy. General theatre instead of specific portrayal. A diametrically opposite angle of approach.

There are many who will condemn the approach at once, holding that no approach to any aspect of the theatre that has not, as its first consideration, the Play—the drama to be produced, the poet's word on paper—is above contempt. At once let it be said that they will be disappointed at the slighter regard in which their paramount subject appears to be held in the light of theatrical tradition. Please let them consider the tradition with an open mind on this point and, if they must seek to make a list to show the order of importance of the things in the theatre, at least restrain their emphasis till we be through with our story.

Returning now to *The Heiress* print: we have decided we must judge it from the point of view, not of the portrayal of the room the dramatist may have imagined his characters to have lived in, but as a theatrical background to some players, linking them and the auditorium they perform in. The set depicted might very well perform such a linking function. Picture it, for instance, in a dark green pattern on a grey or putty-coloured ground with a pale frieze and a cold brown dado. Imagine against it a wine velvet coat, a pink-lilac satin gown, an umber overdress, one waistcoat in canary and one in bottle-green. Such a scheme in a harmonious, not over-committal key—related to the rich faded greens and greys of lichened stone with autumn sun on them—might well have an ineffable element of theatre, and be fine stock for an age that had not yet fallen prey to the demands of our present over-statement.

Here is a scheme in itself ideally unassuming, well fitted to 'suit any play' or at least any with a drawing-room, sitting-room, dining-room, or bedroom, yet possessing a quality immediately ready to exist in paint upon flats on an eighteenth-century stage, framed in its vista of side doors and boxes, and the whole lit with those early candlelights of the playhouse.

In this print, above all others, we have an example of the opposite of naturalism and indeed, it would seem, of realism itself. Here, *par excellence,* is the stage-setting of an interior that is representational in no single detail. Here is the theatrical room that looks not like a room but like theatre. Yet, be it at no moment forgotten, it is a setting that is perfectly consistent with, and indeed entirely suggestive of, the idea of room-interior and it makes its suggestion in a language as satisfactorily theatrical as any playgoer could desire. Here is stock scenery.

Let us return again to our imaginary scene-painter and attempt to sum up the desirable characteristics of his stock-scene design. He would, before all else, have to present something to go on the typical stage of his time, then something that would possess among its leading features what I might describe as a quality of 'all-overness' and the providing of a nice 'lining' for the box of the playing area. Which is to say that a sense of pattern rather than of representation would govern the painter. His work might have something in common with the all-over patterns of wallpaper on the interior of an old doll's house.

Indeed, the analogy of an all-over, hand-painted wallpaper is not amiss here. This scenery had much the same relation to a stage as that wallpaper to an eighteenth-century room. (It is not out of place to recall the delightful hand-painted wallpapers that are so pleasant a feature of the dressing-rooms in the royal theatre at Drottningholm, and one remembers them as providing a very eloquent and decorative 'setting'.)

To provide, then, a highly specialized sort of 'wallpaper', or interior decoration, to the box of the stage was the stock-scene designer's task—not to provide a representation of some outside place whose appearance there happened to be some excuse to import into the theatre. Let us not be accused of forgetting that if the scene-painter were on the other hand called to produce a specific scene (not a stock scene) then other considerations might—or might not—govern his approach. But for the stock-scene designer the above is a pretty likely summary of what might lie behind his work.

There now begins to be apparent an answer to a question sometimes put: Where are the great English scene-designers of the eighteenth century? There are none—or at any rate but very few. The scene-painters were working on a different line from the easel-painters and the picture-makers; they were not providing finished unities, they were providing good linings to this acting-box, and their work, in accordance with the nature of stock scenery, assumed a quality of anonymity.

There was also another point which tended to suppress the individuality of the scene-painter. If we recall the terms of the Great Scenic Controversy we shall see that there was a sort of contempt or jealousy among certain dramatic playwrights for the contribution of scenery. And it would seem that though Jones held his own with Jonson yet, in the end, the dramatists kept the more educated public favour; and the theatrical tradition immediately descending to us is of the playwrights, the actors, and the plays, not of the shows, the showmen, the scene-painters and designers and their uses of the theatre. But an active examination shows that this side too has its tradition, though we must seek for it.

The point of importance at the moment is that there was in the post-Restoration period a large and influential body of men in the theatre, holding such an attitude to their plays and the purity with which they should be presented that—possibly without any special intention—a trend became evident towards the simplification of scenic effect. We emphasize that this is to be felt only in one part of the theatre—that beside it ran contrary tendencies, but they were for the most part held by the other party of the theatre, those who showed spectacle and opera.

So the literary theatre, the theatre of the dramatist, tended in part at least to make for simplified scenery, or at least to hold scenery as a subject worthy of little elaboration, and to be jealously watched for a sign of any competitive self-development.

Hence the English scene-designer was at something of a disadvantage as far as concerned the extending of his craft from strength to strength, from mere adequate existence to vigorous, creative experiment. He was invited, on the majority of occasions, to provide a simplified setting of the stock type, whatever relief he found now and then from special orders for elaborate masterpieces in his own line, issued to him by theatres generally of lesser prestige or at any rate of a younger and hence a more assailable tradition.

Thus the scene-painters of Restoration and Georgian days were not—and never could be—famous for the closeness or truth of execution with which they depicted a given scene. In that sense there were no scene-painters, and indeed no scenic backgrounds. Instead of the record of some vivid portrayer of a particular scene we get a laudatory note of another key; we hear of 'very glorious scenes and perspectives, the work of Mr.

[355]

Streeter, who well understands it', when Pepys pens his note of a performance of *The Siege of Granada. It*, we should remark, is not the portrayal of
an oriental Alhambra where *The Siege of Granada* was set but rather the
producing of a glorious stage background and a thrilling essay in the new
art of perspective. 'From all accounts', says Montague Summers of this
show, 'the decoration' was not perhaps 'strictly correct' but was instead—
and is this not something more?—'sumptuously oriental'. . . . The theatre
was what mattered, not the appearance of the Alhambra. The scene-
painter's business was not scene-illustration but the provision of a stage-
lining.

But we may go even farther than the point taken from Dr. Summers;
the scenery for an oriental play was sometimes so definitely of a stock nature
that it did not even proclaim that note of the oriental—sumptuous or
otherwise. Even this was not thought necessary in *Artaxerxes* (see Pl. 35).
No fame could ever come to the designer of this set; nothing could well
be simpler or less ostentatious.

The dress of the players makes some attempt at a Persian, or at least an
oriental, pretence. But no excuse is taken from the nature of the opera to
indulge in a riot of oriental fantasy or even to arrange, in severity, a few
items of oriental atmosphere to make a scene consistent with the costumes;
instead the stage is furnished with a setting as suggestive of 'stock' as well
might be. Three pairs of the usual column wings and the backscene of an
empty, panelled wall. Here there was no rein given to the imagination of
a scene-designer. This was a play of definite foreign and romantic tang,
but it was put on the stage with a surround of the old pieces of theatre, that
might 'suit any play'—an ordinary interior.

We would again warn the reader against too unimaginative a reconstruction of such occasions. These stock wings and back do not inevitably
mean that the shows were dull. It is of vital importance to avoid conceiving
them as *scenery* in the meaning we use today; they were setting—backings
to a stage, apt for almost any occasion. Their romance and glamour was
exercised there just as potently as in a specially designed Persian vision, but
it was romance of a different nature; it was the romance of the theatre and
its proscenium, its forestage, its boxes, its proscenium doors, and its
lighting, its scenes and its drapes, not the romance of portrayal and
simulation, the romance of a subject, a competitive conception to vie with
the playwright's, of the atmosphere of the site of his dramatic occasion.
No single element of that view was presented at all. The scene-maker
contributed to the theatre, not to the play produced—that was guarded the
playwright's province. As the costumes came out of stock and were an
assembly of what the theatre and the actors had at hand for their business
of acting, and not a harmonized unity of colour and line all from the mind

of a separate and special designer for the occasion, so the scenery, too, came out of the box it was kept in, and had grown up first in its own right as pieces of stage setting, not as illustrations to a writer's idea.

Early scenery, then, was not concerned exclusively with providing a background to any specific scene of dramatic action.

Two very significant references may be brought in support of this statement which may be allowed to crystallize the whole argument of this chapter. They go to show that to the Georgian mind any conception of scenery as the factual background to action was wholly unmeaning and indeed alien to the ideas of the period.

The first reference is taken from a topical article in *The Saturday Review* for 9 May 1891, entitled 'Scenery and Acting'. Contrasting the full scenery of Irving with that of the earlier stage, the writer says:

The fact is that in the eighteenth century, scenery in any true sense did not exist, not merely on the stage, but in fiction, in poetry, in history. In Fielding's novels, some one has said, there are simply 'practical' gates, barns and houses.... In Scott on the other hand, among novelists, as in Carlyle, spite of his hero worship, among historians, the scenery—the groups of people as well as the mere still life—is as important as the actors. This characteristic has naturally found its way to the stage, where not only the chief actors but their environments, social and physical, are demanded.

... Mr. Irving has not only obeyed his own fine artistic sense in the scenic beauty of his revivals, but has also brought the stage into harmony with that larger intellectual movement, characteristic of our time, which demands to see things not in isolated simplicity, but in their origins and surroundings, their social and natural concomitants.

Especially instructive is it to note the implication at the end of this passage that scenic style (which at this period of our review was suffering the long-threatened revolution) changes its nature because of a changing viewpoint in 'that larger intellectual movement characteristic of' the late nineteenth century, which demanded to see things 'not in isolated simplicity' ....

The other reference is again a reference of very considerable historic importance. It is from a quite different source, yet it remarkably confirms the point of the last reference. W. H. Davies in his introduction to Defoe's *Moll Flanders* (Simpkin and Marshall edition, 1933) signalizes Defoe's power of writing a story 'without digressions'; Defoe (he says) does not 'give us long passages of description, like Sir Walter Scott. ... He is so rich in the action of his story that he never requires help in the matter of describing locality. ...' Finally and in culmination: 'He never ... deviates from the telling of his story, like so many authors; and whatever happens to Moll Flanders inside a house is told without any description of its architecture, or its furniture, or whether it is new or old. And whatever happens to her in the open air is told without any setting of wind, sun, rain, or snow.'

A statement more exactly to our point could scarcely be made. The three features of a house-interior which the eighteenth-century writer does not discuss are its architecture, its furniture, its period. It was exactly these features which the eighteenth-century scene-painter ignored in his staging. And, finally, when speaking of the passages concerning Moll Flanders in the open air, the very word itself is used from theatrical parlance—no *settings* of wind, sun, rain, or snow . . .

It is this quality of the eighteenth century that lies behind the nature of its stage scenery. The scenes were stylized decorations not, in the writer's sense of the word, illustrative surroundings to passages of drama. One might add examples at length to substantiate this reading of the Georgians' attitude towards scenery, and in explanation of their—to us—unfamiliar attitude to stock scenery, but perhaps sufficient is said if we recall that even in the Restoration we find exactly the same attitude of cavalier disregard for the exact fitting of scenery to scene-of-action. We find this disregard impressing impartial students who have no argument to test concerning the stock-scene idea; thus in William Grant Keith's study of Webb's scenery for Part One of *The Siege of Rhodes* we read, concerning the design for the opening scene: 'The whole of the action here takes place within the city, but Webb's scene is of Rhodes seen from without, for in this instance, as in all, save one, of the later acts, the scenery serves simply as an illustration of the action, and not its actual setting.' We might, at first thought, have preferred the word 'decoration' to 'illustration' since illustration may convey to some nowadays the idea of representation—which clearly the author does not wish to suggest; otherwise the passage is a perfect summing up of the idea which has grown out of this chapter concerning the early attitude towards scenery. Moreover, it is, pleasantly enough, a summing up based on study of the very show which formed the original and wellspring of all our modern theatre. Perhaps also Mr. Keith was wiser than we in meaning by 'illustrate', not 'to embody in a picture', but to make shining and 'illustrious'—to light up—to *set* off (see *The Oxford English Dictionary*). So few people use the word in its original sense that we may perhaps be forgiven if we misread him.

So much is this true of the Restoration attitude that, in those times, the stage-direction, 'The Scene is So-and-so's House', was probably not intended to convey anything more than it said; not only would there be no indication, nor intention of indication, of whether an interior or an exterior was to be supposed—and (if interior) not only might there be no indication of what room was to be supposed—but it was quite possible, over and above all this, for the dramatist to present an action against one scenic background which involved two separate rooms in the same house successively!

It cannot be over-emphasized how little the Restoration showman considered his stage as representing a fictitious place in a drama. He did not take that approach in any respect—to him his stage was still the players' platform but with added decorative attraction.

To the eighteenth century which followed, the idea of stock scenery was therefore not at all inconsistent; it was in fact a true characteristic of the time. And even in the Victorian era we find stock scenery and—what is to the modern mind something even more unusual—stock scenery which may be mixed with specifically painted scenery. For instance, a special cloth might be used—and used intentionally—with stock wings. We are indeed forced to admit, unacceptable though it be to modern theories, that scenery in the past had a promiscuous quality, was accustomed to associate in many *ménages*, and did not bear itself with any strait-laced propriety— a virgin of all connexions but one. Not only had the scenes themselves a readiness to suit whomsoever took them but the very constituents of a scene were, on occasion, held by no bond of approved relationship but came together from many families without the public finding any scandal. Thus we see the maker of the log-book of the Prince's Theatre, Bristol, listing in 1887 these details for the First Act of *Robert the Devil*: ' "Colleen Bawn" transparent Mountain cloth Water row X—thickness stone wall X 4th Ent. Ship with rostrum L. Whittington felucca ship pieces R & L. Watsons new blue tent piece set LH—Wood wings & borders.' This is more than a stock scene, it is a very anthology or chrestomathy. . . .

With such an approach we may now begin to see that a disposition may well have been present in the past to regard wings as separate entities, drawn from a stock and fitted to a grand variety of backscenes. In most cases there would be some element of suitability in the coupling—tree wings with a landscape, rock wings with a castle—and indeed we some-times find, though comparatively rarely, the note 'Wings to match', but such a note only goes to emphasize that in general wings were not painted to match a specific backscene. We see on reflection that it is in the nature of things that such a scenic system as we have seen growing up through this review would lend itself to such a conception of wings. The run of plays would demand a considerable number of backscenes; some of these would be so special as to have to be newly designed for the occasion, but the majority would fall into a certain range of stock types. Of these backscenes a very few might require special wings, or wings to match, but the great majority again could be reduced to needs of a very simple type and thus could be adequately framed with a choice from a comparatively much smaller stock of wings. Finally, to complete the frame of the wings, the borders above could be of even fewer types—until we find provision made at Plymouth for only three varieties, interior borders, sky borders, and arch-borders.

Before closing this subject we may make two more contributions. The study of wings has led us unavoidably into the province of stock scenery and we may suitably add a note of what a stock of scenes consisted of in the mid-eighteenth century and then conclude with a word from the early nineteenth century which foreshadows the coming revolution against stock scenery.

A valuable and interesting contribution to the former subject was made in a pamphlet published in Dublin in 1758 and entitled *The Case of the Stage in Ireland*. Here we read:

The stage should be furnished with a competent Number of painted scenes sufficient to answer the Purposes of all the Plays in the Stock, in which there is no great variety, being easily reduced to the following classes.

1st. Temples
2ndly. Tombs
3rdly. City Walls and Gates
4thly. Outsides of Palaces
5thly. Insides of Palaces
6thly. Streets
7thly. Chambers
8thly. Prisons
9thly. Gardens and
10thly. Rural prospects of Groves, Forests, Desarts, &c.

All these should be done by a Master, if such can be found: otherwise they should be as simple and unaffected as possible to avoid offending a judicious eye. If for some particular purpose, any other Scene is necessary, it can be got up occasionally.

Little comment seems needed; save perhaps that the gravity of the list strikes one: Temples, tombs, walls and gates, prisons. . . .

The other reference sounds the discontent of the new era; it comes from *The Monthly Mirror* for January 1804, and concerns a performance of *A Bold Stroke for a Wife* at Drury Lane the previous month.

The rising of the curtain discovers Feignwell and his friend Freeman, over a bottle, in a room which, we are to understand, forms part of a tavern; with this I shall not be very severe, but, doubtless, something more is requisite than a small table, two chairs, and a scene, which appears as though the bristles of a painter's brush had not disturbed its surface since the zenith of Garrick's attraction. The next scene is supposed to convey a lively representation of a room in the house of a Quaker; that is Obadiah Prim. To effect this, we have the pleasure of beholding a scene, apparently copied from the gaudy architecture so frequently to be seen in the bed-chambers, and rooms of state, belonging to the chateaus and seats of our nobility—Corinthian pillars, festoons and painted pannels. Can all this convey an adequate idea of the abode of a hosier, and member of a sect, who, as it is well known, and from the words of the authoress of this very play, look upon the luxurious style, and extravagant manners of the age, with an eye of contempt and abhorrence?—Surely not. The same remarks may, of course, be applied to all the scenes, intended to represent the house of Prim, and of Sackbut. The fourth act opens with, what is meant for, Jonathan's Coffee House. This is done by a paltry scene, and two tables, five men at one, and four boys at the other. How well this conveys to the eye the noise, bustle, and confusion, which were the characteristics of that famed resort of stock-jobbers, it is almost needless to observe . . .

It is very clear that the order is changing. These comments speak for themselves as they were intended to. Let us turn to our review again and see how the battle goes in its final stages.

17

DEVELOPMENTS FROM 1860 TO THE
MODERN ERA

★

'A New Stage Stride', 1863—Bad masking at the Adelphi, 1865—The first 'Graphic' plate, 1869—Wings in Garnier's 'Le Théâtre', 1871—The 'Pair of Flats', 1873-5—Moynet's reference to Holland, 1875—Frederick Lloyds's model, 1875—The second 'Graphic' plate, 1880—Percy Fitzgerald and Stage Illusion, 1881-2—Godfrey Turner's affection for flats, 1884—Blanchard, 1885—'H.M.S. Pinafore' in 'The Era', 1887—Buckle on 'Theatre Maintenance', 1888—The Bristol log-book, 1886—William Telbin, 1889—At the Haymarket, 1893—Drops in Benson's tours, 1895—American newspapers, 1895-7—Edwin O. Sachs's 'European Opera Houses', 1896-9—Richmond, Surrey, 1896—'Stage Whispers'—Remains at the Hatcham Liberal Club—Hall's Catalogue, 1931—At the Prince's Theatre, Bristol—Charles Ricketts and the 'New Art Movement in the Theatre', 1901

★

WITH the beginning of the sixties, the battle for a reformation in scenery is on in good earnest. This is a half-century of such conflict and criticism that it is not to be wondered at when, in the 1910's, we find a complete new world begin to open (though rather uncertainly) for the artist in the theatre. This last chapter of our book seeks to present briefly the current news of the progress of this conflict.

Charles Dickens is responsible for our first information. He conducted a magazine called *All the Year Round* in which, on 31 October 1863, an anonymous article was printed entitled 'A New Stage Stride'. In its way it was epoch-marking. It signalled the origin of the cyclorama and pointed to a reform of scenery in every department. It began by reviewing the old system, which it attacked for bad masking above all else. We quote at length:

It is probable that most of us who have been in the habit of going much to 'the Play,' have often felt it to be time that something was done to render the

[362]

illusion of the stage more complete. Those who have ever sat in a stage—or even in a side box—must have over and over again felt that they could see a great deal too much of what was going on 'behind'. We have all of us probably felt dissatisfied with those mysterious side-scenes or wings by which the stage has hitherto been bounded on the right and left. By means of those wings the characters on the stage have up to this time been in the habit of making their entrances and exits, leaving us in an unpleasant state of uncertainty as to whether they were supposed to walk straight through the wall of a banqueting-room—for instance—or whether the banqueting-room had been left, for the sake of ventilation, with no walls at all at the sides. By what mysterious and unaccountable exits the guests used to clear out when Lady Macbeth gave them notice to quit in the banquet scene!

And there was another defect connected with those side-scenes. It seemed impossible to get those which were not in use, at the moment, sufficiently out of the way. Thus it would continually happen that in the midst of a dark forest, a hundred miles from any human habitation, we were rendered unbelieving, and our young illusions were rudely checked, by a glimpse of a bit of pilaster with a gorgeous curtain which had figured in the palace scene a minute before, or by the merest fragment of a light-comedy breakfast-room to be revealed in all its glory in the coming farce.

And then with regard to ceilings and skies, is it not a fact that there are free-thinkers among us who have never been satisfied with those strips of canvas which, hanging in parallel lines across the top of the stage, have so long waved before the doubting eyes of many generations of play-goers? In trying *not* to think that those strips of linen were suggestive of a washing-day, in trying *not* to see those gilded bits of cornice gleaming among the trees of the forest, in resolutely ignoring the man with the paper cap and carpenter's apron, standing ready for action at the wing, we who have sat occasionally at the side of the theatre have had to put such severe restraints upon ourselves, and have altogether had to fight so furiously in resisting the testimony of our senses, that much of our pleasure and interest in the play enacting before us has been sacrificed.

In a word there has been, up to this time, a certain roughness, a want of finish and completeness, about what may be called the boundary lines of the stage. . . .

Next comes the indication of a new system 'which has been for years tested at the principal Parisian theatres' and of its experimental installation at the Lyceum, where 'Mr. Fechter has recently caused to be constructed . . . a stage upon a principle entirely different from any previously tried in this country' (see p. 217).

This new stage is described in picturesque detail. But for all its novelty it turns out to be at first little more than the continental chariot-and-pole system which we already know from Rees in the quotation beginning on p. 220 in our Chapter 11. It seems yet another revival of the mysterious Chetwood innovation. The article treats in full detail of a matter which considerably concerns us, for it gives a comparison of the continental system and the groove system, and in these terms:

Here, then, is the formidable operation of scene-shifting reduced to the most simple of proceedings. Formerly, all that will now be done under the stage was done *on* the stage. There were grooves—raised grooves on the stage—into which the scene was lifted in two halves by staggering carpenters; then other grooves descended from above, into which the tops of the two halves of the scene fitted—not without a very visible crack up the centre. The reader has often from his place at the side of the theatre seen these upper rows of grooves fall over with a flop when they were wanted. The scene at length got successfully, though not without much resistance, into these grooves, and was pushed forward noisily and awkwardly by the carpenters, and was generally successful in retaining a perpendicular position, and not showing *much* of the bare lights and general shipwreck behind. Under the new system no such pushing, struggling, splitting, and joining, will ever be beheld; and among its many advantages, one may specially be mentioned. The old necessity of having raised grooves on the stage, in which the bottom of the scene might slide, prohibited the possibility of pushing any scene or object more than a certain distance from the side. These grooves could never be carried far on to the stage, lest the actors should tumble over them.

This writer does not seem to know of 'loose grooves', for they, of course, could be 'carried far on to the stage', and since they could be removed when there was no scene in them, they were capable of tripping no one provided the scene-shifters did their job. But there is here a contempt for the old system which served the Restoration and Georgian theatres so well. It has ceased to be the marvel it was in Jones's day when it alone made possible the succession of wondrous, glittering spectacles that set his theatre outstanding in our history. It is strange to think that this vaunted new system which revolutionized scene-change was to last in the Lyceum but a few years and then that Irving was to cast out, not this system but the groove-system *again* which had crept back; and then that by the mid-twentieth century this very continental system was to be discovered old-fashioned and an encumbrance even on the Continent itself. But to return to the article; full description follows of the new stage-floor and its traps, then of the two stories of fly-floors above and their catwalks, then of the grid crowning all from which is worked almost the only relic of the old régime that has a kind word—'the immortal green-curtain'. The vast machinery is summed up as being 'all needed, in order that the scene which nightly moves the tears or laughter of the audience may be presented with due effect'. A new angle is thrown for the beams of the footlights, and then a significant word is given to a figure we have noted before:

The banishing from the boards of that abnormal personage, the stage-footman, with his red breeches and white stockings, is an improvement on which we cannot but congratulate the manager of the Lyceum Theatre. It was not pleasant to sit and watch the proceedings of these gentry during a pause in the drama, though it must be owned that they appeared to know their business better than the footmen of ordinary life. With what precision they used to place the table, on which the deed was to be signed, in its exact place; the sofa, again, never had to be removed an inch after it was once put down; the very footstools seemed to be attracted to their right places as if by magnetic force. Still, those footmen used to give one a shock, and bring one's imagination down to the realities of life whenever they appeared, and it is agreeable to think that in future their work will be accomplished by means of trap-doors and other simple contrivances.

It is ingenuous to think of a trap-door being a simple contrivance for shifting furniture compared with a trained, common, human being. Next, box sets and—and this is worth remark—cyclorama sets are foreshadowed:

Many beautiful and interesting effects again will no doubt be achieved on this new stage by means of what may be called 'closed in' scenes. It will be possible to try such effects, not only in the case of an interior shut in above with a ceiling, but in representations of out-door scenery. It is in contemplation at this theatre to dispense entirely with the use of those horizontal strips of canvas which were alluded to somewhat disparagingly at the commencement of this notice, and which are technically called 'borders', or at most only to employ them in scenes so nearly covered in with foliage that they will not appear. In open outdoor scenes, where, for instance, the open country, or perhaps the open sea, extends far away into the distance, the sky will close the scene in overhead: an unbroken canopy extending from a certain point behind the proscenium and high above it, over the stage, and away to where, at the extreme backward limit of the theatre, it mingles softly with the horizon. One may, without being too sanguine, believe that this great arched canopy, spanning the stage from side to side, and from front to back, will lend itself to all sorts of beautiful and truthful effects. With trees, or rocks, or whatever else may be needed at the sides—not, indeed, pushed on in flat pieces parallel to the proscenium, like the separated joints of a screen, but planted here and there, as Nature plants, carelessly and irregularly—it will be possible so to close in an out-door scene, as that there shall be really no flaw or weak place about it, no unfinished gaps to which the scrutinising eye can wander in the confident hope of ascertaining 'how the trick was done'.

It was in the name of naturalism, then, that the cyclorama came into the theatre! And we conclude our extracts from this notable article with the following backward picture:

It is impossible to see 'off', as it is called. Our glimpses of beer-drinking, our visions of prompter's boxes, of flopping rows of grooves, of ladies waiting to go on, of seedy females holding shawls, are over, and done away with. The arrangement of the side-pieces, slanting obliquely away from the audience, and appearing to mingle together in masses rather than to stand carefully separated into regular entrances, renders it quite impossible that any member of the audience situated in any part of the house, should see anything not intended to be seen as part of the illusion. Sufficient entrances for all needful purposes are left among these side-pieces, but they are most carefully masked, and the actor is not seen—unless it is requisite that he should be seen—until he emerges clear upon the stage. . . .

It is a long reference, and a very strange one, with its touchingly trusting faith in perfection in the future and its only partly justified pokes at the formalities of the past that held their romance as surely as the coming innovations were to do in their own time.

[365]

Comment at length might be made on the sentences we have quoted, but there seems little need at this end of our review. The review itself is the comment.

We pass on then to illustration of these old techniques that now are in the balance. As we go we pause to notice a characteristic jibe from the pen of W. S. Gilbert, writing anonymously in *Fun* about Miss Bateman at the Adelphi in 1865: 'When we say that the piece was put upon the stage as all Adelphi pieces are, it will be understood that the audience saw more "flies", "grooves", dead wall, dirty scenery, and unsatisfactory "supers" than they would in any theatre in Whitechapel.' And so to the illustration.

It is to be found in the Christmas Number of *The Graphic* for 1869. This is the first Christmas Number ever produced by *The Graphic*, and the print befits such a special occasion on the part of one of the periodicals which were to achieve a great name in illustrated journalism. The engraving is a full-page plate, containing a wealth of fine work and minute observation. It is entitled *The First Night of a New Pantomime*. (Fig. 34.)

Further, this picture is the first in date of a number we shall discover, now that the falling days of grooves are come, depicting with more or less detail scenes in all of which there appears at an obscure corner, out of the way and amid shadows, some sign at last of the features of the hero of our story. Now that his days are dying, picture-makers rise to record his ancient presence—or rather to portray scenes where his presence, though near forgotten, still lingered, a picturesque remain.

Such pictures are worth collecting, they show all we shall probably ever know of the features of the groove as it appeared to the inquiring human eye exploring among the mysteries of the stage. Much can be learnt from these prints to suggest solutions of earlier problems, and so this example of them merits careful study.

The view presented is across the stage from the left side to the right. We see, from our position in the wings, through between the first and the second grooves. And moreover we are vouchsafed incidentally details of interest concerning the back of the proscenium side.

Looking through across the stage, we see the wall at the far side and, above, the stage-right fly-floor from which descends the beam of a spotlight. Under this fly-floor are visible the greater part of the first set of grooves and, to the right, a portion of the second.

We can distinguish, in the first set, the wing-grooves from the flat-grooves. The wing-grooves are nearer to the audience, they project a little farther towards us than the fixed part of the flat-grooves, and the individual walls separating the grooves have each a rounded end to facilitate the entering of wing-tops. There appear to be three wing-grooves in the set and the

FIG. 34. Print from *The Graphic*, 1869

mass of the wings themselves rising to their housings in the grooves can be dimly seen.

Above the wing-grooves is the tail or leg of an arched border, with a batten of gas-lights behind it. Since we are looking at a scene in which arched borders are used we may expect to find the arms of the flat-grooves raised to their vertical position. And this, in fact, we do.

It is important to realize just what type of scene we are looking at. The fact that it is in a pantomime and the presence of the figure of the girl with crossed arms, raised on a bridge in the beam of the spot, together suggest that we are looking at a transformation scene. That is as much as to say we are not seeing a normal scene of wings and low borders with the backscene on a pair of flats. The flats are all withdrawn and we are looking instead at the downstage limits of something more probably resembling one of Jones's scenes of relieve, and one which is likely to recede in a succession of fretted and wonderful planes to the very back of the stage with its elements seen through a forest of cut-cloths or at any rate under a vista of cut, arched borders.

Some indication of the painting on the scene may be gathered from the face of the wing visible just to the right of the girl. It suggests an elaborate composition of leaves and flowers well in keeping with the fairy 'Realms of Bliss' in painted perspective.

For such a scene wings would be needed as usual, and we see them here, but we also see the low-hung, straight border has given place, under the expanding 'magnascope' property of the groove system, to high arched borders, which mask the tops of the wings only by means of the descending legs at their ends—and these legs are functionally more in the nature of an extension to the height of the wing than part of the across-the-top masking of a border. The 'legged' borders are clearly visible in the print, though the artist has shown no line of demarcation between their extremity and the top of the wings.

It will be noted also in regard to the borders that the normal number has had to be supplemented. This is because the higher the borders on a stage the more are needed to mask a given space or, conversely, the deeper they must all be. In practice one deep border may be more of a nuisance than two shallower ones. And here we see above the girl's head that just in front of the arched border proper, whose legs touch the wing-tops, is a second straight border to mask the top of the one behind.

At the extreme right of the picture is seen the face of one of a pair of flats, withdrawn so as to be out of sight behind the wing. We notice why the wing-grooves are advanced farther on stage than the fixed part of the flat-grooves—in order better to effect just this concealment.

That this half-flat-scene may be one of a group coming at this position we may confirm by turning to the first grooves. Here a set of possibly four flats is seen forming a compact column behind the stooping clown, and with a *length* of lights hung at the back to illuminate the wing behind in the second grooves.

No evidence is to be found in this print concerning bottom grooves, either fixed or movable, but very clear illustration is seen of the hinged arms of the upper flat-grooves reared out of the way to give clear opening for the splendours of the high scene. These groove-arms appear to be of the light skeleton construction which we saw in Contant and which was an alternative to the solider building of the (presumably earlier) type of groove discovered at Bristol. Some idea is conveyed of the pretty considerable size of these groove-arms.

Of the rest we must speak but little—of the drum and thunder-sheet hanging behind the proscenium above the head of the little girl's ward—of the Harlequin's *baton* propped between the timbers of the proscenium side, of the crack-machine like a giant rattle on which Harlequin is leaning, of the 'big-heads' or giant masks on which the small boy is perched. And of the greatest problem—whether this view shows the back of a proscenium door or not. Whatever the interest of these, we have here to deal only with grooves—and with this valuable indication of the type of scene which necessitated the existence of their hinged arms, we turn to our next reference.

Much the same dissatisfaction with wings was being felt at this time in France. For an instance we may refer to *Le Théâtre*, 1871, by Charles Garnier, the architect of the Paris Opera House. Although this book has no connexion with the British stage and deals with a scenic system different from ours, yet it is by a theatrical technician of eminence and it admirably points out an argument against wings that applied equally forcibly, in the extent quoted, to the wings of either country. (The English version is the present writer's.)

If the stage seldom requires to be very deep, on the other hand it can hardly be too broad. On a narrow stage the wings obviously cannot possess much width and they permit the spectator to see between them, as he sees between the columns of a portico, and the parts 'off' are in view. To avoid this great inconvenience it is necessary to bring the side scenes closer to one another and, in consequence, to increase their number, sometimes even to angle them so that they may be opposed to any 'discoveries'. That multiplicity of successive planes is very embarrassing to the scene-painters. It breaks the lines, encumbers the space, and especially forces the scene-plans to be arranged without liberty or variety, governed as they are by the paramount necessity of masking the sides.

Again we have the criticism of the 'artificiality' of wings, of their narrowness and ill-masking, and of the difficulty their successive planes present to a painter aiming to suggest an unbroken side-wall—for scene-painters were now aiming to suggest unbroken side walls instead of the frankly admitted stock decoration that the English were once content to show on the side scenes—and lastly, of the formal limitation their angle and prefixed position on the stage imposed on the free laying-out and arrangement of scene plans.

(And yet, with all this, I am a little sceptical about the embarrassment caused to the scenic artist by the existence of wings. He tackled their nature admirably in the past. He could do so today, enjoying the limitations they imposed and regarding such limitations as the exigencies of his medium and the origin of its form. It was not the scene-painters who objected to wings; it was a growing view of the world that for an imitation to be perfect it ought to be above criticism. That is, however, a personal note. The next two references carry a personal note also, but in a different way. The first of the two passages was one of the earliest that ever came to my notice on the subject of the historical flat scene, and it was the unusual use—to a modern reader—of the phrase 'a *pair* of flats' that helped to confirm me in a belief that what we understand by 'flat' today is something very different from whatever it was that bore the name in the past.)

In an anonymous article in *The Art Journal* on 'Scenepainting in England' (vol. for 1873, p. 27) we read: 'For several years, however, the transformation scene was nothing more than a pair of flats representing the Realms of Bliss in painted perspective.' The reference is to the rich innovations made in the technique of the transformation scene by William Beverley.

Similarly, in an article by Harry Lancaster, apparently printed in *The Furniture Gazette* in 1875, we read apropos the late-eighteenth-century scene-designer, De Loutherbourg, that he 'never, we believe, put brush to a pair of flats in the painting room'.

Next we turn to a piece of information of a different sort. It will perhaps be noticed that since 1707, when the seventeenth-century volume of Pozzo was translated into English, we have had no information whatever about grooves from the Continent. Such earlier continental references as we met dealt indeed only with special theatricals—with experiments and court shows, never with regular public-theatre procedure.

In fact (saving the reference we shall make in a moment), it seems that no countries save Great Britain and, as we shall find, the United States of America ever developed the grooves system in public practice. It became the peculiar method of the English, a respect in which our stage stands unique in Europe.

About this time there appears in France a spate of books dealing in a more or less popular way with the 'secrets of the theatre'. Had we had such a movement from English publishers we might be saved much of the study entailed in this present review. But, however that may be, one of the first of these French books, entitled *L'Envers du Théâtre* by M. J. Moynet, published in 1875, contains, at p. 44, the following: 'En Hollande, on voit jusqu'à six ou huit trapillons à chaque plan. Ces trapillons, posés oblique-ment, se répètent au-dessous des corridors du cintre. La feuille de décora-tion se glisse dans ces deux coulisseaux, ce qui supprime les mâts et les faux châssis.'

Since this contains several technicalities we may be forgiven for making the following suggestion for an English equivalent: 'In Holland one finds up to six or eight *trapillons* in each set (which word "trapillons" is generally to be translated "cut", but here seems to have a suggestion of the groove, since the passage continues:) These *trapillons* lie diagonally and are repeated under the fly-gallery. The scenes slide between these two (sets of) channels, and by this means chariot-poles and frames are obviated.'

Did then Holland, too, use grooves? It is a puzzling paragraph, for we have already seen that the word in French terminology which best seems equivalent to our 'groove' is *costière*. True a *costière* is a very different thing from a groove, being a complete slit through the stage floor, through which projects a mast or pole rising from a carriage or *chariot* running on rails on the floor beneath; on this sliding mast the wing was hung. But Moynet elects to use the word *trapillon*, which corresponds far more closely with Rees's *flap*, to name this Dutch system of two channels (*coulisseaux*), top and bottom, between which the scene-piece runs. For all this, the passage seems to bear no other interpretation than that grooves, or something like them, were known in Holland.

It is very interesting to note that these Dutch grooves are said to be diagonal, as Pozzo's were, and as very few others which we can discover were.

In spite of the suggestion I made above that no series of books dealing with stage technique was published about this period in England, there did appear one volume—and that in the same year as M. J. Moynet's book, namely 1875. In this our next reference is to be found. It was a book by Frederick Lloyds on *Scene Painting*, and it contains diagrams of a typical set of scenery. Here are shown the usual wings and borders, together with two *ground-rows*, a *raking piece*, and a *pair of screens*. These last are interest-ing, because they are profiled at the top as well as the sides, and yet the diagram showing the back view of the two screens points out that the profiling is only carried along half the top of the piece—that half nearer the centre of the stage. The off-stage half is, instead, left plain, and above it is written: 'This straight part runs in the Wing Groove.'

[371]

Grooves were then, on occasion, used to support additional pieces of scenery beyond the regulation wings and flats. Lloyds's book includes a series of plates showing separately all the components of a simple set scene. These are so reproduced that, on turning the page, one sees printed on the back of each piece the carpentry construction with which it is made. These plates have all been photographed separately and the details cut out and assembled in model form and rephotographed (see Pl. 53). Three pairs of wings with their matching borders are shown and, behind, there is what is called a 'screen', either side, one bearing part of a ruined temple and the other a cut-out group of trees. Between these stretches a ground-row bearing a bridge, and in front of it another, very low, ground-row of grass, and in front of this again a small 'raking piece' leading in from the foot of the wing in front of the group of trees on the screen. Behind all the distance is represented on a backcloth. Pl. 54 shows the same model seen from behind with the backcloth and second ground-row removed. Diagrammatic representations of the grooves are added to the model to support the pieces in traditional fashion. Lloyds has marked with a *c* such parts of the scenery as would be covered in canvas, and with a *p* such parts as would be added in profile-board and cut out.

Our next reference brings us to the Christmas Number of *The Graphic* for 1880, which contained a presentation plate. It is hardly likely that its artist ever imagined it would be brought as evidence for a point in the history of stage technique, but in fact it contains at least sixteen points not unworthy of a student's notice. The plate shows a view across the stage from the wings. There is being performed a turn between a clown and a trio of trained dogs. The top-hatted stage-manager is seen in the obscurity of the farther wings. In the foreground a Harlequin is murmuring to a thoughtful Columbine. But above in the distance is a vivid portrayal of a complete set of grooves, with the hinged extension rearing into the air.

Let us turn to this print and, to begin with, consider the wings (Pl. 56).

1. The pieces of scenery in the right foreground show a reasonably similar construction, at the back, to that of ours today. There are, however, interesting differences. Firstly, the timber used seems much thicker than our standard 3 in. by 1 in. The framing of the piece behind the Harlequin is especially heavy, despite the fact that the height of the wings appears to be less than 12 ft. (though this may be artist's licence).

2. We notice also that here is offered confirmation of our supposition that early wings were much narrower than ours; none of those shown seems to be more than 4 ft. wide.

3. Another difference from our modern construction is that at the corner of no piece of scenery here is there to be found that short diagonal cross-

corner brace, generally so beloved of artists, which characterizes the back view of almost all our present-day scene-pieces.

4. Further, the 'rails', as the horizontal pieces across the back of a wing are called, seem spaced a little closer together than we find need for. And the placing of the rails on the back of the two pieces at either side the picture is different. The construction-plan seems to be more haphazard generally than ours—though maybe such discrepancies also lie at the door of the artist who made the picture rather than of the carpenter who made the pieces.

5. Again on this matter of rails: our modern rails are inserted at either end into a pair of shaped cross-pieces, like the short legs of a squat H, which are screwed to the stiles of the wing. These are called *toggles* and are generally about 18 in. long. But the toggle shown here on the piece of scenery to the reader's right is most remarkably long, appearing to be about 4 ft., especially unexpected in such short scenery. The purpose of the toggle is to help keep the piece square, and especially to support the stiles against the strong inward pull exerted by the contracting size-paint on the canvas.

6. Again on the matter of wings, there is to be remarked the curious position of the pair of pieces behind the figures in the foreground. By rights, one would suppose, judging from the other side of the stage, that the piece which would come at this position must of necessity be one half of the pair of flats of which the other is to be seen pushed back, with two more flats, in the flat-grooves on the opposite side of the stage. But a glance at the ground line behind Harlequin's foot shows us not part of a wide flat, but the lower edges of two distinct narrower pieces—presumably wings. Where then are the flats corresponding to those opposite?

7. The last point to be noted concerning the wings is that the wing on the right is tilted and not in its proper vertical position.

8. Turning now to the distant halves of the flat scenes, visible in the opposite flat-grooves, under the reared-up groove extension, we note with very great interest indeed that the centre one of the three is apparently *profiled*, that is, it has a cut edge. How then did it meet its partner when they drew together? It seems only possible that the meeting was not complete and a more or less narrow gap was in fact left between what was, perhaps, two clumps of trees. The gap might be masked by closing another pair of flats behind.

9. Looking upwards we see first of all a rough portrayal of the old-fashioned *gas-batten* or row of gas-jets across the top of the scene.

10. The light from this escapes at the end sideways and forwards to illuminate the back of a border. The border hangs directly in front of the adjacent wing-grooves. It is interesting to notice, in view of what we found in the Plymouth plans, that it is an arched border. This accounts for the fact that the flat-groove extensions are raised, for although the drooping

[373]

ends of the arched border conceal the wing-grooves, it is clear that they would not hide the flat-grooves if these were lowered.

We are inclined to reason from this that what we are looking at is a set scene, because if the flat-groove extensions are all attached to a sole and single barrel—as were those at Plymouth—the turning of this must have raised all the other groove-arms as well; therefore there would be no groove-arm at all in the lowered position. Therefore again there could have been no pair of flats closed across at the back of the scene, and hence the scene must have been backed by a vista into the back recess which, on the analogy of other stages we have studied, we imagine to have been present.

The only alternative to the theory that this was a set scene would be that it was a scene with a backcloth, which could roll up to disclose another, just as a pair of flats could open to disclose a further pair.

11. In view of the number of traps and cuts we have noted in stages of this period, it will be understood that the timbers underneath, which support the stage-floor boards, must run *across* the stage from side to side, not down it from back to front, else the important structural members below would have to be cut into for the traps. The boards of the stage therefore (which must run in the opposite direction to the bearers below) have to be up- and down-stage. In this direction they are correctly shown in the print.

12. Now peer into the shadows. Behind the border and raised groove-arm is the fly-floor with its railing. The upper rail is clearly to be seen in the blackness near the top of the picture.

13. Below this fly-rail there is a patch of the darkness beyond, then below that again is a wide patch of middle-tone before we reach the actual floor of the gallery under which the grooves are fixed. What is this area of middle-tone which seems to replace the lower bar of the fly-rail—or at least to connect this with the fly-floor? We may suppose it is what we should call today an *apron*. An apron is hung from the fly-rails in order to prevent those spectators seated at the extreme side-front from seeing up under the borders into the opposite fly-floor and noticing there the ropes and workings. It is simply a painted canvas, generally sky colour.

14. We turn last of all to examine those objects of our present interest, the grooves; what does the print tell us about them? Firstly consider the wing-grooves. The remarkable point of these is that they do not seem to be formed by projections from a connecting bed, like all those we have met hitherto, but are like a series of five entirely separate battens of wood spaced out at regular intervals. Presumably they must have been bound or stayed together somewhere, but the means for this has escaped the eye of the draughtsman.

There is only one alternative to this. It is that these particular 'grooves' were not grooves proper, but were really on the model of a gigantic horizontal table-fork, between the prongs of which the wing-tops slid. In which case it will very readily be noticed that such a fork would have the immense advantage of accommodating, at a pinch, wings of different heights. This suggestion of a fork is not isolated; we shall find that one of the last references we are to make in our life-story of the groove has a strange link with the present idea (p. 388).

A detail that has not escaped the artist's eye is the interesting point that these battens are provided with tapering ends, which presumably facilitated, in no small degree, the entering of the tops of the wings into the spaces they had to run in.

15. Three odd slits are to be noticed on the down-facing edges of the three intermediate groove-walls of the raised arm, but not on the two outer walls. Here we can only suppose a somewhat botched representation of that form of openwork construction, designed for lightness, that we noticed in the upper grooves in Contant.

16. The final point is negative: look as we may, we fail to find the slightest indication whatever of bottom grooves. It is scarcely likely that an artist, so interested in the world behind the scenes as to note the details of the upper grooves, would have ignored the interest offered to his picture by the addition of lower grooves, had these, in fact, been present. We must conclude that here is another witness to the gradual abandonment of bottom grooves.

Thus, then, may one start hares when one examines an old theatre picture. Here are sixteen perfectly good hares from one *Graphic* Christmas presentation plate to be pursued. The fascination of this study is that, while so much is explored and documented in the way of literary references, yet so many pictorial references still lie unexamined, unexpected even, in the pleasant shades of old prints. The searching of prints is an absorbing investigation indeed, as intriguing as any mystery plot.

The year 1881 saw the publication of a book from which we have had already several occasions to quote—Percy Fitzgerald's *The World Behind the Scenes*. In it there are two references to grooves. Both are of first importance to history; from the one we gain a further note on the failure of grooves to keep up with contemporary scenic developments—together with a valuable suggestion as to the nature of these developments—and the other signalizes so important an occasion that we have already quoted its context in our first chapter as instancing the death of grooves and the passing of the system of visible scene-change.

The first reference begins on p. 2 of the book. Here we are given already a forecast of what is to come, for we find the author, in setting out on his subject, taking pains to say of the scenery of his day that its 'splendours are of an old-fashioned and unscientific kind. Indeed, the attempts of fifty years back belong to a more genuine system of stage illusion than the dazzling displays of our own time, when perfection is thought to be reached. In England, in spite of a certain mechanical skill and deftness, the arrangements of the stage are still of a rather primitive sort; in spite of the blinding glare of the limelight, the profuse colouring thus fiercely illuminated, and the sheen of armour and foil. The scene-shifters are occasionally revealed, "each with half a castle in his grasp," as he pushes the scene back in its groove; the canvas landscape ascends as though it were a vast window-blind, its wooden lath swinging below . . .', and so he goes on. But we have passed an implication that is interesting. It is suggested that the older stage pursued a convention of scenery which fitted well with the artifice of grooves, but that within the half-century 1830–80 some change had occurred in the attitude towards scenery and the conventions of scenic design, that made the old, once-admirably-suited grooves an inconsistence, an eyesore, and a hindrance.

It is with the establishment of this point that we begin really to pierce to the heart of our subject. What really *is* stage scenery? What was it in its early days? Somehow we seem recently to have lost—or become confused over—the significance of scenery in the theatre and today we thrash about in a jungle of controversy, trying to fit the scenes into their proper place in art. What is the place of scenery in the theatre?

To give some sort of answer that will increase the wisdom of modern knowledge is the only end of historical research: our tale of the groove and our examination of all the rest of the scenery that has been brought to being on our stage will go for little if they afford us no aid to such an answer. And so instead of adding another to the theories that come from the lips of essayists on theatrical art we are to see if we can find out anything of what it used to be—of what it originally was.

We find very often that the writers we consult use the phrase Fitzgerald uses here when he talks of the old scenery as belonging 'to a more genuine system of *stage illusion*'. What is this *stage illusion*? What do the words imply? Here is the centre of the whole matter.

A writer of the conservative school of thought today will have no difficulty in giving his answer to the question immediately. He will say, 'Stage illusion is the presenting of an exact picture of real life'. Whereupon the members of the 'advanced' school rise upon him in their wrath and cry that no art is ultimately concerned with reproducing the actual appearance of life, and that the death of scenery would soon supervene if it were prostituted to this heresy.

It is not for us to take sides. But it certainly is for us to take up very seriously this phrase of 'stage illusion', and we may adopt it, at any rate temporarily, to name the principle behind the art of stage scenery. A comprehension of the nature of stage illusion will point us to the goal of all scene-design.

The tenet of the conservative school, mentioned above, has this advantage over that of the other school: that it is stated in unequivocal terms. Whether they are right or wrong, one does know what they mean. But unfortunately no such clarity informs the pronouncements of the opposite camp, consequently their theories are so much the harder to understand, and to refute or accept.

The consistence of the conservative position, which holds that stage illusion consists in deceiving the spectator into thinking he is looking at real life, not painted scenery, seems to rest on the fact that the phrase 'stage illusion' contains a word which is very easily accepted as meaning 'deception'; to give an 'illusion' is apt to be taken to mean the same as 'to give a deceptive appearance'. Hence (they say) stage illusion obviously refers to some sort of treatment that shall make things seem what they are not. This treatment is the treatment meted out to timber and canvas and lit areas of paint that results in making them seem, not fictions in timber, canvas, and paint, representing or suggesting other things, but, in very presence, those things themselves.

To such an extent, then (the conservatives conclude), as scenery reaches this achievement of seeming not scenery but 'the real thing', it is good scenery: and therein lies stage illusion!

But there is another interpretation to be put upon this word 'illusion'; it does not in any wise follow that the illusion specified here is the illusion 'of real life'. The illusion meant may be of something else: the illusion, for instance, not of the presence of reality but of the presence of fantasy. For does not 'illusion', beside signifying a deception, equally signify a vision? The world of stage illusion, then, may be the world of theatrical fantasy, not the world of theatrical imitation.

A further limitation in the conservative's conception of the meaning of the word 'illusion' is that he comes to relate it with something worthless and something ineffectual, like any other imitation. Reality, he says, is *true*, you can bark your shins on it; but illusion is a wisp, a figment, a mere shadow: it is a vanity, a luxurious snare, of no value to a real man, having, above all, no effect whatever (save perhaps one vaguely sedative) upon the business of physical, everyday, positive life.

But the dissenters see a little farther than this. They know that a 'mere illusion' may produce—through the medium of a living organism—a very real effect upon the concrete world, even, instancing psychosis, to the break-up of the health of the only-too-concrete cells of that organism. So they approach the meaning of Illusion with no illusion that they have to deal with a safe and ineffectual power, nor one unworthy of their fullest respect as practical human beings. They will even affirm the *reality of illusion*, stating a truth in a contradiction of terms.

They appear then to be in a better position to solve the enigma than the conservatives, since the conservatives make, it seems, the mistake of under-rating the power and effect of what they claim so easily to define. This illusion is no ineffectual thing. Of that at least the dissenters are sure. Upon any further definition of it they are, however, undecided, or at least divided.

All we can say therefore of Fitzgerald's remark is that a more genuine system of stage illusion may have obtained in the older theatre, but how it was so, and what stage illusion is, are still two of the principal questions we seek to answer in present-day research. Thus we may go on to make some reference to what followed the 'more genuine system' of earlier days as indicated by Fitzgerald towards the end of the same, lengthy, paragraph. And the passage throws a great light on those limitations latent in the nature of grooves which now are beginning to be brought into prominence until at length the grooves come to be regarded as behind the times; old, out-dated, inefficient, spokes in the wheel of progress. The passage, then, has a double interest. It says:

So long as the present principles of scenic representation obtain, and the aim is to give a more and more exact imitation of objects outside, any formal system of mechanics would be found too inelastic to admit of the endless variety required. These demands become every day more and more craving; some new prodigy of imitation is required, and the scenic artist is called on to furnish some monu-mental structure of proportions more vast than has been yet attempted.

And the grooves definitely *were* a 'formal system of mechanics' and they *were* 'inelastic'. There did not seem, in Fitzgerald's day, to be that rejoicing in the limitations of a medium as the chiefest of its qualities which informs the modern movement. Instead he tells us there was a striving for no limits —or for a means of expression that appeared to bow to no limits. A proud means of expression indeed for finite thoughts!

The grooves, it can be well believed, could not stand that pace. They were not invented to transcend the limitations of expression, they were but humble tools introduced by a workman-genius of the Jacobean age, accepted and developed by only less illustrious workmen at the Restora-tion, and maintained as satisfactory under the dignity and downrightness of the Georgians. But they were, all the same, a limited and an inelastic system. And they would not do for the Victorians.

When we come to the second, and only other, reference in Fitzgerald's book, we find the last pretence at abiding them any longer is tossed away. Irving presented the amazing scenic marvels of that double bill, *The Cup*, and the revived *Corsican Brothers*, at the Lyceum in 1880-1. This we have already quoted in full in our first chapter; we repeat the relevant passage now, perhaps with a fuller sympathy with what it concerns. Fitzgerald records Moy Thomas's stating, in *The Daily News*, that—'the economical but comparatively rude system of "wings" and grooves is on this occasion entirely dispensed with, as in the best Parisian theatres; and the scenes are constructed so solidly, and with so many details that . . .' I break off at this casual dismission of an old servant. Just for a fashion—just because it is done in the best circles, in the best Parisian circles—the grooves are 'on this occasion entirely dispensed with'. Alas for the too-familiar half-promise of 'on this occasion'! It was not to be the only occasion. Before scarcely a score of years had passed away the grooves had also passed away—and not only passed away but, a little later, been utterly and universally forgotten; it was as if they had never been.

As we pass we notice that it would seem from Moy Thomas's remark that Fechter's earlier innovations, which had already been so glowingly recounted in *All the Year Round*, and which took place at this very theatre, the Lyceum, had only been temporary, or at least partial; for though we read there that Fechter removed the grooves for a newer system (one also 'tested at the principal Parisian theatres'), yet here we have a categorical statement that eighteen years later the grooves were removed *again* for Irving. And in Irving's grand and far-renowned productions the grooves sank under the onslaught of splendour and *trompe d'œuil*, and passed unwept away, silently into the darkness.

In 1882 Fitzgerald again voiced his opinion about wings and, perhaps unexpectedly, we find him defending them against the new box set. Instead of subscribing to the old cry that it is 'ridiculous to behold the actors making their entrances through plastered walls and wainscots instead of through doors', he counters (in *A New History of the English Stage*, vol. ii, p. 235) that:

This objection, however, opens up the whole question of scenic delusion. I firmly believe that the present system of enclosing the stage, presenting the copy of an actual room, with ceiling, doors, etc., is fatal to illusion. The more general the scenery the better for this end; it should be rather an indication of what is intended, so as to convey a haziness, for the more complete the imitation of real things the less delusion there is. The old mode of entrance from 'the wing' seems to make the boundary between the world off the stage and that on it suitably indistinct; the actor seems to *enter on the scene*—not to come in through a canvas door.

And it was just the 'want of finish . . . about what may be called the boundary lines of the stage' that was inveighed against by the writer of the forward-looking article in *All the Year Round*. Fitzgerald has another point of view. For him the illusion of reality is *not* held to be the ideal aim for scene-makers, and an argument is put up for some alternative of conventionalization that shall accept, and rather stress, the fact that the show is on a stage and the actor is a player in costume before us. In view of our earlier discussion of Scenic Illusion and of the concluding notes we made at the end of our survey of wings we may leave this reference to speak for itself.

Hard upon this—in March 1884—we find a voice raised in affection for the old system, albeit the voice is in a passage of doom more final than any we have yet read. It is the voice of Godfrey Turner in *The Theatre*, saying in an article called 'Scenery, Dresses and Decoration':

I am aware that, a little before my time, these were apt to be somewhat slovenly and unhandsome, and that, contrary to an older practice, the scenic mounting of the drama was almost wholly confined to the painting of wings, flats, and borders, the stage being very meagerly furnished . . . at the beginning, say, of the present century, so little furniture or modelled representations of real objects was there on the boards, that Leigh Hunt, as I remember, spoke of the Kembles and their practice of sitting at a real table in a real chair, as examples of theatrical innovation, and the artifices of a new school. The only scenic backgrounds were flats, run on in pairs, and with greasy black finger-marks down the middle join, which divided as often as not the trim perspective of a gravel-walk. Those dear, dingy old flats, only to be seen now-a-days at the merry matinée or the brisk and bounteous 'ben'! . . .

Dear, dingy old flats!

The next reference is in a passage also containing food for rumination concerning the development of scene-shifting, and an implication that visible scene-change had passed away, as well as an unspoken announcement that the flats are now as good as dead. It is E. L. Blanchard, speaking in 1885:

In the old acceptance of the term the vocation of scene shifter, would seem, in our London Theatres at least, to be relegated to the Dramatic Past. The 'flats' as they were called, pushed on to the stage from grooves at the wings, no longer require the assistance of sturdy men in their shirt-sleeves and paper caps, who could rarely effectually conceal the pair of legs belonging to them, chasing as it seemed the two halves of the interior or exterior they brought together so as to meet exactly in equal divisions. Scenes of late years have been so contrived as to turn bodily round, or else are not changed in sight of the audience . . .

To see the sort of innovations that were in progress at this time we may read this extract from *The Era*, 12 November 1887, where a 'panorama' is used to replace both backscene and wings—bringing us still nearer to the modern cyclorama:

The arrangement of the scene in the revival of *H.M.S. Pinafore* at the Savoy Theatre, this evening will have several remarkable features in addition to those already described by us. The real mast, which stands in the centre of the stage, has been carried right up into the space generally occupied by the sky-borders, which will be done away with, as also will the wings, the latter and the backcloth, being replaced by a panorama of Portsmouth Harbour. The difficulty of lighting thus created will be overcome by the electric light battens being carried up the back of the mast.

The year 1888 was a year of many new departures. A book on the design of theatres was published from the pen of the theatre-architect, J. G. Buckle (who built the Theatre Royal, Stratford, E.15). It was entitled *Theatre Construction and Maintenance,* and there, in his section on Fly Galleries, he gives the following passage marking the revolution that grooves and their scenery were suffering:

The 'grooves' fixed to the underside of the fly galleries in the older theatres, and used for steadying the 'flats' and 'wings', are now almost entirely dispensed with in modern theatres, as they necessitate all the scenes being set parallel with the proscenium. 'Grooves' are still used in a modified form, but are attached to the lower rail of the 'fly-truss', and turn upon a pivot, by which means wings, &c., may be set at any desired angle. Another arrangement is to fix iron sockets to the upper and lower plates of the 'fly-truss', in which a long wood bar, about 3 in. square, works up and down, being fixed in any position by means of an iron pin fitting into a series of holes, specially drilled. At the lower end of this bar is attached a contrivance very similar to an enlarged garden rake. This works upon a pivot and between the teeth the upper edge of the 'wing' or 'flat' is secured. These survivals of antiquated methods are entirely dispensed with in the more recent theatres. . . .

This is an especially interesting reference since it is almost the only one that makes any mention of the attempt of the grooves to overcome their greatest limitation—the imposition of a rigid parallelism on all scene plans. This limitation, in regard especially to wings, was as we have seen un-economical and made adequate masking impossible. The attempt to over-come this limitation took the form of pivoting the upper grooves. (Buckle makes no mention of the lower grooves presumably because they were obsolete by now.) This must have been a clumsy expedient and the experiment was undertaken of replacing the grooves by a sort of inverted fork or rake which, by a system of holes and pins through the handle, could be set at various heights, the inverted head of the fork being pivoted so that the wings could be turned to any angle. But despite their ingenuities, the grooves and the forks are now but 'survivals of antiquated methods. . . .'

We next refer to a Bristol stage-carpenter's log-book, which I had the privilege of examining at the Prince's Theatre some years ago. It belongs to the year 1886, and its bearing upon our subject is not so much to give any new information as to provide us with an example of the name of 'grooves' remaining after their use was gone.

It is a foolscap note-book whose pages are ruled in columns so as to allow six columns to each double-spread for the recording of the handling of the successive visiting shows which are all entered scene by scene. The first column contains a description of the backscene and notes on any special details of set-pieces. The other columns are headed respectively *Grooves*, *Wings*, *Borders*, *Flys*, and *Cellar*. The *Grooves* column contains a single figure, or occasionally a pair of figures, specifying positions, to which we will return in a moment. The *Wings* column contains a short description of the set of wings required, as Wood, Garden, Street, Oak, Pink Domino, or 'match' (that is, 'to match the back scene'). The *Border* column similarly contains a descriptive word; Foliage, Chamber, Sky, and so forth. The *Flys* column gives the special name of the cloth, when used, as Phoenix Park Cloth, Cinderella Corridor, Barraud's Castle Cloth. When no cloth is used the column is usually blank (since flats are already specified in column 1), except occasionally as when we find 'Snow box to work at cues'. The *Cellar* column is almost always empty, but contains a rare mention of a trap or bridge.

But the immediate interest for us is that we see that the *Grooves* column is never empty. Even although a scene may consist of a simple backcloth, hung from the flies, together with the relative wings, yet the position of that cloth is still specified in the *Grooves* column by the figure 3 or 5 or whatever it may be, although the grooves themselves were not used to support it. When the backscene consists of a pair of flats their name is specified in the first column as Street Flats or Barraud's New Library Flats and so forth, and their position is indicated by the number in the *Grooves* column while the *Flys* column is left blank.

Twice in the log-book the *Flys* column has reference to grooves. The first reading: 'At Change of Scene take up 1st Grooves & Proscenium'—no doubt a warning to lift the arms in preparation for a succeeding high scene. The second reference merely reads: '(Grooves down)'.

Thus we receive final confirmation that the grooves gave a sort of geographical name to the separate sections of the stage, the scenery on which was designated as 'in the 3rd (etc) grooves' whether it was of a nature to be supported by those grooves or was independent of them.

The next reference is to a memory of grooves as used earlier and is especially worth considering in detail. It is not an incidental fragment from the biography of an actor, nor the opinion of a dramatic critic; it is the word

[382]

of a practising man of the theatre of the highest eminence in his line. It is by a scene-painter, and marks one of those infrequent occasions when one of the English scene-technicians has forsaken his silence and recorded notes of his own craft in writing.

English stage technicians have very rarely turned for an interval to the pen and written about their work. The craft of scenic presentation still awaits its scribe in our country. As in the other arts (in contrast to the sciences), the literature is by professional writers from the outside, not made up of the accounts and personal expressions of practitioners. One regrets this a little; however non-professional may be an artist's writing, we may be refreshed at the discovery of words on a subject straight from one who knows it as intimately as the workman knows his job. The licensed book-makers' write-ups—so much more easily readable perhaps, but so obviously lacking that authenticity of experience—are too often merely an attempt to render an account or assess some unassessable value.

In the late eighties of the last century *The Magazine of Art* contained a periodic feature headed 'The Art of the Theatre'. To this series William Telbin made several contributions. In one of them is the passage which brings us a glimpse of the old life again at the end of the story. It is, in one sense, as rich a document as any we have, but its riches of meaning are deeply hidden from an uninstructed reader today. For one, however, with an introduction to grooves, it is perhaps the source to which he might turn for his epitaph on the subject of this history.

There were two William Telbins in scenery—father and son. Both were eminent. It is the son, one among the highly skilled group of scene-painters around Irving, as his father had been of those around Kean, who wrote the article. And on p. 94 of the volume for 1889, under the heading 'Scenery', Telbin sets out to defend the new developments in the scenery of his day, and to give his views of its superiority over the scenery of the past. He does not define the new movement in great detail since it was there exemplified in any theatre of the time for his readers to see for themselves. It was not to him a 'new movement' so much as the normal good scenery of his own time.

But we who have followed up this story have already noticed more than once that the promise of a coming change in scenic style was implicit in certain references we have studied. And we are now, in Telbin's time, to know that the change is taking place. All the evidence points to the stage picture of his day as being a different thing, in principle and in physical make-up, from the stage picture of the Restoration.

It was because of the change that the groove lost its vigour and sank into abeyance. But, for Telbin, the groove was still an active memory—superseded maybe, but not yet forgotten.

Here is the passage from his article, which opens by defending the new scenery against the old, and ends by a remarkably interesting reference to the scenic methods that were at that time beginning to recede into oblivion. Telbin begins by saying that contemporary criticism alleges that now 'too much is spent' on scenery, 'that the play is lost in the mounting; that mounting is not the drama, that the setting is not the jewel'. But he will not have this—'Nonsense!' he cries in full career—'Is not poor food better for being well served and well cooked? Is good food less acceptable for being equally well treated? Is a handsome woman less handsome for being handsomely dressed? . . .' He allows we should weaken the effect of *As You Like It* by introducing real streams, but claims 'the more the wood was like a wood, the fitter background would it be for the figure of gentle Rosalind. . . . In Mr. Irving's mounting of "The Corsican Brothers" you have an example of what first-class cooking will do for comparatively speaking poor dramatic meat.' This is enjoyable and vigorous, but now comes his picture of the past:

Now, if managers are not to do their best in the placing of their pieces on the stage, at what distance short of it are they to stop? A true artist knows nothing short of his best. Which among the appliances that science has placed at our service are we to set aside? Gas, and return to oil? Limelights for our moonlight effects, and return to gas lanterns *plus* reflectors? Is electricity to be forbidden entrance at the stage door, and are we to return to old-fashioned grooves in which strips of painting were pushed on parallel with the audience? Would the old spectacle be preferred of scene-shifters charging one another with 'flats' that ran in the long extending arms of the grooves, and dropped down with chains? For my own part I must say that the clatter and the turmoil of the battle of the flats did not add greatly in my mind to the impressiveness of the last act of 'Macbeth.' The unostentatious way in which the scenes change at the Lyceum Theatre is assuredly more in accordance with the better appreciation of the play . . .

These lines are packed with tradition. But before our study of grooves had been undertaken they would have contained for us probably a larger number of obscurities than any other passage of similar length in all the literature of the British theatre. I came upon the passage very early in my study of English scenery and it was partly to elucidate its items that the present work was undertaken. At length these obscure lines of Telbin's can be clarified, and the old ways they mirror so darkly can be better distinguished. But the more we find out about them now the more truly they pronounce an epitaph on the grooves and signal a new era of scenery coming after.

The next item in our obituary is again from William Telbin's hand and again to be found in *The Magazine of Art*, but this time it is a picture, and it is to be found at p. 199 of the same volume, that for 1889. This wash-drawing is printed with an article on scenery, but unfortunately it is not an illustration to any relevant words, and no discussion is made of it in the text. There is only its title which reads: 'Stage scenery as seen from the side boxes thirty years ago.'

Let us apply our method of detailed examination and see what this drawing (Pl. 58) can add to our small knowledge of grooves.

To begin with it out-rivals the *Graphic* print of nine years before in that it pictures the grooves actually in motion. And we may be certain that this representation is authentic, coming as it does from the hand of a past-master of stagecraft. It will be interesting to see if the publication of this drawing will bring to light, from any interested readers, other forgotten portraits of the hero of our history in action in his wonted surroundings. In my own researches this drawing stands so far unique.

It surpasses the *Graphic* print also in that it shows the flats sliding together, under the long descending arm of the grooves.

Up to this moment a reader might perhaps have been forgiven for failing to credit the strange evidence that recreates the old backscenes sliding together from the sides, and closing with the straight line of a join down the middle. It does indeed seem strange to modern procedure. But so it had been from the days of Inigo Jones right up to this period and here in a picture we see it.

We see the whole of one set of grooves attached in their place now, namely the underside of the fly-floor, that gallery running along the sides above the stage. And we see a small part of a second set farther back, showing just between the closing flats. But a curious point is that no store of wings is to be seen in this second set. It is empty. This seems to go to prove that, in spite of what we deduced earlier, the wings were wholly withdrawn from the grooves during the show. And so it presents a problem still to be solved.

But the drawing gives us very welcome confirmation of another theory, namely that the proscenium wings, those painted-curtain side-pieces, were used *additionally* to the scene-wings in the grooves. You will remember that we could see no other way than to make this assumption when we discussed the layout of the Plymouth stage. We found confirmation from Ipswich. Here it is reinforced. That these proscenium wings are here not in grooves is admittedly a guess, but one based on the assumption that the full set of grooves we see in action must be the No. 1 set, since in no stage plan have we ever seen any set of grooves shown so near to the proscenium as the proscenium wings here stand. Moreover, the proscenium wings, of their nature, do not need changing: they are a semi-permanent frame. We noticed in our study of the section of the Plymouth stage that an impossible problem of masking arose at the top unless extra borders were dropped in between the first scene-border and the proscenium. Here now we see not one, but a pair, of these proscenium borders. If these, too, were semi-permanent, like the wings, therein may lie the reason why on the Plymouth grid no provision was made for raising or lowering such borders.

This masking problem presented by the plans, in respect of the great distance back of the first wing position, is solved, and in its solution it brings confirmation of another of our theories, namely the loose regard in which masking was formerly held. This drawing purports to be a view from a box, but it shows much more through the scenery than we are used to seeing today.

Returning to the fly-gallery we find something that looks like a new problem: as we glance along the gallery rail we see that it seems to break out, and then back again, in a sort of bay over the first set of grooves. What the fact of this matter is we cannot tell.

We notice that though there is more than one groove for the wings, yet only one wing is in place; this wing is presumably not drawn back from the last scene (although it is far off in the grooves), but is that of the current scene now closing in. Where the wing from the previous scene is, again we cannot tell.

In the darkness beyond we see dim representations of packs of scenery, but we note with some surprise—and almost distrust—that the artist has shown the pieces all much shorter than would be needed to reach up to fit into the grooves. Is this an error on his part, or are these all short set-pieces?

On the matter of the existence, or not, of bottom grooves the drawing is not absolutely clear, but, though nothing can be seen at the foot of the wings, something of the sort seems fairly certainly to be indicated at the bottom of the flats.

Finally: we took it for granted above that the flats are closing, not open-ing. Our reason for this was that the scene-shifter is seen in the gap between them. Now, in sliding a flat along a groove, one is clearly going to achieve a far smoother movement if one pulls rather than pushes it, that is, if one grasps the forward edge and, taking some of the weight off the toe, leads it along the groove, than if one stood at the rear of the flat and tried to push it away from one. The latter method would be far more productive of tilts and jams and what the French call *saccades*—that staccato series of protests that accompanies the forcible shoving of something that half resists and alternately slips and sticks. Therefore the stage-hand *leads* a flat, not pushes it. Hence the finger-marks at the joining edges which contemporary writers singled out for their anger.

Note the carpenter's hat. It is square. Then it must be a paper hat. We find that carpenters at that time wore paper hats, and if you wish to see how they looked close to, you have only to open your Tenniel edition of *Through the Looking Glass* to see the very thing adorning the head of the Walrus's immortal companion.

The flats and grooves still lingered. In 1893 William Archer, writing of a performance of *Hypatia* at the Haymarket Theatre in *The Theatrical World*, said: 'The scenery is beautiful in design but not altogether happy in execution. It lacks solidity; there is too much flapping canvas about it; and the "flats" do not always "jine". In Hypatia's lecture-theatre, for example, the illusion was sadly marred on the first night by a yawning fissure in the marble gradines.' This gap between the flats is still, even today, a subject for criticism when between the narrower pieces which form the walls of our chamber sets there steals a crack of light because the flats are not properly cleated together. We have noticed above the sweep's annoyance when, according to Clark Russell, he called aloud the prayer to join the flats.

Next, a manuscript note of Dr. W. J. Lawrence's, about 1895, observes with reference to some of the Frank Benson Shakespearian tours, 'Drops have been substituted for flats in front scenes, thus doing away very materially with the disturbing element.'

This world of new departures affects America too, and after what we have found at home we are not surprised to see in *The New York Dramatic Times* for 27 June 1896 that wings are relegated to 'former times' and classed 'artistic monstrosities, designed . . . as a continuation of curtain drapery to reduce the height of the proscenium'. (A thought which is not only the same as that we found in *The Art Journal* of 1853, but which is expressed in exactly the same words so that it seems an unacknowledged quotation.) Thus another subject of our study seems to go out like a light snuffed in the brilliance of innovation—but the wings are hardy pieces; for all the scalding criticism they are still alive today, and we cannot yet write 'finis' to their story.

And for a note relevant both to the general story and to the above crack of light in particular, we have this from America: 'In former times the theatregoer would be annoyed at getting glimpses of light between the frames of the scenery where they meet together at the centre. A strip of steel is now used so as to lap over and cover the crevice, thus avoiding this difficulty.' The reference appeared in one of a series of articles by George J. Manson in *The New York Dramatic Mirror*, 1 August 1896, and it needs little comment.

Two other American references appeared, one the year before and the other the year following. In a Chicago Sunday paper for 19 May 1895 there is a description of the mysteries of stage technicalities for the information of the general reader. In an example of a *Line Plot* (that is, a list of the scenery hanging from the grid and the allocation to each piece of its specific, numbered set of lines) there is quoted: 'One set of lines behind drapery in one . . . One set in three; one set in four.' This is explained later in the text as follows: ' "Drapery in one" is the border hanging in groove one at the "tormentor" wing. "Three" and "four" mean grooves three and four.' The elucidation is succinct almost to the point of obscurity, but the general intention is clear that the grooves were used to designate the various areas of the stage. The "tormentor" wing is the proscenium wing or an extension of it.

The other reference from America is in *The Chicago Evening Post* of 22 January 1897. It reads: 'Formerly the wings ran in grooves . . . Only the old-fashioned theatres have grooves at all now, and companies with modern equipments find them something of a bother when they come to a house where they are still used.'

For the next of the memories, before we turn to Vestigial Remains, we go to Edwin O. Sachs—without any doubt the most painstaking writer on stage engineering that we have had.

His monumental, three-volume, folio work, entitled *Modern Opera Houses and Theatres*, 1896–9, deals almost entirely with brave new constructions of iron and steel. He was a pioneer of fire-prevention in theatres, and therefore he held the little old English wooden stage in contempt. He grants it a brief passage, however, including a mention of the bygone grooves, and an illustration of some value (Figs. 35 and 36).

In some of our wooden stages, so-called 'grooves' are suspended from the underside of the 'fly gallery floors'. These 'grooves' were intended to serve as supports for the top of the scenes and wings, and consisted of wooden frames hinged so as to take up and down, with grooves in them, along which the top of the scene could slide, and be held as if in a fork. The 'grooves' are, however, I am glad to say, now considered out of date, as the scenes are generally arranged in a different way. They are, however, shown upon the illustrations, as they have not yet been quite forgotten. When 'grooves' were used, it would be well to note, the 'scenes' had to be set at right angles with the side walls, or parallel with the curtain line, enforcing a very stiff and unnatural effect in many of the scenic pictures, and greatly hampering the scenepainter.

Later in the book we find the nature of the 'different way' in which the up-to-date scenery was then beginning to be supported: 'The brace . . . is the method which has superseded the grooves . . . . primitive makeshift for the antedeluvian groove. . . .'

We notice here with interest that no mention whatever is made in all the above of *lower* grooves. They seem to have been completely forgotten.

But . . . 'the antedeluvian groove'! How art thou fallen from Heaven, O Lucifer, Son of the morning!

The illustration in Sachs, showing the grooves, is, after the detail of

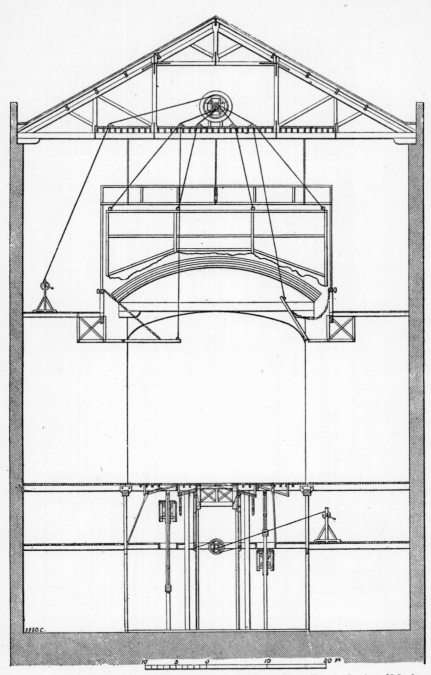

FIG. 35. Type of English wooden stage, cross-section. From Sachs, 'Modern Theatre Stages', *Engineering*, 1896

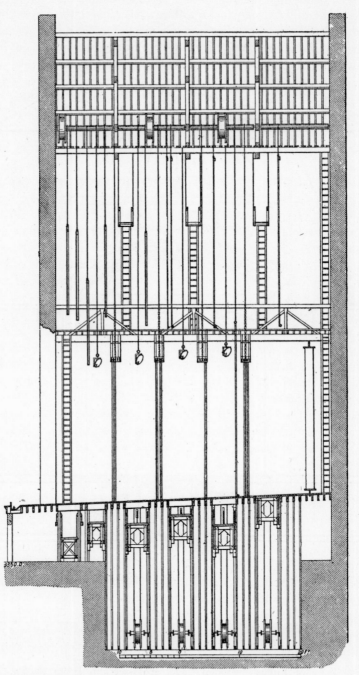

FIG. 36. Type of English wooden stage, long section. (From Sachs, op cit.)

Contant, generally self-explanatory. It consists of a section across the stage from the front, together with one from the side. We notice in the front section that the grooves are stayed out from under the fly-floor by two stays, with diagonal braces between them, so that they will take scenery 24 ft. in height, although the fly-floor is 29 ft. above the stage. We notice again the use of chains to prevent the flat-groove arms from falling beyond the horizontal, and we see the lines raising the arms, going up to a barrel, but here the appearance must surely be deceptive, for it seems to indicate that they go up to the very same barrel as that to which the border-lines are attached.

The side section shows the sets of grooves to the number of four, as is so commonly found, and we also see a cloth hung 'in the fourth grooves', that is to say, just in front of that set of grooves. We may also notice the three ladders rising from the fly-floor to the hanging *catwalks* that span the stage some 47 ft. up. But possibly the chief point of the drawing is that no vestige whatever is here shown of any bottom grooves.

The history of the bottom grooves is now capable of a temporary summary: for both wings and 'flats' Jones used full bottom grooves, the flat-grooves extending right across the stage. Foulston omits the centre part of the flat-grooves, making them in two short parts. Contant reduces the grooves to mere parallel strips with no intervening special beds and reduces flat-grooves and wing-grooves to the same. Telbin seemed to reduce their employment still further and confine them to flats alone, and now in Sachs there are none present at all.

A point nearly as important is that this section affords confirmation of what was uncertain in Contant's fragmentary diagram of the grooves and stays under the fly-floor in Fig. 29. There we noted that he seemed to suggest, somewhat to our surprise, that wing-grooves in the upper sets had become identical with flat-grooves—not only was there no distinction in shape, but there was none in function either, for the one set of four grooves was used to take either kind of scene-piece.

This Sachs now confirms; for in each groove position there is now only one simple set, each containing, as far as it is possible to decipher, four grooves.

Here then is a further simplification of the system. Not only have the bottom grooves now disappeared entirely, but the top grooves have been reduced to the simplest uniformity. In this respect this side section shows an advance on those of the full theatres given in Contant's second volume, where, in the upper sets, flat-grooves and wing-grooves were still differentiated.

By the mid-1890's, in England as in America, those houses 'where they are still used' were becoming increasingly rare, and there is one uncommon print which, intentionally or unintentionally, seems to stress this growing rareness. It is a print showing the grooves in a *View of the Auditorium of the Richmond Theatre from the Stage* (Pl. 55). Its details we will briefly remark in a moment, but first a—possibly very relevant—curiosity of date has to be noticed.

The print bears, beside the above title, no lettering save the signature: 'F. Cornman Delin^t et Sculp. Feb^r. 1896'. If the picture is of the Richmond theatre on the Green, in Surrey (as the details of the auditorium indicate it is), then one remembers with interest that, according to Frederick Bingham's pamphlet on that theatre published in 1886, the building which is shown in the print was demolished in 1884. Since the date of the print is 1896, one wonders why a picture was published of a theatre that had vanished a dozen years before, and upon what evidence that picture was made.

I must, however, dismiss the query, only pausing to wonder if here is some indication of an antiquarian mind recording a memory of earlier times, but for a purpose that is obscure unless it be to mark a dying fashion. Suffice it to say that this mind—whether antiquarian or no—clearly belonged to someone who had seen grooves.

For here in the picture are the backs of three pairs of wings and one pair of proscenium wings, the back of a typical green festoon curtain, and the auditorium beyond. The timber-framing of the wings is clear to see and shows, among other things, the diagonal cross-corner brace at the upper corner of each piece. Something else is also shown. Drawn exactly parallel with these braces is an exactly similar set of members but projecting up in the air above the inward corner of each wing. Just why are these pieces drawn so exactly parallel with the braces? It seems to indicate an emphasis in the draughtsman upon the fortuitous that makes us question either his knowledge or his sense of pictorial composition. But there is no doubt that these upper members are intended to represent the up-reared arms of a set of grooves, whose fixed portions (confused here with the wing-tops) hold the heads of the pieces of scenery.

The technical dependability of the sketch is clearly suspect, but one wonders how true is the indication that the proscenium wings ran in a special groove that spanned the proscenium opening continuously. If this could be relied upon, here would be a curious harking-back to Hogarth's great groove in the *Indian Emperor* print.

The reference that almost ends this strange, eventful history is brief. In R. J. Broadbent's *Stage Whispers*, p. 179, we read, most curtly, that 'grooves' equals 'forks' and no more. At first we might express surprise. What does this mean? Admittedly we laid the table-fork under contribution ourselves to give an analogy of the prong-grooves of the *Graphic* print and a foreshadowing hint was also contained in the reference to Buckle, p. 381. But here is the word come into a theatrical vocabulary as a thing in itself— and a thing to explain which they take the old appellation of 'grooves'— and surely take it in vain!

Yet it is perfectly just. For, for a short transition period between the supersession of the grooves and the adoption of the brace, there was a practice in which the wing-top was supported between two prongs projecting down from an arm, or directly from the fly-floor. And in this connexion we come to an odd footnote to our history that owns a touch of pathos.

I was once invited to prepare a recommendation for the improvement and modernization of a small stage at the Hatcham Liberal Club, New Cross. There, during my examination of the old fittings on the stage, I noticed above my head two horizontal battens running diagonally from either front corner to points approximating to the positions of the two edges of a somewhat narrow backcloth. These battens were each furnished at three points along their length with a curious small metal downward projection. Here is the back view of one of them (Fig. 37).

At first they puzzled me. Then I saw they were for supporting the tops of wings. But they were so shaped that not only could a wing be pushed between their two prongs and set at the old angle of wings, parallel with the front of the stage, but it could be turned to the modern diagonal position. This, however, was not all. The strip of metal was divided at the lower end into what might be called three legs with the centre one removed, and, of the two fork-prongs left, one was bent at right angles for about an inch before it turned down again, parallel with its fellow, towards the ground. Hence the three wings on each side could, because of this formation of their supports, each be fully swung through a quarter of a circle in their forks, as on a central pivot, so that now they presented their edges to the audience —and of course in that position they lined up and became the parts of a continuous side-wall to a chamber or room set. These ingenious forks, then, could take either exterior tree wings, facing the audience, or a row of chamber flats in positions nearly at right-angles to the trees, and forming the unbroken side-wall of a room.

The fork principle is rarely alluded to now, though it must be in the memory of most stage managers and carpenters who have reached years of discretion. It was primarily a shift used by small theatres, but it was so far accepted in standard procedure as to be illustrated among the many details of modern stage equipment in the 1931 trade catalogue of The Hall Manufacturing Company, one of the biggest makers and suppliers of professional stage equipment in London, where there is shown a sort of manifold fork whose prongs are short, down-projecting, hardwood rollers, for the easy entering of the heads of the flats. The item is No. 150 in the catalogue and is called 'Fork ends for wings' (see Fig. 38). The fork is not, however, reproduced in the catalogue of 1936, but in the enlarged booklet of the firm produced in 1947 a strange survival, or resurrection, of the 'fork ends' is to be seen. The form is exactly similar to those in the earlier catalogues, but their use, when fixed to some convenient elevated support, is now recommended for keeping separate the heads of individual members of a pack of flats when they are stored in the wing-space, so that any one can be drawn out at need without disturbing the others. It is curious to see

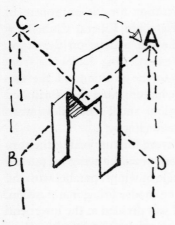

FIG. 37. Sketch of fork allowing pivoting of wings.

FIG. 38. Fork ends for wings as shown in Hall Manufacturing Co.'s catalogue of 1931

that that apparently secondary use of the old grooves as a store for scenery, as well as an 'engine' for the movement of pieces in use, should have survived longest of all, even if only in that curious vestigial remnant—the forks.

Here is a strange burst of desperate adaptiveness to spring from a dying system, rather pathetic in its sacrifice of its own body, and the truncation of its once noble timber mass to a little tin plate with bobbins, in the effort to keep up with those too-exacting demands of modernized, increasingly naturalistic, increasingly untheatrical scene designs.

One can see, now, how close to real principles were those little arms of the toy theatres of our boyhood that held the wings. They were simple strips of wood, split at one end and at the other pivoted with a nail to a bar running above the side of the stage. One slipped the wings in them and turned them to a suitable angle. In some models, too, the cardboard back-scene was held at the top by a pair of wooden strips a fraction of an inch apart. The whole principle was much more like that of the old stage than

[394]

is generally realized today, even by those who are fortunate enough to possess one of Benjamin Pollock's original Juvenile Theatres, still obtainable only a few years ago, just as they had been made when Stevenson wrote 'A Penny Plain and Twopence Coloured'.

We add a footnote.

There was to be seen in the Prince's Theatre at Bristol an odd variant of the groove system. The Prince's has been demolished by bombs. But I am very glad to be able to add this photograph at the end of the story.

At intervals along the fly-rails of the Prince's Theatre (which was built in 1867) there rise up great vertical baulks of timber. One of these is seen in the foreground of Pl. 57, and two others, very dimly, across the well of the stage, against the opposite fly-floor. In this photograph the proscenium is outside the picture to the reader's left.

The interest of these timbers is that the inner face of each has a vertical groove, or slot, with metal lips. These slots had not been used in the memory of anyone in the theatre, but in a conversation with one of the older stage-hands I was told that he had heard how, once, horizontal battens had run across the stage between each pair of timbers with their ends sliding up and down in the slots. Each such batten bore a groove on its lower face. He told me the purpose had been to drop one over the heads of a row of flats—meaning, in this instance, narrow flats of the modern sort—of which there might be three or more in the back wall of a chamber set. How near this hearsay information is to the facts we cannot be sure, but we seem to have here some sort of variant of the grooves adapted to fit the new and narrower flats that had been coming into use. It would seem only to have been an experimental measure, for in the memory of all on that stage, flats had been supported in the modern way—with braces from the floor.

To conclude our review by meeting an odd form of the groove is in itself not surprising, but when we see how very close in appearance this last form is to the groove we found pictured in Hogarth's painting of the children's performance in 1731, we reflect upon the freemasonry among stage-hands that the grooves seem to symbolize, and wonder whether this final example is a most ancient survival of method or an independent invention a hundred and fifty years after.

To lead these long adventures justly into modern times is a grave task. Our subject in this review has been changeable scenery; but we have accepted, almost without noticing, an implication that the word 'change-able' meant '*visibly* changing', for that was its import through all the long period we have covered. As such, changeable scenery has now come (or seems to have come) to its end. It is so rare in the twentieth-century theatre as to be virtually unknown. Its dynamic contribution to the unfolding of a dramatic plot is no more employed.

Yet, of course, scenery is still changeable; it is only that the spectacle of the changing has vanished from the theatre. We hide all changes with a curtain. The concentration has shifted from the changing scene as a dynamic part of drama to what is really a temporary, static scene, complete in itself, presenting its own subject with an appearance of permanence so that its capacity for alteration is, as near as may be, denied. The concentration is now not on the transformation of scenes but on the unity of the individual set and its suitability to the part of the play. Such unity and suitability have become so greatly thought of that the nature of the single prospect itself as a picture is that by which one judges the merit of a scenic decoration today. And the standpoint from which one judges is almost exactly similar to that from which one judges an isolated picture in an art gallery. Each scene design comes to be considered as a work of art.

This new conception marked our attitude to stage scenery at the beginning of this century, and it thus brings an end to our story and, at the same time, a beginning to another idea of scenery altogether which needs to be studied (and has indeed already been much studied) on its own. It is valuable to notice that the conception of scenery-design as one of the arts is a new conception.

How much is this conception a final truth? And what does it mean? *Is* designing scenery an art?

We will offer one final reference to our readers. It is evidence of this very question, but the reference will not contain—neither shall we attempt —any answer. In the theatre today we do no more than supply the material for an answer, and the material (which is our work) is not yet finished. We have before in our review seen theorists confounded by the event as time caught up with them. The present times have their theorists—and among these are inspiring prophets—but the appeal of scenery to the present writer is the appeal of its physical practice in the theatre rather than of its spiritual significance as an art and he is not prepared to speak in such detail of that. He therefore turns to the last item of his evidence, intending it only as evidence of the existence of a question.

In *The Contemporary Review* about 1901, Charles Ricketts, a distinguished member of the new school of scene-designers, published an essay entitled 'Stage Decoration'. In his *Pages on Art*, published in 1913, he printed a final text of this essay with certain alterations which were slight but significant. In its original form the opening of the essay read (and it seems a clear expression of the ideas of 1901):

I have often met with the question: 'Is there an art of stage decoration?' Should the setting of plays be different, if so, what should be the difference?

This sense of dissatisfaction is in part felt; it is sometimes due to the hearsay of better things abroad; it points to a probable change or to a need obscurely felt by all. Is there an art of the stage, some guiding principle, some new secret which would tend towards greater fitness and beauty in the setting of the poetic drama? . . .

Ricketts attempts his answer. For it the present reader is referred to Ricketts's book, whence he must make his own judgements.

What is interesting to me is that I had this passage pointed out to me by my revered friend, the late Dr. Gordon Bottomley, and I once quoted it in a short paper. I received a characteristically gentle and thoughtful rebuke; for Dr. Bottomley wrote: 'I feel to blame for sending you the "first state" of Ricketts' essay from "The Contemporary Review"; for I have misled you. I have checked it with the final text in his "Pages on Art", published in 1913, and I find it makes his meaning so much less ambiguous that I have been unable to restrain myself from correcting your quotation by it. I am really sorry about it; for it dishes your point about "obscurity"; but it is fairer to Ricketts—isn't it?'

The 'final text' of 1913 reads:

I have often met with the question: 'Is there an art of stage-decoration?' Should the setting of plays be different, if so, what should be the difference? This sense of dissatisfaction is in part felt; it is sometimes merely due to the hearsay of better things abroad. Is there some guiding principle which would tend towards greater fitness and beauty in the stage setting of poetic drama?

How far justified was this removal of the reference to the 'obscureness' of the need it is difficult to say. Had the practitioners of 'The New Movement in the Theatre' seen a light by 1913? Or was it only that the need was then more clearly felt?

But let us, again, rather than offer theories, note the facts. Ricketts removed the reference to 'a probable change . . . a need obscurely felt by all'. Gordon Bottomley, out of his great belief in the New Theatre, felt it fairer to Ricketts to accept his cutting of the reference to 'obscurity'. But neither Ricketts nor we are really any clearer yet what the art of stage decoration is—or whether it lies at all in the way we design changeable scenery. We still feel *obscurely* the need of 'better things'.

And thus I am forced to one personal theory at last in this review, which is perhaps relevant since it springs out of the review. It seems from my work in the theatre that the road towards satisfaction lies not in the re-designing of scenery, whether static or changeable, nor in any restatement of the way of representing the scene-of-action in a play, though it may on occasion include all these things. Reform of scenery alone is not reform of the stage. Scenery is a joy in the theatre, but not the whole. I look forward rather to finding what satisfactions come from the new designs of *stages* (and theatres to fit them) that this and that pioneer today is slowly bodying forth for the people. I should say that as we come nearer to adding another, and contemporary, flowering to the tree of which the forms grouped in Fig. 1 are the earlier fruits—in so far shall we be carrying on and enriching the tradition of the theatre.

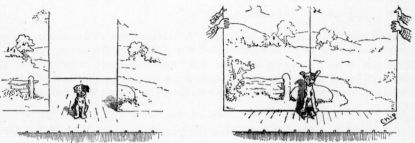

A MOVING SCENE.

FIG. 39. The end of a tail. (From a late-19-cent. American newspaper)

INDEX

PRINTED IN
GREAT BRITAIN
AT THE
UNIVERSITY PRESS
OXFORD
BY
CHARLES BATEY
PRINTER
TO THE
UNIVERSITY